WORLD OF SPORT

SPORTWATCHER'S GUIDE

The publishers gratefully acknowledge the
assistance of London Weekend Television
and *World of Sport* in the preparation of
this book.

First published 1981 by
William Collins Sons & Co. Ltd.
London · Glasgow · Sydney · Auckland
Toronto · Johannesburg

ISBN 0 00 411653 4

Printed in Great Britain by Butler and
Tanner.

WORLD OF SPORT

SPORTWATCHER'S GUIDE

INTRODUCED BY DICKIE DAVIES
EDITED BY PAUL WADE

Collins

Contributors

The Editor

PAUL WADE is a sports broadcaster and journalist. While with the BBC World Service from 1963 to 1978, Paul Wade covered Olympic, Commonwealth, All-African, Asian and Pan-American Games, Athletics and Soccer World Cups, and other major international sporting events. He is now a freelance journalist and sports correspondent for London's Capital Radio.

The authors and advisors

NEIL ALLEN: Sports columnist, London *New Evening Standard;* he has covered every summer Olympics since 1956.

ROB ANDREW: Australian Olympic field hockey player.

HOWARD BASS: Winter sports journalist, author and broadcaster. Special correspondent for *The Daily Telegraph* and *Sunday Telegraph.*

REX BELLAMY: *The Times* tennis correspondent and author of 'The Tennis Set'.

BARRY BLOXHAM: Australian Surfwear Co.

JOHN BURNS: Press Officer 1982 World Cycling Championships.

RICHARD CALLICOTT: International Secretary, English Volleyball Association.

CHRIS CARTER: Leading British motorcycling journalist.

CYRIL CARTER: Former British gymnastics international.

FRANK CHARNOCK: Amateur Fencing Association official.

MAX CRABTREE: Director, Dale Martin Wrestling Promotions.

ERIC CROSBIE: Secretary, English Bowling Union.

P. R. DAVIES: Consultant Editor of *Badminton;* National Coach, Badminton Association.

RICHARD EATON: *The Times* racketsports correspondent.

CLIVE EVERTON: Editor, *Snooker.*

TOM FOY: The Archery Centre of London.

MARY FRENCH: National Technical Officer, All-England Netball Association.

JOHN GOODBODY: Staff Correspondent, UPI Paris Bureau; author of six books on sport.

DICK HAWKEY: Chairman of the British National Coaching Committee and Chairman of the International Rules Committee, the Squash Rackets Association.

JOHN HELM: BBC Radio sports producer.

ALASTAIR LACK: Broadcaster and MCC member.

RENTON LAIDLAW: *New Evening Standard* golf correspondent.

JO MANSER: Former Cambridge University Boat Race cox.

GENEVIEVE MURPHY: *The Observer* equestrian correspondent.

ROSALYND NOTT: *The Daily Telegraph* waterski correspondent; Editor, *Power Boat and Waterskiing.*

FRANK PAGE: *The Observer* sailing and motoring correspondent.

CHRIS REA: Former Scotland and British Lions Rugby International.

GORDON RICHARDS: Public Relations Committee, International Canoe Federation.

GERALD SINSTADT: Granada TV soccer commentator.

OSCAR STATE: Vice-president, International Weightlifting Federation.

ATHOLE STILL: ITV swimming commentator; *Sunday Times* swimming correspondent.

CLIFF TEMPLE: *Sunday Times* athletics correspondent.

DEREK THOMPSON: ITV horse racing commentator.

JOHN TIMMINS: General Secretary, British Handball Association.

JERROLD TRECKER: TV sports commentator and journalist, USA.

Additional research

KATHERINE ARNOLD

NICK PRIESTNALL

Dickie Davies writes:

It's my great pleasure to introduce the WORLD OF SPORT SPORTWATCHER'S GUIDE.

ITV Sport always tries to broaden the horizons of the sporting world for viewers in this country. Each year we cover upwards of eighty different sports, some familiar, others more obscure, from this country and, through our international contacts, from every continent.

This guide is aimed to provide background information on all sports which are regularly covered on TV. It explains the rules, looks at the skills, and spells out the terminology.

It hopes to provide a service which, in the nature of things, we cannot always give on TV. Though, when we show American football, for instance, we try to lay down the basic principles before we go into the item, detailed analysis of this marvellous but complex game would take up all the airtime that should be given to the actuality coverage. And it is plainly impossible to interrupt the action to explain finer points of a game which to some might be a total novelty, but to others a particular favourite.

This book is aimed to cater for everyone — for enthusiasts who need to check up on matters of specific fact, and for people who have come newly to a sport on TV. It is written by expert journalists, officials of various sports, and by TV broadcasters. All of them know how to present their material in a clear, concise and attractive manner.

I know that I and my research team will be referring to it when we need to check up the details of a sport we are presenting, and I am sure that all viewers will find it a great help before, during and after sports transmissions. It's a book to browse through, to refer to — and to keep on hand whenever there's sport on your television.

How to use this book

Your **SPORTWATCHER'S GUIDE** provides easy reference to each sport, so that you can consult the book quickly and easily as you watch a new sport for the first time, or when you have a question about a sport you are watching for the hundredth time!

Each sport is listed in alphabetical order in the table of contents opposite. Several sports are listed under their various popular names — 'Soccer' for instance, is also listed under 'Football' and 'Association football', but each refers to page 203, where it appears under 'S' for 'Soccer'. A few entries do not appear in aphabetical order in the book itself. For instance, Canadian football is really a version of American football, and follows right after its 'parent' sport. Similarly, Pool and Billiards are found under Snooker.

Official rule books run to many pages for every sport, but here — for all the main sports — you can find out:

 where the sport takes place,

 the equipment the players use,

 how they win,

 what the basic rules are,

 what skills and

 what tactics are required by top-class performers, and

the words the TV commentators use to describe the sport.

Contents

AMERICAN FOOTBALL

Defence ○
S = safety
CB = cornerback
LB = line backer
DE = defensive end
DT = defensive tackle

Offense ●
T = tackle
G = guard
C = centre
TE = tight end
SE = split end
QB = quarterback
WR = wide receiver
RB = runningback

A typical formation. The quarterback can pass to his wide receiver who would be running downfield, or else he can use one of his running backs to rush with the ball. The line backers would try to get through to sack the quarterback; the corner-backs and safeties defend against long passes and runs.

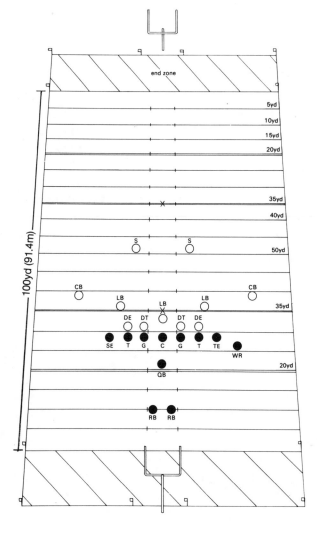

There is no sport like American football. Although it has its roots in games like rugby, it has developed in 100 years into something technological and computerized. Every strategy on the field is planned by coaches on the sidelines, so that it is almost like a violent game of chess. Quite simply, 11 men attempt to carry an oval ball over their opponents' goal line by passing or running with it. The opposition is allowed to tackle them, and so effective are they that teams are given four attempts at moving the ball a mere 10yd (9m approx), let alone the length of the 100yd (92m approx) long field!

Play starts and stops every few seconds with players regrouping before starting another play. The violent collision of the players as they try to batter their way upfield has produced helmets and padding that make the already oversized athletes look positively superhuman. Although the two teams can each have only 11 men on the field at any one time, every player's role is highly specialised so the coach has a pool of 45 players that he can call on to carry out his complicated tactical plans. Many players are on the field for a matter of seconds before trotting off as colleagues come on to deal with some new situation. The team with the ball is referred to as the *offense,* the opposition as the *defense.*

The game is virtually exclusive to the United States which boasts a professional league that attracts millions of spectators both through television and in the stadium. Played from August to January, it is also immensely popular at schools and colleges. There are even many studious arguments that consider American football reflects the American way of life. But, although the players may look like something from outer space, only superb athletes who have tremendous physical strength allied to speed, ballhandling ability and sheer inspiration can make it to the top.

1 The Field

Modern technology has affected all parts of the game and, although it is traditionally played on grass, more and more teams have artificial surfaces which are less affected by bad weather. The goalposts which were always 'H' shaped are often modernized. After all, it is only the space above the crossbar and between the posts that counts when kicks are taken. So to avoid players injuring themselves the posts have lost their 'legs', which have been replaced by a single curving cantilevered support. The lines which mark off the field into 5yd sections are for the benefit both of the spectators and the players who use the *gridiron* lines as a guide to whether a team has made all or part of the necessary 10yd to be able to retain possession. The dimensions of the field are always uniform.

AMERICAN FOOTBALL

2 Equipment

Players wear an extraordinary amount of padding in the North American game. Begin with a helmet, designed to protect the head from direct blows, equipped with a face mask. Also mandatory is a mouthpiece, usually dentally fitted.

Players then strap on shoulder pads, kidney pads, thigh pads, knee pads; heavy tape protects any joint which can be bent in the wrong direction.

Cleated shoes, a light, numbered jersey and tight-fitting pants (to hold the bulky pads in place) complete the outfit.

3 Winning

The toss of a coin decides which team has the choice of kicking off or receiving the ball. Then play starts with a kick-off from the 35 or 40yd line. This gives possession to the opposition straight away because they usually catch the ball. Their task is then to advance the ball upfield at least 10yd (9.14m) in four attempts called *downs.* If they succeed they have four more attempts at another 10yd. If they fail, they then have to give the ball to their opponents. As the object of the game is for the offensive team to cross their opponent's goal line, they also want to keep them away from their own line. Therefore, if there seems little chance of making the 10yd in four downs, a team will give up possession by kicking the ball as far as possible away from their own goal line, forcing the opposition to begin their attack deep in their own half of the field. They are really like two armies trying to gain territorial advantage in order to strike for the opponent's base.

There are two ways of gaining the 10yd. Holding the ball tightly, a player can run upfield as far as he can before being stopped by a tackle. The second and more spectacular way is by *passing* the ball, throwing it forward through the air for a *receiver* to catch. This move often covers more than 30yd (33m approx) in one fell swoop. However, if the ball is caught by the defense (an *interception*) they take possession. If

The quarterback (12) gets three seconds to release the ball if he is lucky. He must ignore the threat of 83, assuming his teammate, 40, will block him while he looks for pass receivers downfield.

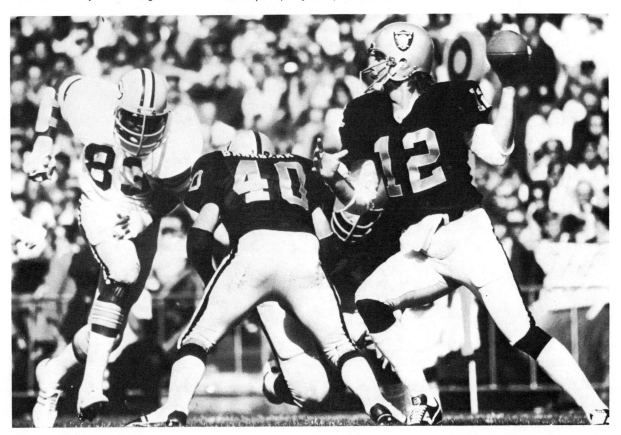

AMERICAN FOOTBALL

no-one catches the ball, the pass is *incomplete* and no *yardage* has been made, but a down has been used up.

In any four downs, players might try a combination of running and passing. Again, like two armies, the idea is always to try to confuse the defense into thinking an attack is coming from one direction and then to attack from another.

When a team takes the ball across the opposition's goal line they have scored a *touchdown* which is worth six points. Each touchdown may be converted by a *place kick* taken in front of the posts which is worth an additional point. There is a variation in school and college rules which permits a team to try to run or pass for two points from the three yard line (3m approx) instead of kicking for the single point.

If attackers get near their opponents' goal line but feel they cannot make the requisite 10yd, they can attempt a *field goal* instead of giving away possession by kicking. The field goal is worth three points and is kicked from any spot on the field. The ball is *snapped* back by the centre to a player who holds it for a specialist kicker to strike from distances as far as 50yd (45m approx) away from the goal line.

One other way of scoring involves the defense, which may force a player carrying the ball backwards behind his own goal line. Tackled in this way, the player gives away a *safety,* worth two points to the other team.

The game is played in four *quarters* of 15 minutes each. Although the nominal time of a game is an hour, the clock only runs when the ball is in play, so most games last nearly three hours. If at the end of this the score is tied (level) in a professional game, an additional 15 minutes is played, the first score producing a winner and ending the game.

 Rules

Although there seems to be more violent physical contact in football than most other sports, deliberate roughness, punching, kicking, tripping etc. are forbidden. The umpires, dressed in black and white striped shirts throw a *flag* or handkerchief on the ground when they spot an infringement of the rules. Because the game is based on the idea of advancing a few yards at a time, penalties are easy to award. If the offending team is on the attack, they would be moved back 5, 10 or 15yd depending on the seriousness of the offence. So a team might find itself trying to make 20yd on the next play with only three downs left. If the defending team breaks the rules, the attackers could be moved upfield 5, 10 or 15yd, so making their first down automatically. However, a penalty can be turned down by a team if it is not to their advantage.

Once a player has caught the ball on a kick-off he tries to run back up the field towards the opponent's goal line. His teammates try to give him room to run by blocking opponents who are streaming down the field trying to tackle the man with the ball. It is possible for a player to catch the ball from a kick-off

No.31 is running round left end. He should gain several yards, as he has men in front of him (67, 85) ready to block opponents.

The scrimmage is quite formal. Everyone on both teams must be behind the line of scrimmage. The centre has his hands on the ball. The quarterback stands behind him and shouts a series of coded instructions which conform to specific moves or *plays* that his side has learnt. He might call out '59-red-blue-hut!' On the word 'hut' the centre *snaps* the ball back between his legs straight into the quarterback's hands and play is under way. Occasionally, the quarterback might use an *audible,* and change his tactics at the last moment as he spots a flaw in the opponent's defensive formation. He would shout out a new set of coded instructions that were audible to his teammates.

Many of the moves are executed so quickly that only the television slow motion action replay can show the sleight of hand that is often used by the quarterback. He can *fake a hand off* (disguise handling the ball) to a *running*

The quarterback has a small white cloth pinned to his front to keep the ball and his hands dry. He can throw the ball accurately 60-70 yd (55-64m), even under pressure, as he imparts spin on it with his fingers.

A pass play: This wide receiver has evaded his marker and waits for the ball to reach him. However, the cornerback is stretching for the ball too, hoping to intercept the pass from the quarterback.

and run all the way to score a touchdown, but he will usually be tackled soon after catching the ball. Under college rules, as soon as any part of his body (except his hands or his feet) are forced to the ground, play stops.

The player has been *downed,* the *tackle* has been *made.* In the professional game, a player can keep going even if he is half-tackled and the referee will only stop play when his forward progress is halted. The players then go into a *huddle* as the quarterback tells his teammates what play he will set in motion.

The defenders often do the same though this only takes a moment as the defensive formation is fairly standardized. Both sides line up facing each other about one foot (30cm approx) apart at the *line of scrimmage.* This is an imaginary line running through the tip of the ball straight across the field. It is from this line that the ball must be advanced 10yd. On the sidelines two men carry a chain 10yd long which has a tall pole with a flag on it at one end (which is placed level with the line of the scrimmage) and a similar pole to show how far the team in possession has to go.

The chain does not move, but a third official has a pole called a *down marker* that indicates how far play has moved. A number shows which down is being used at the start of the next play.

AMERICAN FOOTBALL

back or *drop back* to position himself for a forward pass.

As players are allowed to block opponents, the man with the ball will often follow a colleague whose job is to clear a path for him through the opposition. Sometimes players attempt to cover only 2 or 3yd (2 or 3m approx) by squeezing through a small gap in the defensive wall. For the long forward pass, receivers sprint upfield, away from the line of scrimmage and run *a pattern* designed to throw off any *pass defenders.* The quarterback must be behind the line of scrimmage when he throws and must deliver the ball with pinpoint accuracy to his receiver who is

A wide receiver doing his job. He has leapt to catch a forward pass from his quarterback. As long as he holds on to the ball the pass will be complete.

often travelling at top speed at the moment he goes for the catch.

There are rules to prevent players taking unfair advantage by trying to move forward before the ball is snapped, though one player is allowed to run sideways behind the scrimmage line. Defenders can use their arms to tackle but the offensive team must not hold; blocking from behind *(clipping)* is illegal, as is *pass interference,* when a player interferes with a man who is

trying to catch a forward pass. The only ways a defender can stop a pass getting to a receiver are to block him straight after the snap or to get between him and the ball. Best of all, he might intercept the pass!

5 Skills

Every position on the field has specialist skills. From this point of view, American football is the most demanding sport in the world. Players do not so much *play football* as play specific positions such as *offensive guard* or *defensive tackle.*

However, coaches need players who are quick, whatever position they play. Speed over 40yd (35m approx) is measured as this is considered to be the furthest a big defensive line man will have to run to grab an opponent. It is not unusual for a defender to be quicker than an offensive player. Mobility is crucial too. The ability to move quickly to the side or even backwards is vital in a game where the slightest gap between players can be exploited.

Quarterback: he is the general on the field of play and has to have tactical awareness. Although he carries out the instructions of the coach, he usually calls his own plays. If a coach wants to suggest a move, a substitute player will relay the message from the sidelines. The quarterback initiates all of the attacks. He must not only be able to pass well, throwing overhand for distances as great as 60yd (54m approx) but also quickly. It is estimated that he has three seconds at most to release the ball. He has to be able to run with it and withstand hard tackles. The key man in the side, he must never lose confidence.

Linemen: the biggest men in football; often ranging in height to 6ft 8in (2m approx) and weighing close to 275lb (125kg) they utilize their strength and size to try and keep equally big men away from their backs and pass receivers.

Backs: primarily of two types, big and strong for straight ahead running and blocking, smaller and quicker for wide running. An extremely difficult position to play, the running back is also vulnerable to leg injuries because he may be tackled by as many as three men at a time, a combined weight of 750lb (340kg) if he's unlucky.

Down linemen: refers to the defenders who adopt a crouching stance

directly opposite the offensive line. Their job is to detect where a play is going and stop the advance of the forwards and running backs.

Line backers: quicker, often more wiry men in the 6ft 4in (2m) 225lb (100kg) range, who must be fast enough to catch running backs and defend against passes, strong enough to fight off the blocks of 275lb (125kg) opponents and then make tackles. They have a difficult job and the good ones get very well paid for it. They are the defensive counterparts of quarterbacks, the glamour men.

Pass receivers: although the ends and wide receivers specialize in catching forward passes, nowadays the running backs are also key pass receivers.

Safeties: primary pass defenders who must stay with speedy receivers and prevent thrown balls from being caught. Because they are the last line of defense and mistakes are all too apparent to the naked eye, this is no job for the faint of heart. They must be sure tacklers. Players rarely play in more one position as the game is so specialized.

 Tactics

These are always developed by the coach who has as many as nine assistants concentrating on specialized areas of play. Each team has a *play book* which is full of secret plans of offense and defense. All the players have to learn these before the season begins and they also have to learn the terminology by which all these plays are known. Every play outlines a specific task for each player and these are practised time and time again so that they can be executed perfectly during a game. They are too numerous and complex to be listed but a play book might contain diagrams like those overleaf.

Tactically, a coach must recognize the strengths and weaknesses of both his own team and the opponents'. He might decide to *keep the ball on the ground* and *rush* with it, wearing the defense down. Other coaches might be more flamboyant and *go to the air,* passing

The hand-off. The quarterback takes the ball from his centre, and turns quickly to hand the ball to his running back, running to the left.

13

AMERICAN FOOTBALL

the ball as often as possible, relying on the skills of an oustanding quarterback and receiver. Incidentally, a quarterback often passes not so much to a receiver but at a spot where the pass receiver is expected to be. A ball that sails harmlessly over the sidelines or straight to an opponent could be less the fault of a quarterback than the receiver, who failed to be in the right place at the right time.

Down: the name for each play. A team has four downs in which to gain 10yd, the reward for which is another four downs

Field goal: worth three points, is a place kick from anywhere on the field that goes between the posts

Forward pass: football's most exciting play, a thrown ball from behind the line of scrimmage to any one of five potential receivers; because a pass is a free ball, there is danger of an *interception,* which takes place when a defender, rather than an attacker, makes the catch; this means the defender's team gets possession of the ball

Fumble: when a runner loses possession of the ball before he is stopped by tacklers. A free ball; everyone goes for it

Incomplete pass: a forward pass that is caught by neither an attacker nor a defender; a down is used up, the yardage remains the same

Line of scrimmage: except for kickoffs, every play in football originates from a different spot; this spot is marked on the sideline and determines the distance needed for a first down; equally important, all forward passes must originate from behind this line

Punt: a kick from the hand that usually takes place on fourth down when a team feels it cannot gain the necessary 10yd in order to continue the attack; good punters average about 40yd (35m approx) per kick, while good punt returners are happy if they average 10yd (9m) per return

Quarter: the unit of play, 15 minutes

Safety: the ignominy for the attack, being trapped behind its own goal line, costing two points

10 yards to go: the distance needed on first down in order to get another set of downs. Each succeeding play may reduce the yardage. You will hear terms like 2nd and 7, 3rd and 4, 4th and 2. The first part of the phrase is the down, the number after is the yardage remaining to be gained in order to get another first down

Time out: time is automatically stopped following many plays (an incomplete pass, for example) so that actual playing time is not wasted while the ball is being recovered. In addition, a team may request a time out for players to consult with the coaching staff

Touchdown: football's major score, worth six points. ∎

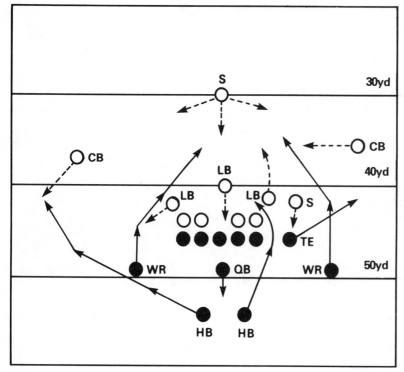

Defense	○
CB =	cornerback
S =	safety
LB =	linebacker

Offense	●
QB =	quarterback
WR =	wide receiver
HB =	halfback
TE =	tight end

An all-out attack by ●. The quarterback moves back with the ball ready to throw to one of five possible receivers. One halfback goes wide to the left, the other cuts through the line looking for a pass over the middle; the two wide receivers cut back towards the inside while the tight end goes wide to the right.

Most coaches have a set pattern of play for every situation they find themselves in, so rival coaches study old films of their games in case they can anticipate a move when the teams meet; some professional teams even hire computer experts to program opponents' moves. *Spotters,* usually assistant coaches, sit high up in the press box using their bird's eye view of the field to analyse both teams' strengths and weaknesses. Their information is relayed by telephone or walkie-talkie radio to the head coach who is down on the edge of the field with the players.

It really is a tactical game! In the end, however, it is the ability of a player to time his leap in the air to catch a ball one-handed in the end zone, or the persistence of a runner as he spins out of tackles and *runs to daylight* looking for the slightest hesitation in defense, that can turn a game.

To the uninitiated there may seem no difference between Canadian and American professional football, but such a suggestion would cause a patriotic outburst in the northern portion of the New World. Canadian football *is* different, both technically and in spirit.

Because there is one more man on a team (12 instead of the 11 used in the United States) and because the field is considerably larger — 110yd (100m) in length plus deep end zones in Canada, as compared to 100yd (90m approx) and short end zones in the USA — and wider — about 15ft (5m) on the average in Canada, the Canadian game is considered more 'wide open'. Because only three downs in Canada (instead of four in the USA) are allowed to gain 10yd (9m approx), the accent is far more often on the *forward pass,* on *end runs,* and on surprise or *trick* plays. One other technical difference allows backfield runners to move before the ball is snapped into play by the centre, an advantage to the ball-carrier that is not present in the United States game. Yet another difference is that kicks are always run back in Canada; there is no *safety catch,* but would-be tacklers must stay 5yd (4.5m approx) clear of the kick receiver until he touches the ball.

Does it all add up to a different game? Not in essence, though the Canadian variation in scoring which allows for a single point to be scored whenever a ball is kicked into the end zone and without the opposing team being able to run it back into the field of play does inject a bit more excitement into the closing stages of particularly close games. The two versions of football still depend very much on strength and power, good passers and good receivers, and running backs who can escape the clutches of tacklers and gain yardage. The differences between the games are outweighed by the similarities, though the manner in which passes and end runs dominate in Canada does present a visually more attractive spectacle in the opinion of Canadian and even many US observers.

The difference in 'spirit' is even more noticeable. Because college sport is not of major importance in Canada — much more akin to university sport in Great Britain, for example — spectators identify totally with the nine professional teams which make up the Canadian Football League, rather than with local university teams. The Grey Cup, the annual championship game, is played in late November and has become the occasion for an annual, week-long party that sees Eastern or Western Canadians travelling across country to the site of the game, which varies between Vancouver, Toronto and Montreal. There is a Grey Cup parade and other festivities which combine to make the week one of the major social events in Canada's sporting year.

The game has had some successful television exposure in the United States, but interest in it lies primarily among Canadians. To avoid the game being dominated by products of American college *football factories,* their number is strictly limited, and the remainder of the playing rosters must be native-born Canadians, many of whom are part time football players and full time workers. The leading quarterback in Canadian football, for example, was for many years an Ottawa mathematics teacher. That, too, is a major mark of difference between the CFL and the professional NFL of the United States of America. ■

CANADIAN FOOTBALL

Basic Rule Differences

Canada	*USA*
1 12 men per team	1 11 men per team
2 Three downs for 10yd (9m approx)	2 Four downs for 10yd (9m approx)
3 All kicked balls must be returned to the field of play (one point to kicking team if not returned)	3 Kicked balls over the end zone line are out of play (no penalty for no return)
4 Motion allowed before start of play by potential ball carrier and other backfielders	4 No motion allowed before start of play by potential ball carrier

With more room to move and fewer downs than in the US version of the game, Canadian football has the reputation of being more open and exciting.

AUSTRALIAN FOOTBALL

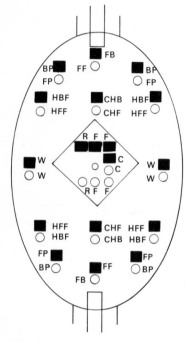

Field of play

FB = full back
FF = full forward
BP = back pocket
FP = forward pocket
HBF = half back flanker
CHB = centre half back
CHF = centre half forward

W = wing
C = centre
F = follower
R = rover

Attracting *Finals* crowds in excess of 100,000, this is the most popular participant spectator winter sport in the southern states of Australia. The fans expect to see spectacular *high marking* (catching); bruising body clashes, as no protective clothing is worn; accurate kicks covering in excess of 60yd (55m); high scoring and 100 minutes of non-stop action from the two teams of 18 players.

The oval field, which usually doubles as a cricket field, can be up to 200yd by 150yd (180 by 135m). Four wooden posts stand at each end, with no cross-bars. The inner two posts are the *goalposts* and the outer two the *behind posts*. These are 7yd (6.4m) apart. A 10ft (3m) diameter circle marks the centre of the field and this is enclosed by a 50yd (45m) square. There are further markings in front of the posts for the *goal square* which is 10yd (9m) deep.

The ball is oval, like a rugby ball, 29½ in (73cm) long and weighing between 16 and 17oz (475g approx). Sturdy shirts, shorts, socks and boots are worn, rather like rugby players' uniforms.

If an attacker kicks the ball between the goal posts a *goal* (six points) is scored. Any kick at any height counts. A *behind* (one point) is scored if an attacker kicks the ball between the goal and behind the post or if the ball somehow touches a player on its way through the posts. If a defender accidentally propels the ball between his own posts, a behind is awarded to the attackers. It is not uncommon for both teams to score in excess of 20 goals and as many behinds.

The team with the higher number of points is the winner: e.g.

20 goals (× 6) + 24 behinds = 144 points defeats
22 goals (× 6) + 11 behinds = 143 points

There are few rules in this flowing game. Players can move the ball by running with it, as long as they bounce it every 10yd (9m approx) which can be a pretty skilful move with an oval leather ball! They are allowed to kick the ball and *handball* (or punch) but throwing the ball is against the rules.

Passing to a team mate is often done by kicking and this produces the characteristic exciting high jump or *high mark* as players leap to catch the ball. A clean catch gives the player an unimpeded kick. The *field umpire* gets play under way at the start of each period and after a goal is scored by bouncing the ball in the centre circle where four members of each team try to gain possession.

When a behind is scored, the ball is put into play again by kicking it out of the goal square. Although it looks as if anything goes, free kicks are given for grabbing an opponent around the neck, shoulders or

legs; for either not releasing the ball when firmly held or for dropping the ball when tackled. Lying on the ball, pushing, tripping or hitting the man with the ball or deliberately obstructing the player without the ball — all these are penalized, with a free kick ... as is time-wasting.

A fair tackle of the man with the ball is a shoulder charge, and a hold round the waist.

To complicate matters, some checking or *shepherding* is allowed. To prevent an opponent from tackling a teammate who has the ball, a player can block him as long as he is within 5yd (4.5m) of the ball.

If the ball is kicked out of play on the full, without hitting the ground first, the defender nearest the spot gets a free kick. However, a ball that bounces before going over the boundary line is put back into play by the *boundary umpire,* who turns his back on the field and hurls it back high over his head where the players battle for possession.

Time wasting by arguing with the umpire and similar fouls when free kicks are awarded are penalized easily — the umpire advances the kick 15yd (14m).

The 18 players each have specific roles. The three *forwards* are the most creative while the three *half forwards* have to be elusive. The three *centres* need both speed and agility but the three *half backs* are the spring board needing strength to both clear the ball from the central area and halt attacks. The three *full backs* must be strong, safe and reliable as the last line of defence. The stars of the side tend to be a trio that follows the ball all over the field. Known as the *ruck,* they consist of two tall *followers* who try to tap and punch the ball to the *rover,* the most important man on the field.

As the quickest way to goal is straight up the middle, the best players tend to be there because this provides the best angle for goal kicking. As goals can be kicked from 60yd (50m), play moves quickly. Conversely, in defence the ball is played away from the centre towards the sidelines.

Many of today's teams use the accuracy and fluidity of handball in attack and defence, rather than risk losing possession by kicking. Skilled sides can compensate for their lack of height this way but despite this, possession changes frequently. There is no offside rule and in good, dry conditions it is a tremendous spectacle; wet conditions, however, can reduce the game to a muddy kickabout. ∎

RIGHT: Daley Thompson, 1980 Olympic decathlon champion, in the discus.
PAGE 18: Power and speed are the basic factors in American football.

To most people, archery means Robin Hood and Little John shooting at the Sheriff's men in Sherwood Forest, but the sport has moved on a long way since then. The skill is much the same, but the equipment has changed a great deal. The old longbow has gone, to be replaced by bows getting their power from glass-fibre and sending their aluminium arrows at over 200kmph (130 mph). Archery isn't a sport requiring hard physical effort, more a continuous and sustained application of muscle and skill, so you will see people of all ages taking part in an archery competition. There are few spectators.

just above the handle. This helps the archer to aim at the target.

Bows are categorized by their *weight* or *draw-weight,* which indicates the force needed to hold the string drawn right back. A bow would be marked 15kg at 71cm (32lb at 28in) to show that when an arrow 71cm (28in) long is drawn back properly the archer's fingers would be holding up the equivalent of a 15kg (32lb) weight.

1 The Target

Made of compressed straw, the *target* has canvas stretched over it marked in five circles of colour — yellow at the centre, then red, blue, black and white on the outside. Each band of colour is divided into two, so there are ten rings which score from ten in the centre down to one on the outside. The target is 122cm (4ft) across for the 60m, 70m and 90m (65yd, 75yd, 98yd approx) events but only 80cm (2ft 7½ in) across for the shorter events. The yellow in the centre of a target is always called a *gold.*

Well-balanced competitors straddle the white line when taking aim. Note how the nose and lips touch the bowstring, all part of lining up with the target.

2 Equipment

Apart from the basic bow and set of arrows, archers use a *tab* or shooting glove to prevent the bowstring making their fingers sore and also a *bracer* to stop the string hitting the bow-arm. Sometimes the string can hit the chest or shoulder so a protective *chestguard* is worn. Don't forget that the bowstring can reach 200kmph and that can cause large bruises.

Modern bows have a number of gadgets attached which increase accuracy. The most noticeable are the *stabilizers.* These are rods screwed into the bows with small weights attached which help to stabilize the bow when the string is released. Modern bows also have a sight on the front projecting 20cm (8in)

LEFT: American star Mike Tully, having pushed on the pole to clear the bar with his legs, must now straighten his body and arms to complete the vault.

3 Winning

It is very simple to win at archery. Archers aim to get more of their arrows nearer to the centre of the target than anyone else. Each arrow scores according to where it hits the target. If an arrow cuts a dividing line between two rings then it is given the higher score. In international competitions governed by FITA men shoot two *rounds* of 144 arrows. Each round is made of three dozen arrows at a target 90m (98yd approx) three dozen at 70m (65yd approx) away, three dozen at 50m (55yd approx) and three dozen at 30m (33yd approx). Women also shoot three dozen arrows at four distances, but these are slightly shorter, 70m, 60m, 50m and 30m (75yd, 65yd, 55yd and 33yd approx). Archers usually shoot off six arrows in each turn, called an *end,* before taking their scores. When they are shooting at the smaller target from 50m or 30m, then only three arrows are shot because

An arrow in the centre of the target scores 10 points. Each ring decreases in value down to one point at the edge. Competitors extract the arrows by twisting and pulling.

RCHERY

the gold could get overcrowded and good shots might be deflected! At the Olympic Games, a good total for men over two *FITA rounds* would be about 2500 from their 288 arrows; for women about 2400 from 288.

4 Rules

Rules cover the equipment and dress as well as safety precautions. These are so basic that in top class competitions archers would never break them.

5 & 6 Skills & Tactics

Archers have to reproduce the same mechanical action with every shot. They have a series of moves — *nocking, hooking, drawing, holding* and *loosing,* that's to say placing the arrow on the bow, placing the fingers on the string, drawing the string back, aiming and shooting. If any move feels wrong, the archer will always stop and start the whole series all over again.

The modern archer relies on a variety of stabilizers and a special sight to control the powerful bow.

Unless you are an archer, it can be hard to tell who is shooting well. The one who looks as though he is shooting every arrow exactly the same with no variation in style is probably in the lead, and the easier it looks, the better he is shooting. The leaders are the ones pulling their arrows out of the gold!

7 Words

Bouncer: an arrow that hits the target and bounces off
Cutter: an arrow that lands on the dividing line between two rings
End: one archer's turn, shooting three or usually six arrows
Fast: short for 'hold fast'; when an archer hears this he must stop at once
FITA: the Fédération International de Tir à l'Arc, the world governing body
Gold: the centre of the target, never called a bull's-eye
Grouping: a cluster of arrows 'grouped together' on the target
Hanger: an arrow that doesn't penetrate the target very deeply and hangs down
Perfect end: six arrows landing in the gold
Pinhole: the exact centre of the target, marked by a dot
Quiver: pouch for holding arrows. ■

Track events decide the fastest human over a set distance, while field events test competitors' ability to throw and jump the furthest or the highest.

1 The Track

With metrication more and more prevalent, the standard track is a circuit 400m (437yd approx) long; with the exception of the mile, world records are only recognized over metric distances. Most new tracks, and certainly all those used for international competition, have an *artificial surface.* This is usually a rubberized compound that can be used in any climate.

All races are run counter-clockwise, so that the curve is always away to the left of the runner. The exceptions are the short sprint and hurdle races over 100 and 110m (or 100 and 110yd), where the *straight* or *straightaway* in front of the main stand is used. The same *finishing line* is used for all races.

Eight *lanes,* to separate competitors, are marked out on the track. Other marks include those for *staggered starts.* In races which start on a bend (200 and 400m) it may look as if some athletes have been given an advantage, starting ahead of their rivals. But to counteract the effect of running wide round a bend, the starting lines in each lane are staggered, and each athlete is starting at an identical distance from the finish.

been missed by the human eye.

In order to time races *electrical timing* is used. The human timekeeper, pressing a stopwatch at the start and finish of a race, is being superseded in most international meetings by electrical timing, which is started automatically by a connection to the starter's pistol, and the results of which can be read off from the photo-finish picture to the nearest one-hundredth of a second. In fact, in events up to 400m only performances recorded by a fully automatic electrical timng device are now acceptable as world records.

For the sprint and hurdle events up to 200m (or 220yd), as well as the long and triple jumps, the speed of the wind is measured by a special gauge. If the following wind is blowing at more than 2m (or 6ft 6in) per second, then any record time or distance cannot be ratified as it would be *wind-assisted.*

When it comes to equipment, men and women wear shorts and athletic vests which must be clean and non-transparent even when wet. Identifying numbers are allocated at a competition and must always be visible and are usually pinned on the chest and back. Although several runners (notably Africans) have competed successfully barefoot, most athletes wear some sort of special shoe. *Spikes* or spiked running shoes vary from event to event as well as with the individual's preference. Spikes can be a maximum of 2.5cm (1in) long with four in the sole and two in the heel. Plastic or rubber padding is often inserted to protect the heel bone in jumping events, but the sole must never

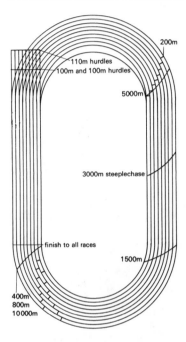

Starting lines are marked on the track

2 Equipment

For the sprint events, *starting blocks* are used by most competitors. A starting block is a device, usually made of metal, which can be screwed or nailed to the track just behind the starting line, and against which the sprinter can press his feet at the start to improve his initial momentum. The foot plates are angled and adjustable according to the physique and preferred starting position of the individual athlete. At major meetings like the Olympic Games the starting blocks themselves have an electrical built-in *false start detector,* which can indicate whether any athlete's foot has left the blocks even fractionally before the gun sounded, an offence which might otherwise have

be more than 13mm (½in) thick, with the heel only 6mm (¼in) thicker than the sole. In the throwing events or even long distance running events, a flat rubbersoled shoe is worn.

The modern starting block is electronically wired to detect if an athlete's foot leaves the block early.

ATHLETICS

Track & Field

Sprints & Relays

For 1 & 2 see page 23

The sprint events of 100, 200 and 400m (or 100, 220 and 440yd) are the shortest, quickest races on the track and field programme with sheer blazing speed being the most important factor in determining the fastest human between two points. The relays, 4x100m and 4x400m, are races between two or more *teams,* each consisting of four athletes who have to run the same distance in turn, passing a hollow metal *baton* or stick, about 30cm (1ft) long, cleanly from runner to runner without dropping it.

long as all three baton *change-overs* during the race have been accomplished within the permitted *zones.* In sprints and relays a photograph often decides placings in top events.

4 Rules

All sprint races are run in lanes, and the only exception to this is on the last three stages of the 4x400m relay, where the teams can *break* (leave their lanes) for the inside lane on the back straight of the second runner's lap. Otherwise, they cannot set foot in anyone else's lane during a sprint race.

Coming out of the blocks at the start of the 100m, the runners look up and drive forward with their arms and legs.

3 Winning

Runners in the 4 × 400 relay are allowed 10m to build up speed but must exchange batons in the 20m takeover zone marked on the track.

The winner is the athlete who gets his or her torso (as distinct from an arm, head or leg) over the finishing line first. In the case of the relays the winner is the team whose final runner gets his or her torso over the finishing line first, as

A good baton change in the relay. The incoming runner has slowed down slightly but is stretching to reach his teammate.

The races must begin from a stationary start, with the officials satisfied that all competitors are quite still before the starting pistol is fired. If an athlete is judged to have moved before the pistol sounds, the starter fires a second shot to signify it was a *false start,* and the runners have to stop and return to the assembly line. Any runner charged with causing two false starts is disqualified.

The starter for the sprint races gives two commands: the first is 'on your marks' at which the competitors move up to the starting line and settle themselves comfortably in their starting blocks, resting on one knee, with their fingers behind, but not on, the line itself. The second command is: 'Set!', at which the resting knee and hips are lifted and most of the body weight is moved forward on to the arms. It is an uncomfortable position, but one which the sprinter is rarely asked to hold for more than two or three seconds before the gun sounds. Good use of starting blocks can contribute to an explosive start, but a simple standing start is usually permissible, as long as the toe is not on the starting line and the athlete remains still in the 'set' position.

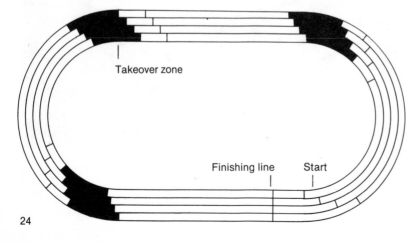

Takeover zone

Finishing line   Start

In a 4x100m relay, the baton has to be passed three times within the single circuit of the track, and a 20m long *take-over zone* or *relay box* is marked in each lane at the point at which the takeovers are to be made. Any team not completing its takeovers within the designated boxes is disqualified.

In the 200m, and to a certain extent in the 400m, running the curve is a skill. Runners must keep in lane, but run as close to the line as possible.

 Skills

To reach top speed in a 100m race (about 45kmph (28mph) for men, 40kmph (24mph) for women) from a motionless start takes around 40m, but even that speed can be held for only 15-20m before the runner almost imperceptibly begins to slow again. However, the successful sprinter maintains relaxed form at top speed and in the closing stages tries to avoid tightening up the shoulders, jaw, neck and arms, which would lead to tension and inefficiency. Relaxation under even the tightest competitive situation is vital and the correct use of a *dip* finish can win a close race.

The dip is a deliberate lean forward with the chest a metre or so from the finish in an exaggerated effort to get the torso across the line first. But if it is misjudged and employed too early, a race can be lost because the sprinter slows as soon as he uses it. If he dips too far forward, he can end up flat on his face on the track! ■

Although the runner in white has won, he makes sure by dipping at the line and thrusting his chest forward to break the tape.

ATHLETICS

Track & Field

Sprints & Relays

ATHLETICS

Track & Field

Middle Distance

1 & 2 see page 23

Middle distance running races are those situated in the no man's land between the sprints and the long distance races: the 800m (or 880yd) and 1500m (or 1 mile). And contrary to one light-hearted opinion, they are not the events where athletes need 'neither speed nor strength'; they need both.

3 Winning

The events are straightforward races, run anti-clockwise on the track and though usually easier to judge than sprints, the principle is the same: first competitor to get his or her torso over the finishing line is the winner. Intermediate times are called by an official timekeeper at the end of each lap, and before the last lap a bell is rung (or, in the USA, a gun is fired).

4 Rules

When runners are travelling at speed round a bend accidents occasionally happen. Here one woman has been tripped and brings another competitor down with her.

The first bend of the 800m is usually run in lanes to avoid unnecessary risk of collision at the start, but as the competitors pass the red flags at the beginning of the back straight they can *break* for the inside lane. Breaking too early, however, would cause disqualification.

After that it is virtually every man for himself, and although deliberate physical contact or obstruction is forbidden, the sheer speed at which top

class athletes are travelling, with each trying to get into the right position, means that the occasional elbow clash or push is inevitable. In an 800m race, for example, the competitors are often running only a few seconds slower than in a 400m (or 440yd) race, where they have lane divisions. At 1500m the pace is relatively slower.

5 & 6 Skills & Tactics

Pacemaking. The pacemaker is whoever takes the lead early in the race, as he is the athlete dictating how fast the rest of the field will be running. The preferred tactical position for most athletes is to be just behind the right shoulder of the leader, however, and in general terms the early pacemaker in a top class race seldom wins. It is easier to follow than to lead, and although the disadvantage of leading was thought to be mainly psychological, increasing scientific evidence suggests that on even a relatively calm day, a pacemaker actually creates a slight suction breaking through the wind resistance for the following runners.

So why should anyone want to lead? The answer is that sometimes no one does! Instead, particularly in a 1500m (or 1 mile) race, the field will almost jog around the first lap with no one wanting to take on the pacemaking role. Anything slower than 60-61 seconds for the first lap of an international 1500m race suggests this reluctance, and the race will instead become a battle of nerves to see who will succumb to the urge to pick up the pace first.

In certain races, usually special invitation events, or races where one or more competitor is hoping to run a record time, a pacemaker or *rabbit* may be surreptitiously included in the field with the specific task of setting a good speed for the opening lap or two. He then often drops out or slows down and leaves the serious contenders to finish the job with the momentum he has started. Such pacemaking is officially frowned upon, but it is difficult to prove the difference between deliberate planned pacemaking and an athlete's individual decision to run the opening laps very fast. And many world records, including Sir Roger Bannister's breaking the *four minute mile barrier* in 1954, have been accomplished with carefully orchestrated pacemaking. ∎

The long distance events for men are the 5000m (or 3 miles) and the 10,000m (or 6 miles) on the track, and the classic marathon 42,195m (26 miles 385yd) on the road. For women, the 3000m (1.86 miles approx) on the track and the marathon on the road are both now widely contested internationally, and in 1984 the first women's marathon will be run in the Olympic Games.

For 1 see page 23

2 Equipment

Long distance runners have often been innovators in athletics kit, because of the extreme nature of their event. Vests are often cut to the minimum, with white preferred as it reflects the sun. Lightweight, brief-cut shorts reduce the chances of leg-chafing, as will some dabs of petroleum jelly. Shoes are as light as possible without risking foot injury, and some track runners have raced internationally in bare feet in the past.

The most common sight in marathons now is the mesh vest, which allows air to flow more freely to the body for cooling purposes on a hot day. This may also bring its own related problem of chafed nipples, however, and many marathon men cover the affected parts with an adhesive bandage.

3 & 4 Winning & Rules

In international championships, like the Olympic Games, the entry is sometimes so big that heats have to be run even for the 25-lap 10,000m, with perhaps only the first four or five in each heat qualifying for the final itself.

5 & 6 Skills & Tactics

The first runner to cross the line is the winner. The long distance events are fought out largely on stamina, with each

man trying to run at a pace which — over the length of the race — will wear down his rivals. Yet international runners are now so fit that the result of a race is sometimes only decided in the final lap at a pace just slightly below sprinting speed. Consequently, many athletes with little basic speed are looking more and more towards the marathon, which is still the refuge of the strong runner who has more stamina than speed.

On the track, by contrast, the even-paced runners are those who can often set records on their own; but when faced with rivals who are ready to either speed up or slow down the race at different stages, they can crack up. The eventual winner of a distance track race up to 10,000m is very rarely out of the leading group throughout the race. Unless the pace being set is suicidally fast, no athlete with hopes of victory will normally let the leaders get away from him. So watch for the smooth-moving, relaxed runner amongst the leading group. His breathing will not be laboured, and if any gap opens, he will be the first to close it.

In the marathon, because of its relatively greater length, it is possible for a runner to *move up through the field* and win. The testing time comes between 28 and 36km (18 and 22 miles), the point at which many runners suddenly *hit the wall.* This is the time when all the glycogen, an energy-source in the muscles, has been exhausted, and the body starts to draw instead on its fat reserves for fuel, which can be a painful and tiring experience after two hours of running. Marathons often change dramatically in the last 10km (6 miles) and even in the last 400m (¼ mile) as a runner who has paced himself better catches a tired rival.

7 Words

Fastest losers: in qualifying heats, the conditions for entry to the final are sometimes *first six in each heat, plus two fastest losers.* This means that whichever two athletes outside the first six had the fastest times go through.
Split times: the time taken at different sections of a race, which can indicate whether the final time is likely to be a fast or slow one.
The diet: the *carbohydrate-loading diet* or *the diet* is a special week-long preparation to artifically increase the body's energy-giving glycogen reserves. ∎

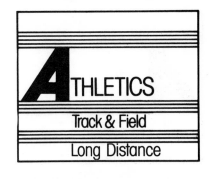

In the marathon, refreshment stops are set up every five kilometres. Competitors use the plastic bottles to squeeze water into their mouths or over their heads to counteract dehydration and heat.

ATHLETICS

Track & Field

Hurdle Events

1 The Hurdles

The standard hurdles events are the 110m and 400m for men (110yd, 440yd) and 100m and 400m (100yd, 440yd) for women. They are really sprint races with an added difficulty — or, rather, ten added difficulties in the shape of metal barriers with wooden tops which have to be hurdled by every competitor. The 3000m (1¾ miles approx) steeplechase, which is only run by men, is a gruelling middle distance event with 28 solid timber barriers, plus seven water jumps to be negotiated in all.

2 Equipment

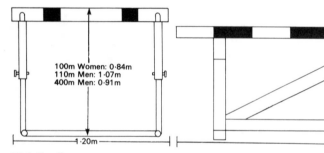

100m Women: 0·84m
110m Men: 1·07m
400m Men: 0·91m

←1·20m→

High Hurdle

←————— 3·66m —————→

0·91m

Steeplechase Barrier

3 Winning

The last three hurdles in the 400m event often trip up the tiring athlete. The muscles are tightening and the stride pattern falters.

In each case, the first runner across the line is the winner.

4 Rules

In the *hurdles* races every competitor has to stay in his or her lane. The trailing of a leg around the side of a hurdle, rather than over the top, is not allowed, but there is no limit on the number of hurdles which can be knocked down during the race, as long as it is not deliberate. In fact, it is quicker to hurdle a barrier properly than to knock it down, because the impact can throw the athlete off balance.

In the *steeplechase,* where the barriers are more formidable and, unlike hurdles, are not designed to fall over when struck, the runners are allowed to put one foot on top of the barriers when clearing them. However, few of the leading steeplechasers do so, except at the water jump, which is a permanently-sited obstacle, 0.914m

(3ft) high, with a 3.66m (12ft) wide expanse of water on the far side. It is virtually impossible to clear this hurdle without putting one foot on the barrier and then driving off hard. There is no penalty for landing in the water — it only slows the athlete down.

5&6 Skills & Tactics

The 400m hurdles is actually an easier race for spectators to follow than the 400m *flat,* despite the fact that the hurdles are arranged on a staggered start around the first bend. Each hurdle is the same distance away from the starting line in each lane, so whichever athlete is *first to rise* at each flight of hurdles is leading.

The fluent rhythm of today's top level hurdlers disguises the difficulties of this

High hurdling times are not much slower than sprints because competitors do not jump over the obstacles but flow over them. The secret is in the rapid lift of the leading leg and the ability to force it down on the track again in one smooth movement.

type of event. Until you see someone hurdling badly, you can never really appreciate someone who is hurdling well. The main aim is not to hurdle as high as possible, but rather to clear the barriers with speed and efficiency and the minimum of interruption to the running action. Time spent in the air is time wasted, and the top hurdlers skim the top of the barriers.

The action involves a fast *step-over* action of the leading leg. A sideways swing of the rear (or take-off) leg then follows through, lifting the thigh as high as necessary (but no higher) to clear the barrier, and get back into the sprinting action between hurdles as quickly as possible. Tremendous mobility of the hips is needed. But in all hurdles and steeplechase events, fatigue increases as the distance passes and the number of dramatic falls seen at the final barrier over the years is a reminder that these events are never won until the first runner is safely across the finishing line.

The steeplechase is demanding because the obstacles break up the rhythm of the runners. The more efficient the hurdling style, the better. To clear the water competitors put one foot on the hurdle and drive forward.

away and on the correct take-off leg.

In the 400m (or 440yd) hurdles, for example, the first hurdle is 45m (or 45yd) from the starting line, then each hurdle is 35m (or 40yd) apart, which leaves a 40m (or 35yd) run-in to the finish. Between the hurdles in the first half of the race, the athlete may try to run exactly 13 strides, so that he always reaches the next hurdle on his *take-off* foot. But in the second half of the race, where he is increasingly tired, his stride will become shorter and to ensure that he still arrives on the correct foot he may make a conscious decision to switch to 15 strides between the remaining hurdles. Some hurdlers have the ability to lead with either leg, so they can switch to 14 strides. ∎

7 Words

Stride pattern: stride patterns are the key to successful hurdling. The athletes do not just charge headlong at the barriers and hope for the best. They have evolved in training a set number of strides between the hurdles, so that they reach each barrier the right distance

ATHLETICS
Track & Field
The Jumps

All three events involve a running jump for either height (high jump) or distance (long and triple jump), with solely the human body to produce all the explosive power, aggression and strength needed.

1 The High Jump Pit

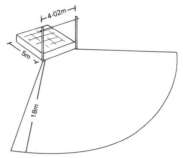

High Jump Fan

2

Take off in the straddle style, where the jumper faces the bar, drives off on one leg straight up in the air and rolls over the bar.

Using the straddle the jumper has rolled over the bar, lifting her take-off leg over. Note the arm positions, well away from the bar.

2 see page 23

3 Winning

The high jump is the odd event out for three reasons. Firstly, and most obviously, because vertical rather than horizontal distance is measured. Secondly, because the event is based on success or failure, with the athlete attempting to jump over a cross bar at a set height (which can have only two outcomes: he succeeds or he doesn't). And thirdly, because the athlete can have unlimited successful attempts. The winner is the last remaining jumper in the competition.

4 Rules

In the high jump the competitors can choose their opening height at which to begin jumping, and also forego an attempt at any height if they wish. But once they have had three successive failures, they are eliminated. The take-off has to be from one foot only, and the run-up can be made from any angle on the semi-circular approach area known as the *fan*. Check marks are allowed on the fan to help the jumpers to reach their take-off point on the correct foot.

Some athletes may *win on the countback.* In a tie situation officials examine their cards and put one athlete ahead of another on the basis of fewer failures.

Once the flopper's body is above the bar the shoulders begin to drop and the legs have to be straightened to flip over the bar.

5 Skills

One of the two most popular methods of high jumping is the *straddle* in which the jumper clears the bar face down, virtually rotating the body length-ways around it. The *Fosbury Flop,* the other high jumping method, involves a head-first clearance, crossing the bar on the back, and landing on the neck and shoulders. It was first used by 1968 Olympic champion Dick Fosbury.

1 The Long & Triple Jump Pit

When the judges examine the take-off board very closely after an athlete has taken a long or triple jump, they are looking at the layer of plasticine which is placed next to the edge of the board to see whether any spike marks have been made by the athlete's shoe indicating a *foul jump*. If they find marks, a red flag is raised and the jump is void.

2 see page 23

2 see page 23

3 Winning

In the long and triple jumps, all the competitors have to put their efforts into a maximum of six trials, and the winner is the athlete whose best jump is further than anyone else's.

4 Rules

Both the long and triple jump involve straight approach runs to a white-painted take-off board. Again, only a one-footed take-off is allowed, and as the distance jumped is always measured from the edge of the take-off board nearest to the sandpit, the jumper aims

A triple jumper at full stretch. Having hopped on his right foot for the first part of the jump, he is now doing the step, trying to maintain height before driving off on his left foot.

to get on the board, and as close to the edge as possible on each jump without going over it.

If the jumper's toe goes over the board, that attempt is not measured, although it is still counted as one of the six trials. It occasionally happens that a jumper fouls every jump.

On every jump, just before landing, the jumper shoots out both feet in front of him to gain some extra distance, but he must not overbalance and fall back, as the measurement will be taken from the mark he has made *nearest* to the take-off board. If he puts a hand back to steady himself, for instance, his hand mark, and not his feet marks, will be measured as his jump if it is closer to the take-off board.

The take-off board for the triple jump (formerly known, and more accurately, as the hop, step and jump) is sited much further back than the long jump board. The competitor takes off on one foot, lands on the same foot (the Hop), takes a long step to land on the other foot (the Step) — still on the runway — and then lands on both feet in the pit for the Jump.

5 Skills

The long jumper needs speed down the runway as well as good lift from the take-off board. Speed + height = distance. A good jumper must sprint flat-out with head up, not *looking for the board*. Once in the air some jumpers try to put in a stride in mid-air *(hitchkick)* while others hang momentarily before swinging their arms and legs forward violently before landing. Again the head should be up, not hanging backwards.

The triple jumper needs less height than a long jumper because if he goes too high in the Hop, he will lose speed for the Step. Strength and balance are essential to counteract wind.

ATHLETICS
Track & Field
The Jumps

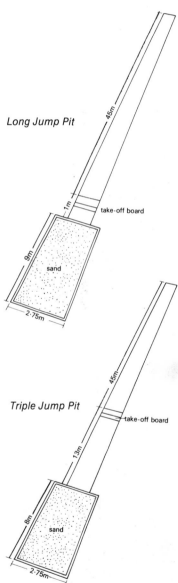

Long Jump Pit

45m

1m

take-off board

9m

sand

2·75m

Triple Jump Pit

45m

take-off board

13m

8m

sand

2·75m

The jumper has put his hand back. As the jump is measured from whatever part of the body lands nearest to the take-off board, the jumper has lost about a yard or metre on this attempt.

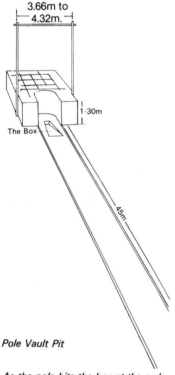

Pole Vault Pit

As the pole hits the box at the end of the runway, it bends alarmingly, taking the full weight of an athlete travelling at speed.

This is often described as 'gymnastics on the end of a pole' because the athlete uses a fibreglass pole, about 5m (16ft approx) in length, and weighing approximately 2kg (4lb approx) to lever himself up to and over a metal crossbar held at a measured height by adjustable uprights. He lets go of the pole at the moment of clearance, and lands on a specially-made 1m (1yd approx) high foam-rubber landing bed. Only men take part in this event.

1 The Pit

The runway is usually 45m (50yd approx) long with a *box* sunk into the ground for the pole. The crossbar weighs 2.2kg (5lb approx).

2 Equipment

Poles are made of fibreglass and come in various lengths to suit individual competitors. The amount of *bend* or *spring* in the pole can vary too and vaulters often have a selection to hand for warm, cool or windy weather conditions. They are usually slightly curved, with sticky tape binding at the bottom and near the top for a hand grip.

3 & 4 Winning & Rules

The competitor who clears the greatest height wins. The total number of vaults is irrelevant, except in deciding a tie between several athletes who have cleared the same height.

Each athlete can choose the height at which he wishes to enter the competition once the officials have announced the opening (starting) height, and the graduated amounts by which the bar will be raised at the end of each round.

Once any vaulter has had three consecutive failures, he is eliminated. These may well be all at one height or, if he chooses, he may pass after one or two failures and take his remaining attempt(s) at a greater height. But as

soon as a third consecutive failure is recorded he is out. He is then credited with the best height he has cleared.

If two vaulters have cleared identical heights, whichever has had fewer failures at that height is placed the higher.

5 & 6 Skills & Tactics

The approach run, from a runway at least 40m (44yd approx) long, has to be fast and correctly timed. As the vaulter arrives at the pit, he inserts the far end of the pole into a special sloping box, which has been sunk into the ground to a depth of 200mm (8in approx) between the uprights. This action is called the *plant* as he literally plants the pole into the ground, and by pulling hard on the pole with his own body weight, he creates a pronounced bend in it, which represents stored energy.

At the same time, he lifts his feet and hips up towards the crossbar, and as the pole begins to straighten out again, carrying him up with it, the pulling action develops into more of a push, as the vaulter virtually performs a handstand on top of the pole for a brief second. As he tries to thrust his body over the bar, he has to remember to push the pole away from him as he lets go of it. If it falls forwards and knocks the bar off, even if he were well clear, it would count as a failure. But if the pole falls forward into the pit without dislodging the crossbar, is it still a clearance.

The wind is a hazard; even when it seems calm at ground level it could still be very gusty 5.5m (18ft) up in the air. Cold weather is also detrimental to good vaulting, not only because of the adverse effects on the muscles, which is relevant to all events, but because the vaulting poles bend less easily at lower temperatures. They can even snap in mid-vault!

Because of the difficulties peculiar to the pole vault, an international competition can last a long time; eight hours or more is not unknown at a major international competition.

Therefore the competitor is then faced with a decision as to whether to get in a *safe* vault early on at a lower height, or to save energy for later greater height, with the greater risk of failure or that weather conditions may have deteriorated by the time he would otherwise vault. ■

Competitors take in turns to throw the javelin for distance and judges measure each valid throw to the nearest centimetre. Every competitor is allowed at least three throws, often six, but sometimes if there are more than eight people taking part, only the leading eight are permitted the further three throws. At a major meeting like the Olympic Games, however, a separate qualifying competition may be held in which every competitor who throws beyond a certain predetermined distance is allowed to compete in the final.

1 The Runway

36·50m

2 Equipment

A javelin consists of three parts: a metal head with a sharp point, the shaft (made of metal or wood), and cord-bound hand grip. From its widest part, approximately the centre of gravity where the grip is situated, the javelin tapers gradually to the metal head and the rear tip, but it has to be circular in cross section throughout.

The men's javelin is 2.6-2.7m (8ft 8in approx) long and weighs 800g (28oz); the women's 2.2-2.3m (7ft 5in approx) and 600g (21oz).

3 Winning

At the end of six rounds the thrower who has recorded the longest distance

wins, the next longest is placed second, and so on. In the event of a tie for any place, the judges consider the tying athletes' second best throws to decide.

4 Rules

The javelin is thrown from a runway 20-25m (33-38yd approx) long, and the competitor has to release the implement and come to a halt before reaching the white *scratch line* marking the end of the runway. He must not cross the line, or touch the ground in front of it, otherwise the throw is ruled a foul. The javelin has to land point first, making a mark in the turf even if it does not stick in, to be declared valid and measured. If it lands flat and makes no mark, the throw is void.

The last long stride puts the power into the throw as the athlete pulls the javelin through, using the full leverage of his torso and legs.

5 Skills

In the javelin, as in all the throws, the moment of release has to be an explosive one as athletes are powerless to do any more to improve the throw once it has left their hand. The thrower pulls back the throwing arm four strides before the moment of delivery, and on the final stride brings it through fast for the actual throw, while at the same time trying to *flight* it; a trajectory too high or too low will cause it to fall short. ∎

ATHLETICS

Track & Field

Javelin

ATHLETICS

Track & Field

The Throws

The competitors take it in turns to throw the hammer, discus or shot for distance and judges measure each valid throw to the nearest centimetre. Every competitor is allowed at least three throws, often six, but sometimes if there are more than eight people taking part, only the leading eight are permitted the further three throws. At a major meeting like the Olympics, however, a separate qualifying competition may be held in which every competitor who throws beyond a certain standard distance is allowed in the final.

Shot Put

Discus

Hammer

About to deliver the discus, this athlete braces his left leg to use it as a pivot. His arm whips round and the discus spins off the first finger.

1 Competition Areas

Because of the difficulties of spectating from a distance, the throwing areas usually have arcs marked with tape at, say, 60, 70 and 80m to give spectators a rough indication of each throw's length. An indicator board near the throwing circle shows the competitor's number, the round number, and the distance of each throw after measurement.

2 Equipment

The *shot* is spherical, smooth, and made of solid iron, brass, or any metal not softer than brass. The *discus* is made of wood or other suitable material with a metal rim which has to be rounded in a true circle; the centre of the discus is thicker than the rim, giving it the overall appearance of a tiny flying saucer.

The *hammer* consists of three parts: a completely spherical metal head, a length of wire not less than 3mm (1/10in) in diameter connected to the head by means of a swivel, and a grip (or handle) connected to the wire by a loop. Gloves for the protection of the hammer thrower's hands are permitted, but not for the discus or shot.

3 Winning

At the end of six rounds the thrower who has recorded the longest distance wins, the next longest is placed second,

and so on. In the event of a tie for any place, the judges consider the tying athletes' second best throws to decide.

4 Rules

The shot, discus and hammer are all thrown from *circles,* circular concrete slabs in the ground. The shot, which looks like a small cannonball, has to be *put* rather than thrown, with one hand. It is held close to the chin, and the hand is not allowed to drop below this level during the action of putting. A white wooden *stopboard,* positioned round the front edge of the 2.13m (7ft) wide circle helps the athlete stay in. He can touch the inside of the stopboard with his toe but not the top, and he must leave the circle by the rear half after each throw.

The discus rules stipulate only that it must be thrown from a 2.5m (8ft 2½ in) wide circle, and land in the area formed by a 40 degree arc from the circle, but not the precise throwing method. In practice, a 1¾ turn technique is normally used, with the thrower gripping the discus in the spreadeagled fingers of one hand. He also has to leave by the rear half of the circle on completion of the throw. In the shot and discus, throwers must not tape their fingers together to get a better grip and have to show an official their hands before each throw.

The hammer, like the discus, has no set method for throwing according to the rule book, other than that it must be thrown from the circle, commencing from a stationary position. In general, hammer throwers, gripping the hammer handle with both hands, swing it around twice to get it moving, then turn three times in the circle to accelerate the hammer and then finally release it. There is actually no limit on the number of these turns, and some throwers use four, but the width of the circle itself is the restriction. If a thrower loses his rhythm he may start his *wind-up* again, as long as the hammer has not touched the ground outside the circle. The competitor must not leave the circle until the hammer has landed, and then only by the rear half.

5 & 6 Skills & Tactics

Most throwers know when they have just achieved a good distance from the *feel* of the throw, and their reactions give a good clue even before the measurement. Likewise, they may sometimes deliberately step out of the front of the circle to save officials the trouble of measuring what they know is a poor throw.

For good technique in the shot put, watch for a full extension at the waist in delivery, and a long follow-through with the putting hand after delivery. In the discus, watch for a long and loose throwing arm; the further away the discus is from the body during the turn, the faster it is travelling, and the further it should go when released. Likewise with the hammer: its head is kept a long way from the body by use of straight arms as acceleration is gained through the turns. The hammer is swung through an angled plane, low at the back of the circle, high at the front.

A demonstration of the shotputter's action which also shows a couple of flaws. The left foot and left arm are too high so the throwing distance would be shortened.

A hammer thrower turns fast with arms fully stretched so that the weight is swung through the biggest arc possible.

7 Words

Cage: for safety reasons, a C-shaped cage is erected around the throwing circles at the hammer and discus to prevent any accidentally released implements from flying into the crowd or on to the track

O'Brien technique: the orthodox method of shot putting, in which the thrower starts with his back to the throwing area and *glides* across the circle to deliver the shot

Rotational technique: a relatively new method, in which the shot putter turns in the circle like a discus thrower before releasing the shot

Stopboard: the 10cm high wooden step in front of the shot put circle, which helps prevent the athlete toppling forward and out of the circle. This is not used in discus or hammer. ∎

ATHLETICS

Track & Field

Pentathlon, Decathlon

For 1 see page 23

The male athlete has to be strong enough to put the shot, throw the discus and javelin, and fast enough to sprint 100 and 400m. He needs enough stamina to run 1500m as well as sufficient agility to hurdle, and, as here, high-jump too.

The *multi-event* competition, as it is called, is a two-day mini-tournament to find the best all-round track and field athlete. It tests speed, strength, stamina, agility, technical skill and, of course, the ability to handle an arduous competitive situation, through a series of widely ranging events. At the highest level the winner cannot have a single *weak* event.

2 Equipment

Multi-event athletes need far more equipment than other athletes. Even though items like shot, discus and javelin will be provided, they still lug around huge bags containing different types of spiked running shoes, high jump shoes, javelin boots, their scoring tables, tape measures, and a thousand other things. It is vital to keep supple, so athletes also take blankets and sleeping bags into the arena with them to try to get some rest and warmth between events.

3 Winning

Each individual performance in the events earns the athlete a certain number of points, calculated by reference to special *international scoring tables.* For example, in the men's decathlon, a 100m run in 11.25 seconds earns 745 points, a time of 11.26 seconds earns 742 points, and so on. It is the total number of points from these 10 events which really matters, not the individual placing of the athlete in any of them. Similarly, the women compete in five events (the *pentathlon*), although their multi-event is being increased to seven events, the *heptathlon,* from 1981.

The breakdown of events is as follows:

Decathlon — men:
1st day — 100m; long jump; shot put; high jump; 400m
2nd day — 110m hurdles; discus; pole vault; javelin;1500m

Pentathlon — women:
1st day — 100m hurdles; shot put; high jump
2nd day — long jump; 800m

Heptathlon — women (from 1981):
100m hurdles; shot put; high jump; 200m; long jump; javelin; 800m

A good illustration of how the tables work is the following set of results from the 1976 Montreal Olympic decathlon, in which the American Bruce Jenner set a world record:

First Day	Performance	Points
100m	10.94s	819
Long J.	7.22m	865
Shot	15.35m	809
High J.	2.03m	882
400m	47.51s	923
First day total		4298

Second day	Performance	Points
110m Hurdles	14.84s	866
Discus	50.05m	873
Pole Vt.	4.80m	1005
Javelin	68.52m	862
1500m	4m12s	714
Two-day total		8618

4 Rules

The rules are virtually the same in each case as for the individual events, except that in the throws and the long jump only three trials per athlete are allowed. Also a competitor is allowed to commit up to three false starts in a race before disqualification, as opposed to two in the individual event. Obviously dis- qualification is a disaster as it means zero points for that event, compared to the 800-900 points to which the athlete must aspire in each activity. Likewise, failing to clear any height at all in the pole vault or high jump is a similar tragedy — no points.

5 Skills

The 1500m for men and the 800m for women is traditionally the final event, into which the tired competitors can pour their last ounces of energy. By middle distance standards, the per- formances are rarely eye-catching, but then middle distance runners don't usually warm up by throwing, vaulting, jumping or hurdling! The multi-event competitor has to be strong enough to cope with the throwing events, but not too bulky to high jump or hurdle. The opening event of the second day is testing too, because an athlete needs to be very supple to hurdle well, whereas he might be a little stiff from his efforts on the first day.

Apart from the physical problems, the decathlete/pentathlete has to be able quickly to get over any setback or disaster, and proceed to the next event straight away. A specialist sprinter may only need to be in the right frame of mind for ten seconds, but a decathlete has to keep himself at a physical and mental peak for two days. ■

ATHLETICS
Track & Field
Pentathlon, Decathlon

In the past, slim girls have been able to do well in the pentathlon despite an inability to put the shot convincingly. When the heptathlon is introduced it will put emphasis on strength rather than speed.

ATHLETICS

Track & Field

Walking, Cross Country

A perfect example of the heel-and-toe action required of a walker, who must always have some part of his foot in contact with the ground.

Race walking takes place both on the track and the road, but the major international competition distances are 20km (12½ miles approx) and 50km (31 miles approx) on the road, which are Olympic events. The 50km is 8km (5 miles approx) further than the marathon men run, so it is the longest race on the Olympic programme. Race walking for women is gradually growing in popularity, but so far is not included in any major international games.

In hot conditions walkers often wear white sunhats and light-coloured kit which reflect the sun's rays. In international races of 20km or more, refreshment stations are provided for the walkers at 5km (3 mile approx) intervals to prevent possible dehydration through sweating. The walkers wear thick socks to prevent blisters, and well-heeled shoes are needed to withstand the constant pounding of a long road race.

The events are straightforward races, given the restrictions of the rules defining race walking, and team events (not included in the Olympics) are decided by giving the first finisher one point, the second finisher two points, and so on. With an agreed number of finishers from each club to be counted, the team with the lowest total wins (e.g. 1st + 3rd + 4th + 6th = 14 points, beating 2nd + 5th + 7th + 8th = 22).

'Walking is a progression by steps so taken that unbroken contact with the ground is maintained.' In other words, the toe of the rear foot must not break contact with the ground until the heel of the advancing foot has touched down. This line between maintaining contact and breaking it can be a very fine one, and judges are appointed to watch the competitors' feet at various stages of a race to ensure that contact is being maintained. Additionally, the leg must be straightened momentarily at the knee on each stride, and the officials have the power to disqualify any competitor they consider is not walking fairly. The walker's forward progression is, in fact, a matter of leverage, using the heels and toes as points of resistance to the ground, with drive from the rear foot being very controlled.

The race walker's hip action, which may appear somewhat eccentric at first sight, has a definite purpose. The *wiggle* is a deliberate rotating of the hips to bring about a longer stride than is possible in ordinary walking, and the trunk has to remain erect, leaning neither forward nor back as such a lean would restrict the stride length. The whole action must be smooth: a jerky race walker is wasting energy, and

multiplied by the 1100 strides per km (or 1800 strides per mile) he will take, that is a lot of energy to waste. ∎

CROSS COUNTRY races are held over open country, fields, forest paths, and heathland, to provide competition on a constantly varying terrain, challenging both in gradient and surface. Most international-class races for men are staged on courses approximately 8-12km (4-7 miles) long, and for women from 3-5km (2-3 miles), with the annual world championships taking place each March. Cross country running is no longer included in the Olympic Games, although many of the world's top runners excel both over the country and on the track.

Cross country is a winter sport, so competitors often wear several layers of clothing to try to maintain body heat. Woollen hats and gloves are frequently worn on the coldest days, but the most important thing is keeping a foothold on a wide range of surfaces often encountered within one race. In heavy mud, or on grass, spiked shoes are ideal, but shoes with *waffle* soles are fast gaining popularity for varied ground conditions. They have dozens of small lightweight rubber studs spread over the sole, and are suitable for anything from road to mud.

Most individual events are straightforward races, but a team competition is often held in conjunction. Each club or country is asked to nominate, say, six of its athletes in the race as its team. If it is agreed that, say four men will actually score in the team competition, then the finishing positions of whichever are the first four of those six nominated runners home are added together to make that team's total, e.g. 1st + 3rd + 9th + 15th = 28 points. Therefore the team with the lowest total wins. Even the runners who are not included in the scoring four can play their part by overtaking rival runners and helping to make their opponents' score greater.

An alternative cross country team event is the relay, where usually about four to six stages are run, all on the same course. No batons are used, but the incoming runner has to touch hands with the outgoing runner to make the *change-over*.

The course, often consisting of a number of repeated laps, is marked by flags and arrows which have to be closely followed. Taking a short cut means disqualification. At the end of a race, the winner is ushered down a temporarily constructed channel, usually made of fencing or rope, and known as the

ATHLETICS
Track & Field
Indoor

Although cross country running is often regarded as a winter training exercise for the summer track season, there are athletes who are specialists, able to run efficiently and well in slippery and muddy conditions over undulating terrain.

finishing funnel. It is just wide enough for one runner, and as each of the following competitors crosses the finish line, they are *funnelled* on down the same route, at one end of which their number and finishing position is noted by officials

In wet conditions, watch for the athlete who appears to glide over the mud rather than get bogged down in it. A relatively fresh runner can be spotted by his ability to produce a high knee lift and vigorous arm drive on hills. ∎

INDOOR ATHLETICS, using tracks half the size or less of outdoor circuits, has developed from being simply a winter training exercise to get away from bad weather, into a mini-international competitive circuit in itself. In North America it is a major spectator attraction, and in Europe, the other continent where it has really caught on, there have been European indoor championships and international matches since the 1960s.

Some of the track events are necessarily cut-down versions of their outdoor equivalents. The 60m or 65yd replaces the 100m, for example, and the 60m hurdles is the indoor version of the 110m hurdles. Not only is there just limited room to race, there is also limited room to stop in the sprints! None of the standard throwing events, apart from the shot put, can be held indoors — for obvious reasons! And even the putters often have to use a leather-covered shot to prevent damage to the track. The longest running event is usually only 3000m or two miles, over 15 or more laps of the small track.

The banked tracks themselves are usually wooden-based with a synthetic rubberized surface. Because they are largely hollow underneath, many runners find that they give an extra bounce to their stride. But running fast round a tight bend, even with the banking, can be a tricky business, needing considerable experience. Often the shorter runner with the lower centre of gravity will be able to handle the indoor circuit better than a long-legged runner who may always have his measure outdoors. Tactics play a considerable part, especially in the middle distance races, where it is far more difficult to overtake on the tight bends than on an outdoor track.

Indoor 'world records' are not officially ratified, but the prevailing conditions in some cases can even be superior to outdoors. There is no wind to disrupt the pole vault, or indeed any event. And because of the limited space, the jumpers and vaulters often have to start their run-ups from halfway up a banked track, giving them increased momentum. Outdoors, turning such disadvantage into advantage in this way would not be possible.

The fact that the athletes are much closer to the spectators than outdoors means that the atmosphere of an indoor meeting is subsequently much greater, and the field events athletes in particular feel they hold more of the centre-stage than they normally do in an outdoor stadium, where they are sometimes only figures lost down one end. So it is occasionally more than a training exercise; it can also restore lost pride! ∎

Indoor events favour competitors with fast starts, as distances are only over 50-60m for the sprints.

BADMINTON

Badminton is akin to lawn tennis and squash. It has some of the blistering overhead power-shots of tennis and some of the subtle, deceptive touches seen in squash. It is one of the fastest-growing participant sports in the world. The aim is to volley a *shuttlecock* back and forth over a net with a racket until one side is unable to return it into court.

Badminton offers three varied games — each with its own distinctive magic: *singles,* men's and ladies' *doubles,* and *mixed doubles.* It has a contrasting variety of strokes which at one moment power the shuttle from the racket at up to 100mph (160kmph) and at the next caress it a few inches with net-skimming, micrometer accuracy. It demands a sprinter's start, masterful deception, chess-like tactics, a marathon runner's stamina and the reflexes of a panther.

1 The Court

The singles court is not as wide as the doubles court, but in singles the *service courts* are longer than in doubles, as they stretch all the way to the back *boundary line.*

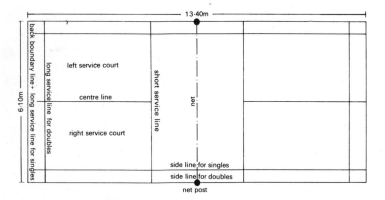

net post

2 Equipment

The lightness and fragility of both racket and shuttle are part of badminton's charm and the very essence of its fast, whippy, and deceptively wristy strokes.

The majority of rackets have metal frames. The shaft is of steel or carbon fibre to give maximum controllable

whip. Strung drum-tight with finest natural gut, they weigh only 3-4oz (100-128g).

Even more fragile is the game's missile — the shuttlecock. The base is of domed cork, covered in white leather and inside is a tiny lead pellet without which it would not fly properly. Into this base are set 16 goose feathers, inter-linked and strengthened with glued thread. It takes two geese to provide the perfectly matched feathers for a single tournament shuttle, which weighs roughly $\frac{1}{10}$oz (3g).

3 Winning

The first person to win two out of three games wins the match. In each game the winner is the first to 15 points (11 points in ladies' singles). *Points can be scored only by the serving side.* The player in the right-hand half-court always serves (diagonally) first. If the *rally* or series of shots is won, a point is scored and the server moves to the left-hand court. The same player, alternating sides, continues to serve until a rally is lost. Service then goes to the opponent. (In doubles, the serve would pass to the partner. If a further rally is lost, the serve then passes to their opponents, who continue in the same way.) The serving sides's score is always called out first by the umpire: 2-1, 3-1, 4-1, etc. In doubles, after the first server loses a rally, *second server* is added to the score: '4-1 second server'. (The side commencing a game initially have only one serve; thereafter, two as outlined above.)

In singles, the player serves from the right-half court when his score is even; from the left when it is odd.

Badminton is like several other racket sports which use the idea of *setting* in close games. If the score becomes 13-13 the non-server(s) can either play straight through to 15 or *set* (i.e. play an additional five points, to 18). This also applies at 14-14, but only a further three points may be played then (i.e. to 17). In ladies' singles setting is at 9-9 or 10-10 for a further three or two points respectively.

The decision to set or not depends on the state of the game. In doubles, when opponents both have serves in hand, a pair will invariably decide to set. This means that the opponents will have to get three of five points (rather than one or two) for victory, so the *setting pair* have a better chance of regaining service. When the opponents are second server, it may be decided to *play straight through* because:

The server is weak or nervous
The receiver is very effective at counter attacking
This bold decision could upset the opponents
The receivers are tired and would not want to protract the game, or it is felt that the opponents cannot maintain their long run of points that brought them to setting.

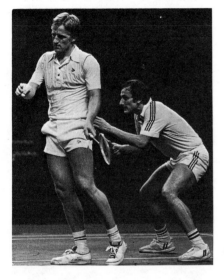

With his partner about to serve, the player on the right concentrates on his opponents. Both players are in the middle of the court.

4 Rules

There are several possible faults connected with serving. Unlike tennis, the server must serve underhand with no part of the shuttle above his waist and the racket clearly pointing downwards. He must have both feet on the floor within the service area. The receiver is also limited in that he may not move before the shuttle is hit or take any action which otherwise distracts or delays the server.

Players must not hit the shuttle before it crosses the net or touch the net under any circumstances while the shuttle is in play. The shuttle may not be hit twice on the same side of the net (either by the same individual or by the two members of a pair).

5 & 6 Skills & Tactics

SINGLES

The basic aim in singles is to force an opponent to run around the court by playing deceptive and good length *clears* and *drop-shots* to the four corners. Patience and stamina are essential because it can take 10-20 strokes to force a weak return or create a vulnerable opening. A *smash* is then used to try to end the rally. As a shuttle decelerates rapidly the smash is seldom used from behind the back doubles service line except by very powerful players. Even the fastest pin-pointed smash is often nonchalantly returned with an almost *dead racket* as a close *net-shot* or hit wristly *cross-court* away from an unbalanced opponent.

The high serve is occasionally varied with low ones but these do leave the deep back-hand open to attack. With an effortless flick of the wrist, most top players use a range of back-hand clears, drop-shots and smashes.

While one player covers the net, his partner smashes.

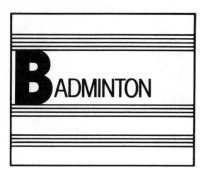

BADMINTON

To hurry his opponent into error a player may use *jump smashes* or *drops* (thereby gaining also a steeper angle), *flat* (horizontal) attacking clears, lobs and deceptive strokes.

Women lack the power and the speed of men so they cannot finish rallies so decisively. Consequently there are longer, tense battles fluctuating from attack to defence and back to attack. It is a war of attrition in which stamina and concentration matter as much as power.

LADIES' AND MEN'S DOUBLES

In ladies' and men's doubles positional play changes rapidly — from side by side when defending, to back and front when attacking. For the opening three or four strokes both pairs optimistically maintain back and front positions, jockeying to win dominance with downward or flat strokes. The serves are generally low, tape-caressing and to the corners, varied with occasional flicks and drives. The receiver's aim is to meet the shuttle early and hit down or flat to attack. His partner, racket up, bounces up and down equally aggressively at the net, ready to make acrobatic interceptions. He seizes every opportunity to *dab* down; if he cannot, he will play a tight *upward net shot* hoping to force a lift to his point-hungry partner.

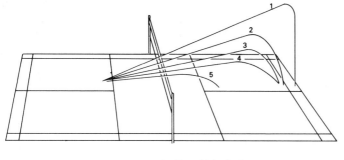

1 Very high singles serve
2 High doubles serve
3 Flick serve
4 Drive serve
5 Low serve

An attacking clear played from the back boundary line.

MIXED DOUBLES

This is a different game again — one in which delicacy and deception play a greater part.

To prevent the woman being out-gunned by the stronger, faster man she plays 95 per cent of the game at the net. Although the area she has to cover is small, her task is twice as difficult as the man's; cramped and crouching, she has half the time to decide whether she can control or should leave to her better-placed partner a shuttle which is travelling twice as fast as it will be when it reaches the man.

The top-class net player has many attributes: the ability to outface the most aggressive male receiver with low serves, often backhand, and deceptive flick serves; to attack high or low serves, playing them down flat or so accurately that the net cannot be at-

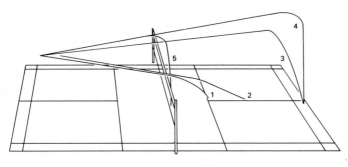

1 Attacking drop-shot
2 Smash
3 Attacking clear
4 Defensive clear
5 Floating drop-shot

1 Push-shot
2 Drive-half-court
3 Drive-full-length
4 Drop-shot at the net

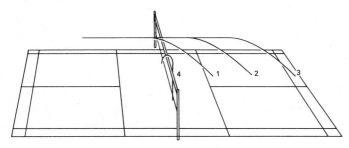

tacked. So too with the rest of her game. With her partner having to cover two-thirds of the court it is imperative that she does not *lift* the shuttle.

The man, serving from further back than in men's doubles, tries to outplay and out-position the lady — the potential weak link. He launches an all-out attack on her serve in an endeavour to break her confidence. If his own partner is strong and quick she stands just to his left and behind him when he receives. Then if he is drawn into the net she takes over at the back — but only temporarily. She then hits down and quickly regains her position at the net.

A back and front pair's sidelines are vulnerable, especially the area between the two opponents (known as the *divorce area,* for obvious reasons). As the man is the sole back-court defender, he too keeps the shuttle down with straight half-court pushes to confuse and draw his opponents from the centre before launching fast cross-court drives. If the shuttle is lifted short, he smashes steeply; if deep, he plays fast drop-shots to the divorce area. In defence he must have a quick eye, a strong back-hand and the ability to play shots close to the net with real accuracy.

Words

drop almost vertically down the other side
Stab: as in *upward* but racket stabs under shuttle turning it head over heels so making it difficult to hit cleanly
Push: deceptively like the *drive* but hit more gently to fall between net and back players or just over the net
Read: stroke anticipated or observed just before actual impact
Round-the-head strokes: strokes where racket meets shuttle over left, rather than

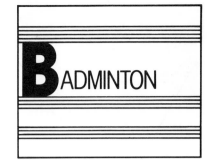

Putting everything into this drive, the nearest player seems to have caught the opposition flat-footed.

Backhand: stroke played on left side of right-hander
Bird: nickname for the shuttlecock
Clear: overhead stroke hitting shuttle from base-line to base-line
  Defensive: hit high to give striker time to regain his base
  Attacking: hit fast and flat to hurry opponent
Drive: attacking side-arm stroke played flat at roughly tape-height from about mid-court; used mainly in mixed doubles
Drop-shot: deceptive overhead stroke hitting shuttle from base-line just over net
Kill: win rally with smash
Lob: underhand clear hit high and deep as answer to *drop-shot* or *smash*
Net-cord: stroke when shuttle hits tape and topples over
Net shots: played from and/or to the net:
  Dab: shuttle above tape height dabbed wristily downwards, fast and steep
  Upward: shot of great delicacy stroked fractionally above tape to

right, shoulder; strong alternative to backhand strokes
Serves: opening stroke of each rally or exchange of shots:
  High: hit hard to drop vertically on back service-line so blunting attack and opening up court; used mainly in singles
  Low: hit gently to skim the tape and drop just beyond the front service-line so forcing a lifted return
  Flick: similar action to *low serve* but wristily flicked, fractionally before impact, just above reach of receiver
  Drive: again, similar action to *low* serve but last-second jab drives shuttle flat and fast into a gap
  Backhand: low, flick or drive
  Advantages:
  1 unusual
  2 forward point of impact gives receiver less time
  3 white shuttle in front of white clothing difficult to spot quickly
Smash: overhead stroke hit downwards powerfully and steeply to gain outright winner
Tape: white band on top of net. ∎

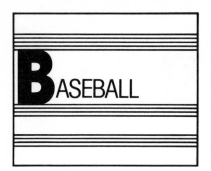

BASEBALL

Baseball is a sport where no action happens slowly. It is a summer game that is quicker than the eye, enhanced by the television replays which allow the viewer time to study what really took place. A game of strategy and endless permutations, so difficult to play well and so easy to play for enjoyment, baseball is tremendously popular in the United States, Latin America and Japan.

Combining nine individuals of differing skills into a team for an eight-month season, professional baseball is interesting for two distinct reasons. There is the drama of league competition with teams pursuing the championship *pennant* and an ultimate place in the *World Series* (America's championship playoffs). Then there are the performances of the individual players as they seek honours in *batting, fielding* and *pitching,* the three distinct skills which make up the game.

Above: standard positions

Below: the field markings

1 The Field

This is divided into the *infield* and the *outfield*. A square, called the *diamond*, is the centre of the action. At three corners of the diamond are *bases*. The bases, canvas bags pegged to the

ground, are at 90ft (27.4m) intervals on three corners of the square made by *home plate, first base, second base* and *third base.* Home plate is a five-sided slab of whitened rubber. The front edge, which faces the pitcher, is 17in (43cm) wide. The sides are 8½ in (22cm) long and the two rear edges which meet at the intersection of the foul lines are 12in (30cm) long. The bases are circled counter-clockwise from right to left by the *batter* when he attempts to score a *run.* In the middle of the diamond, 60ft 6ins (18.4m) from home plate, is the pitcher's *mound,* approximately 16in (40cm) high, from which the ball is thrown to the batter.

Beyond the immediate square is the *infield crescent.* The area around the pitcher's mound is grass, as is the outfield, but the surface between the bases and extending about 20ft (6m) between the green areas is dirt. This provides a surface for players running from base to base to *slide* into the base.

The outfield, surrounded by a fence about 10ft (3m) high, is vast and grass-covered. Distances down the two *foul lines* which mark the limits of the playing area *(left field line, right field line)* average about 330ft (100m), while the furthest distance is directly opposite home plate, often as great as 460ft (140m).

There is also territory outside the two lines, which is designated *foul territory.* A fielder may go into this area to take a catch, but since the area is small and bordered by spectator seats, this is usual only in the case of balls hit straight into the air and drifting off into the foul regions.

All baseball stadiums are different sizes so there are no uniform distances to the fences but all the distances around the bases and from mound to plate are mandated by the rules. It is also not necessary for the surface to be grass. In fact, several modern stadiums in North America are covered with artificial turf, giving rise to arguments about its effect on the game. Balls struck onto the turf move much more rapidly than off grass and require fielders to stand much further away from the batters.

Artificial turf does have one clear benefit: it is almost always in playable condition. Baseball cannot be effectively played on grass in the rain and tradition holds that the professional game is not played during inclement weather. The popular expression 'taking a raincheck' comes from the practice of allowing spectators to use their tickets for a rescheduled game.

2 Equipment

A bat, a ball and a glove are essential items. Safety demands a batting helmet and a good, snug-fitting uniform.

The batting helmet is worn by the hitter and the base-runner to protect the head from thrown balls. It is vital.

The uniform consists of tight pants and socks which protect the legs when sliding or falling in attempts to field batted balls.

The bat is made of wood, usually ash. Gloves are made of leather and must be flexible with a webbed pocket to trap the ball. The ball itself is white and hard, about the size of a cricket ball, 9-9¼ in (22.5-23.5cm) in circumference, 5-5¼ oz (142-149g) in weight.

Special *cleated* (studded) shoes are worn on natural fields, athletic shoes (gym shoes) on artifical surfaces.

3 Winning

The object of the game is to score more *runs* than the opposition. Each team gets nine turns at bat (called *innings*) during a game, but extra innings will be played to determine a victor if scores are level after nine. The visiting team always bats first.

In order to score, a batter must successfully complete the circuit of all four bases. Each time he does it, it counts as one run. When he is *up at bat* a batter stands close to home plate and receives deliveries from the pitcher. An umpire is behind the plate to determine whether the pitch could have been hit *(a strike)* or is too high or wide *(a ball)*. Four balls constitute a *walk* and allow the batter to reach first base automatically. He can also reach first base (or even further) by hitting the ball safely into fair territory. The batter must *always* run when he hits the ball into fair territory; this gives the defenders their chance to get him out. If he reaches first base, his successful hit is called a *single;* if he reaches second base, a *double;* third base is a *triple;* and if he can make it all the way round in one go, a *home run.* Any hit over the fence into the crowd is automatically a home run, although the batter jogs round the bases just to confirm it.

The pitcher has released the ball, which is halfway to the batter. The catcher is obscured by the umpire, who wears face and chest protection. He hovers behind the catcher to decide whether a pitch is a ball or strike.

Baseball

Once *on base,* he is now called a *runner* and there are several ways to advance. He must go forward to the next base when he is *forced* by another runner advancing behind him; or he may attempt to advance on his own, simply racing toward the next base and trying to beat the defence. This is called *stealing* and can be done at any time once a man is on base. If there is a man on each base, the bases are *loaded* and a home run at this stage would score four runs as the three men on base would get home safely as well as the batter.

The defenders can get a batter out in three main ways.

1 *Struck out.* Each batter has three strikes before he is out. A strike is registered every time the umpire signals that a pitch crossed home plate in the *strike zone* (between the armpits and knees of the batter) or when a batter swings and misses. The first two *foul balls* (hit into foul territory) count as strikes; after that foul balls are not counted.

2 *Caught.* If the ball is hit into the air (a *fly ball*) and is caught before hitting the ground, the batter is out.

3 *Off Base.* Once the ball is hit, a batter must be on base to be *safe.* He will be out if he is beaten to a base by a fielder catching and throwing the ball to the baseman who must be touching the bag. A runner who is touched with the ball when off base is also out.

Once three men are out irrespective of how many are *on base,* the side is retired and the other team bats. An inning is completed when both sides have had three men retired.

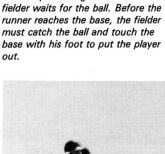

No. 23 sprints to get on base as the fielder waits for the ball. Before the runner reaches the base, the fielder must catch the ball and touch the base with his foot to put the player out.

The balance between attack and defence in baseball is maintained by a simple equation: it is much harder to hit than to defend. A good batter reaches base only three times in every 10 tries, so the number of runs scored in a game is not very high. Typical scores are 5-3, 7-4 and 3-1 and it is not unusual for teams to fail to score at all. When that happens the winning pitcher has pitched a *shutout.* Of course there are days when the batters seemingly cannot fail and ocassionally scores do reach double figures.

Rules

The pitcher must keep his foot in contact with a rubber plate on the mound; this keeps him the required distance

The pitcher in action. Although his rear foot was on the rubber plate on the mound as he wound up, he rocks forward on delivery.

from home plate. He must not rub anything on the baseball in order to make it do tricks on the way to the plate. Examples would be scuffing the ball on his pants or applying perspiration to make it swing.

Similarly, a batter must not apply any substance to the hitting surface of his wooden bat, although the handle may be rubbed with pine tar to improve the grip.

No batter or baserunner can interfere with a fielder's attempt to play the ball. Fielders are allowed to dive or leap for any balls, including reaching among the spectators in order to take a catch, but they must not obstruct the runner. The runner may employ any subterfuge such as pretending to steal a base, trying to

disturb the pitcher by jumping or walking away from his base, but he must not physically interfere with play.

There are a lot of technical rules, of course, but they govern specific instances. The spirit of the game says that the pitcher and fielders try to get the hitter out and the batter tries to get safely on base and then score runs.

Four umpires are stationed around the bases to make decisions. The most difficult are those determining whether a runner reaches a base before the ball does. Baseball tradition allows for some argument over these decisions but it also says 'the umpire is always right'.

Skills

Every baseball player is both an attacker and a defender, but there are special skills with all of the positions. Batters must be quick to spot different kinds of *pitches,* able to judge which pitches will be in the strike zone and which ones to ignore. A *free swinger* tries for distance so as to beat the pitcher with sheer strength. These men are often the home run hitters. They also tend to strike out a lot. A more controlled batter will try to place the ball in a specific direction, using a shorter swing. While this batter won't hit as many runs, he may well have a higher *batting average,* the statistic which shows how many times he hits *safely* (gets to first base) in relation to his times at bat. For instance, 10 in 30 tries is written as a .333 average.

Fielders are grouped in two categories: *infielders* and *outfielders.* Infielders ring the bases. The *first baseman* is vital since most *outs* are recorded there. He must be sure-handed though speed is not vital. The *second baseman* and *shortstop* play similar roles but need good speed to reach balls hit hard and fast into their areas. The *third baseman* has a difficult job since he is quite close to the batter and he must consistently make long throws across the diamond to first base, so he must have a *good arm.* All of the outfield positions call for speed and good judgement since the primary task of the deep fielders is to catch balls hit in the air and to prevent hard hit balls from finding gaps between them. Each outfielder, of course, must be able to throw well over a long distance.

The *catcher,* clearly, is a specialist. He must handle each pitch thrown and

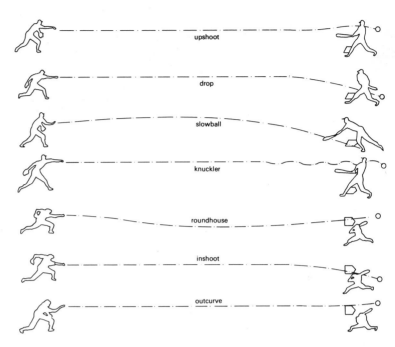

The pitches used in baseball

help his pitcher by presenting a target for each delivery. In addition, the catcher *runs the defence* because he is the only man with the entire field in front of him.

The pitcher is the most specialized of all. He may try to use sheer speed (a *fast ball*) or a variety of pitches which swing in the air. They include the *curve* (which moves away from the batter), the *drop* (which falls just before reaching the batter), the *screwball* or *inshoot* (a curve moving into the batter) or the *slider* (with a late dip away from the hitter). These are the major pitches but few master all of them. A good pitcher usually has control of two or three and mixes them often to keep the hitter guessing.

The pitcher winds up on his mound. He looks over his left shoulder at the target area, the strike zone.

BASEBALL

AMERICAN LEAGUE

Cleveland   010 100 000—2 7 2
Toronto   010 420 10x—8 12 0

Garland, Monge (8) and Diaz; T.Underwood and Cerone. W—T.Underwood, 8-16. L—Garland, 4-10. HRs—Toronto, Howell (13), Mayberry (21).

Oakland   000 000 200—2 3 0
Chicago   200 000 12x—5 11 3

Keough, Heaverlo (8), Hamilton (6) and Heath; Dotson, Hoffman (8), Proly (8) and Colbern, Foley (9). W—Dotson, 2-0. L—Keough, 1-16. HRs—Chicago, Washington, (13), Squires (2).

California   100 000 000—1 7 0
Milwaukee 000 100 10x—2 7 0

Tanana, Montague (7) and Downing; Slaton and Moore. W—Slaton, 15-8. L—Tanana, 6-5. HR—Milwaukee, Thomas (42).

Seattle   000 500 100—6 13 1
Kansas City 001 200 000—3 9 3

Dressler and Cox, Stinson (9); Splittorff, Eaton (5), Martin (7), Quisenberry (8) and Porter. W—Dressler, 3-2. L—Splittorff, 13-17. HR—Kansas City, Wilson (6).

Boston   000 021 000— 3 9 1
Baltimore   920 200 00x—13 15 1

Fans follow baseball by reading the box scores. Flashed up on TV and printed in newspapers, these shortened versions show that in the first game Cleveland were the visitors (batting first), that they scored runs in the second inning and again in the fourth - a total of 2. They had 7 hits and 2 errors. Toronto, the home side, won with one run in the second, four in the fourth, two in the fifth and an eighth run in the seventh inning. The 'x' in the ninth shows that Toronto did not have to bat in their final inning as they had already won 8 - 2.

Garland started pitching for Cleveland but was replaced by Monge in the eighth; the catcher was Diaz. Underwood pitched for Toronto, Cerone was the catcher. The winning pitcher was Underwood, who has now won eight games and lost sixteen this season; Garland has won four, lost ten. Howell scored a home run for Toronto, his thirteenth of the season; Mayberry's was his twenty-first.

The catcher crouches behind home plate. He wears a protective face mask, a chest protector held in place by the straps, and leg guards. His mitt is larger than other fielders' mitts. The catcher is the major tactician on the field.

6 Tactics

Within the game, defensive placement of fielders is most important. This is where the manager and coaches come in as they study opponents to determine where batters are likely to hit the ball and then place fielders in those spots.

The catcher is the major tactician on the field. Using a series of coded signs, he suggests pitches which the pitcher refuses or agrees to with a shake or nod of the head. The defensive team has a variety of other tactical decisions to make, but the most important is when to change pitchers.

If the starting pitcher is ineffective or tiring and giving up hits, he will be replaced by a *relief pitcher,* a specialist who works only a few innings at a time. These relievers are so specialized that managers will call on a left-handed pitcher to probe the weaknesses of just one hitter, then bring in a right-handed pitcher for the next batter. Most teams carry nine or ten pitchers and might expect to use three or four in any one game. Once a pitcher has been relieved he cannot pitch again in the match.

The batting team must also decide whether to use the power game, going for a big inning of many runs, or try to squeeze out runs one at a time. The latter strategy involves the use of *sacrifice bunts,* when a player makes a deliberate out, dropping the ball down in front of him in order to advance a runner in a scoring position. Weaker hitting teams will employ these stratagems. Coaches at first and third base tell the runners when to stop and go because the runner's back is often to the fielder.

The batting team's manager can also *pinch hit* at any time, that is, send in a substitute hitter for a weak batter, or a left-handed batter to face a right-handed relief pitcher. These permutations are possible because each team will have about 16 batters, only eight of whom start any game.

7 Words

Batter: he bats in sequence with other team members; a good batter is one who hits safely three in every 10 tries

Big inning: what results when a team puts several hits together; anything more than three runs an inning is a big inning (the record, incidentally, is 17 in the major leagues)

Bunt: when the batter tries to hit the ball very softly so as to deceive fielders who are playing too far away from him; difficult to do

Double: a hit for two bases

Error: a mistake by a defender who fails to take a chance to put a batsman out

Fair territory: the area where the fielders are stationed is fair; balls hit in this area count as good

Fly ball: a batted ball struck in the air; if caught, the batter is out; if it clears the outfield fence, it's a home run

Force play: when a runner must try to advance because a batter hits the ball fairly; two men can never occupy the same base, so the first one on a base is forced to leave when another takes his place

Foul territory: the area outside the lines, where there are no fielders except the catchers, is foul; a player may make a catch here, but balls which fall in this area cannot count as hits

Grand slam: a home run with three men on base, baseball's ultimate hitting weapon

Hit: a batted ball that eludes the defence, lands safely and allows the runner to reach base

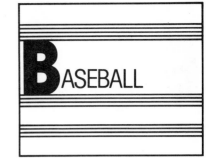

BASEBALL

Home run: a hit for all four bases, usually a ball struck out of the park altogether, clearing the fence which surrounds the outfield

Inning: divided in halves, the top belonging to the visiting team, the bottom to the home team; the home team always bats last

Knocked out of the box: when a pitcher is forced to leave the game because the other team is getting too many base hits

Line drive: a hard-hit ball that goes between, or just over, infielders

Line up/Batting order: the card which tells who plays, which position they play, and the order in which they bat; prepared by the manager for each game

No-hitter: the pitcher's ultimate weapon, when he gets a team out nine times and allows no batter to hit safely; very rare

Out: the retirement of a batter or runner, three of which are needed to end each team's time at bat (half-innings)

Pinch-hitter: substitute batter

Pitcher: he starts the play by delivering the ball in overhand fashion to the batter from a mound; there are two kinds of pitchers: *starters,* who work every few days, and *relievers,* who may pitch each day for short spells

Pop up: a ball hit straight up in the air, usually caught by an infielder

Run: scored by a batter who reaches first base safely, then advances to second, third and home without being retired, before three batters are out in an inning; no run can be scored while a third out is being made

Single: a hit for one-base

Steal: advancing from one base to another while the pitcher is delivering the ball to the batter; it's hard to do, but speedy runners make it a speciality

Strike out: three swings and three misses by the batter; he's out

Triple: a hit for three bases

Walk: when four pitches are judged to be not in the hitting zone by the umpire the batter can walk to first base. ∎

At bat, the left-handed batter with a protective helmet; his wrists are cocked ready to swing into the ball. He stands sideways on to the pitcher.

BASKETBALL

Basketball has the vigour and creativity of soccer, plus the attraction of constant scoring. Inventor James Naismith, a Canadian by birth, would probably not recognize the multi-million dollar arenas built across America to house his sport, which began with a couple of peach baskets nailed to a balcony in a YMCA College in Massachusetts, but he would still recognize his game, so little has changed in 90 years.

Basketball is a handling game, with five players on each side who score by tossing the ball through a round hoop that is 10ft (3.05m) off the floor. This makes it a tall person's game, though highly skilled shorter players can also be effective.

1 The Court

The court is rectangular with a surface of wood or rubberized composition material. It is divided into two by the *half court line.* At each end of the court is the target. This is the *basket,* an orange metal hoop with a loose string net hanging down, which is fixed to a *backboard* of clear, hard plastic. The basket actually protrudes 5ft (1.20m approx) into the court and is 10ft (3.05m approx) above the floor. The area marked out on the floor under each basket is called the *keyhole.* No attacking player can stay inside this area for more than three seconds. This rule stops the big players from waiting under the net and so keeps the game moving.

Waiting for the tip-off, C and 3 are opposing centres, 4 and 5 are guards defending against forwards A and B. E and D defend against 1 and 2.

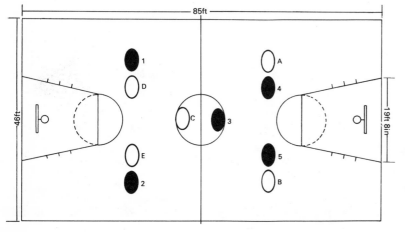

2 Equipment

Most of the expense is the creation of the indoor playing area, which must have the court, the baskets and the backboards. The individual needs only a pair of indoor athletic shoes with good rubber soles and a simple physical training outfit. The orange ball is about 30in (75-78cm) in circumference and weighs about 22oz (600-650g).

Ankle and knee wraps are occasionally worn, but no padding may be used at all, except for soft elbow and knee guards. Any wraps to protect an injury (such as a cut or muscle pull) must be soft so there is no danger to other players.

3 Winning

Bird's eye view of a scoring attempt. Three members of each team are under the basket, while the two far ones are ready in case the ball does not go in.

Every time a player *shoots* the ball into the basket his team gets two points. The ball must go through the hoop from the top and can be bounced off the backboard. After a foul, the fouled player may be awarded two *free throws,* which he takes from the *free throw line.* An unhindered shot, each is worth one point.

The game is played in two halves of 20 minutes, though the American professional game consists of four 12-minute quarters. If the score is level at the end of regulation time, extra periods of five minutes are played until one side wins.

A free throw. Note the flip of the wrist to impart slight backspin. The ball tends to drop sharply when it hits the backboard -hopefully into the basket!

4 Rules

There are simple differences between professional and college rules in North America and some slight variations in the rules played in international competitions, but they are only technical. The idea of the sport holds true regardless of which set of regulations is used.

Each team has five players on court at any one time. Substitutions are allowed at any time so the squad may consist of as many as 12 players. A coach sends on a substitute for tactical reasons or to replace a player who is injured or tired from the fast pace of the game.

The game begins with a *jump ball* when the referee throws up the ball, and two opposing players jump to gain possession by tapping it to their own players. Once a team has the ball the players try to move up the court towards their opponents' basket by passing or *dribbling* the ball. Dribbling is a basic skill which looks easier than it is. A player with the ball has to bounce it off the floor each time he takes a step but can only use one hand at a time. As soon as a player uses both hands to hold the ball he must pass or shoot and cannot start dribbling again.

While one player has possession of the ball his teammates manoeuvre themselves into good scoring positions. The shooter may be hindered by a defensive player but direct physical contact is not allowed during a shot at the basket. At the same time, a defender may not block the ball on its downward flight toward the basket — this

stops the tall player using his height to an unfair advantage.

Defenders who do make physical contact with their opponents, or attackers who deliberately collide with defenders, are charged with *personal fouls.* Once a player has committed five he can take no further part in the game. An American professional player *fouls out* after six. If the collision occurs as a player is shooting for the basket, two free throws are awarded as well as a personal foul.

Lesser fouls are known as *violations* and these include intentionally kicking the ball, *travelling* (taking more than 1½ steps without bouncing the ball), and infringements of two special time rules. Teams are required to play attacking basketball because of these two rules: a team has to leave its own half within 10 seconds of gaining possession of the ball, and it must shoot for the basket within 30 seconds (international rules), or 24 seconds (American professional rules) of bringing the ball into play. No such shooting rules exist in American university basketball.

After a violation, the opposing team is given possession and they *bring the ball in* from the side line nearest the spot where the offence occurred. A team also loses possession if it lets the ball go *out of bounds* (off the court) and after a basket has been scored. The ball is brought back into play at the spot where it went out of bounds; after a basket, this would be from the end line.

5 Skills

Although anyone can shoot and everyone has to defend, the five players on each team have specific roles. *Forwards* must be good shooters from the sides and corners since they play mainly to the right and left of the basket. They must also be good at *rebounding,* which is regaining possession of the ball as it bounces off the backboard or ring after an unsuccessful shot.

Centres are usually the tallest players, must be consummate rebounders and generally are the top scorers. When attacking they are waiting for passes from their teammates so they tend to play with their backs to the basket and must be able to spin quickly to shoot. On defence they are often the last player between an attacker and the basket so must be adept at blocking shots without fouling.

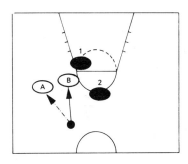

The Screen. B passes to A and runs into the gap between A and his marker 1. A then shoots as his teammate screens the defence.

A scoring attempt has failed, so the dark-shirted attacker and his opponent go for the rebound. Timing and aggression are vital as defenders should never allow attackers a second chance to shoot.

BASKETBALL

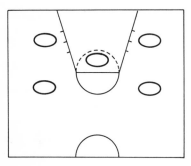

This zone defence, the 2-1-2, is used most of all. With one man in the middle of the free-throw lane, two men guard the backboard and two men stand level with the foul line. The man in the middle can drop back to help with rebounding. The disadvantage is that he would not be up with play on a fast break.

It is almost impossible to stop a well-executed jump shot. Here the player is well clear of his challengers, sees the basket clearly and shoots at the peak of his jump.

The lay-up shot is considered the easiest shot of all because the closer a player is to the basket, the better is his chance of scoring. Here he 'lays' the ball up against the backboard, angling it so that it rebounds into the basket.

The two *guards* play behind the three forwards. They are the creative players, the playmakers, who are often quicker and shorter. They concentrate on passing the ball to their forwards and centre under the basket but must be able to shoot from medium range (25ft/8m) to draw out defenders. Good guards also lead the *fast break* from defence to attack.

All players must be able to pass accurately over short and long distances or by bouncing the ball past an opponent or teammate. There are several identifiable shots, including the *lay up* where the player dribbles in under the basket and shoots at very close range and the stationary *set shot* taken from about 15-25ft (5-8m) away from the basket. The most common is the *jump shot* where the ball is released in mid-air as a player jumps to get clear of an opponent. The *hook* is more complicated because the player's back is to the basket as he swivels and shoots in one movement with a hook of the arm.

6 Tactics

Basketball teams must make two vital decisions: what kind of attack to employ and what kind of defence to play. Each decision will determine how the game proceeds.

There are three attack options. First, a team may elect to play a slow, patterned game, utilizing as much of the time available on each offensive movement. This style of play favours a good passing team, one that is able to get people free for easy scoring chances by a series of manoeuvres. The slower style can also be used to negate a height disadvantage, since fewer attempted shots means fewer eventual rebounds, which are likely to be grabbed by the taller opponents.

Second, a team may choose a *race horse* style of play, relying almost totally on the fast break. In this manner, usually preferred by tall teams, the ball is moved into the attack zone as quickly as possible and the first available shot is taken. These teams depend on their speed to beat the defence and on their height to control rebounds.

Third, a *controlled fast break* may be employed. In this style, a team will advance quickly if the opportunity is there (whenever the defenders are immediately outnumbered, for example), but may play the slower game if the running opportunity is not present.

Most have a recognizable offensive pattern for which the opposition chooses the appropriate defence.

Few teams are truly adept at both the *pattern attack* and the fast break.

There are two fundamental defences: the *zone,* where a player protects a designated area of the floor rather than marking an individual player, and the *man-to-man,* which involves the close shadowing of a rival in the offensive court. The zone is most effective against teams which like to pass and cut through areas since the individual players are not drawn out of position when they are protecting areas of the court; the man-to-man requires greater physical endurance, speed and agility, but is generally thought to be the most effective defence if it can be played well. Clearly, a man-to-man needs five quick defenders, while a zone might disguise the lack of speed of a player or two.

Each defence can be extended to cover the entire playing surface and is called a *press*. The *zone press* is especially effective at trapping players behind the 10-second line, but is vulnerable to the long pass and the fast break; the *man-to-man press* is obviously a physically demanding tactic, so is rarely used for long.

RIGHT: A Soviet player goes for the basket in a game against the USA.
PAGE 54: A four-man bobsleigh at the end of its run at the Winter Olympics.

There are specific tactical roles for each team member. A standard offensive play is the *pick* where one attacker, acting as a *screen,* keeps defenders at bay. This gives his team-mate an unimpeded shot. Defenders must learn to slide or move away from their own man to double up on the man with the ball, but this can only be done when all of the defenders are working in unison. The same is true for *switching* in a man-to-man defence, where defenders foil the pick by exchanging defensive responsibilities. Clearly a lot of practice and understanding are necessary for it all to work.

It is easy to recognize defences, harder to spot the attack. If a man shadows his opponent everywhere, then it's man-to-man; if attackers are allowed to move through the defence in the direction of the basket when they do have the ball, it's a zone. The fast break attack is noticeable for its high speed emphasis, of course, but it takes more than just a couple of exposures to the sport to pick up the more intricate patterns of the controlled attack teams. They have an immense variety of styles, an entire vocabulary that is more for the devoted follower of the game than the first-time viewer.

7 Words

Assist: a pass that results in a basket being scored
Back court: the defensive zone
Boxing out: the art of keeping the body between the basket and the attacker; close marking
Buttonhook: change of direction as player doubles back on himself
Defensive rebound: a rebound caught by defenders
Double team: when two defenders mark one attacker, usually the star player
Drive: to attack at full speed
Dunk shot: when a player jumps very high and literally stuffs the ball through the hoop
Fake: to feint
Field goal: a successful shot during normal play, worth two points
Free throw: uncontested shot from free throw line, worth one point; must be taken by player fouled, unless injured

LEFT: Wearing the yellow jersey, the race leader attacks the hill climb.
PAGE 55: England cricket captain Ian Botham clips a ball to leg.

Game clock: runs whenever ball is in play, stops when ball is out of bounds or when foul is committed; so 40-minute game takes about two hours including interval
Goal tending: striking the ball on its downward flight to the basket; illegal
Jump ball: the method of starting play; the ball is tossed up between two players who try to tap it back to their teammates
Pattern offence: slower attack with players moving to designated spots to execute pre-planned plays
Personal foul: after five of these, a player is out of the game (six in American pro league)
Pick/Screen: an offensive manoeuvre using one player to block for another, without making contact; a player places himself between the defender and his own teammate who has the ball
Pressure defence: coverage all over court; usually defenders do not bother to harass attackers beyond the halfcourt line, allowing the 10-second rule to do it for them
Shot clock: the 30-second (or 24-second in American professional game) clock which limits time a team may possess the ball without shooting; failure to shoot in the allowed time costs possession
Stalling: slowing play down by maintaining possession (usually in US college play)
10-second line: the halfcourt line; teams have 10 seconds to cross this line after obtaining possession in defensive zone
Time out: when play is stopped, often for teams to discuss tactics
Travelling: taking more than 1½ steps without dribbling; penalty, loss of possession. ■

BASKETBALL

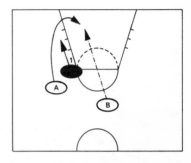

Player A uses the button hook as he goes for the basket. He sprints for the endline, then shakes off 1 as he turns back quickly to take a pass from B.

As he drives for the basket, this player shows how the ball should be kept low as he dribbles, using the fingers, not the palm of the hand.

Bobsleigh

The big dipper at a fairground demands little courage compared with the daring descent of a sled as it hurtles down a slithery zig-zagging chute of ice. Sleds are manned by crews of two or four.

off the track — an error that has caused fatal accidents in the past. Most courses now have the major bends electrically iced, but totally artificial tracks tend to be slow and 'safe' and therefore unpopular with experts.

The secret of recording a good time on a bob-run is to take the fastest line. Travelling too high or too low on the wall of ice can add unwanted fractions of a second to a run.

1 The Courses

Championship courses are a maximum of 1200m (1300yd approx) in length and include at least 15 banked turns. The ice-walled banking at the sharpest bends can be about 6m (20ft approx) high, topped by an overturning safety lip to minimize the chance of shooting

2 Equipment

Today's sleds are precision-built machines of steel and aluminium resting on two pairs of rounded runners, the ones at the rear on a fixed axle while those at the front are turned by sensitive ropes.

The crew seats are only 20cm (8in approx) above the ice, behind stream-lined fibreglass cowlings which reduce wind resistance and afford some protection in the event of a crash. Sleds must be no more than 67cm (2ft 2¼in approx) wide and their length is limited to 3.8m (12ft 5in approx) for crews of four and 2.7m (8ft 10in approx) for twos. The two-man is called a *boblet*. Speeds exceeding 150kmph (90mph approx) are achieved, so riders wear protective knee and elbow pads as well as crash helmets and goggles.

3 Winning

International championships comprise four runs for each sled, usually two a day on consecutive days, the lowest aggregate time deciding the winner, and even after four descents the outcome may be determined by mere hundreths of a second. For major championships each nation may enter three sleds per event during training but only two may compete in the actual championship.

4 Rules

Any advantage which heavier crews may have is eliminated by rules stipulating the maximum combined weight of bobs with their crews as 630kg (1389lb) for fours and 385kg (847lb) for twos. Within these limits, additional weights may be bolted to the sled to assist a lightweight crew.

5 & 6 Skills & Tactics

There are several ways in which crucial seconds can be saved. One is obviously in steering — going into turns at the correct angle without rising higher up the banking than necessary. This is where course familiarity allied to driving skills counts so much and therefore there are always four official training days on a course prior to a championship.

The brakeman at the rear needs to check the runners and work in perfect coordination with his driver, which is why the same pair tend to stay together for several seasons. The skill of synchronizing weight transference to control movement and assist the steering is more pronounced in four-man crews, when the two middle men play a more vital role than is evident.

They are by no means simply human ballast. The faster the sled goes, the more the crew has to lean inwards as one man, and this unison of movement is acquired through team training and mutual understanding. Watch for a crew not leaning together and you will know their time will suffer.

Often underrated is the importance of the start, where technique can easily win or lose the event. The electric timing begins 15m (16yd approx) after the start and all riders including the driver have to push the sled forward with the aid of rear and side handles before leaping into their seats. Perfect teamwork is required in this, an art of its own, to ensure a speedy getaway without rocking the sled or getting in each other's way. This is so important that most teams practise starts in simulated conditions well before the season starts.

Loudspeaker announcements give each crew's intermediate time at various points on the course and the first time is of special interest because it always indicates whether the start has been satisfactory.

7 Words

Ballast: extra weight added by crews who have less than maximum allowed
Bob: popular name for bobsleigh
Boblet: a two-man bobsleigh
Brakeman: rear member of crew who coordinates start and finish
Cowling: fibreglass hood, steamlined for extra speed
IBF: International governing body, International Bobsleigh Federation
Middle men: middle two competitors in four-man bob
Starting block: brakeman pushes off this at start. ∎

BOBSLEIGH

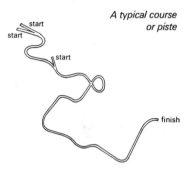

A typical course or piste

The piste snakes round a mountain-side and even crosses itself once. There are three entry chutes offering alternative starts.

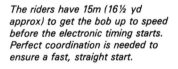
The riders have 15m (16½ yd approx) to get the bob up to speed before the electronic timing starts. Perfect coordination is needed to ensure a fast, straight start.

BOWLING

Bowling has made the transition from pure fun to high competition with the advent of big-money tournaments. A culmulative-scoring game, the object is to knock down more *pins* than the opponents by bowling a large, heavy ball down a special *lane*. Bowling is a test of skill and stamina over a five-day professional tournament.

A bowler may still not be regarded by many as much of an athlete, but he or she must be consistent to first weather the qualification tournament phase, then shift mental gears for all-out competition.

2 Equipment

The bowling building has specialized lanes, pin-spotters, *air-jets* for drying the hands during competiton to ensure a better grip, and scorecards, some projected upon a screen for easier viewing. However, the ultimate in modern bowling equipment even eliminates the need for a screen — a computer does the job!

1 The Lane

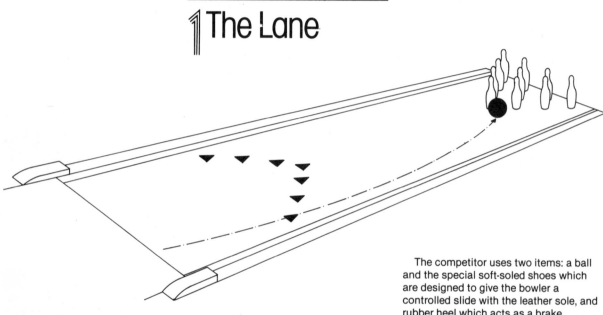

A bowler must have an almost mechanical delivery time and time again. He uses the arrows, or range-finders, to aim the ball. The ideal target is the pocket between the head pin and its immediate neighbour.

The playing area is a lightly-oiled wooden surface 62ft 10⅜in (19.16m) long and 42in (1.06m) wide. It is bordered on either side by a *gutter* which catches any balls that leave the lane itself. At the top of the lane is a *foul line* about 16ft (5m) from the start of the walk-up area where the bowler begins his approach. The bowler may not step over this line.

At the far end of the lane are the 10 pins, each 15in (38cm approx) in height and 15in in circumference, arranged in a triangular format with the pin closest to the bowler called the *head pin*. Each pin weighs between 3lbs 3oz and 3lbs 10oz (1.42 and 1.64kg) and is now usually made of laminated wood covered in plastic. The automatic *pin spotter* sweeps the lane of pins knocked down and re-sets those still standing after a delivery. The ball comes back automatically on the *ball-return track*.

The competitor uses two items: a ball and the special soft-soled shoes which are designed to give the bowler a controlled slide with the leather sole, and rubber heel which acts as a brake.

The ball, weighing 16lb (7.26kg), has three holes for the thumb and the middle two fingers. The remaining fingers rest on the surface of the ball, so that it is rather like cupping a large grapefruit in the hand, using the outside fingers for stability and the inside fingers for grip. Bowling balls can be made to an individual's specifications, so that the holes are drilled the right distance apart for greater comfort. A *wrist support* is often worn to keep the wrist and arm straight.

3 Winning

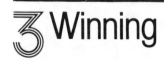

A game is played over 10 *frames* or turns. A bowler is allowed two attempts in each frame to knock down all 10 pins. Each pin knocked over is worth one point — but bowling has evolved a rather more complicated scoring system to reward the good bowler. If the bowler knocks over all 10 pins in a frame a bonus system comes into operation, so that he or she can score more than 10 in that frame. This is how it works:

If a bowler knocks down all 10 (a *strike*) with the first ball, he gets 10 points plus whatever he scores with the next two deliveries. These two deliveries also count in their own frame.

If a bowler knocks down all 10 with two balls (a *spare*) then he gets 10 points plus whatever he scores with his *next delivery*.

If a bowler still has a pin or pins standing after the two deliveries, he has rolled an *open* frame, the bane of his existence.

In this case there is no bonus earned, the score is simply the number of pins knocked over in two attempts.

If a strike is scored in the tenth frame, a further two deliveries are allowed. Obviously, at the end of 10 frames, the highest total score wins.

What's a good score? The professional bowler must average around 210 per game to be a winner. A perfect game in the sport is 300 pins, a succession of 12 strikes. It is not unusual for a professional bowler to have done the 300 game more than once in a career, but such games are infrequent enough to be dramatic.

Rules

The epitome of simplicity. Players must roll the ball down the lane, not throw it, and they cannot step over the foul line when releasing the ball. If they cross the foul line, no points are scored for that ball.

Like golf, bowling etiquette demands quiet and respect for all competitors from fellow bowlers and spectators alike.

Skills

More subtle than it appears to the naked eye, a bowler's technique is compounded of consistency, spin and speed. The first requires a good bowler to find each alley's *groove,* the spot where the ball seems to be radar-guided into the area most likely to produce a strike, and to keep rolling into that same spot. This requires a steady approach and slide to the foul line and a release of the ball that is gentle, not at all jerky.

Spin involves *lift* with the fingers and is imparted to the ball at the moment of delivery. The *pocket* between the head pin and its partners is approached from a point just to the right or left of that first pin and no bowler rolls his ball straight at the head pin. Instead, he attempts to *hook* the ball into that region, spinning it from right-to-left or left-to-right down the lane. Most bowlers have their own degree of hook and this is one debatable difference in technique.

In order to assist the bowler, small *arrows* or *rangefinders* are set in to the lane to help the bowler aim — in fact, he aims at these, a quarter of the way down the lane, rather than the distant pins themselves.

The main skill at the top level is coping with the oily surface of the lane. As the oil dries out during the game so the lane takes more *break,* as the ball grips and curves more. All lanes are 39 boards wide, so a bowler talks of a *seven board break* perhaps. If there is

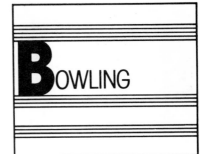

Before international contests, all balls are carefully weighed and measured.

A typical scorecard, showing how points are accumulated.

FRAMES	1	2	3	4	5	6	7	8	9	10	TOTAL
	A ✕	7 2	8 ╱ B	6 3	A ✕	A ✕	5 3	5 ╱ B	6 −	7 ╱ ✕	
RUNNING TOTAL	19	28	44	53	78	96	104	120	126	146	146
EXPLANATION	10 +7 +2	=19 +7 +2	=28 +10+6	=44 +6 +3	=53 +10 +10 +5	=78 +10 +5 +3	=96 +5 +3	=104 +10+5	=120 +6	=126 +10 +10	
	10 + strike bonus next 2 balls	Less than 10 scored no bonus	10 + spare bonus next ball	Less than 10 scored no bonus	10 + strike bonus next 2 balls	10 + strike bonus next 2 balls	Less than 10 scored no bonus	10 + spare bonus next ball	Less than 10 scored no bonus	10 + spare bonus next ball	

BOWLING

excessive oil, the ball may only curve or break three boards; this could increase to 10 boards when the oil has dried out. So the bowler may have to deliver from a different spot, adjust the amount of lift or use a softer ball (that has more traction) or a harder ball that won't break as much.

Showing intense concentration as he lines up on the arrows or spots inset in the lane, this bowler has turned his wrist sharply on releasing the ball to get it to curve inwards as it rolls towards the pins.

6 Tactics

None really, because the bowler is very much on his own. He might have the option of playing safe at some point during the match, electing to accept an open frame rather than attempt a difficult spare conversion, but that would be about it. Bowling is straightforward; on every delivery a bowler wants to knock down every pin.

7 Words

Alley: old-fashioned name for the playing area, now called a lane
Foul line: the line about 16ft (5m) from the start of the walk-up area where a bowler begins his approach; the bowler may not step over this line when delivering the ball
Frame: the units which make up each section of the game. It consists of two attempts to knock down all 10 pins; the tenth frame has two extra attempts if a strike is scored
Gutter: the area on either side of the lane that catches a badly thrown ball
A gutter ball will hit no pins as the gutter is below the level of the lane
Kegle, kegler: slang names for pin and bowler, derived from old German words
Open frame: failure to knock down all 10 pins with two deliveries
Pin-spotter: automatic machine which picks up the pins after each ball, re-setting those not knocked over and clearing off those that are down
Spare: knocking down all 10 pins with two deliveries
Strike: knocking down all 10 pins with one delivery
300 Game: a perfect game, the highest score in bowling, achieved by rolling 12 consecutive strikes. ■

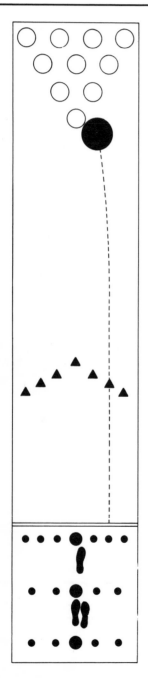

Most bowlers use the 4-step approach, without a long run-up.

T he idea of rolling an object along the ground towards some sort of target has been for centuries a gentle way of passing time with a friend or opponent. Bowls on a flat grass lawn is a sophistication of this simple pastime because of the considerable skills involved in controlling the heavy composition ball or *bowl* so that it finishes up on the exact spot the player intends. It may be slow but it is immensely cunning.

All bowls are shaped slightly on one side to give them a *bias* so that they curve as they run down the green. Indoor bowls on an artifical surface has developed rapidly in countries with poor climates, while in the north of England there is a local variety of the game called Crown Green bowls, where a rise in the middle of the lawn gives bowlers an added hazard and play is across the green in any direction.

The surface of a green is usually a little below that of the surrounding area, so a small bank encloses it, with a ditch between the green and the bank. The ditch is filled with clean pebbles, and helps to drain the green.

The game is played up and down strips called *rinks,* each 19ft (5.5m approx) wide, so six games can usually be played side-by-side at the same time. Fine string indicates the boundary between the rinks.

Because they are exposed to sun, wind and rain, all greens have different characteristics. Some are regarded as *fast,* others *slow,* depending on the amount of moisture in the ground, the type of grass and even the length of the grass, which is trimmed very short.

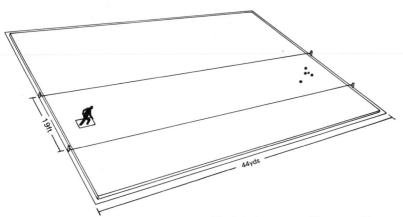

B OWLS

2 Equipment

Grey or white flannel trousers and a jacket are usually worn by men; skirts

1 The Green

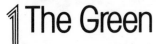

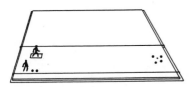

Singles: two players with four bowls each

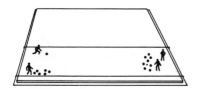

Pairs: four players with four bowls each

and jackets by women. Shoes must be flat soled so as not to damage the green.

Bowls are black or brown with an identifying colour dot or *eye* and are quite heavy in the hand, usually between 3 and 3½lb (1.5kg approx) and a maximum of 16½in (419mm) in circumference. Made of vulcanized rubber, there are five standard bowls (numbered 1-5) each with a different grade of bias which comes from the slight shaping of one side of the running surface. Contrary to popular belief, the bowls are not weighted in any way. The smaller eye on the side of the bowl indicates the biased side. The *jack* or target is white, weighs 8-10oz (227-283gm) and is 2½in (6.35cm) in diameter.

BOWLS

draw

trail

drive or firer

The basic deliveries

Although it is early on in this singles match, the bowls are clustered around the jack. A point is scored for each bowl nearer to the jack than the nearest one of an opponent.

after 18 ends. In *Fours* or *Rink Play* the four players on each side have only two bowls each and have 21 ends in which to amass the most points.

Winning

Competitors are trying to get more of their bowls nearer the jack than their opponents. A point is scored for each bowl nearer to the jack than the nearest one of an opponent.

After all the bowls have been delivered down the rink, players start again by playing back the other way, so saving time as well as wear and tear on the green. Each round is called an *end*.

There are four sorts of competition. In *Singles* (one against one) each player has four bowls and the first one to score 21 points wins. In *Pairs* (two against two) each player has four bowls and combines with his partner to try to score as many points as possible over 21 ends. In *Triples* (three against three) each player is limited to three bowls and the winners are the team with most points

Rules

The length of the target (jack) varies from end to end because a toss of the coin decides who should have the privilege of *delivering* the first jack. This small hard ball is bowled out smoothly and can end up anywhere between 25 and 40yd (23 and 35m approx) from a small rubber mat.

Bowlers must keep one foot on or above this mat as they deliver their bowls. Succeeding jack deliveries are made by the winner of an end, so the winning side can dictate the sort of game they want to play. Once the jack has come to rest, it is centred. The jack must travel 25yd up the rink or else the opposition get the chance to deliver it. However, any bowls that travel less than 15yd are removed from play.

Once the jack is in position, the *lead*

players on each side take turns to deliver their full quota of bowls. Then the second players, third players and finally the captain, or *skip*, who always plays last. The idea is to build up a *head*, a pattern of bowls surrounding the jack where some bowls are defensive and intended to block an opponent's attempt at rolling his bowl up to the jack. Any bowl that touches the jack is called a *toucher* and is marked with chalk, so that even if the bowl is knocked into the ditch later in the game it is still *live* and counts at the end of a match. Otherwise bowls that end up in the ditch area are *dead*, and do not count.

Crown Green bowls has the same objectives as Lawn bowls. The main difference is that play takes place diagonally across the raised *crown* of the green and in the main is played in singles. Each player has two bowls and the first one to 21 points wins.

5 Skills

The delivery of the bowls should be a smooth, underhand action. Experience builds up a feel for the conditions, the amount of *green* or curve needed to put the bowl on the spot required. The speed of the green is important. A *9 seconds green* is, in fact, slower that a *12 seconds green* because the longer a bowl keeps running, the faster or less resistant the green is. The three basic shots are the *draw*, designed to move the bowl on to the jack; the *trail*, where a player deliberately pushes the jack away from a cluster of opponent's bowls towards his own; and the *firer* or *drive*, a hard shot designed to break up an opponent's good position by sheer force.

6 Tactics

These vary depending on whether a player is involved in singles, pairs, triples or fours, though there are ploys common to all four games. By moving the mat and the jack about, a player can dictate his preference for playing over a long or short distance. The skip will dictate tactics by standing at the head and indicating where he wants his colleagues to deliver the bowl. Some bowlers run after their bowls after delivering them, as if they are trying to encourage their bowls — a useless though colourful move!

7 Words

Blocker: bowled short intentionally to block opponent's bowls
Bumper: on delivery, the bowl bumps against the ground
Dead bowl: not being a *toucher,* comes to rest in the ditch, or within 15yd (14m approx) of the mat, or even outside the rink
Draw: the line of a bowl, including the curve effected by the bias
Green: refers to width of rink bowler uses to curve bowl into the head; also playing area
Heavy: a bowl delivered too hard
Jack-high: level with the jack
Kitty: another word for jack
Merry: see *Heavy*
Pinching: too straight a delivery, not enough curve
Rink Director: Australian term for skip
Shot: the bowl closest to the jack; *to have shot,* to be in the lead
Tuck-in: to move jack behind or amongst bowls so it is difficult for opponent to score
Well-paired: to place a bowl near an opponent's to prevent possible large score
Wood: old-fashioned word for the bowl which used to be made of wood. ∎

Several games can be played simultaneously on a green. This player stands on the mat, about to step forward and deliver his bowl.

BOXING

It is not surprising that boxing is big time on the television screens of most of the world. Millions of men, women and youngsters can relate to the skill and courage needed in the boxing ring. It is a simple sport to follow with only two competitors — the boxers — and one official — the referee — to watch.

Boxing can be defined as fist fighting with padded gloves (to protect the hands rather than give weight to punches) by two men in a roped square.

Amateur boxing has slightly different rules from *professional* boxing including a maximum of three rounds for each contest, and comes into its own every four years when the Olympic Games are televised. There are also amateur World Championships.

between the light-heavyweight and heavyweight.

The International Amateur Boxing Association recognizes the following 11 weight divisions for the Olympic Games and world amateur championships:

Light-flyweight: not over 106lb (48kg)
Flyweight: 112lb (51kg)
Bantamweight: 119lb (54kg)
Featherweight: 126lb (57kg)
Lightweight: 132lb (60kg)
Light welterweight: 140lb (63.5kg)
Welterweight: 148lb (67kg)
Light middleweight: 156½lb (71kg)
Middleweight: 165lb (75kg)
Light heavyweight: 178½lb (81kg)
Heavyweight: over 178½lb (81kg)

1 The Ring

The four-sided fighting or boxing area is known as the *ring* after a fenced-off area of ground in London's Hyde Park used for impromptu fights in the 18th century.

The three-roped ring is on a raised platform, 14-20ft (4.27-6.1m) square for professional contests and 12-16ft (3.66-4.88m) square for amateur contests.

The vests and large gloves show that two amateur boxers are in action. The man on the right is a southpaw. He should get his punch home over his opponent's left lead.

Boxers only take on opponents of the same weight, so there are basic weight division limits. Boxers have to be inside the weight limit on the morning of the fight. In professional boxing they are:

Flyweight: up to 112lb (50.8kg)
Bantamweight: 118lb (53.5kg)
Featherweight: 126lb (57.2kg)
Lightweight: 130lb (59kg)
Junior lightweight: 135lb (61.2kg)
Junior welterweight: 140lb (63.5kg)
Welterweight: 147lb (66.7kg)
Junior middleweight: 154lb (69.8kg)
Middleweight: 160lb (72.6kg)
Light heavyweight: 175lb (79.4kg)
Heavyweight: over 175lb (79.4kg)

Other divisions recently instituted, but without universal recognition, include a light-flyweight and super-bantamweight, and a new division called the cruiserweight division.

2 Equipment

Boxing gloves usually weigh 6 or 8oz (170 or 227g) in professional boxing with a maximum of 10oz (283g) for divisions above welterweight in amateur boxing. Hands are further protected by wrappings of soft bandages and adhesive tape under the gloves and the boxer wears a rubber gum-shield inside his mouth. It is compulsory for all boxers to wear an abdominal protector cup inside the shorts.

All boxing federations have their own rules restricting the use of medical substances in corners by *seconds* (assistants) so that there shall be no unnecessary risk to the boxer. The second's basic equipment usually includes white petroleum jelly, sterile swabs, a concentration of adrenalin (1/1000 to water), and an ice bag. With the increasing illegal use of drugs in sport, boxing officials keep a close eye on all medical aids.

3 Winning

The boxer, stripped to the waist in professional boxing but wearing a vest if he is an amateur, aims to win either *on points* by scoring more blows with the knuckle part of the glove on the *target* (defined as 'any part of the front or

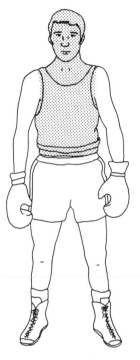

The target area

sides of the head or body above the belt line'), or to outclass his opponent so that he is no longer able to defend himself. A *knock-out* occurs when a boxer is down and is *counted out* by the referee within 10 seconds.

There is no single governing international body in professional boxing, which leads to occasional disagreement over the rules and, even more often, as to who is the true world champion. However, the most common way of scoring a round is what is termed *10 must,* which means the referee and/or ringside judges must give 10 points to the winner of each of the three-minute rounds. There is a minute's rest between each round.

The loser of the round — the boxer who has scored fewer blows to the target area — gets, say, eight or nine points depending upon how often he scored. However, a round can be scored *even.*

The points for each round are added up to decide the winner, so a bout can end with honours even as a *draw* or *no decision.*

World and British professional championships are staged over 15 three-minute rounds, but European professional championships have recently been limited to 12 rounds as an experiment. In amateur international boxing bouts, all over three three-minute rounds, the winner of each round gets 20 points, the loser proportionately less and there can be no drawn verdict at the finish. In the Olympics there are five ringside judges and a referee who controls the bout, but does not decide who the winner is.

A boxer may win through a *points*

The boxer on the right, gumshield showing, has penetrated his opponent's defence with a powerful right cross.

decision, a knock-out, referee *stopping* a contest, *retirement* or through a *disqualification,* because his opponent has committed a foul. A boxer must not hit below the belt, on the back of the neck (known as a *rabbit punch*) or with the open glove, or with the head, shoulder, wrist, elbow or arm. He must not, of course, be hit when the referee has brought the boxing to a temporary halt nor must he be hit after the bell has sounded to end a round. If a boxer is on the floor when the bell sounds, the 10-second count continues.

BOXING

The jab or left lead

This is the punch that does most point scoring, as the boxer tries to keep his opponent at arm's length while looking for an opening.

The straight right

If a boxer can evade his opponent's left jab, he will throw the straight right to the undefended side of his opponent's head.

The uppercut

A boxer needs to be in close to his opponent to be effective with the uppercut, which starts low down and is aimed at the chin.

The left hook

This can be the most damaging punch, aimed either at the opponent's temple to stun him, or to the ribs to wind or weaken him.

 Rules

As there are at present two different world governing bodies of professional boxing, interpretations of the rules and judging will differ slightly depending upon which state or country is staging the bout.

The two main organizations recognizing their own world championships are the World Boxing Council, started in Mexico City in 1963, which includes among its members federations from Latin America, North America and the Orient as well as the European Boxing Union and the British Boxing Board of Control, and the World Boxing Association, which originally was formed by some American states but now holds its own championships in various parts of the world.

Watching a bout on TV you may see a referee warn one of the boxers for fouling. This could be for holding, failing to break from a *clinch* (close-quarter interlocking of the two boxers' arms), punching to the kidneys, striking an opponent who is either down or in the act of rising. Generally, the refereeing of amateur international boxing may seem stricter, or fussier, depending upon the feelings of the viewer, than in the professional sport. The top professional referee is often dealing with more experienced boxers boxing at a slightly less hurried pace because the bouts are scheduled to last longer.

 Skills

Boxing has its own technical language like any other sport. The *orthodox* boxer does most points scoring with a *left lead* or *jab* to the head or body and then tries to find an opening for a following right hand because that is likely to have more power. From the straight left or jab comes the left *hook,* when the arm is bent at right angles so that the glove explodes on target. A *southpaw* is a boxer who stands with his right foot foremost and *leads* with his right glove. Southpaws are in the minority, but they include many past amateur and professional champions. The four basic punches are the *straight blow,* the *hook,* the *swing* (a round arm blow) and the *uppercut,* when the boxer slightly bends his knees and brings the bunched gloved hand up in a straight line to chin or body from the floor.

Think of the left hand as scoring

points or making openings but also as a defensive counter-attack when it brings an on-rushing opponent to a sudden painful halt. Think of the right hand as the heavy gun, but remember the right glove is a vital part of defence as it can be used to block or deflect the other man's left leads.

'Any fool can fight but very few can box' is an old saying worth bearing in mind when watching the sport. The boxer aims to hit his opponent without being hit in return. Apart from blocking punches with his forearm, shoulder or glove he will try to *duck* or *slip* punches with a slight movement of his head — sometimes so slight that, unless you are watching very closely, you will believe he has been hit. Body punches, which a boxer uses both to decrease the stamina of his rival and sometimes to bring his opponent's head forward, can be blocked with the elbow as well as by pushing the blow aside with half-open glove.

Cuts near the eyes of a boxer do not necessarily mean the bout will be stopped by the referee. It depends upon the seriousness of the injury or sometimes upon the view of the ringside doctor. In his 'corner', outside the ring while the boxing is going on, the boxer will have two or three seconds (in professional boxing one of them will be his manager), who are there to refresh him during the minute's rest between rounds. Apart from rubbing him down, giving him a drink of water and passing on swift advice, they will attempt to treat any cuts sustained by the eyes or to the head. The most frequent cause of such injuries is a collision of heads. If they are caused by a deliberate *butt* then the boxer responsible will be seriously warned or even disqualified by the referee.

6 Tactics

The TV commentator will often talk about *feinting,* when one boxer pretends to land a blow to get his opponent off guard and hits him with the other hand; and *combination* punching, a rhythmic sequence of up to six or seven swift successive blows to head and body.

Counter punching is a vital ingredient of success. One of the best known counters, though difficult to perfect, is a *right cross* over the opponent's *left lead.* The boxer aims to slip the in-coming left lead by letting the punch slide over his right shoulder and then pivots his body and throws the right counter with his wrist snapping down on impact. The best counter against a southpaw (the boxer who stands right foot foremost and leads with his right) is not a right hand punch but a left hook coming from outside the southpaw's own line of vision. Remember that the best champion boxers often trap their opponents into making mistakes and then punish them for it with counters rather than simply launching all-out attacks.

BOXING

7 Words

Backpedal: to move backwards out of range
Canvas: the floor of the ring
Combination: series of deliberate punches
Cornermen: see *Seconds*
Cross: a hook with a right hand
Cup: protecting lower abdomen, worn under shorts
Distance: the full number of rounds
Gumshield: guard for teeth worn by boxers in mouth
K.O./knock-out: when a boxer is hit so hard that he cannot recover within 10 seconds
Neutral corner: one of the two corners not used by the boxers for resting between rounds. When one boxer knocks another down, he must *retire to the neutral corner* until instructed to box on by the referee
Points win: to win by boxing better, scoring more blows to the target area
Purse: prize money put up by promoter for the boxers
Reach: length of boxer's arms; determines if he stands nearer or further from opponent
Ring: where contest takes place
Seconds: boxer's assistants in corner
Southpaw: boxer who leads with right glove, with right foot forward
Spar: to practise boxing, usually wearing protective headgear
TKO: (American) technical knock-out, when the referee stops fight because boxer cannot defend himself properly
Towel, throw in: when boxer's second indicates he wants to end the bout to save the boxer from further punishment
Uppercut: punch starting low down and delivered upwards to chin
Weigh-in: usually on morning of fight, to check boxer is within correct category. ■

Feet planted solidly on the canvas, the boxer on the right is set to throw a left hook to the unprotected side of his opponent's head.

Canoeing

& Kayaking

anoeing, the oldest form of boating, originated with the dug-out canoes of prehistory and developed into the sophisticated birch-bark canoes of the American Indians and seal-skin kayaks of the Eskimos. However, it was not until Rob Roy McGregor built his canoe in the 1850s that canoeing started in Europe. Present-day canoeing has developed into an Olympic sport with fairly separate disciplines, each with several classes of boat. These classes fall into two categories: *kayaks* and *canoes,* known in Britain as *Canadians.* Canadian canoes, 'C' boats, are descendants of the Indian craft. Competitors kneel in these and paddle with a single blade. Kayaks, 'K' boats, originate from the Eskimos' craft and competitors sit down and paddle with a double-bladed paddle. Each class is subdivided into events depending on the number of paddlers per boat — (1, 2, 4, 7, etc) — K1, K2, K4; C1, C4, C7.

1 The Course

The disciplines of competition canoeing are *slalom* and *wild water* racing, held on rough waters, and *sprint* and *marathon,* which are held on flat water. Sprint racing is run over three distances — 500m, 1000m, 10,000m (550yd, 1100yd and 6½ miles approx) — though the 10,000 event is reduced to 6000m (3¾ miles approx) for women. Marathon events are over a distance of about 20km (12 miles) though Britain also stages the Devizes to Westminster race of 200km (120 miles). While wild water races are run over a distance of approximately 8km (5 miles) down rapids on a river, slalom is a test of a canoeist's ability to read and use the water on a course or a particular rapid.

Different courses provide different conditions for the canoeist. Sprint rac-

This canoeist has a waterproof spray deck round his waist as he slaloms through the rapids and gates. Leaning out of the canoe, he is trying to drag his craft sideways, using the paddle as a lever.

ing is affected by cross-winds and many courses have wind breaks included in their design. Marathon paddlers can gain advantage by knowing the local conditions, such as which side of the river to be, which corners to cut, etc. Slalom and wild water racing are graded by the severity of the rapids, but changes in the river's water affect the size of the rapids. A rainy week has caused problems with many a slalom!

2 Equipment

Equipment for wild water canoeing is based on safety: personal flotation aids and crash helmets are compulsory; and many paddlers wear waterproof anoraks for warmth. In all disciplines, except sprint racing and marathon, fibreglass canoes have superseded wooden or canvas canoes. The paddles are made from a variety of materials with the emphasis on strength and lightness. Competition canoeists also wear a *spray deck* which seals the canoeist in his cockpit and prevents water entering the boat.

3 Winning

Sprint racing is rather like the 400m (or 440yd) in running as it is run in heats and the competitors are obliged to stay in lanes. However, for competitors eliminated in the opening round there is a *repêchage* or rerun for losers, which may enable a paddler to enter the final by the back door. The marathon is comparable to distance running events, with a mass start (which can be spectacular to watch) as well as all the tactics — when to make a break for it, whether to lead or not.

Wild water canoeing can be seen as the canoeist's cross-country event, except that competitors set off at one-minute intervals and the results are obtained by the use of synchronized watches. A slalom course is generally about 800m (½ mile) long on a rough river with not more than 30 *gates* (poles suspended from wires hanging across the river), some no more than 1.2m (4ft approx) wide, which the canoeist must negotiate without touching. Gates have to be taken in the correct order and presentation (either with the canoe going forward or in reverse), and even making the canoe travel upstream as well as downstream. Time penalties are incurred for touching a pole or taking a gate incorrectly. These penalties vary from 10 seconds for touching a pole to 50 seconds for missing a gate, and are added on to a competitor's time. In all events it is the fastest competitor who wins. However, in slalom, each competitor has two runs, with the better run counting.

4 Rules

In all events canoeists may paddle whatever design of canoe they prefer, provided it conforms with certain regulations and measurements. There is a minimum length restriction on all boats. A maximum length restriction applies to wild water racing and sprint boats. Sprint and marathon boats have a minimum weight requisite as well. Other regulations apply to the competition — in the shorter distances in sprint racing the canoeist is not allowed to ride the wake, *wash hanging* as it is known, of another canoeist. But this practice is permitted, in fact is a consummate skill, in marathon racing. Slalom and wild water racing are *against the clock* on individual runs so wash hanging is impossible, though a competitor who has been caught up must not baulk the faster paddler but make way for him. In slalom, if a canoeist capsizes and falls out he is automatically disqualified for that run. In wild water racing, however, a canoeist may get back into his boat provided he has no outside assistance, stays in the *confines of the river bank,* and carries on; the only penalty is the time lost.

5&6 Skills & Tactics

Canoeing is physically very demanding and in terms of all-round muscular strength and heart/lung endurance, canoeists rank among top athletes. The upper body, especially, has to be powerful though all muscles are used — the legs for anchoring the body and enabling the canoeist to rotate his trunk, the stomach for resisting the rotating caused by the pushing and pulling from the arms. A stylish paddler will push his

arms out rigid, keeping his body steady all the time and not allowing the arms to cross the centre line of the boat. The strongest competitors usually win, despite any tactical manoeuvres.

7 Words

Back-paddling: stroke pushing the paddle forward to reverse direction or resist a current
Brace: recovery stroke with paddle pushing on the water to prevent capsizing
Deck: top of enclosed canoe
Draw stroke: paddle is dug into the water away from canoe/kayak and drawn inwards thus pulling the boat sideways
Eskimo roll: used to right capsized kayak
Feathering: turning paddle blade sideways on, to cut down wind resistance
Ferry gliding: technique for moving across a current
Free gate: marked with black and white rings, it can be entered in either direction
Gate: in slalom runs, two poles hanging down from a wire. Competitor must keep red and white pole to port; green and white to starboard
Grade: river rapids are graded from 1 (easy) to 6 (virtually impossible)
'J' stroke: 'J'-shaped movement in water
Portage: carrying a canoe/kayak around awkward rapids, waterfalls, etc.
Telemark turn: a fast turn, using the paddle as a pivot. ∎

CANOEING
& Kayaking

In the sprint races on flat water, the kayak is open. The competitor uses a double-ended paddle.

The canoeist uses a single-bladed paddle, kneels on one knee and races over 500m, 1000m and 10,000m.

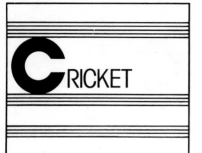

CRICKET

Cricket is an ancient game and therein lies much of its charm and its popularity as a sport. This bat and ball game must also be the only game in the world where the players stop for lunch and tea. Not only that, but a top class match played over five days more often than not does not produce a winner! It is an immensely complex game and is unusual in that even the slightest change in weather conditions can have a major effect. Despite this, cricket is successfully played in countries with climates as different as England, India and the West Indies.

The pitch is marked out with white lines. The bowling *creases* are 22yd (20m approx) apart and in the centre of these are the *stumps*. A white line known as the *popping crease* runs 4ft (1.20m approx) in front of the bowling crease. This has two functions. First, the bowler must have some part of his front foot behind it when he bowls the ball; second, the batsman is safe while his foot or bat is grounded behind the popping crease, otherwise he is *out of his ground* and could be dismissed. The line of the popping crease stretches sideways to infinity so that the batsman can still get home even if he runs wide of the pitch. The bowler must bowl

1 The Field

Cricket is usually played on grass. A well-tended *square* in the centre of a field is rolled and mown to provide several strips 22yd (20m approx) long and about 3yd (3m approx) wide. Each strip is called a *pitch.* The pitch plays a major part in cricket because the ball is bounced off it, and how it reacts to varying weather conditions often determines the course of the game. Certainly a captain will always *inspect* the pitch before tossing a coin to decide which team bats first. So the care and maintenance of the pitch is a job for a skilled groundsman.

The pitch with typical fielding positions for a right-handed batsman facing a slow bowler.

The wicket

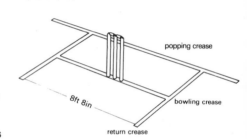

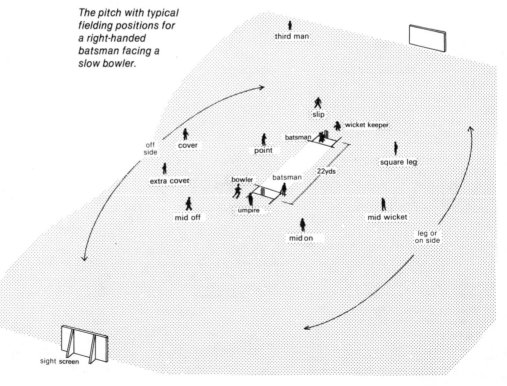

between the *return crease* and the wicket.

The set of three wooden stumps set in the ground at each end of the pitch are referred to as the *wicket*. These stumps are 28in (71cm approx) high and make a target 9in (23cm approx) wide. Two small pieces of wood called *bails* rest on top of the stumps. Ideally the cricket field is oval, with the *boundary* 75yd (70m approx) from the wicket.

2 Equipment

The basic requirements for a game of cricket are a *bat* and a *ball* and two sets of stumps. The bat is made of wood, and is flat on one side, rounded on the back. The handle is made from cane and covered in a rubber grip. Bats vary in weight, according to the preference of individual batsmen. The ball has a cork centre, wrapped with twine and covered with shiny red leather. The heavy seam joining the two pieces of leather is exploited by bowlers to make the ball swing in the air or spin off the pitch. The ball has to weigh 5½-5¾oz (155g approx) and be 9in (23cm) in circumference. The shine on the ball goes after a while and then slower bowlers would use it, whereas fast bowlers always use it when it is still shiny.

Cricketers usually wear white or cream shirts and flannel trousers and sweaters. Socks are also white, as are boots of either canvas or leather. The most dramatic addition to equipment is the *helmet,* because several batsmen have been hit on the head in recent years. The helmet, complete with visor, is now used extensively by first class batsmen, and can also be used by fielders positioned close to batsmen, particularly on the leg side.

A batsman always wears an abdominal protector — a hard metal or plastic *box,* a *thigh-pad* and white *pads* or *gloves* to protect his hands. The wicket-keeper has an equal amount of protection, and wears not only pads, but also large leather gloves to catch the ball. And finally, the umpires wear short white

The bowler has finished his run-up and is delivering the ball. He pivots on his left leg, keeping his left shoulder up as his right arm swings over in an arc. The arm must stay straight so that the ball is bowled, not thrown. By having his left leg slightly bent and by leaning to the left, this bowler is losing height in his delivery.

coats, and keep an array of aids to help with the game — spare balls, a cloth, pencil and notepad, and a simple calculator, coins or even pebbles to count the balls bowled in an over.

3 Winning

Cricket is played between two teams of 11 players. As in baseball, one team bats and attempts to score runs while the other team *bowls* a ball at the batsman to try to get him *out*. Whereas the action is concentrated on one spot in baseball, there are two target areas in cricket. After a bowler has bowled an *over* (six *balls* in most countries, eight in some) from one end of the field, another bowler bowls an over from the

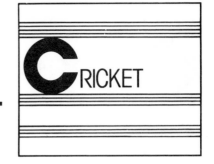

Bowled! The batsman has played a poor shot and the ball hits the wicket. The balls fly in the air as the wicket-keeper watches.

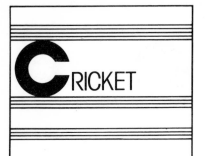

CRICKET

other end. The fielders change positions after each over, too. There are always two batsmen out on the field, one at each end of the pitch. To score a run after one batsman hits the ball, they must both run to the opposite end, so that they have changed places. That completes a run. They can run once, twice, three or even four times per hit and scores can be quite high. Every batsman's ambition is to score a *century* (100 runs) in an *innings!*

The batsman can score runs by hitting the ball to any part of the field — even behind him. If he hits it hard enough to go over the boundary line, he scores *a*

Caught! The batsman has tried a leg-glance but it looks as if the short-leg fielder will catch it in his right hand.

boundary which is worth four runs if it touches the ground before going over the line, or six runs if it clears the line (like baseball's home run). Then batsmen do not have to run up and down four or six times — the runs are awarded automatically.

In a game that lasts for a specific time, it often does not matter if a batsman is not scoring runs quickly. He can play defensively by stopping the ball dead with his bat or just pushing it away gently. If the ball is inaccurate, he can ignore it and let it go past him. He can do this as often as he likes. Even if he tries to hit the ball and fails, it does not matter.

The bowlers and fielders are trying to get 10 of the opposition batsmen out. They have several ways. The bowler can *bowl* him — get the ball to hit the wicket and knock the bails off. He can tempt the batsman to hit the ball into the air so that it is *caught* by a fielder. Even if the ball snicks the edge of the bat, a batsman can be caught behind the wicket.

The bowler can lure the batsman out of his crease so that the wicket-keeper *stumps* him by hitting the wicket with the ball. If, however, he has his bat or foot grounded behind the white line of the crease, he would be safe. If a ball (under certain circumstances) would have hit the wicket but the batsman's leg gets in the way, he could be out *l.b.w., leg before wicket.*

If the batsman hits the ball and is trying to score a run but he or the other batsman fails to make it to the safety of the opposite crease, he can be *run out* if the ball hits the stumps before he gets home. There are other ways of getting a man out but these are rare.

An innings ends when 10 out of 11 batsmen have been dismissed. The other team then bats and tries to score more runs. Top class matches, labelled *first class,* are always two innings per side played over three, four or five days so the run totals of the two innings are added together. If the game is not completed by the agreed *close of play* time, a *draw* is declared. If the match ends with the final scores level and the final innings of the game complete, a *tie* is declared. This is very rare. Most games begin in mid-morning, break for lunch and tea and close about 6pm. In recent years *limited over* cricket has become popular. Instead of a time limit, each side has a certain number of overs (between 40 and 60) and the winner is the side that scores most runs. These games are designed to be completed in one day.

 Laws

The laws of cricket have evolved over many years and are extremely complicated. *Wisden,* the cricketer's record book, requires over 20 closely typed pages to print the present laws, so any short introduction is bound to be incomplete. There are laws to cover the equipment, ways of scoring runs and dismissing batsmen. Then there are stringent regulations concerning the care and maintenance of the pitch, including the necessity of covering it in case of rain. The duties of the *umpires* are clearly defined. These two men are the sole arbiters of any decision that has to be made. They decide when a player is *out* if a member of the opposing team *appeals* by shouting *'How's that?'* They also check the legality of a bowler's delivery which must be straight-armed at the moment the ball is released; one of the bowler's feet must also be behind the crease. They decide when play should stop, either for rain or bad light, and when play should resume.

5 Skills

THE BATSMAN: His job is to score runs and this is done by playing a variety of strokes to the *off* side and to the *leg* side of the field — to right or left field for a right-handed batsman. He also has to defend, and ensure that he does not lose his wicket. There is a stroke designed to counter almost every sort of ball that is bowled. These are in two categories. If the ball *pitches* or lands out of reach, *short* of the batsman, he rocks back and plays *off his back foot.* If the ball is *well pitched up,* near the batsman, he pushes his left leg forward to play the ball (assuming he is right-handed). Of course, sometimes the batsman, in the case of a *swinging* ball that curves in the air, or a ball that is too wide to reach, will take no positive action.

The main attacking shot is the *drive,* played with the full face of a vertically *straight bat* against the ball and with the weight of the batsman's body on the front foot. The *pull* and the *hook* on the leg side are also attacking shots as is the *cut* on the off side, a shot that sends the ball anywhere in an arc between *third man* and *cover point.* The *forward defensive* stops the ball. Attacking strokes off the back foot are generally deflective shots that send the ball behind the wicket.

THE BOWLER: His job is to take wickets. The *fast bowler* aims to beat the batsman by sheer pace. The *medium-pace* and *slow bowlers* use guile; the former by moving the ball *through the air* and *off the pitch,* the latter by trapping the batsman through *spin* and *flight.* The secret of good bowling is *length* and *direction.* A *good length ball* denies the batsman the chance to play forward or back with confidence. A well-directed ball is aimed accurately at the line of the stumps, or at a selected spot just outside that line.

THE FIELDER: The importance of fielding may seem less obvious to the spectator, but teams ignore it at their peril. Here the key member of the team is the *wicket-keeper.* A good *fielder* can save his side 20 or 30 runs in an innings by stopping attacking shots.

6 Tactics

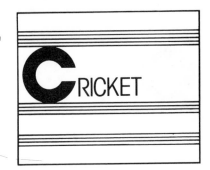

THE BATSMAN: In general he tries to *build an innings.* On coming into bat he is content to stay at the wicket and *plays himself in* while he tests the bowlers and the conditions of the wicket. When he has settled in, he will try to increase the tempo of his run scoring, as his confidence increases. However, batsmen at different numbers in the batting order often have different

An attacking stroke. The batsman has played off his back foot and steps forward as he aims the ball through the covers, with a full swing of the bat.

roles to play. The opener wants to lay a secure foundation for the innings by *seeing the shine off the new ball.* As the shine goes, the ball swings less in the air and is less menacing. But the batsman coming in at number six or seven may well have little time to study the bowling. His instructions will be to increase the rate of scoring, and to succeed he may have to use unorthodox shots. In the context of the game, a quick innings of 35 runs may prove as valuable as an opener's innings of 70. As

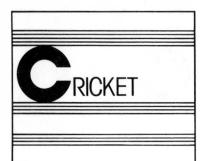

CRICKET

all the players bat, the *tail-enders* are usually bowlers who are not specialist batsmen.

THE BOWLER: He tests the batsman from the moment he arrives at the wicket. A fast bowler may bowl a *bouncer* that whizzes past the batsman's head. He may try a *yorker* that is aimed to pitch under or just beyond the bat as the batsman plays his stroke.

A slow bowler loops the ball in an arc through the air to confuse the newcomer before he has found his feet. Any bowler has a whole range of techniques to take wickets: he can intimidate by bowling at the batsman's body; he can change the pace of a ball by bowling faster or more slowly than the batsman anticipates; he can disguise his wrist action to produce a ball that spins in an unexpected direction; and with the aid of the captain, he can adjust the field placing to surprise or bewilder his opponent. A bowler usually aims to exploit a batsman's weakness in technique or concentration, although on occasion he may play to a batsman's strength in the hope of inducing carelessness through over-confidence.

THE CAPTAIN: His skills are required more on the field than off it. In the pavilion, the captain can do little other than alter the batting order (legal in cricket and tactically important) and try to inspire his team. But on the field, his role can be vital and nowhere more so than in *bowling changes* and *field placing*.

The captain can call upon a wide range of tactics to disrupt the batsman. He can introduce a new bowler to *break a stand* where two batsmen have settled in; he can switch a bowler from one end to the other and even have a fast bowler at one end and a slow bowler at the other to try to upset the batsmen's rhythm. *Field placing* is of equal importance. A fielder called up from the deep field to a close catching position can lead to a vital wicket; a deep fielder

moved further back to the boundary can save runs. With these tactics, the captain tries to put pressure on the batsman, and if that fails to take wickets, he can set a defensive field to restrict the runs to a minimum.

7 Words

Cricket has its own language, much loved by those who play and follow the game. It is a mixture of precise technical meanings, historical usage and slang: a combination that can be bewildering.

All-rounder: a player who is good at both batting and bowling

BATTING

Collapse: when several batsmen are out in quick succession
Duck: out for no runs; the batsman out for a duck
Face: one batsman *faces* a bowler, is in strike; his companion is the non-striker
Gardening: when a batsman prods the wicket with his bat to flatten bumps and holes that may have appeared
Guard: the position of the bat relative to the stumps as the batsman faces the bowler; so that he is always in the same position, the batsman marks the ground near the crease with his bat
Innings: refers both to the individual effort of a batsman and the collective effort of the team
Mark, get off the: score the first run of an innings
Partnership/Stand: number of runs scored while two batsmen are at the wicket
Ton: 100 runs, a century

BOWLING

Bouncer: a fast ball that is usually *pitched* short and bounces high round

---

A cricket scorecard. It shows that England batted first and then dismissed India for 202. Having made 334, England declared their second innings closed with eight men out. This set India 437 runs to win . . . But time ran out for the visitors who still needed 8 runs to win with two wickets in hand. The scorecard shows how each batsman was dismissed — c, caught; b, bowled; lbw, leg before wicket; st, stumped. It also shows the score when each wicket fell and the performances of the bowlers. Kapil Dev, for example, bowled 32 overs (O), of which 12 were maidens (M); he conceded 83 runs (R); and took 3 wickets (W), those of Boycott, Gower and Bairstow. He also bowled one no-ball (NB) and one wide (Wd). So after five days hard work . . . the result was a draw!

August 30 31 September 1 3 4. The Oval. Match drawn.

ENGLAND

	1st Innings		2nd Innings	
G. Boycott	lbw b Kapil Dev	35	b Ghavri	125
A.R. Butcher	c Yajurvindra b Venkat	14	c Venkat b Ghavri	20
G.A. Gooch	c Viswanath b Ghavri	79	lbw b Kapil Dev	31
D.I. Gower	lbw b Kapil Dev	0	c Reddy b Bedi	7
P. Willey	c Yajurvindra b Bedi	52	c Reddy b Ghavri	31
I.T. Botham	st Reddy b Venkat	38	run out	0
J.M. Brearley	b Ghavri	34	b Venkat	11
D.L. Bairstow	c Reddy b Kapil Dev	9	c Gavaskar b Kapil Dev	59
P.H. Edmonds	c Kapil Dev b Venkat	16	not out	27
R.G.D. Willis	not out	10		
M. Hendrick	c Gavaskar b Bedi	0		
	l-b9, w4, n-b5	18	l-b14, w2, n-b7	23
124.5 overs	Total	305	116.5 overs Total (8 wkts. dec.)	334

1st inns: 1—45 2— 51 3— 51 4—148 5—203 6—245 7—272 8—275 9—304 10—305
2nd inns: 1—43 2—107 3—125 4—192 5—194 6—215 7—291 8—334

India Bowling	O	M	R	W	NB	Wd	O	M	R	W	NB	Wd
Kapil Dev	32	12	83	3	1		28.5	4	89	2	2	2
Ghavri	26	8	61	2	4	1	34	11	76	3	5	
Bedi	29.5	4	69	2		1	26	4	67	1		
Yajurvindra	8	2	15	0		1	2	0	4	0		
Venkataraghavan	29	9	59	3			26	4	75	1		

INDIA

	1st Innings		2nd Innings	
S.M. Gavaskar	c Bairstow b Botham	13	c Gower b Botham	221
C.P.S. Chauhan	c Botham b Willis	6	c Botham b Willis	80
D.B. Vengsarkar	c Botham b Willis	0	c Botham b Edmonds	52
G.R. Viswanath	c Brearley b Botham	62	c Brearley b Willey	15
Yashpal Sharma	lbw b Willis	27	lbw b Botham	19
Yajurvindra Singh	not out	43	lbw b Botham	1
Kapil Dev	b Hendrick	16	c Gooch b Willey	0
K.D. Ghavri	c Bairstow b Botham	7	not out	3
B. Reddy	c Bairstow b Botham	12	not out	5
S. Venkataraghavan	c&b Hendrick	2	run out	6
B.S. Bedi	c Brearley b Hendrick	1		
	B2, l-b3, w5, n-b3	13	B15, l-b11, w1	27
79.3 overs	Total	202	150.5 overs Total (8 wkts.)	429

1st inns: 1— 9 2— 23 3— 47 4— 91 5—130 6—161 7—172 8—192 9—200 10—202
2nd inns: 1—213 2—366 3—367 4—389 5—410 6—411 7—419 8—423

England Bowling	O	M	R	W	NB	Wd	O	M	R	W	NB	Wd
Willis	18	2	53	3		1	28	4	89	1		1
Botham	28	7	65	4	1	3	29	5	97	3		
Hendrick	22.3	7	38	3	2	1	8	2	15	0		
Willey	4	1	10	0			43.5	15	96	2		
Gooch	2	0	6	0			2	0	9	0		
Edmonds	5	1	17	0			38	11	87	1		
Butcher							2	0	9	0		

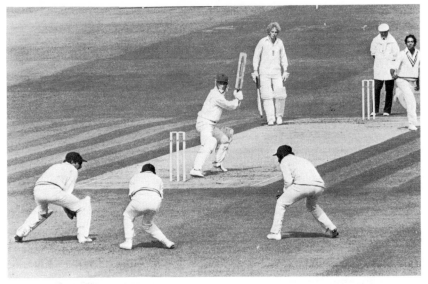

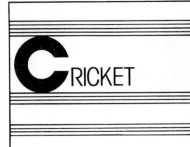

CRICKET

Caught in the slips! First slip has caught an edged shot by the batsman. Note the wicket-keeper standing back to the fast bowler, the umpire at the far end, and the bowler who has completed his delivery and runs off the closely-mown pitch.

the batsman's head

Full toss: a bad ball that does not bounce before reaching the batsman

Hat-trick: three wickets with three successive balls (unusual)

Leg-break, leg-spin: a ball that deviates from leg to off when it hits the ground

Long hop: a bad ball that is very short and easy to hit

Maiden over: an over when the batsmen fail to score; good for a bowler

Off-break: a ball that deviates from off to leg when it hits the ground; for a right-hander, this would move in to him

Over the wicket/round the wicket: indicates which side of the wicket the bowler bowls; *over* means that the bowling arm is nearest the wicket; *round* is away from the wicket

Pace: fast bowling

Seamer: medium pace bowler who moves the ball by angling the seam of the ball

Takes his sweater: when a bowler finishes a spell of bowling and puts on his sweater to keep his muscles warm

FIELDING

Backing up: a fielder covering a colleague in case he misses a throw to either wicket

Dolly: an easy catch

Howzat!: an appeal to the umpire by the fielders; 'How's that?' means 'Is he out?'

Overthrow: a bad throw that allows batsmen to make extra runs

Extras: runs scored as a result of errors by fielding side

Bye: when the ball evades the wicket-keeper and the batsman runs even though he hasn't hit the ball

Leg bye: when ball hits batsman's leg and he runs (as above)

Wide: when a bowler bowls so wide that batsman cannot reach it, the umpire signals wide, a run is added to the score and an extra ball is added to the over. ∎

If the ball hits the stumps, the batsman on the left will surely be run out. The batsman only needs to have his bat grounded over the white line to be in, so he stretches to make it. If both batsmen cross, and reach the other end of the pitch, a run is scored.

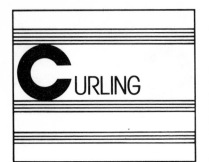

CURLING

The sight of broom-wielding players brushing the ice feverishly in front of a disc-shaped stone as it glides across the ice, spurred by excited shouts of 'soop, soop' is enough to convince the casual observer that curlers are mad. But initial mirth gives way to considerable respect when the intricacies of the game are understood.

Curling was pioneered in Scotland and is now popular throughout North America and most of Europe. This four-a-side team game is basically akin to bowls, using stones on ice in place of wooden balls on grass.

Each stone has smoothly curved edges and a metal *striking-band* around it to withstand wear and tear when colliding with others.

The only specialized apparel is suitable footwear. Shoes need soles capable of gripping or sliding to suit individual preference. Shoes with spikes that could damage the ice are banned.

 Winning

Alternating with their opposite numbers, the curlers *throw* stones up the ice towards the *tee,* or *button* as it is called in North America. Sixteen stones are played from each end *(head),* two

 The Rink

A sport for both men and women, curling combines accurate delivery of the stones as well as tactical sooping to alter their pace and direction.

The ice area used for a game, 138ft (42m approx) long and 14ft (4.25m approx) wide, is called a *rink.* Somewhat confusingly, each team is also termed a *rink.* At either end of the playing area is a circular target *(house)* with a radius of 6ft (1.83m), the centre *(tee)* of each being 38yd (34.75m) apart.

from each of the eight players. The object is to finish a head with stones nearest the tee, a point being scored for each stone lying nearer than any opposing stone, none being eligible which are clearly outside the house. Players then play back down the ice to the other tee.

 Equipment

You will not see a stone lifted from the ice very often because it weighs up to 44lb (19.9kg), can be 4½in (11.42cm) high and 1yd (1m approx) in circumference. The metal handle with which it is set in motion is detachable and interchangeable so that either side *(sole)* of the stone can be used.

Rules

A match is usually played over 10 or 12 heads or for a certain period of time. The player delivers his stone from a metal plate *(hack),* but must not cross the *hogline,* marked 11yd (10m approx) from the hack. If the stone does not reach the far hogline, it is deemed a *hog* and is removed from the ice.

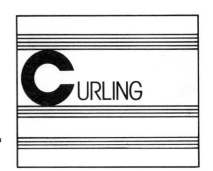

 Skills

The team captain is the *skip* who masterminds the strategy throughout. He tells his teammates when and how much to *soop* or sweep. Sooping just ahead of a moving stone can change its pace and direction, the friction temporarily melting the ice in front of the stone. Strong sweeping can change a stone's course enough to pass a *guard* (stone blocking opponent) and to increase the stone's distance dramatically. Both teams can soop whenever their stones are moving or when an opponent's stone passes the *sweeping stone*.

The other particular skill is in delivery. The curler grips the handle with eyes on the skip's broom, which will indicate where to aim. Drawing the stone back with an underarm pendulum swing, he brings it forward to release it with a smooth follow-through action.

Normally starting from a sitting posture, he rises to put all the body weight on the forward foot, swinging the other slightly to the side to counter the stone's weight. Some players slide as far as permitted before releasing the stone. The moment of release and manner of turning the handle controls the degree of draw to right or left.

 Tactics

It is one thing to deliver a stone to come to rest within the house, quite another to plan for it to be still there at the conclusion. This dictates the basis of tactics, so the intelligent use of a short-placed stone *(guard)* to protect one in the house becomes a key factor and the last of the 16 stones played is, more often than not, the most vital.

Each player tends to specialize. The *lead* delivers the initial stones and the *number two* and *number three* adapt their method of approach according to the developing situation, either striking an opponent's stone, drawing to the house or playing a guard.

The last to deliver is the skip. Holding his broom as a guide, he stands behind the house showing the members of his team the spot to aim for. He is replaced by the next in command when playing his own stones.

At the moment a stone leaves the player's hand, the other two players in the side wait with their brooms to sweep the ice on command from the skip. A notable difference from lawn bowls is how direction and pace may be influenced.

7 Words

Besom, broom or *brush:* for sweeping ice, made of horsehair in Europe, cornstalks in North America
Bonspiel: a match featuring several teams
Button: see *Tee*
Crampit: see *Hack*
Draw: turning the handle as the stone is delivered imparts draw or swing; also a shot with sufficient weight to reach the house
Granite: another name for stones which are made of granite
Hack: small metal implement embedded in the ice from which a curler throws a stone
Head or *end:* a complete series of 16 stones in one direction
Hog: a stone that does not reach the hogline or minimum distance and is then removed from the ice
House: the target, circles on the ice
Kiggle-kaggle: a stone that wobbles as it runs
Lead: first player on a team
Pebble: the dappled surface which is essential to provide a controlled curve to stones, made by spraying ice just before play
Pot-lid: stone on the tee
Rink: either a team, or area where game is played
Skip: captain of team, and last man to throw
Strike: a fast stone thrown to knock opponent's stone out of position
Tee: centre of house. ■

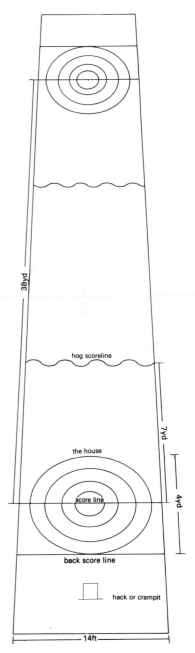

Curlers often follow through with their delivery to ensure a smooth release.

CYCLING
Track

Ever since the bicycle was invented. it has been used for racing. In some parts of the world, notably Western Europe, professional cyclists are highly paid, top-class athletes. Principally, there is trackracing in a stadium, road racing, and cyclo-cross, a sort of cross-country on a bike. There are male professionals in all three and although there are no women professionals in any of these, women amateurs compete on the track and the road.

TRACK EVENTS: the major events feature the *sprint*, the *tandem*, the *individual pursuit*, the *team pursuit*, the *kilometre time trial*, *points* and the *motor-paced event*.

A hardwood track. The ends are banked more steeply than the sides and it is as the sprinters come out of the bend that a break usually takes place.

1 The Track

Indoor cycle tracks have wooden surfaces; outdoor tracks are made of African hardwood, cement or asphalt. The world championships standard length is 333m (365yd approx). Some tracks are twice this length; others as short as 250m (275yd approx).

Cycle tracks are steeply banked. The incline in the straights is never less than 12 degrees and around the bends this increases to as much as 55 degrees. The minimum width of an internationally-approved track is 7m (23ft approx).

Three lines are marked around the track. The blue band 20cm (8in approx) wide painted around the inside of the track is not part of the competitive area. The continuous red line painted on the track surface 90cm (1yd approx) from the inside edge is known as the *sprinters line*. The narrow blue line, marked around the circumference of the track one-third of the distance from the inner edge of the track, is the *stayers line*. Cyclists travel counter-clockwise and once a sprinter positions himself on the stayers line he can only be passed on the right. The purpose of this rule is to cut down on accidents.

2 Equipment

The racing bike is a fine piece of pre-cision engineering — light but strong. The alloy frame may be less than half a millimetre (1/16in) thick! Gears are made of metal alloy and tyres (called *tubulars*) have a fine latex inner tube and are fitted to the wheel rim with adhesive. The wheel rather than the tyre is changed after a puncture.

Track bikes have no gears or brakes, and are designed for sheer speed, weighing about 8kg (17½lb). To go with lighter machines, clothing is made less wind resistant — jerseys and shorts are made of nylon and silk.

3 Winning

Sprint: this is normally contested by two riders at a time over 1000m (1100yd approx), three laps of a 333m (365yd approx) track. However, riders use the first 600-700m (700yd approx) as a gentle warm-up for the final sprint over 200m (220yd approx). Sprinters play a cat-and-mouse game, often standing still daring an opponent to take the lead. But, in the end, the first man over the line wins. Run as a knock-out com-petition, the winner of each round is the one who wins two out of three heats. Timings are taken on the last 200m but are irrelevant in knock-out competitions.

Tandem: on a bicycle built for two, to the same rules and tactics as the sprint, but over 1500m (1640yd). Both individual and tandem sprints are often decided by photo-finish with the width of a tyre separating the two machines.

Pursuit: two riders start on opposite sides of the track and are really racing against the clock rather than each other. Women race over 3000m (1¾ miles approx), amateur men over 4000m (2½ miles approx) and professional men over 5000m (3 miles approx). The winner is the fastest cyclist over the distance, or the competitor that catches up with his opponent.

Team pursuit: four men on four bicycles race over 4000m (2½ miles approx). The winners are the team with the first *three* men home.

Kilometre time trial: only amateurs take part in this race *against the clock* over one kilometre (⅝ mile). There is only one rider on the track at a time and he goes flat out to get the fastest time. The riders are *seeded* on the basis of past form, so that the slower men go first and the faster ones later. The fastest competitor wins.

Motor-pacing: riders are *paced* by motorcycles, which act as windshields so that they can cover up to 72km (45 miles) in an hour. Both amateurs and professionals take part in events which are run either for one hour or over a fixed distance. A bell sounds when the hour is up or the distance has been covered, and then the first man over the finishing line wins.

Points: this is an event for up to 25 riders who crowd on to the track and race up to 50km (30 miles), collecting points as the first three pass the finish line on each lap. Therefore the rider who accumulates the most points wins, not necessarily the first man across the line at the end of the race. On the last lap, points are doubled.

Rules

Sprint and tandem: riders draw to decide who will lead out — the leader must travel at least at walking pace. Punctures, falls or mechanical troubles allow re-starts. During *standstills* a rider who moves back more than 20cm (8in approx) is penalized by being made to lead for a lap or until the bell rings when there is only one lap to go. This penalty is signalled by two pistol shots. A rider who forces another off his machine is disqualified and the other awarded the heat even if he has not passed the finish line.

Pursuit (individual): in elimination heats the event is re-started for punctures, falls or mechanical break-downs in the first 30m (32yd approx); after 30m the rider involved drops out. In the eighth and quarter finals any rider catching his opponent must go on to finish the distance in order to record a time for the pairings in the next round.

Pursuit (team): each team consists of four riders. The rider on the inside of the track leads his team until the first *relay,* a way of pacing the race, when the first man rides up the banking and returns to take fourth position, and a teammate sets the pace for a while. Riders are not allowed to push one another — the penalty is disqualifica-tion in the heats and relegation in the finals. Three men must complete the course.

Kilometre time trial: if any event is not completed because of (say) rain, the times of those who have ridden are dis-regarded and so the whole event is re-run. If a rider punctures, falls or has mechanical trouble, he is allowed to ride again after the next five men have

ridden to give him time to rest. No rider is allowed more than two re-starts.

Motor-pacing: in the case of an accident to either machine (cycle or motor-cycle) or a puncture or fall, the cyclist is allowed to keep warm by cycling gently around the track while any repairs are carried out. Any rider who drops more than 10 laps behind in the finals is disqualified.

5 & 6 Skills & Tactics

Sprint: sprinters will use the steep banking to gain speed to swoop past the man ahead and below. If he is ahead a rider may ride *high* to force his opponent behind to follow and stay up with him: this way the front man (always looking over his shoulder) can be the first to swoop away. Often a rider

A lot of track racing takes place indoors at night. The centre of the arena is stacked with bicycles, spare wheels and refreshments as competitors flash past on the steeply banked track.

CYCLING

Road

will force his opponent to take front position, perhaps by a standstill and a war of nerves, because it is more often the man who comes from behind who wins the sprint.

Pursuit: the tactics are either/or: EITHER you set such a pace at the start that your opponent (when he realizes your game) is too far down to make up the time OR you let the other fellow lead slightly and keep edging him to alter his pace so that when he starts to tire you put on your reserve of pressure.

Kilometre time trial: the one event that requires more *hate* than the pursuit. The kilo man has to hate an inanimate object — the clock. He has no tactics, but requires great riding skill and finesse to clip fractions off seconds. The slightest *wheel wobble* can lose a world or Olympic title.

Motor-pace: the riders require enormous staying power to follow a motor bike for an hour at an average speed of 70kmph (45mph) — and a lot of judgement in deciding whether to go from the front or come with a late challenge. Often it is the man who has ridden the race half a lap or so behind the leader who just beats him on the line.

Points: these riders require absolute bike control and track discipline. Every one of perhaps 25 riders is anxious to be first over the lap line, maybe 175 times. The lap sprints decide the points, but what decides who is at the front of the group to contest these lap sprints is the tactical thinking a lap before. ■

Although a roadman's bike is somewhat heavier than a track bike, it is also specially built. Riders carry refreshments as they cover as much as 280km (175 miles) in a day.

In road races, the *field* (which can number as many as 200 riders in the Olympic Games and is usually about 150 in a professional event like the Tour de France) starts en masse and covers a set distance either on one day or several days. A road race over more than one day is called a *stage race* or a *tour*. Racing is on normal roads, obeying regular rules of the road — but generally with police assistance halting traffic and traffic signals. The longest stage race in the world is the Tour de France (June and July) which lasts 26 days and covers about 3500km (2200 miles). There are also *time trials* on the road as well as the track. Riders start (usually) at one minute intervals to race against the clock — individually or in teams of four. Another form of road time trialling is to ride individually for a set time, such as 12 or 24 hours.

1 The Course

Road race circuits or courses are chosen (where possible) to include a mixture of flat roads, hills and descents. In world championship road races the width of the road must never be less than 5m (5½ yd approx) and in the last kilometre (½ mile approx) before the finishing line the width must be at least 8m (8½ yd approx). In world championships the maximum road race distances are — women 70km (45 miles); amateurs 190km (119 miles); professionals 280km (175 miles).

2 Equipment

Road machines are stronger than track bikes. They have 10, 12 or even more gears, using two chain wheels and five or six or more sprockets on the rear *block*. Road bikes are made for comfort, weighing about 10kg (22lb) with accessories for drinking bottles, quick release hubs (for fast wheel changes during racing) and pump pegs.

Road racers' jerseys have back pockets for food; all shorts have chamois leather inserts in the seat to prevent chafing on the saddle. Shoes have steel plates on the soles to slot on to the pedals.

A lightweight crash helmet with jaunty cap and light gloves complete the outfit.

3 Winning

Stage races (more than one day) have several classifications. Most important (to most people) is the individual winner — the rider whose daily stage times, added together, are lower than anyone else's. Allowance will have been made for bonuses deducted and penalties added.

Second most important category (except to the East Europeans who consider this their prime target) is the team class. This is decided, as in the case of the individual, by adding together the times of each stage of the best three men in each team each day. Teams have between 4 and 12 riders.

The points winner is the rider who has accumulated the best aggregate daily placings. The King of the Mountains is the rider who has collected most points on the designated hill climbs. The Hot Spot Sprint is contested at designated spots on the daily course where a line marks the sprint. Points are awarded to the first three across.

All these classifications — except the points — occur also in one-day races.

4 Rules

The full rules of road racing are as long and involved as those for the track.

Riders are allowed to help one another — exchanging food and drink or waiting to *pace* back to the bunch a rider who has punctured or who has had an accident. But pushing is forbidden. So is *taking pace* from, or hanging on to, vehicles. Dangerous riding (such as *boring* and *switching* in front of others) is not allowed.

5 Skills

More than any other sporting cyclist, the road race man must have the stamina of thousands of miles spent training — without this background his guile and cunning will help little. The finest physical skill of the cyclist — trackman, time triallist, cross-countryman or roadman — is the gift of

dedication to the often lonely pounding out of a daily 150km (100 miles). This cycling strength is harder won than the hardest race.

6 Tactics

The roadman cyclist, with the stamina of those thousands of training miles in his legs, can now go out to win his race with his head. His skill and cunning may beat his physical betters. On stage races he must keep in his mind the relative and cumulative times of his closest challengers. In all road races he

must use his wits to judge which break to join (not wasting energy by joining everyone who goes *up the road*). He must decide when to leave a break and go for a lone win — whether to fragment his break into a composition more of his choosing — and where to position himself among others if there is a group sprint for the finish.

7 Words

Bit and bit: small groups of riders take it in turn to ride at the front, giving wind shelter to the followers; after a spell the front man drops to the back of the group

CYCLING
Road

Cyclists are constantly watching each other, waiting to see who tries to make a break. Then they have to decide whether to go with him, or whether to stay with the bunch.

CYCLING

Cyclo-cross

Break: group of riders which has ridden clear from the main field

Bunch: the entire field of riders, or (after a break) the largest group on the road

Classic: certain one-day races in Europe that are traditionally regarded as the best

Commissaire: race official or judge

Cowboy: a rider who breaks the unwritten rules of etiquette

Domestique: member of a team whose job is to work for the team leader

Echelon: riders following in line ahead (and usually at an angle across the road) to protect each other from a cross-wind

Honking: out of the saddle and standing on the pedals — usually up stiff climbs

Off the back: riders who have fallen back from the main field

Pacing: riding behind another to take shelter from the wind

Prime: pronounced 'preem' — a point on the course or route at which there are special prizes; usually mountain tops or sprints

Yellow jersey: the French call it *maillot jaune* — the yellow shirt worn by the race leader. ■

When it comes to a steep hill, competitors just pick up their bikes and run. Having to combine riding and running is a severe test of stamina.

Cyclo-cross is really road racing over rough country and over obstacles like fences, streams and ditches. Most courses include sections of normal roads. There are no rules that insist when riders must pedal or carry their machines: both — whichever is on the ground — must reach the finish line together.

Cyclo-cross courses are normally about 32km (20 miles) long. Artificial obstacles are put in the way — a gate, a felled tree — to force riders to dismount and carry their cycles. However, these obstacles must not (according to international rules) be so difficult as to make riders 'perform feats of acrobatics'. Cyclo-cross bikes are generally road bikes with heavier knobbly tyres, guards to prevent chainwheels coming off and perhaps specially-designed brakes to prevent clogging by mud. Cyclo-cross is always a one-day event so the first man to pass the finish line after the required distance or number of laps is the winner. He may pass the finish aboard his bike or on foot, carrying his machine. Races last about an hour. The cyclo-cross rider has to combine the roadman's tactics with his own particular judgement of when to ride and when to carry his machine. An extra metre run, or one more turn of the pedal, can decide a race. ■

arts used to be a game that was played just for fun in clubs and pubs all over the world. Now the skills of the best players have been recognized and publicized by television. Throwing pointed arrows at a board can earn professional players a comfortable living. For the spectator the appeal of darts is its incredibly fast tempo. There is a quick build-up to the climax. Then, wham! One player hits his winning shot, everyone cheers, and they're off again.

1 The Board

The board is usually made of compressed fibres. In international competition the board used is the *clockboard*. Each segment is given the value of the number on the edge of the board but there are two strips that increase the value of a dart when it lands there. The narrow outer strip doubles the value, the narrow inner ring trebles it. The tiny *bull's-eye* at the centre of the board is worth 50 points, the bigger bull's-eye, 25 points.

The board is hung on a well-lit flat wall or stand with the centre of the bull 5ft 8in (1.73cm) above the floor. Players throw with their toes touching the back edge of a raised wooden strip on the floor called an *oche* (pronounced: *ockey!*), placed a distance of 7ft 9¼in (2.37m) from the face of the board. Players who prefer to throw from behind the oche are allowed to do so.

2 Equipment

Most leading players throw slim-line darts made of tungsten mixed with another metal (copper or nickel) to form an alloy. The most popular weight range is from ½ to 1oz (18 to 28g). The advantage of *tungstens* is that their slimness makes it easier to group them closely, such as in the treble 20 bed. The three *flights* which balance the dart were usually made of trimmed goose feathers but plastic is now used.

3 Winning

Each player throws three darts in turn. Unlike most sports where competitors

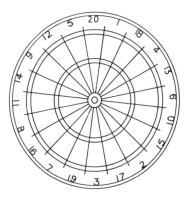

The clockboard

The player concentrates on the target. He has to be decisive when the pressure is on him.

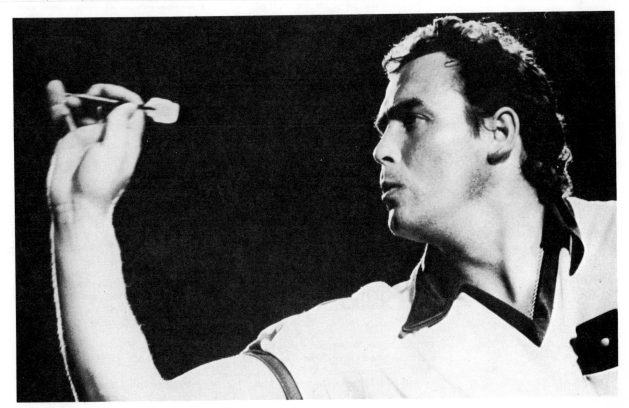

DARTS

try to amass points, darts players usually start with 501 and reduce their score down to zero, but they must finish exactly with a *double.* Take this sequence where Smith is playing Jones:

Smith	Jones
501	501
416	401
356	356
236	273
96	133

Each player has thrown twelve darts. Smith has 96 points left, Jones has 133. Every number less than 159 can be finished in three darts and every number less than 99 can be finished in two darts. So both players could finish at the next attempt.

Jones has little room for manoeuvre. He wants treble 20 with his first dart to leave himself 73 (133 minus 60). Now he must go for a high, odd-number treble (such as treble 11) so he can finish on double 20.

Smith's 96 is not too complicated. He should try for treble 20, then double 18. If he hits single 20 with his first dart all is not lost — he is on 76 with two darts left. That can be achieved with a treble 20 and that mandatory final double, the double 8. Of course, he would be in trouble if he hit treble 5 instead of treble 20 because that would leave him 61 . . . The combinations go on and on. It all happens in a flash.

The professionals often aim to finish on double 20 or double 16. Double 20 because many find it easiest to hit, double 16 because it halves to 8, 4, 2 and 1. So, if they hit single 16 when aiming for double 16, they can go straight on to double 8 and so on.

Rules

In international matches players need not start on a double but they must always finish on a double. The bull's-eye counts as double 25 for a finish.

Skills

Players pick up a dart as if they were picking up a pen to write, so that it's comfortable in the fingers. The dart is thrown with a sharp movement of the arm, like driving a nail in with a hammer.

Tactics

Professionals always concentrate on treble 20. Therefore 100 scored means two darts in single 20 and one in treble 20. A player on his way to winning a major tournament will average about 100 in his turn. Someone might even hit the maximum of three treble 20s, 180.

It is very difficult to get three darts into the treble 20 *bed,* but the player keeps on trying until he is looking for his winning double. There is no point in pacing his score, like a middle-distance runner might pace himself. Boom! In he goes wanting a *ton* (100) or more. Players may vary the actual physical pace of their game. A top pro facing a fast-throwing opponent might, quite legitimately, slow the action down to try to upset his opponent's rhythm.

Note how many darts a player needs to throw to complete his 501. A potential champion will average less than 20. Fifteen darts for 501 is exceptionally good but the crunch comes, of course, with the finishing double. No top player would be happy to take more than three darts to get the final double.

Words

Bust: to score more points than needed to go out; player loses the rest of his turn

Check-out: to finish; 'check out in 15' is to win in only 15 darts

Double: a dart landing in the outer ring of the board

Double start: a game where players are required to hit a double to start

Double top: double 20 because it is the top of the board

Flights: the three feathers that balance the dart in flight

Flying start: a game where players start straight away without the formality of a double

Leg: one game of 501; players might play a match of five legs: the first to win three legs wins the match

Toe the oche: to begin play, e.g. 'Toe the oche at 11am'

Ton: 100

Treble: a dart landing in the inner ring of the board

Wire dart: a dart that hits the board and bounces out. ∎

DIVING

The ability to overcome gravity, even for a second or two, has aroused man's excitement and imagination ever since he first observed the freedom of birds in flight. Diving is one of those activities which gives the opportunity of enjoying the sensation of flying, while the water provides a relatively 'soft' landing area. Competitive diving is split into two separate parts: *springboard* and *highboard*.

On this reverse dive, the competitor must have all her limbs perfectly positioned and controlled as she goes into a backward somersault before straightening out.

The object in both forms is to jump upwards, as high as possible, from the board and to perform different kinds of aerial gymnastics which end in a completely straight, head or feet first entry which causes as little splash in the water as possible. Apart from the *set* dives, which must be performed in any competition, the spectator should look for the greatest number of somersaults and twists performed with style and control. It is the effortless grace, perfection and ease of execution of extremely difficult dives that is the greatest attraction of this sport.

1 The Pool

In springboard diving a very flexible aluminium alloy board is used, to help the diver jump higher into the air to give more time in *flight*. This board is 3m (10ft approx) above the surface of the water. At top level, highboard diving is performed from a solid platform 10m (33ft approx) above the pool, which must be at least 4.5m (15ft approx) deep. A spray or sprinkler system agitates the surface of the water during dives so that divers see the surface clearly from the highboard. Otherwise they would see only the bottom of the pool!

2 Equipment

The only piece of equipment available to the diver, apart from the boards themselves, are a swimsuit or pair of trunks, which should be made of close-fitting, light and flexible material, capable of withstanding the rigours of diving without falling apart or, worse, falling off!

The hurdle: before take-off, the diver jumps to gain the maximum spring from the board. The higher a diver gets, the more room there is to perform twists and somersaults.

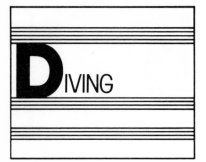

DIVING

Winning

All the different dives have a particular *tariff* value based on their degree of difficulty. They are divided into six groups: one, the handstand group, applies only to the highboard; the other five apply to both springboard and highboard.

Forward dives (rotating forwards from a forward takeoff).

Back dives (rotating backwards from a backward takeoff).
Inward dives (rotating forwards from a backward takeoff).
Reverse dives (rotating backwards from a forward takeoff).
Twisting dives (any of these four with the diver spinning in mid-air as well as rotating).

Throughout the dive, the body must be held in one of three positions: straight; *piked* (where the diver touches his toes in mid-air); and tucked (knees bent up onto the chest). In dives which involve a somersault and a twist, a *free* position is used. In the more complicated dives, the speed of the movement makes it almost impossible to see the actual position of the diver's body. Television's slow motion replays have made the appreciation of this graceful sport so much easier!

In springboard competition a dive from each of the main groups (the set dives) must be performed. Then the diver attempts the *voluntaries* (men six, women five) which can be as complex or varied as the diver wants. So men perform a total of 11 dives, women 10.

In highboard competition men complete four set and six voluntary dives, women four set and four voluntary.

Major international competitions have seven judges, each of whom awards a mark between 0 and 10. They are concerned with the style and execution of the takeoff, flight through the air, somersaults or twists, and entry into the water.

When they have awarded their marks the highest and lowest are discarded and the remaining five are added together. The sum is multiplied by the tariff value and the result is the final score for each individual dive. The scores for each of the dives are added up and whoever has the most points overall wins.

RIGHT: Commonwealth champion Chris Snode demonstrates the perfect pike position in a practice session.
LEFT: This diver must bend more at the waist and straighten her arms to perfect her dive. Slow motion replays have made it possible for the viewer to spot such vital details in diving.
PAGE 90: Spanish superstar Severiano Ballesteros rarely holds back when driving off the tee.
PAGE 91: Top three-day rider Captain Mark Phillips battles to control 'Town and Country' on the cross-country course, the gruelling second stage of equestrianism's toughest competition.

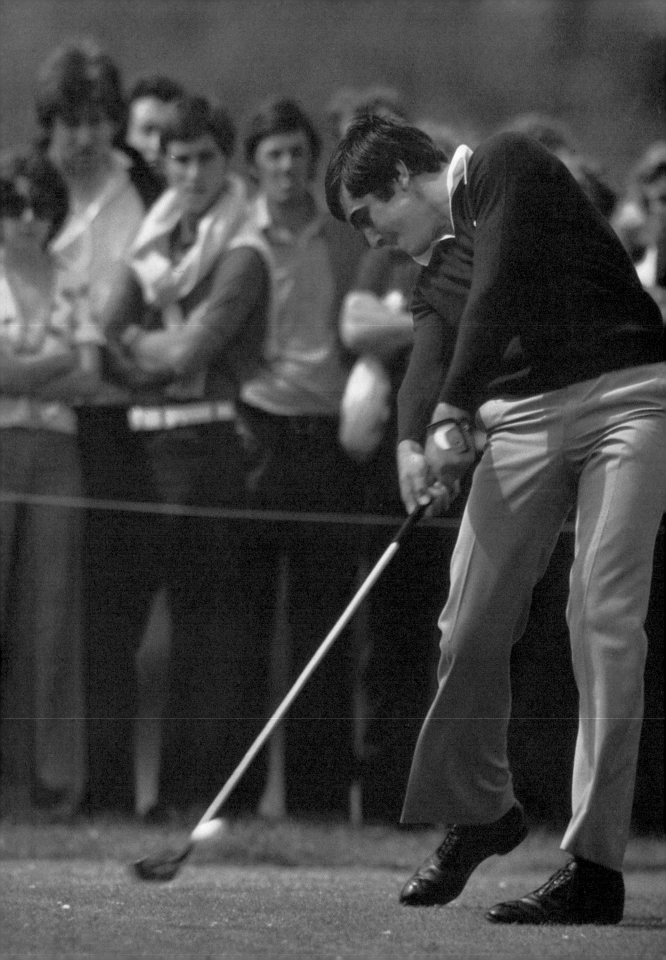

4 Rules

All dives must be performed without any assistance and are graded quite carefully:

Completely failed
(e.g. not the intended dive)   0 points
Unsatisfactory (e.g.
extremely poor performance with a flat body contact
with the water)   0.5-2 points
Deficient (e.g. poor
execution, extremely poor
entry)   2.5-4.5 points
Satisfactory (e.g. passable
execution, little height)   5-6 points
Good (e.g. standard and
correct execution, a
little splash on entry)   6.5-8 points
Very good (e.g. high flight,
crisp execution, entry
with little or no splash)   8.5-10 points

5 Skills

A good diver will display confidence, style and perfect control, to such a degree that the performance of even the most difficult dive looks extremely easy. It is sometimes possible to judge the capability of the competitor just before the dive itself — look for signs of nervousness or tension, especially on the face; fidgeting or pacing up and down on the board; standing for an excessively long time before taking off. These are all indications that the diver may be finding things too difficult. Look for the amount of height gained from take off and for signs of poor control and technique, such as *snatching* too quickly into a somersault and *opening out* too late or early for a head-first entry. When the diver enters the water, look to see whether the body is too arched or whether it is bent, see if the feet enter the water at exactly the same spot as the hands; whether there is a splash, or if the water *rips* so that it is difficult to spot the point of entry. Most divers *punch* their way into the water, gripping their hands together as they plunge into the pool. The latest method is more difficult. Called the rip dive because it only leaves a ripple on the surface,

LEFT: Nina Shaposhnikova, one of the USSR's star gymnasts.

divers keep their fingers pointed as they arrow downwards; then they attempt to part the water on impact, almost as if they were swimming to the bottom! An American invention, it requires split-second timing and only the best in the world use it successfully. In every dive the legs should be held firmly together with toes pointed throughout.

6 Tactics

A diver can often win a competition by performing relatively simple dives perfectly. A higher tariff value (a more difficult dive) is often unhelpful, sometimes disastrous, if the execution is not exact. Competitors submit a list of their dives, and the order in which they will be performed, to the referee. By choosing to perform the more difficult manoeuvres early on, a diver can put pressure on other competitors — but only if the execution is perfect. This is the mark of a real competitor. Poor competitors will often leave their more difficult dives until last because they are nervous about them or are afraid a mediocre attempt will upset the rest of their dives.

7 Words

Backdive: where diver has back to pool on takeoff
Break-out: when diver changes position in mid-air
Entry: the moment of hitting the water
Feet-first: not all dives require competitors to go in head first
Header: a head first dive, as opposed to feet first
Hurdle: the diver's spring or jump at the end of the springboard, leading into the final takeoff
Over/under twist: twist too far/too little and enter the water at an angle
Reverse dive: where diver takes off facing forward but somersaults to enter water facing backwards
Swallow/swan dive: a forward dive where arms are stretched wide until just before entry
Tariff: degree of difficulty of a dive ranging from 1.1 to 3.0 which is multiplied by judges' score to get a final mark for a dive
Tower diving: US name for highboard event. ■

DIVING

Show jumping might have been designed specifically for television. It is spectacular and skilful and simple to understand, with an inbuilt climax in the timed *jump-off* with which most competitions end. People who have never ridden a horse in their lives can appreciate this sport which combines the skills of both the horse and its rider as they cover a set number of fences in an arena.

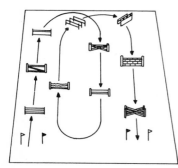

A simple course

1 The Course

An outdoor arena is used, usually 150 by 125m (164 by 137yd approx) but a minimum of 90 by 60m (or 100 by 65yd approx). The fences are set up using the whole length and breadth of the arena. Indoor arenas should be a minimum of 60 by 30m (or 65 by 33 yd approx). The course designer has much the same role as the compiler of an examination paper. The designer asks the questions, while the riders and horses have to find the answers. Rather than test the horses by merely putting the fences at the maximum height allowed by the rules, the ability of the contestants should be tested by awkward turns and distance problems, so that a horse needs to shorten or lengthen its stride between fences that are close together. Good courses are designed to sort out the best horse, not eliminate all of them!

Course designing is particularly difficult in major contests, like the Olympic Games, in which the standard of competitors covers a very wide range.

Both horse and rider are balanced, and looking forward to the next fence.

The designer needs to make the course sufficiently difficult to test the best horses, without causing havoc among those at the other end of the scale. The maximum length of a course (measured in metres) is the number of obstacles multiplied by 60.

2 Equipment

At international level the rider wears: a riding cap, white shirt and tie, jacket (usually scarlet for men and black for women), breeches and boots. The horse requires: bridle, saddle and protective coverings for his forelegs (usually both *tendon* and *over-reach boots*).

3 Winning

The idea is to clear all the fences in the prescribed order and inside the time limit. Horse and rider are penalized for knocking down any part of a fence (four faults) or putting one or more feet in the water or on the landing tape (four faults) at a water jump. If a horse refuses to jump a fence or runs past it the first *refusal* is penalized with three faults; the second with six faults and the third with elimination. If the horse or rider falls the penalty is eight faults. The time faults are calculated by giving one quarter of a fault for each second (or part of a second) over the *time allowed*. There is also a *time limit* which is double the time allowed. This would rarely be exceeded at top level, as the rider would never force the horse to continue if it had made so many refusals or errors that it was going to be over the time limit.

4 Rules

All international contests are judged under the rules of the Fédération Equestre Internationale (which is the ruling international body for equestrian sport). There are three main types of competition: (1) contests which primarily test jumping ability but also use the time taken as the deciding factor. Time counts in the first round or (more often) in the first or second jump-off held when two or more horses finish equal. A steady *clear* round (one with no faults) is therefore better than a fast one with four faults. (2) *Puissance* contests which test high jumping ability only. During successive jump-offs for a puissance, the fences are gradually reduced to a minimum of two (one *spread* and one *upright)* and these are made progressively higher, like the high jump in track and field athletics. (3) Contests which put a premium on speed and agility, in which faults are converted into seconds. The rules for international contests stipulate a minimum weight for both men and women over the age of 18 of 75kg (or 165lb), so lead weights may be added under the saddle as in horse racing.

5 & 6 Skills & Tactics

The most stylish riders are those who sit quietly and communicate their wishes to the horse with the minimum of movement. It may look more spectacular to leap out of the saddle at every jump, but riders who adopt the acrobatic style are less in control than those who are more orthodox. However there are riders, even at top level, who do not have good style — but still win!

The horse should maintain an even rhythmic stride and his back should be rounded when jumping. The height of a fence governs how far away the point of take off should be. The ratio is usually one-third, so that a horse would jump a 2m (or 6ft) fence from 66cm (or 2ft) away.

Unlike horse racing, there is no perfect build for a show jumping horse. It has to be brave and have plenty of spring in its hindquarters.

Before each competition, the rider walks the course very carefully, pacing the distances between any fences that are particularly close together in order to know whether the horse will need a shortened, normal or lengthened stride. When speed is decisive, the top riders save time by audaciously cutting corners so that they take the shortest possible route. This is always more effective than a headlong gallop because time gained on the straight sections of the course is wiped out by time lost on the turns.

The draw in a timed jump-off is generally considered to favour the rider who goes last. But those drawn early will try to cancel the advantage by jumping with such speed and precision that they demoralize their remaining opponents. If a rider has two horses in a competition he or she will usually ride the better one second, so that any tips learnt from the first ride can be used for the second. Rhythm is important, and a rider will put a horse into a rhythm before going through the start. To make sure that his or her horse is supple, before an event a rider will often use dressage exercises.

7 Words

Combination: an obstacle comprising two or three fences, all of which are within 12m (or 39ft 4in) of each other

Double: a combination of two fences close together, requiring two quick jumps in succession

Jump-off (or *barrage):* a second (or later) round in which those lying equal first compete against each other; in most competitions time is decisive in either the first or second jump-off; the number of obstacles is often reduced and their height increased

Over-reach boots: protective rubber rings worn by horses to prevent injuries caused by the toe of a hind foot striking the heel of a fore foot

Oxer: fence made of poles and hedge. A *double oxer* has poles on both sides of the hedge

Puissance: a contest that judges jumping ability only, without time being used to decide the result

Spread: any fence that combines width and height

Stand-back: to take off a long way in front of a fence

Tendon boots: protective coverings worn by horses to prevent injuries caused by the toe of a hind foot hitting the back of a foreleg

Treble: a combination of three obstacles placed close together. If a horse refuses any part, all three fences must be jumped again

Triple: a spread made of three horizontal poles which are higher at the back than the front, like a staircase

Under: a horse that gets under a fence is taking off too close to it

Upright: a vertical fence (e.g. a gate) which doesn't incorporate width as well as height

Withers: ridge between horse's shoulder blades, point from which horse's height is measured. ∎

It takes less than a second for a horse and rider to clear an obstacle. At take-off the reins must be slackened in order to allow the horse to stretch its neck and head. By leaning forward and coming out of the saddle, the rider takes his weight off the horse's hindquarters. He must then stay still in midair, but on landing straightens his legs.

95

EQUESTRIAN EVENTS

Dressage

Dressage is the art form of equestrianism. It involves training horses to a high level of gymnastic coordination and control, with a continual striving for perfection. The Fédération Equestre Internationale says that: "The object of dressage is the harmonious development of the physique and ability of the horse. As a result it makes the horse calm, supple, and keen, thus achieving perfect understanding with its rider. These qualities are revealed by: the freedom and regularity of the paces; the harmony, lightness and ease of movements; the lightening of the forehand and the engagement of the hind-quarters; the horse remaining absolutely straight in any movement along a straight line and bending accordingly when moving on curved lines." Few achieve such perfection.

1 The Arena

Different tests are set for the different standards of competition, with the more difficult movements reserved for the Grand Prix which is described as an 'expert competition'. The tests take place in an arena measuring 60m by 20m (or 66 by 22yd) with letter markings around the outside. The sandy surface is raked before each competitor enters the arena, so that the pattern of hoof prints shows up clearly, and a central strip is rolled flat as a guideline.

The dressage arena. The letters mark the points where competitors execute required movements.

2 Equipment

For the rider: top hat, shirt, hunting stock, tail coat, breeches, boots and spurs. For the horse: double bridle and saddle.

3 Winning

From the moment the horse and rider canter into the arena, they are being assessed by the judges. First, they halt and salute. The horse should be perfectly still at the halt and all movements should be crisp. Horse and rider then complete a set pattern of complex moves which the rider has memorized. The letters around the arena mark the turning points as the horse walks and trots, sometimes in straight lines, sometimes at an angle, sometimes in a circle. The horse also changes strides so that the left leg leads instead of the right. Then there are *pirouettes,* where the horse circles with its hind legs remaining on the spot, or the *piaffer* where the horse trots on the spot. In the *passage* the horse moves in a slow, controlled trot, springing lightly from one diagonal pair of legs to the other. The judges are again saluted at the end of the test.

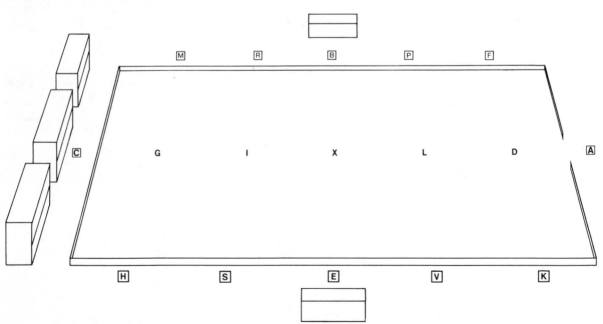

Throughout these tests, the judges expect the horse to be light on its feet, quick to respond yet not looking as if he is being controlled. Balance and rhythm are vital, so that the horse glides around the arena. The rider must be equally graceful to complete a good-looking partnership. The pattern of hoofprints is also studied to assess the ability of the horse.

Each movement or group of movements is marked by the judges from 0 (unmarkable) to 6 (perfect). These marks are then totalled to give the final score. Each test usually comprises about 20 movements.

4 Rules

The rules for international competitions are drawn up by the Fédération Equestre Internationale. The FEI compile and publish the official tests and how they should be executed. There is no minimum weight for the riders in the dressage competitions.

5 Skills

The qualities of the best dressage horses can be seen in the freedom and regularity of the paces; the harmony and lightness of the *forehand* (front legs) and the controlled strength of the *hindquarters* (rear legs). The rider should remain as still as possible so that the horse gives the impression of doing what is required of its own accord.

6 Tactics

Top dressage riders can make a performance in a test look better than it is by covering up any *resistance* or disobedience from the horse. This can be done, for instance, by correcting the horse using the legs on the side that the judges cannot see.

Immaculately turned out, this horse and rider are relaxed and in perfect harmony. This disguises the immense concentration necessary at international level.

7 Words

Grand Prix: the most demanding of the dressage tests, with advanced movements such as Passage and Piaffer included

Kur (Free style): a competition in which there is no set test; riders have to include certain movements but can choose their own sequence

Passage: a slow, very elevated trot, which is recognized by its moment of suspension between each stride

Piaffer: similar to the Passage, but performed on one spot without any forward movement

Pirouette: a movement in which the horse turns a full circle, with the inside hindleg acting as a pivot

Track: the line in which a horse moves; this can be straight or on *two tracks* where the horse walks at an angle so that its forelegs and hindlegs trace different tracks. ■

EQUESTRIAN EVENTS
Dressage

Originally designed as a test for army officers' chargers, it is still the best all-round test of a horse and rider. The horse has to be calm and obedient on the first day when the dressage section takes place. On the second day, it needs courage and stamina for the speed and endurance phase, and on the third day its condition is tested with show jumping. The rider, too, is tested for courage, fitness and technique.

1 The Courses

On *Day One* the dressage lasts about 10 minutes and takes place in an area marked in the same way as for a specialist dressage event. If there is a large entry, two days may be taken up. *Day Two* is divided into four parts, all timed independently, and designed to test the speed, endurance and jumping ability of the horse. Phase A is over 16-20km (or 10-12½ miles) of roads and tracks. The route must be covered at a rate of 240m (or 262yd) per minute at a brisk trot or canter. Phase B is over a steeplechase

The gruelling cross-country phase can often take its toll of horses and riders, especially in muddy conditions. Riders often remount, despite a 60 point penalty, and press on.

course of about four fences, and is about 4km (or 2½ miles) long. Each fence is jumped three times at a gallop and time is important. Phase C is a repeat of Phase A. Then there is a 10-minute break when each horse is checked for fitness by a veterinary surgeon before the gruelling final phase. Phase D is an 8km (5 mile) gallop across country. The fences are solid and water jumps and walls are included as well as steep banks and *drops* where the horses jump a fence and then land lower than the take off point.

Some fences are built at right angles. The cautious rider will jump these in two parts: the bold will attempt to clear two in one go, and at the angle where they join. Flags mark the fences with the white to the left and the red to the right.

Day Three is relatively easy. The show jumping is designed not so much to test the jumping ability of the horse but more its suppleness after the previous day's exertions. This is where all the hours spent training the horse for perfect control are put to the test. The contrast between the brightly coloured show jumping fences and the previous day's solid natural obstacles also tests the horse's ability to adjust to different conditions.

2 Equipment

There is correct dress for each of the three phases. Dressage: top hat or riding cap, shirt and hunting tie or stock, tail coat or hunting coat, gloves, breeches, boots and spurs. Cross-country: crash helmet or riding cap, polo neck sweater, breeches and boots. Show jumping: riding cap or top hat, white shirt and hunting tie or stock, hunting jacket, breeches and boots, as well as a stopwatch to keep an eye on the time limits.

The horse requires: protective coverings usually worn on the forelegs in the cross-country and show jumping phases.

3 Winning

Dressage: marks from 0-6 are awarded by a panel of judges who are looking at the quality of the paces, the obedience of the horse and the *seat* or posture of the rider. There are also points deducted for exceeding the time limit. The marks are then averaged and deducted from the maximum possible total. A special multiplying factor is applied to give the rider's penalty score. *Steeplechase and Cross-country:* just as in show-jumping, penalties are given for refusals at fences. Twenty penalties for the first refusal, 40 penalties for the second and elimination for refusing a third time. If the horse and/or rider fall within the *penalty zone* around each fence, that counts as 60 penalties. The rider has to memorize the course thoroughly since taking the wrong course results in elimination. For each second over the *optimum time* on the steeplechase course, 0.8 of a penalty point is added, and for each second over the optimum time on the cross-country course, 0.4 of a penalty point is added.

Show jumping penalties are awarded if a fence is knocked down or a horse's foot goes in the water at a water jump (five penalties). A refusal (including *running out* or *circling*) would result in 10 penalties the first time, 20 penalties the second and elimination the third. If the horse and/or rider fall, 30 penalties are scored and for each second over the time allowed, a quarter penalty.

 # Rules

Under the international rules of the Fédération Equestre Internationale, all riders in senior three-day events must have reached their eighteenth birthday and must carry a minimum weight of 75kg (or 165lb) for all sections of the competition except the dressage. Because it is such a demanding event, horses must be officially examined for fitness before the start, again before they set out on the cross-country course, and finally on the morning of the show jumping phase.

Skills

Skills are built up over years, so that a rider and horse work together as a unit. The best riders display a bold and positive approach to the riding of cross-country fences and usually manage to find a few places where they can save time.

 # Tactics

The speed, endurance and cross-country phase involves a fine judgement of pace, so that the horse conserves enough energy to finish the course without running out of steam. Riders therefore look for ways of saving time on the cross-country course, rather than pushing their horses on at a speed that would drain their resources. In international team contests, most countries have their supporters positioned round the course so that they can send back word about any fences that are proving troublesome.

 # Words

Box: an enclosure where riders prepare for the start of the speed, endurance and cross-country phase; it is also used for the ten-minute compulsory halt before the cross-country, during which the horses are examined for fitness
Broken down: term used to describe a horse that has badly strained or ruptured the back tendons in one or more of its legs
Circling: refusing an obstacle, by circling before it
Combined event: any competition that comprises two of the three of the usual three-day event phases
Cross-country: a test on a prepared course in open country and over fixed obstacles
Multiplying factor: this varies between 1 and 2½ and is applied to the dressage marks so that this phase can be made to exert 'the correct influence on the whole competition'
Penalty zone: the area surrounding steeplechase and cross-country fences in which penalties are incurred for a fall
Refusal: refusing to jump an obstacle by coming to a halt, circling or running past it
Roads and tracks: these constitute the endurance aspect of a three-day event; there are no jumps, but the route must be covered at a rate of 240m (or 262yd) per minute
Running out: refusing to jump an obstacle by riding past it
Steeplechase: a test over fences that are similar to those used on regulation steeplechase courses. ■

When landing, the rider takes his own bodyweight with his knee joints and by straightening up his body helps to take pressure off the front part of the horse.

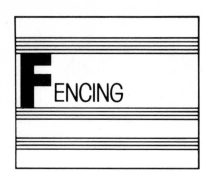

FENCING

To train for war and for duelling men practised with blunted or covered weapons; modern fencing as a sport evolved from this. Today fencing lives on solely as a sport. It retains much of the flourish and exhilaration of the duel, but the danger of injury has been eliminated.

Because much of the ritual and formality has been left behind, it is now a modern, dynamic and athletic sport. The great appeal of fencing, apart from its romantic past, is that it involves the total human being. A fencer must constantly analyse defence and attack to devise tactics to outwit the opponent. Fencing demands uncompromising attention and offers mental and physical challenge of the highest order.

2 Equipment

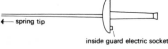
foil
← spring tip
inside guard electric socket

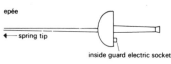
epée
← spring tip
inside guard electric socket

sabre

types of handle

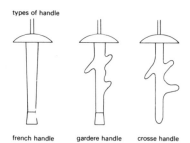

french handle   gardere handle   crosse handle

The foil is 1.1m (43in) long with a maximum weight of 500g (17½oz); the épée is also 1.1m, maximum weight 770g (27oz); the sabre is 1.05m (41in) and weighs 500g maximum.

1 The Piste

Fencing is confined to a long, narrow mat. Both fencers stand behind their *on guard* lines at the start of a contest or after a *hit* has been registered. If a fencer is forced back over the *rear limit* line twice, a penalty hit is conceded so a *warning* line is marked 2m (2yd approx) from the rear limit. Although fencers can side-step or turn slightly, they can never reverse positions during a bout.

Over a protective undergarment (plastron) the fencer must wear a white jacket and knee breeches made of strong canvas; the long glove on the fencing hand is soft leather. The mask has a wire mesh visor. For foil a metallic jacket is worn which reacts to the electronic equipment used for registering hits.

3 Winning

Three weapons are used in modern fencing — foil, épée and sabre. Each has different characteristics and the style of fencing differs radically but the scoring system is the same for all three. Hits are recorded AGAINST the fencer hit, not FOR the fencer scoring, so the competitor with the higher score next to his name would be losing.

Bouts are usually won by the first fencer to score five hits in a six-minute contest, eight hits in a ten-minute contest, or ten hits in a 12-minute contest. Shorter contests are usually

preliminaries while longer contests are finals or the later stages of a *knock-out* tournament like the Olympics. If the requisite number of hits is not scored when time is up, the competitor in the lead wins. If scores are level, the first hit in extra time wins it. Competitors often begin with a series of *pools* where each fencer takes on the others in the group one after the other. Traditionally a final pool of six fencers is considered the best way of producing a worthy champion but the Olympics have a straight knock-out competition featuring the best 32 fencers.

4 Rules

FOIL
Fencing with the foil is governed by conventions dating back from the 18th century, the chief of which is that if both fencers are hit simultaneously, the attacker alone scores. The target for foil is the whole of the trunk, front and back. Hits *arriving* on the head, arms or legs stop the bout but do not score. To be valid, a hit must arrive with the point on the target and with sufficient force to depress the spring tip, which resists a pressure of 500g (1.1lb approx).

Classically, fencers stand sideways on, presenting opponents with less of a target, and keeping opponents literally at arm's length.

The attacker is the fencer who FIRST straightens his arm with the point continuously threatening the target. The defender then only has the right to hit when either he has parried the attack or the attacker has missed. There are exceptions to this rule — if the attacker bends his arm interrupting the attack, or if the attack is of more than one movement and the attacker is hit with a *stop hit* or counter thrust.

The electrical apparatus has a white and coloured light for each fencer. The lights indicate to the President (official watching each bout) who struck first and which part of the body was hit. A white light denotes an *off* target hit and coloured lights (red or green) indicate hits on the target. Hits that land on the guard of the weapon, or on the piste on which they are fencing will not register.

EPEE

This is the duelling sword. Hits are scored with the point only. The target includes every part of the fencer. Bouts are fought under the conditions of a duel without conventions; any hit counts. Simultaneous hits count against both fencers. The spring tip of an épée will resist a pressure of 750g (1.5lb approx). As in foil, hits on the guard of the weapon or on the piste do not register.

SABRE

This is the cut and thrust weapon. Hits are made by cutting with the whole of the front edge of the blade, or with the first third of the back edge nearest the point, or with the point of the weapon. The target is all parts of the body front and back above the line of the hips.

Sabre is fought under similar conventions to foil, the attacker being the first fencer with his arm straight threatening the opponent's target.

To date there is no method or apparatus for judging sabre electrically, therefore it needs four judges, who watch for hits arriving and the president controls the bout as well as deciding on the priority of hits.

Skills & Tactics

Because of the speed of the sport, it may at first be difficult to follow the play. Do not try to watch both fencers; concentrate on one at a time, preferably the attacker. If his attacking move is parried, see how

quickly he assumes the defensive role in order to parry his opponent's *riposte* before returning to the offensive.

A fencer must know by reasoned observation or by intuition just when to attack. He must be constantly judging and changing distance to be in a position to attack and score; he must be aware of how far and when to step in in order to disconcert his opponent's preparations to attack. He must deceive without being deceived; he must develop tactics and counter-tactics to meet lightning-fast reactions which may themselves be nothing more than clever deceptions to draw him into making a mistake in distance or timing.

7 Words

Assault: a bout
Attack on the blade: preparation to attack by beating or pressing against the opponent's blade
Balestra: a short jump forward
Barrage: a tie or fight-off
Broken time: a deliberate pause made between two movements of an attack
Compound attack: an attack which includes one or more feints
Corps à corps: when two fencers come into bodily contact
Engagement': the crossing of the blades in contact with each other
Feint: a movement of the blade meant to resemble an attack and whose purpose is to draw a reaction
Flèche: an attack made by running rather than a step, or lunging
Judges: those whose duty it is to watch for hits and to assist the President
Lunge: a classical leg action enabling the fencer to reach his opponent.
Parry: defensive action with the sword to deflect the opponent's offensive action
Phrase: a sequence of fencing movements exchanged between two fencers
Piste: the area on which fencers fight in competion
Preparation to attack: a blade, body or foot movement which opens the way for an attack
President: the umpire or referee at fencing
Riposte: the offensive action which follows a successful parry
Salle: fencing club
Second intention: to lure the opponent into attacking rashly so that the fencer can counter-attack
Touché: The word used to acknowledge a hit. ∎

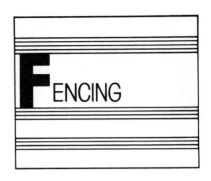

FENCING

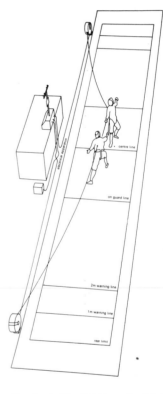

The piste is 14m (46ft) long; 2m (6ft 6in) wide

FRISBEE DISC

The idea of spinning a plastic disc to a companion has developed from a pleasant recreation into an organized, competitive sport with several different games. In the USA, even dogs have their day with the National Canine Catch and Fetch Championships!

Circular, with a lip underneath, discs are made of a tough but slightly flexible plastic. For competition, there are five recognized sizes. The 97g (3²/₅oz) is for the younger player for *Freestyle* and *Maximum Time Aloft;* the 119g for distance and accuracy; the 133g and 141g are all-purpose models; and the 165g is the regulation disc for *Ultimate.*

The fundamental skills are throwing, catching and *delaying.* The three basic throws are the *backhand, sidearm* and *overarm* or *wrist flip.* The backhand produces clockwise spin for righthanders while the other two make the disc spin anti-clockwise. Apart from the basic catching technique in front of the body with one or two hands, there are *trick catches* such as behind the neck or back or even under the leg! The development of delaying tactics such as the *nail delay* has opened a new range of options in freestyle play. This involves catching the spinning disc on a finger nail and keeping the spin going.

FRISBEE DISC GOLF
Instead of using a club and ball, players design a course with trees, bushes and water to test the individual's ability to get from the *tee area* to the *pole area* in the lowest number of throws over an 18-hole course. Although a marked tree or lampost can be used as a target, in competition a 5ft (1.5m) tall pole with a metal basket and chains is required. One point is counted each time the disc is thrown and when a penalty is incurred. A run up and follow-through is allowed on each throw, but the disc must be released with one foot on the *lie,* the spot where the disc previously landed. A disc that lands *out of bounds* or more than 6ft (2m) above the ground can be brought back into play at the cost of a penalty stroke.

ULTIMATE FRISBEE
Played by seven players a side, *Ultimate* is a fast-moving team game where points are scored by scoring goals. The idea is to pass the disc from teammate to teammate until it is caught by a player in the *end zone,* the 30yd (25m) deep area at each end of a 40yd × 60yd (35m × 55m) field. As it can be played on any surface, some players may like to wear helmets, hats or gloves but these must not endanger the safety of others. Consisting of two 24–minute halves, Ultimate lasts longer because the clock is stopped for time-outs, injuries, fouls etc. If a player catches the disc cleanly, his team retains possession. If he drops it or it goes out of play, possession goes to the other side. If the disc falls untouched to the ground, the opposition also takes possession. Players must not walk, run or take steps with the disc and must always pass through the air, not by handing the disc to a teammate. Grappling for possession is not allowed — this is an energetic but clean sport.

INDIVIDUAL CONTESTS
Players can throw for *distance* from a marked *throwing* or *foul line,* which must not be crossed when throwing. Then there is *TR&C* (Throw, Run and Catch) where the player tries to achieve the maximum distance between throwing the disc, then running after it and catching it cleanly. *MTA* (Maximum Time Aloft) is timed from the moment of throwing to the moment the player catches it again, while *Freestyle* is a five minute programme of skills and tricks that should blend with accompanying music, like a freestyle ice skating programme. Fellow players mark performances from 1 to 10 based on difficulty, creativity and flow of movement.

Players often talk about *self-caught flight* where one person both throws and catches the disc in one hand as in TR&C and MTA. Look out for the *thumber,* a specialist throw of great power and speed made with the thumb pushed hard inside the rim of the disc. Then there is *tipping,* when the disc is bounced in the air with a touch of the finger, elbow, knee, toe, head ... or any other part of the body! And what about the *air-bounce* when the disc is thrown hard downwards so that it bounces on air, rises and hovers! ∎

Competitors take frisbee throwing very seriously. Note the concentration required, and the special boots.

Wrestling, tripping and punch-ups were a major part of Gaelic Football until formalized rules were issued by the Gaelic Athletic Association in 1885. The modern game can be compared to rugby and soccer. Two teams of 15 battle it out for 60 minutes with a 10–minute interval at half-time.

only bounce the ball once before giving it to another player. Attackers must not enter the parallelogram ahead of the ball. Kicking, tripping and pushing are illegal but a shoulder to shoulder charge is a fair challenge. A foul results in a free-kick at the place of infringement or a penalty from the middle of the 14yd (12.8m) line where the attacker tries to boot it past the goalkeeper to score a goal.

1 The Pitch

The grass-covered pitch, the goals and the *square* or *parallelogram* are the same size as in Ireland's other favourite sport, Hurling. There is a free-kick line 50yd (approx 45m) from each goal-line.

2 Equipment

Players wear a club strip like rugby or soccer players with numbers on the back of their jerseys. The ball, like a soccer ball, is round and leather-covered; its circumference is 27-29in (68.5-73.6 cm) and its weight is 13-15oz (368-425g).

3 Winning

The ball can be punched or kicked into the goal (under the bar) for three points (a *goal)* and over the bar for one point (a *point).* After a goal the game is restarted by the defending side kicking off from their 21yd (19.2m) line; after a point, a defender kicks off from his own square.

4 Rules

Players hit the ball with their hands or kick it with their feet either on or off the ground, although only the goalkeeper can pick it up directly from the ground (and then only within his parallelogram). Players may not throw the ball, so they pass it by hitting it with an open hand, fisting it, passing it from hand to hand, or bouncing it while running. Up to three steps may be taken before the ball must be kicked or bounced. After a high catch (often spectacular, like a mark in Australian Football) a player may

5 & 6 Skills & Tactics

The skills are similar to those employed in soccer (and many other team ball games) and are based on control of the ball and fast, accurate passing. Players cover the whole pitch and so need a strong positional sense, good anticipation, sharpness in attack and, of course, stamina.

7 Words

The parallelogram: the goal area (also known as 'the square')
To hop the ball: to bounce the ball with one or both hands
Free-kick: awarded after an infringement
Penalty kick: awarded after a foul within the parallelogram. ∎

As throwing is illegal, players pass the ball by hitting it with their fist or open hand.

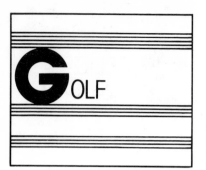

GOLF

There are references to Scottish shepherds playing a form of golf in the 16th century. They fashioned clubs from branches of trees and hit roughly-shaped balls into holes dug at random in the ground. From such crude beginnings, the game has become much more sophisticated. Physical it may be, with a golfer walking, on average, 5 miles (8km approx) during a round, but it is also a thinking man's game. Ninety-five per cent of golf is mental. It takes intelligence to work out the best place to hit a drive, the best way to play a hole. Scoring well depends on more than hitting the ball well.

The game demands complete concentration for as long as maybe four hours — concentration on the apparently simple task of getting a small ball into 18 relatively small holes in as few strokes as possible.

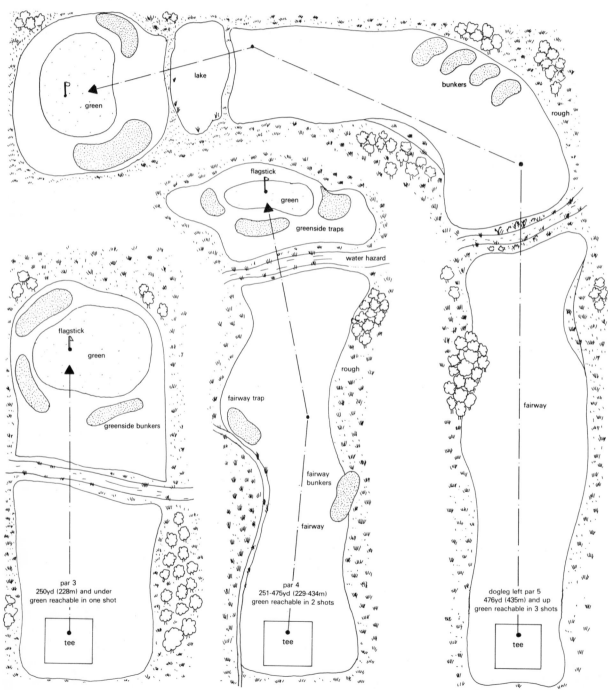

par 3
250yd (228m) and under
green reachable in one shot

par 4
251-475yd (229-434m)
green reachable in 2 shots

dogleg left par 5
476yd (435m) and up
green reachable in 3 shots

A golfer is always on his own — if he plays badly, there is no one to blame but himself. A simple game, but perhaps the confusing aspect is the special language golfers use.

1 The Course

The standard number of *holes* on a full course is 18. Each is made up of three distinct sections: the *tee,* the *fairway* and the *green.* The tee is a flat, well mown area about 6yd (5m) square where the golfer strikes the first shot at each hole. This is the only time the ball can be placed on a small wooden or plastic peg (also called a *tee*) making it easier to hit. Having *driven* off the tee, the golfer hopes the ball lands on the fairway, the stretch of ground that runs from the tee to the green. The grass here is cut short, but is bordered on both sides with *rough* or longer grass which starts about 3in (8cm) high and can become knee deep. There is a premium, then, on driving reasonably accurately off the tee because the further off-line a shot is, the more severely the golfer is punished.

In addition to the rough there are other *hazards* a golfer must avoid — hollows filled with sand on the fairway called *bunkers, water hazards* such as lakes, streams and ditches as well as trees and bushes. All these are strategically placed by golf course designers to catch the badly-aimed or struck ball.

The third part of a hole is the *green* which has the actual hole, 4¼ in (10.8cm) wide, sunk in it, marked with a tall stick and flag. Greens are very smooth so that the ball can run along the ground to the hole. On average, about 50ft (15m) across, they can undulate or slope gently. The texture of the grass, even the direction in which it grows and is mown, can affect the ball as it rolls towards the hole. Some holes are long and test the ability to hit a ball a long way, others are short and demand even greater accuracy. All require accurate *putting* on the greens, to *hole the ball* in as few strokes as possible.

Courses vary enormously throughout the world, and there can be several types in one country. In northern Europe, and to a lesser extent in America, there are *links* courses built beside the sea. These courses are firm underfoot so that a ball, when it lands, runs on... and on... and on. These conditions mean players frequently have to play *pitch and run* shots, bouncing a ball short of the putting surface to let it roll up to the hole. In contrast, there is the *parkland* course, an inland course, where the grass is thicker, the ground softer and the greens more yielding or *holding.* Here the golf ball runs only a few yards (metres) after landing and stops or even screws back when it hits the green. In these soft conditions, golfers can play *target golf* — hitting the ball right up to the spot where they want it to land, knowing it will stop there.

Inland courses are usually protected from the wind by trees or hills, but links courses are wide-open and vulnerable to the worst weather. Winds can switch direction at the seaside more than once in a round, completely changing the character of several holes. A feature of the heathland course, which is built inland, is clinging heather and broom.

A driver has a solid wooden head that helps to hit the aerodynamically-dimpled ball a long way. The ball has a hard but rubberized core.

Some bunkers can be small or, like this one, swallow the ball up. The golfer uses a special flat wedge to get under the ball, which can get 'plugged' or buried in the steep sandy face of the trap.

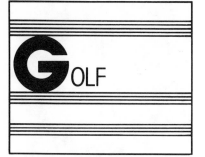

GOLF

Putting may look easy, but it is often the hardest phase of a golfer's round. Golfers try all sorts of grips and swings to find one that gives them consistency for both long and short putts.

Scorecard

2 Equipment

One aspect of golf which is not standard is the size of the ball, *dimpled* to make it fly through the air with aerodynamic efficiency. In America and on most professional tours the 1.68in (42.7mm) diameter ball is used. This is the so-called *American-size* ball, which plays better in coarse grass. In some countries, like Britain, a smaller ball, 1.62in (41mm) in diameter, is used which is easier for an average player to control in the wind. In addition, there are weight and velocity restrictions.

Golfers have several clubs, all designed to move the ball in different ways in different conditions. To start off there are four *woods* with big, solid heads. Used for distance, the No.1 wood is the *driver,* the 2 and 3 woods have slightly more loft in the head, for use off the fairway and the 4 wood is used when recovering from light rough.

There are nine *irons* (with steel heads) for the fairways, numbered 1 to 9. Somewhat confusingly, the lower the number, the further the ball should go. The lowest numbers have longer shafts and a less lofted or angled clubface so that when they hit the ball the trajectory is lower and longer. On average, a golfer hits a 2 iron about 200yd (180m), going down about 15yd (13m) a club to the *wedge* (sometimes called a 10 iron) which reaches about 90yd (82m). The low numbered irons are called *long*

irons, 4 to 7 are *medium irons,* and the rest are *short irons.* The wedge has a very short face and is used to cut through sand, to get under the ball and lift it clear. On the green, a *putter* is used, light-headed for fast or slick surfaces, heavier on slow surfaces.

Most professionals use clubs with lightweight steel shafts but sometimes they use graphite, which reduces torque, makes for extra whippiness and, if struck properly, can make the ball go further.

3 Winning

Most major golf championships are decided by *stroke-play* with players adding up their scores for each of the 18 holes, with the lowest total winning. Golfers do not mark their own scores so cards are exchanged between players at the start of a round and are returned and checked at the end, before being signed and handed in to the official recorder. In big tournaments, four *rounds* of 18 holes, played over four days, decide the winner. To make things more exciting, only about half the field plays on the final two days, the higher scorers having been eliminated.

If two or more players finish level there is usually a *sudden death* play off. They play as many extra holes as necessary to determine the winner, who is the first golfer to win a hole, by getting the ball in the hole in the fewest strokes.

In *match-play,* a less popular form of the game among the professionals, golfers play each other in a knock-out tournament and scoring is on a *holes up* basis. Player 'A' may take 3 strokes and win the hole from Player 'B' who takes 4. Matches usually end when a player is ahead by more holes than there are holes left to play, 4 and 3 (four up and three to play).

It is always possible to tell how well a golfer is doing at any stage of a round, because each of the holes has a *par rating.* This is the score a good golfer should make. There are three ratings — par 3, par 4 and par 5. A par 3 is up to 250yd (228m) long from tee to green. The green should be reached with one shot, leaving two putts to *make par.* A par 4 hole is from 251yd (229m) up to 475yd (434m), and requires two well-struck shots to get to the green, while the par 5 hole is anything over 475yd and needs three good hits to reach the

Player						Handicap				
Competition						Date				

Hole	Name	Yards Length	Par	Player's Score	Strokes Allowed	Hole	Name	Yards Length	Par	Player's Score	Strokes Allowed
1	St Medan	385	4		4	10	Erinview	313	4		10
2	Dasher's Den	373	4		7	11	Puddle Hole	163	3		17
3	Muckle Skelp	542	5		4	12	Dunskev	388	4		2
4	Captain's Leap	157	3		15	13	Sandeel	283	4		12
5	Plateau	362	4		6	14	Glenside	293	4		3
6	Portree	367	4		13	15	Campbell's Gamble	101	3		18
7	Gorsebank	165	3		16	16	Rickwood	377	4		5
8	Flyover	279	4		11	17	Greenfield	284	4		14
9	Hillcrest	298	4		8	18	Journey's End	509	5		9
Out		2928	35			In		2711	35		
						Out		2928	35		
Signature of Marker						Total		5639	70		
Signature of Competitor						Less Handicap					
						Net Score					

putting surface. Top professional golfers will often hole the ball in one shot less than par, which is called a *birdie*. If the golfer manages to *get down* in two less than par, that is an *eagle*. The rare *albatross* or *double eagle* denotes a three under par effort. There is no bonus for achieving birdies or eagles — they are just part of golf's jargon. If a player does badly he would record a *bogey,* one over par, or even a *double bogie,* which is two over.

In order to tell how well a golfer is doing, say on the ninth hole compared with one on the fifteenth, TV commentators usually talk in terms of *par*. The golfer would be so many strokes *over* or *under par* at any stage of the round.

ball and drop it without incurring a penalty, as this is *casual water.*

Because putting is so important golfers are permitted to repair plug and pitch marks on the putting surface — these are the marks made when a ball plunges into a green. On the green a player is allowed to pick up the ball and clean it before putting. Once a ball is on the green, players may *mark* the ball, putting a coin or disc on the ground and removing their ball in case an opponent's ball hits it.

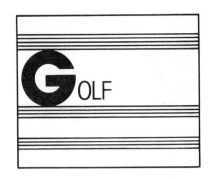

GOLF

4 Rules

Rule one emphasizes the simplicity of the game which consists of playing a ball from the teeing ground into the hole by successive strokes in accordance with the Rules. The next 40 rules deal with the awkward situations that golfers get themselves into, as well as limitations on equipment, etc. A golfer can carry a maximum of 14 clubs, though the composition of the set is up to the individual. Only one replacement is allowed if a club is broken accidentally when hitting a shot. Other rules cover good manners, requiring that players do not try to upset opponents in any way or try to waste time.

The ball must always be played from where it *lies,* from where it landed. If it is impeded by branches or long grass, that's hard luck on the golfer. Loose stones, leaves or twigs can be removed but at no time must the ball be moved or else the golfer suffers a penalty of one stroke, which is added to the score. At times, of course, the ball lands where it it impossible to play — behind a tree, in a pond or even *out of bounds,* off the course. Then *stroke and distance* come into play. If a drive is hit out of bounds, a player can use another ball and drive again. This would be counted as the third stroke — the first and second drives plus a penalty stroke.

If the ball is in an awkward lie, a player can move two club lengths away and drop the ball over one shoulder. This also incurs a penalty of one stroke but could be safer than trying to bash the ball out of trouble. If there is snow or ice or a pool of water on the green, due to heavy rain, a player can move the

Driving from the tee, the golfer has to allow for the wind, clear the rough in front of him and even try to curve the ball in the air, as well as hitting it as far as possible!

Below: How loft of club affects shots; with little loft the ball goes a long way without rising, with a lot of loft the ball rises sharply.

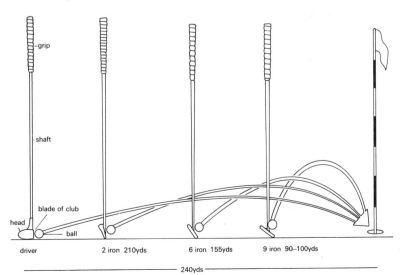

grip

shaft

blade of club

head

ball

driver   2 iron 210yds   6 iron 155yds   9 iron 90–100yds

240yds

5 & 6 Skills & Tactics

While average amateurs strive to hit the ball reasonably straight, professionals may not always want to. If a hole curves

altogether — it is a *fresh air* shot, which actually counts as one stroke.

Just as there is no right or wrong way to swing the golf club, so there is no right or wrong way to putt, except that croquet-style (straddling the line of a putt and swinging pendulum-style) is not allowed. Some golfers rap the ball into the cup with a distinct jabbing movement, others prefer to stroke the ball smoothly.

This golfer is using an iron to chip the ball onto the green. If he had decided to use a putter from that position, Americans would call it a Texas wedge!

to the right or left a shot may be *shaped* in that direction. The choice of which shot to play could be affected by the strength and direction of the wind. If a golfer *fades* a ball, the shot goes intentionally from left to right; if over-done, this is a *slice* or *cut* shot in which the ball moves more dramatically left to right and into trouble. If the ball is hit straight out right, then it is *pushed* or *blocked*.

Many golfers, on the other hand, play a natural *draw*, a shot which intention-ally moves right to left. If not controlled, the shot becomes a *pull* or a *hook*. If he drives off violently to the left it is a *quick hook*, or *duck hook*, one of the most destructive shots in the game.

On average a golf professional will drive a ball 280yd (255m) but downwind this could approach 400yd (360m) if the fairways are sunbaked.

A player using a short iron to hit a steeply arced approach shot on to the green may hit instead a more shallow-curved shot right over the green. This is *thinning it* and means that the ball was hit with the bottom edge of the club instead of the face. If a shot is hit *fat* because the club took up too much turf before hitting the ball, it will be short of the target. If a shot is hit off the angle between the clubhead and the shaft, it is *shanked* and will go off to the right. This is the most demoralizing shot in golf. To *toe* a shot means to hit it off the end of the clubface instead of flush in the middle. If a player misses the ball

7 Words

Ace: a hole in one
Address: stance of golfer before hitting ball
Borrow: the slope on a putting green
Caddie: person employed to carry club and advise on shots
Chip: a shot hit with medium iron close to the green
Cup: another name for the hole
Divot: a sliver of earth taken up when an iron shot is played correctly
Dogleg: hole with sharp bend to left or right between tee and green
Fore: a warning shout before a drive or shot is played
Pin: another name for the flag in the hole
Handicap: not used in professional play, where all players are of equal ability; in amateur games, a system of bonus strokes is used so that players of differ-ing standards can meet on equal terms
Short game: the play up to and on the green
Marshal: official who keeps spectators in order at tournaments
Nineteenth hole: popular name for bar in the clubhouse
Open: a tournament open to amateurs and professionals. ■

Olympic gymnastics, sometimes called artistic gymnastics, is all about perfection. In gymnastics there is no pure and objective method of selecting winners. There is no direct confrontation between individuals or teams, no confrontation between the performer and a stopwatch or measuring tape, because performances are assessed by judges.

Gymnastics, generally regarded as one sport, is really two sports in one. The men's competitions demand a different type of performance from the women's. Men's gymnastics is all about strength, control and difficulty, whereas women's gymnastics introduces artistic and interpretive elements.

above floor level. *The rings:* constructed of wood (or similar material), they are hung by cables, usually from a frame, swinging freely 2.5m (8ft 6in approx) from the floor. *The high bar:* sometimes called the horizontal bar, undoubtedly the most exciting piece of Olympic apparatus for spectator and gymnast alike. At least 2.4m (8ft approx) long, the bar is made of tensile steel firmly supported on uprights 2.5m above the ground.

The women compete on four pieces of apparatus. *The floor:* as for men. *The vault:* exactly the same as used for the men, except that it is set *sideways on* to the run-up and is only 1.2m (4ft approx) high. *The beam:* 5m (18ft

GYMNASTICS

Perhaps the most demanding position on the rings is the crucifix, or cross, where the body must be perfectly still and controlled, with the arms horizontal, shoulders and hands in line.

1 The Apparatus

The men perform on six pieces of apparatus.
The floor: exercises on a 12m (40ft approx) square area of carpet. *The vault:* the simplest and shortest of all gymnastic events. The *horse* is 1.35m (4ft 8in approx) high and 1.6m (5ft 2in approx) long, an oblong box well-padded, covered in leather and standing on wooden legs. *The parallel bars:* two flexible wooden rails set parallel to each other at a maximum height of 1.7m (5ft 4in approx) above ground level and adjustable in width to suit the needs of the individual performer. *The pommel horse:* sometimes called the *side horse,* it is of the same general construction as the vaulting horse, except that it has two handles (of wood or similar material) set parallel 40-45cm (16-18in approx) apart in the centre. The top of the handle should be 1.22m (4ft approx)

Placed sideways on for women's competition, the vaulting horse is used lengthwise for men.

GYMNASTICS

approx) long and only 10cm (4in approx) wide at the top, the wooden beam is set on uprights 1.6m (5ft 4in approx) from floor level, and covered in chamois leather to give a good grip. *The asymmetrical bars:* sometimes called the *uneven parallel bars,* they are two oval wooden rails 2.4m (8ft approx) long and are set parallel to each other, the low one set 1.5m (5ft approx) from the ground, the high rail 2.3m (7ft 8in approx). An adjustable screw between the uprights enables a gymnast to vary the distance between them to suit her own height.

Below: the pommel, or side horse, makes tremendous demands on the strength and control of a gymnast, who must not let any part of his body, except his hands, touch the horse during the 30-second routine.

Above: the male gymnast's strength is tested in the parallel bars as he swings and turns using all the apparatus. At some stage in the routine he must let go completely. The bars themselves are flexible, to help competitors with swing.

Although both sexes compete on floor and vault, the nature of these performances is somewhat different. On the floor, men concentrate on *tumbling* agilities with little artistic interpretation. The women must set their routine to music, introducing more artistry. Vaulting is the closest the sexes come to competing in similar ways, but even then the men vault the length of the horse, the women across the width.

2 Equipment

Both men and women wear leotards, a one-piece costume made from a flexible material and forming straps on the shoulders for men and usually sleeves for women. The men must wear specially designed white trousers when performing on the apparatus, although for floor and vault, shorts are allowed.

When performing on the rings, high bar and asymmetrical bars hand guards made from leather are often used to prevent blistering and tearing the hands, and to help maintain a secure grip. A white powder may also be rubbed onto the hands before starting a routine. This is magnesium carbonate, which absorbs sweat and oil from the skin that would cause the gymnast to slip. It also prevents the hands sticking to the apparatus when they are moved.

Gymnastic shoes (extremely flexible) or socks should be worn during a performance, although women often compete in bare feet. They may step into a box and shuffle their feet before attempting the beam or vault. The box contains granules of resin which stop their feet from slipping.

3 Winning

Most competitions are divided into two parts: the *set* exercises and the *voluntaries.* The sets are designed and issued to the gymnasts well in advance of the competition. Often, in order to qualify for the competiton itself, they must show a complete mastery of these exercises, plus a suitable standard of performance in the voluntary routines. Voluntaries are constructed by the gymnasts themselves and should be difficult enough to bring the best out of the competitor.

Four judges mark the performances on each piece of apparatus and give scores in whole units and tenths, with 10 the maximum (e.g. 8.9; 9.7). When the marks have been decided, the highest and lowest are discarded and the competitor's final score is the average of the remaining two. This may be in hundredths (e.g. 9.2 plus 9.3 averages out to 9.25). If the marks vary a lot from judge to judge, the referee will query the discrepency and occasionally marks are altered. In top class competition the television cameras often focus on the glamour events like the floor exercises or the parallel bars. Although the best performance on each piece of apparatus usually wins a gold medal, gymnasts themselves hold the *overall winner* in high esteem. That is the competitor with the best total of marks on all pieces of apparatus, six for men or four pieces for women. In big international events there is also a team prize for the best country, calculated by adding up the best five performances (teams must have six competitors) on each piece of apparatus.

The gymnast is judged from the moment of stepping forward to begin an exercise until the final stance completes the routine. Apart from the elements of difficulty the judges look for the demonstration of agility, spring, strength, twist and swing. Starting with a full mark of 10, points are deducted for movements that are too simple, show needless repetition, lack of control, breakdowns in the routine and any sign of too obvious effort and strain. Each piece of apparatus makes different demands upon the gymnast.

4 Rules

Each element in a performance is awarded a *degree of difficulty,* decided by the International Gymnastic Federation (FIG). The stages of difficulty for men are:

A Reasonably difficult (i.e. tucked back somersault)
B Difficult (i.e. back somersault straight
C Extremely difficult (e.g. back somersault with two twists, or double back somersault)

Each routine must contain a set number of each category (in the Olympic Games, at least two 'C'

movements in any one routine). Similar categories are used for women's gymnastics (e.g. 'C' = superior difficulty), and there are similar requirements in the construction of a routine.

MEN
Floor: the routine must contain *tumbles,* balances (held for at least two seconds), linking movement, and must display height in all somersaults, movements requiring suppleness and those requiring strength. The routine should be constructed in order to cover all parts of the area, and should last for a minimum of 50 seconds and maximum

In one and a half minutes, women gymnasts execute moves that are closely influenced by ballet and modern dance.

GYMNASTICS

of 70 seconds. A bell or whistle sounds when 60 seconds have elapsed.

Vault: a springboard (beat board) is used to provide additional lift and may be placed at whatever distance from the horse a gymnast prefers. A vault is made up of four parts — the take-off, flight onto the horse, hand contact with the horse and flight off the horse. The landing must be performed with both feet held together and there should be no additional steps taken. Only one attempt is allowed for each competitor.

Parallel bars: the routine should consist of swinging movements, flight (when contact is lost from the bars with either one or both hands) and *held* positions. A springboard may be used in order to mount the apparatus.

Pommel horse: a routine should consist of continuous swinging movements without the legs touching the horse including double leg circles (circling movements with the legs held out horizontally, straight and together) and

Although the beam is quite narrow, girls now perform on it as if it were the floor! In training there is a foam bed below; in competition there is no protection.

circles or sideways movements of individual legs (e.g. *shears,* a scissor-like action of the legs). Double leg cirlces are the most important and all parts of the horse should be used.

Rings: swinging movements, held positions and demonstrations of strength should all be included in a performance. There should be at least two handstands, one using strength and one a swinging motion, and one major strength movement (e.g. the *crucifix).* All stationary positions must be held for at least two seconds.

High bar: continuous swings, both forwards and backwards, make up a routine. There should be changes of grip, twists around the vertical axis *(pirouettes),* and the gymnast should let go of the bar at least once. A large mattress filled with thick foam (called a *crash mat)* may be put in front of the high bar to serve as a landing area. With top competition demanding more spectacular moves, this is vital for safety especially as one small slip could result in a head first landing.

WOMEN

Floor: the requirements are the same as for men but the routine is set to music and contains a major element of dance. Judges look for a good artistic interpretation of the music as well as degrees of difficulty in tumbling.

Many consider the horizontal, or high, bar to be the most exciting men's exercise to watch. Gymnasts pack as many swings and circles into a routine as they can.

Vault: the requirements are the same as for the men except that two attempts, which can be two different types of vault, are allowed with the higher score counting.

Beam: this is the only piece of apparatus for which the men have no equivalent. Extreme concentration is necessary to perform a routine containing a leap (with good height), at least one handstand (of any variety) and the usual requirements of agility, balance and dance demanded of a floor exercise — all on a beam only 10cm (4in) wide! A springboard may be used to mount the beam.

Asymmetrical bars: much like the men's high bar, the routine must be as continuous as possible (although a slight pause may occur when standing on the lower bar). Close circle movements, where the body comes into contact with a bar, a handstand and at least one motion where the gymnast lets

Although the women are only in action for about 30 seconds, the uneven bars is one of the must physically punishing events. The hands get calloused and the thighs and groin receive constant bruising contact.

go of the apparatus completely should all be included. A springboard may be used by the gymnast to mount this apparatus also.

Skills & Tactics

Although assessing the marks for each performance is extremely difficult, especially at top level, it doesn't take an expert to see the difference between a good and an exceptional performance. Good gymnasts will appear to defy gravity, the best just ignore it. Excellent gymnasts never lose balance and their movements will appear crisp, fluid and effortless. But even top class competitors can commit major errors, such as stopping, falling off the apparatus (especially the beam and the pommel horse), *over-rotating* a somersault or making an imperfect landing at the end of a performance.

At top level a gymnast must display elements of risk and originality as well

GYMNASTICS

as virtuosity. Many will perform techniques never seen in competition before and if these are truly original and are potentially dangerous, the movement may be named after them. This was the case with Olga Korbut of the Soviet Union, whose back somersault on the high bar of the asymmetricals became known as the *Korbut back*.

Gymnasts can never show fear; confidence always contributes to success.

7 Words

Bridge: arching the body up on the hands and feet with the chest upwards

Cross or *crucifix:* a test of strength and control hanging on the rings, forming a cross with the arms out to the side
Diamidov: on parallel bars, a full turn starting with a swing and ending with a handstand
Dislocation: hanging by the arms in front of a bar with the hands gripping backwards
Dismount: way of getting off piece of apparatus
Element: a movement
Flic-flac: a backwards handspring
Hecht: a vault doing the swallow or swan dive; dismounting from the asymmetrical bars
Layout: the body fully extended
Pike: a 'V' made by bending the body forward at the hips with both legs straight
Planche: lifting body on the arms alone keeping it horizontal; a test of strength and balance
Reuther board: springboard used for mounting apparatus

The floor exercise should use as much of the mat as possible.

Scale: balancing on one leg
Straddle: spreading the legs apart
Stutz: on the parallel bars, reversing direction, starting with a swing and ending with a handstand
Travel: on the pommel horse, the gymnast's movement along the apparatus
Tsukahara: vault named after Japanese gymnast, where gymnast twists after take-off to change direction and then somersaults off the horse
Walkover: backwards or forwards, a cartwheel on the spot, head on, rather than sideways on
Yamashita: vault named after Japanese gymnast, where a pike is executed as vaulter leaves horse. ∎

Handball is one of the simplest games in the world and unlike its cousin, soccer, no special boots are needed. It began as an outdoor eleven-a-side game but now the indoor seven-a-side game is far and away the more popular. Wherever the climate is warm enough, the seven-a-side game can be played on any firm, flat surface outdoors. Quite simply, the players move the ball about, bouncing and dribbling it and passing at great speed, the object being to get near enough to goal to try to hurl the ball into the net.

However, there is one rule in handball that makes it markedly different from soccer. Players are not allowed to enter the *goal area*, a semi-circle or 'D' surrounding the goal and patrolled by a goal keeper, so most play features a defensive wall of players on the edge of this semi-circle all trying to keep out a fast-manoeuvring group of attackers. Apart from that, the rules conform to many similar ball games.

 The Court

The court is 20m wide and 40m long (22 by 44yd approx) with a clearly marked halfway line. The goals at each end are solidly built, 2m (6ft 6in) high and 3m (9ft 9in approx) wide with a net at the back.

The important markings are:

The *goal area line*. Only the goal-keeper can stand inside the 'D'.
The *free throw line*. At goal throws, free throws and penalty throws, attackers must stand outside the free throw line.
The *penalty line,* which indicates the spot from which penalty throws are taken.

2 Winning

Players wear simple shorts and shirts with gym shoes. Some players wear knee and elbow pads to prevent abrasions. The ball is made of inflated leather, weighs 425-480g (15-17oz) and has a 58-60cm (23-24in) circumference, about the size of a No.3 soccer ball.

The handball court showing its markings and dimensions.

3 Winning

As the idea is to score goals by hurling the ball in to the goal, the team that has scored the most goals at the end of the match wins. The whole of the ball has to cross the line between the posts and under the crossbar to count as a goal. Goals can be scored in open play or from the penalty line. They all count as one goal. The restriction of the goal area leads to some spectacular shots at goal. This is because players are forbidden to set foot in the goal area, but they are allowed to cross the line in mid air! As top class players can power the ball at

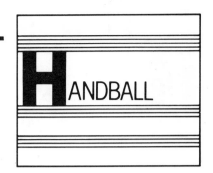

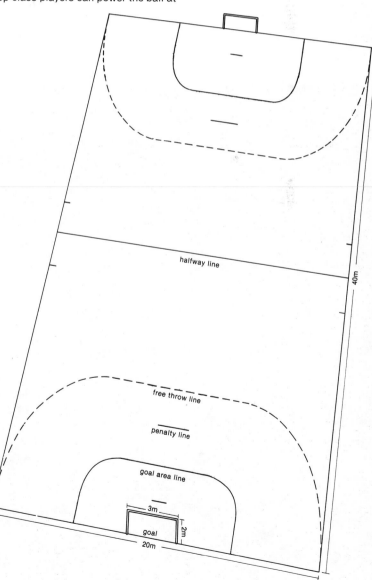

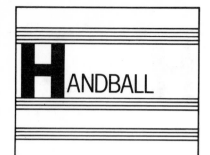

HANDBALL

speeds about 115kmph (70mph) they dive through the air to fire the ball at goal before crashing full length to the ground.

4 Rules

Play begins from the centre of the court with the team that won the toss electing to throw or defend. For men, play is divided into two 30 minute halves; for women play lasts 25 minutes each way. Although there are only seven players on court at a time for each team, five substitutes are freely available and freely used due to the hectic and tiring pace.

Attack: the ball is moved about by passing, but if an individual decides to move with the ball he or she can take three steps but must then bounce the ball. After a further two steps the ball must be passed. If the player stops, the ball must be released after three seconds. Rules like this ensure that the game is played at top speed all the time. Unlike soccer, there is little midfield play and no offside rule, nor are there any *goalmouth scrambles* as these are eliminated in the *goal area*. Players are also forbidden to make the well-known defensive move in soccer of passing the ball back to the goalkeeper. The award of a penalty throw dissuades that action!

Defence: As soon as a team loses possession it goes on the defensive. The most defensive formation has six players in an arc on the edge of their goal area line. More scope for breaking up attacks would have five players in the wall with one roving in front of them, trying to intercept the ball as well as cutting down the area the attackers can manoeuvre in. Most skilled teams can afford to have four defenders back with two players thrown forward. This *4-2 formation* forces attackers to be more imaginative and quick in their manoeuvring.

The obvious way of gaining possession is by intercepting a pass. However, one hand can be used to knock the ball away from an opponent, although snatching or grabbing at the ball is penalized. Tripping, tackling or grabbing the opponent with the arms are all illegal, though obstruction with the trunk of the body is allowed, even if the player does NOT have the ball.

As soon as one side has possession, the other side funnel back to the edge of their goal area. The goalkeeper can keep the ball out of his goal by almost any means except kicking it, though he can block the ball with his legs.

Fouls: simple fouls (failing to bounce the ball after three steps etc.) are punished by the award of a free throw to the opponents, taken where the offence occurred. Defenders should then stand 3m (10ft approx) from where the throw is taken.

More serious fouls (violent play etc.) are punished by the award of a penalty throw from the penalty line. This means that one player has an unhampered throw at goal from 7m (23ft approx) with only the goalkeeper to beat. The penalty taker cannot take a run-up and he must throw from behind the line keeping one foot on the ground. Top class players rarely miss.

There is also suspension for ungentlemanly conduct. A player can be sent off for two minutes, so a team would then have only six players on court. The third

Although no player other than the goalkeeper can set foot inside the goal area, this player demonstrates the classic handball shot where a midair dive is allowed as long as the ball is in the net before the player touches the floor.

time a player is suspended, he is off for the rest of the match.

Out-of-play: if the ball goes over the side line, a *throw-in* is awarded against the side that touched it last. If the ball is propelled over the goal line by an attacker or the defending goalkeeper, the goalkeeper takes a *goal throw,* with his opponents restricted to an area beyond the free throw line. If, however, a defender somehow propels the ball over his own goal line, a *corner* is awarded to the attackers. Their thrower then takes the corner from the side of the field that the ball went out of play. He or she stands right in the angle at the corner of the field and usually passes to a teammate though a goal can be scored direct from a corner.

Skills

Although ball handling ability is vital, it is useless unless it can be allied to accurate passing and powerful shooting. Players who can pass, dribble or shoot with either hand will always have an advantage as they are harder to block.

Tactics

Although strength and speed are obvious attributes in handball, it is often the subtler moves that can make the difference. Pretending to shoot but flicking the ball to a nearby colleague at the last instant can open up a chink in the defensive armour; *jump shots* that give the impression that a mid air shot is coming get defenders lining up to block — then suddenly, the attacker feeds a line player in a better shooting position. The *side* throw gets the ball round a defender, the *dive* shot launches a player at goal, while in the *fall* shot a player keeps one foot on the floor but falls away to one side in order to get a lower angle on the shot.

The court is quite large so the team that can use every part of it will have more room to outmanoeuvre opponents, and fast running wing players are an asset. Top class goalkeepers will have not only defensive qualities but should also be able to set up a *fast break* by saving a shot and immediately throwing out an accurate pass to a teammate.

Words

Centre: player in the centre of defence
Corner throw: taken when the ball is deflected by a defender (excluding the goalkeeper) over his own goal line
Court player: all players excluding goalkeeper

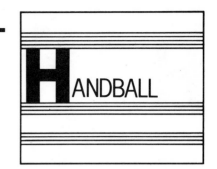

Distributor: see *Playmaker*
Free throw: awarded for minor breach of rules and taken from where offence occurred.
Jump shot: a shot for goal when player tries to get above defending players
Line player: player in the attack who works his way into the defensive wall getting as close to the goal line as possible
Penalty throw: awarded for serious breaches of the rules and taken from the penalty line. The thrower must throw at goal and only the goalkeeper can defend
Playmaker: player who sets up all the moves and ploys in attack
Referee's throw: the referee bounces the ball between two players when he is undecided as to which side committed the foul
Seven metre line: the penalty line
Three second rule: ensures that the ball is passed or bounced within three seconds. A free throw is the penalty for holding the ball too long
Throw off: the way a game is started at the beginning of each half and after every goal is scored
Wing player: player at the end or corners of defensive wall. ■

One way to beat the wall of defenders is to go over their heads to shoot between their upstretched arms.

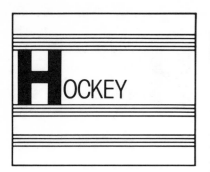

HOCKEY

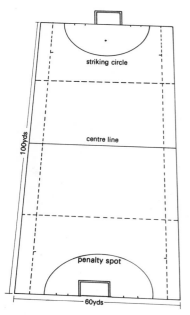

For greater control this player is holding his stick low down. He can only use the flat side of the stick to hit the ball.

F ield hockey is played between two teams of men or women, each with 11 players. The object of the game is to propel a small hard ball, similar in size to a cricket ball, with a stick curved at one end, into the opponents' goal and thus score. The team which scores the higher number of goals wins the game, which normally lasts for two periods of 35 minutes; teams change ends after the first half has been played.

The game, which is primarily one of skill rather than strength, has an abundance of thrills with 160kmph (100mph) shots at goal and daring saves by goalkeepers, coupled with the brilliant and delicate touches of ball control and the speed of movement of the game as a whole.

1 The Field

In front of each goal is an area called the *shooting circle* but usually referred to as the *circle.* Goals can only be scored from shots made inside this area.

Grass is the most common playing surface but artificial turf surfaces are becoming more common. The near perfect artificial surface has revolutionized the game as fewer errors are made in stopping or controlling the ball, which is thus in play for a greater percentage of the game. This makes for a better spectacle but also makes greater demands on the fitness of players.

2 Equipment

The stick: the curved head is made from a smooth-grained hardwood. Into this is glued a laminated handle (often of Sarawak cane) to prevent jarring. The striking face is flat. The weight of a stick varies from 12-23oz (340-652g) for women and 12-28oz (340-749g) for men. The average length is 3ft (91cm) and the whole stick must be passed through a ring with a diameter of 2in (5.10cm).
The ball: is white, hard and weighs about 5½oz (156g). It as about 9in (23cm) in circumference, which is slightly larger than a baseball but the same size as a cricket ball. For international matches a leather-covered ball is used.

3 Winning

In hockey, the team which scores the greater number of goals is the winner, with all goals being of equal value. Unlike most games, a goal in hockey can *only be scored from within a restricted area,* the *shooting circle,* when the ball has been hit by or glanced off the stick of an attacker inside the circle. The only exception to this rule is that no goal can be scored directly by the player taking a penalty corner. If you see the goalkeeper stand aside and let the ball go into the net, you can be sure he believes the ball has not been touched by an attacker inside the circle, so the 'goal' will not count. If the scores are tied at the end of the game in which a winner must be found, then periods of extra time may be played. If, after this, the scores are still tied the result may be determined by a series of penalty strokes taken by five players from each side shooting alternatively. The side that scores more goals wins.

4 Rules

As hockey is played with a stick and a hard ball, it can be dangerous. The rule concerned with conduct of play is specific on this point, so a player must not hit wildly at an opponent. Barging, tripping and deliberately wasting time are also fouls. A player, other than a goalkeeper in his own circle, must not stop or deflect the ball on the ground or in the air with any part of his body.

The ball moves pretty quickly and so two umpires are used, one in each half of the field. One of the umpire's hardest decisions concerns the *obstruction rule,* which states quite simply: 'A player shall not obstruct by running between an opponent and the ball or interpose himself or his stick as an obstruction.'

The point is that if one player obstructs another and the umpire does not penalize the offence, it may lead to frustration because there is often nothing the obstructed player can do to redress the situation, other than commit a foul himself. With the advent of tactics involving *man to man marking, shadow obstruction, shepherding* or *blocking out,* such frustration can be dangerous if the cause is not recognized and the offender penalized.

Apart from obvious fouls mentioned above, umpires also have to watch for *offside.* A player of the same team as the *striker* or *pusher-in* is in an offside position if, at the moment when the ball is hit or pushed-in, he is nearer to his opponent's goal line than the ball, unless he is in his own half of the field or there are at least two opponents nearer to their own goal line than he is.

The penalty for most fouls is a *free hit* awarded to the opposing side. This is taken where the infringement occurred and no opponent is allowed within 5yd (4.55m) of the striker. In certain circumstances the umpire may award a penalty corner or *short corner.* The attackers must remain outside the circle until the ball has been played. Then it must be stopped (not necessarily motion-less) on the ground by an attacker or touch the stick or person of a defender before a shot can be attempted. The traditional use of the hand to stop the ball at short corners, or even during the flow of play, is to be abolished from September 1982. This should speed up play and can be directly attributed to the increased use of smooth artificial surfaces, where the ball is more easily controlled with the stick.

If, in the umpire's opinion, there has been an *intentional foul* by a defender in his circle, or a goal would probably have been scored had an *unintentional foul* not been committed by a defender in his own circle, the umpire may award a *penalty stroke* to the attackers. The penalty stroke is a *push, flick* or *scoop* stroke taken from a spot 7yd (6.40m) in front of the goal by an attacker against the opposing goalkeeper who must not move until the ball has been played. The remaining members of both teams must stand beyond the 25yd (22.9m) line during the taking of the stroke.

Occasionally umpires may not see a foul but more frequently if they do not blow for an infringement they are playing the *advantage rule* which states quite simply that they shall refrain from enforcing a penalty if they think that by enforcing it an advantage would be given to the offending team.

When the ball is sent over the goal line by an attacker and no goal is scored, the game is restarted by a defender hitting the ball from the spot exactly where the ball went out of play and within 16yd (4.64m) of the goal line. On the other hand when the ball is sent unintentionally over the goal line by or off a defender who is within his own 25yd area and no goal is scored,

a corner is awarded to the attackers. The same rules apply as for a short corner, except the ball must be hit or pushed along the ground from a spot on the goal line within 5yd of the corner flag on the side of the goal that the ball went out of play.

When the ball crosses the side line, the game is restarted by a player of the team opposed to the player who last touched it in play, pushing or hitting the ball in from the spot at which it crossed the side line. At the moment when the push-in is taken no players of either team may be within 5yd of the ball.

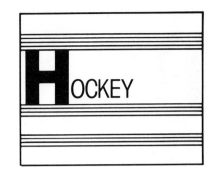

5 Skills

The first essential of a good hockey team is its ability to maintain possession of the ball for as much of the game as possible. The skills fall into two categories: individual and team. Each individual must be able to bring a fast-moving ball under close control and make an accurate, well-timed pass to a teammate. In passing, a player will often *feint,* or *dummy,* with a deft movement of his body or stick in order to mislead the opposition. Except when passing over a great distance, most players will use a *push* rather than a *hit,* because a push can be better concealed and executed more quickly, as the stick does not have to be drawn back as it would be to make a hit.

Against well trained opposition, possession is not enough; it is also necessary to beat an opponent while keeping full control of the ball. The player who can do this is said to have good

The player with the ball has his stick 'reversed', as he can only strike the ball with the flat side of the blade.

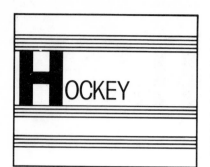

HOCKEY

stickwork or *ball control*; he is the one who appears to have the ball glued to his stick. An attacker needs the shooting skill (and flair) to take his chances well. Some players must also develop the ability to *convert* a penalty corner or a penalty stroke into a goal; the psychological pressure on a player taking the latter is often extremely heavy.

Tackling, or dispossessing an opponent, is another important skill. When making a tackle a player must ensure that he is always on balance, ready to turn and run with his opponent or run back into defence. To be caught off balance and left stranded is a cardinal sin for any player, but particularly when in defence.

Because hockey can only be played with the left-hand face of the stick, the ball is mainly played on the right side of the body. However, the ball often has to be played from the left side and this requires the ability to turn the stick quickly. Players on the left side of the field in particular must develop the skill of using the *reverse stick*, turning the stick upside down.

A good goalkeeper will kick equally well with either foot. A confident *goalie* (goalkeeper) will be able to kick shots coming straight at him well clear of the circle. However, when he has to stretch to reach a shot aimed at the corner of the goal, he cannot also kick the ball all in one action. Therefore he tries to drop the ball down so that he can clear it before it is snapped up by an attacker. If an attacker has broken away and all the defenders have been beaten, the goalkeeper may decide to leave his goal to cut down the angle and tackle the attacker single-handed on the edge of his circle.

The individual skills of the players must be combined in order to develop the teamwork which is essential for winning games. By discussion and the practice of moves in training, each player knows where he should be when his own team possesses the ball and when the opposition possesses the ball.
Set corner plays are also developed for push-ins and free hits.

6 Tactics

The more traditional or *orthodox* system, favoured by Asian teams, uses five attackers and five defenders plus a goalkeeper. In the last decade or so, in order to counter the stickwork of the Indians and Pakistanis, a *marking* system, favoured by European and Australian teams, has emerged. The marking systems vary but a common formation is to have four forwards, five midfield players who mark opponents man-to-man, a sweeper and a goal-keeper.

In an orthodox team a defender's position is determined by the location of the ball. One defender will approach the attacker who has the ball, while the others position themselves with the following things in mind — not being eliminated by a pass, being able to move quickly to an opponent should he receive a pass, and ensuring that he is closer to his own goal than the ball. Primarily, each defender is concerned with a zone of the defence area and will involve himself with any opponent who has the ball in his zone.

Orthodox teams like to attack with five forwards distributed evenly across the width of the field. The ball is passed out to either wing, hoping to draw the defence outwards, thus making space for the attacker to go through the middle; on the other hand, if the defence does not move out, the wing may go round the defence. The ball can then be crossed to an inside forward to score. When this is not possible, much use is made of square and back passes to retain possession, while trying to find an opening.

In a marking system the defender's aim is to mark an opponent man-for-man to prevent him gaining clean possession. Unlike the orthodox *zonal* approach, a defender's position is determined by the running of the man he is marking. The only defender who positions himself according to the

At a short corner, six defenders are usually allowed behind the goal line. As soon as the ball is struck, three sprint out to try to smother the shot while the goalkeeper and two backs guard the goal.

location of the ball is the *sweeper* who covers his team from behind to gather in any loose ball or to tackle any opponent who still has the ball after evading his marker.

In attacking against a marking system players endeavour to evade their marker by deft changes of speed and direction of running. This is difficult so frequently the ball is passed into open space for a teammate to run on to. Another alternative is for an unmarked defender, with the ball, to *overlap* his forwards by running into the attack area with the ball.

With more and more time being spent on tactics and fitness, it has become more difficult to score *field goals,* though on artificial turf surfaces more goals are being scored, including field goals, from open play. To counter this, tactics have been developed to win penalty corners by deliberately pushing the ball onto a defender's foot or forcing an obstruction within the shooting circle. Teams now spend hours perfecting the three elements of converting penalty corners: the push out, the stop and the hit. So corners and penalty strokes can be engineered but converting them needs to be rehearsed extensively.

Such is the fitness of players today that the distinction between orthodox and marking systems often becomes blurred especially if a team is slow in mounting an attack or delays too long in taking a free hit. The team without possession will mark as many opponents as possible. Despite this qualification, the distinction between the two is still valid; in the former, a defender is concerned with a zone, while in the latter, a defender follows his man wherever he runs.

7 Words

Back-tackling: forwards, after an attack breaks down, running back to help their defenders
Indoor hockey: popular in Europe as a winter training exercise, it now has tournament status. Played with six per side, it develops skills as the ball must be pushed not hit, and can only be lifted when shooting within the circle
Linkmen: term describing the two midfield players in the 4-2-4 system who link the defenders and forwards
Mixed hockey: popular recreational game with set numbers of men and women

playing together.
Sticks: when the stick is raised in a dangerous manner above shoulder height
Feint (dummy): deft movement of the stick or body to wrong-foot an opponent
Field goal: scored from open play as opposed to the conversion of a corner, penalty corner or penalty stroke
Flick: propelling the ball into the air with a flick of the wrists
Marking system: defenders are

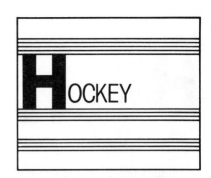

concerned with man-to-man marking of opponents, irrespective of the location of the ball
Orthodox system: defenders are more concerned with a zone of the field rather than a particular opponent. Sometimes referred to as 'five-three-two-one'
Overlap: a defender, possessing the ball, moves past several of his marked forwards, into the attack area
Push: propelling the ball along the surface and not in the air
Reverse stick play: turning the face of the stick over in order to play the ball on the left side of the body
Scoop: propelling the ball into the air with a shovelling movement of the stick
Solo run: a player controlling the ball in such a way as to get past several opponents by himself
Stickwork (ball control): the ability to control the ball at rest or on the move and so defeat an opponent
Tackling: attempting to dispossess an opponent who has control of the ball
Trapping: stopping the ball motionless with the stick. ∎

The player on the left is about to try to hit the ball away, while the man on the ball will use his wrists to flick the ball rather than hit it. His pass will be quicker, as he does not have to swing the stick.

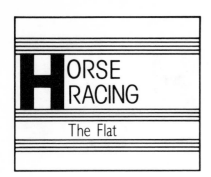

HORSE RACING

The Flat

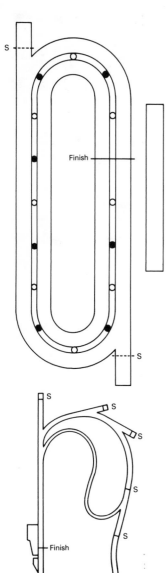

S = start points

The regular, oval circuit of a typical American course contrasts with the twists and turns and undulations of the English Derby course at Epsom.

Racing is a truly international sport enjoyed in many parts of the world. It all began in Great Britain where the *thoroughbred,* the fastest and most stylish of all breeds, was originated. The different types of racing are *flat racing, hurdling* and *steeplechasing,* and *harness racing.* Courses vary greatly; European courses are all grass, while in the USA they race on dirt. Jockeys' styles also vary around the world.

BETTING

Racing revolves around betting because a percentage of all money bet goes back into the sport to provide prize money and new grandstands. In Britain there are two main types of betting, the *bookmaker,* and the *tote.* At the racecourse, the bookmaker puts up his stand which consists of a blackboard showing all the horses names with a price chalked up alongside each name. When you bet, you take the price offered. If your horse is 8 to 1 and wins, you will receive £8 back for every one £1 you stake.

On the other hand, the tote or *pari-mutuel* as it's called in France, is run as a pool with all the stake money totalled up and a proportion paid back in winnings. This is used in most countries round the world. There is usually a minimum stake (say one pound or dollar) and you can place that to *win,* to *place,* or *each way.* Win means win only. Place means a return if your horse finishes in the first 3 (for 8 runners or more; first 2 for 5 to 7 runners; but 4 and under, only a win counts). Each way (*show* in USA) means win and place combined, so £1 or dollar each way means a totaly outlay of £2 or dollars. In *forecasts* or *quinella* you have to name the first and second, and of course this greater degree of difficulty offers a greater return.

There are also special bets involving horses in different races. A *double* — name 2 horses that must win, and then the winning odds are multiplied together. A *treble* — 3 horses that must win with the odds multiplied. A *Yankee* — 4 horses, 2 of which must win and a total of 11 bets, so a 5 pound or dollar stake costs 55 pounds or dollars. A *patent* — 3 horses, 1 of which must win. Since 7 bets are involved, a 5 unit stake costs 35 units. *Ante post betting* is for big races. Bets can be placed months ahead of a race so that better odds are obtained but the horse may not run, and so the *punter* (gambler) loses his money.

All races are recorded in form books, noting the finishing order, jockey, weight, going, distance, etc., but these are very complicated and expensive. For the occasional racegoer, the daily racing paper is cheaper and much simpler.

Flat racing takes place in spring, summer and autumn, so the European flat racing season runs from March to November. British gambling laws allow no racing on Sundays, although in the rest of Europe this is traditionally the day for big races.

All horses are given the same birthday — January 1st of the year of foaling in the Northern Hemisphere, and August 1st in the Southern Hemisphere. Horses must be at least 2 years old to race. The minimum distance is 5 *furlongs* (five eighths of a mile or 1000m) but on the European continent there are races over 4 furlongs (800m). The maximum distance is 2½ miles (4km).

1 The Course

Courses vary in shape and size: some are right handed, some left handed, some a figure of 8. Few are perfectly flat, the majority having undulations and turns. Each racecourse stages, on average, 20 days racing a season, ranging from just a single day to 5 consecutive days at the big meetings.

In France there are 4 big tracks in and around Paris, with racing at one of these tracks 6 days a week. In the USA, racing tends to be *centralized* at each racecourse, where the racehorses are trained and 5 meetings a week are staged for up to 3 months. This is possible because unlike the European grass racecourses, the Americans race on dirt; after each race the track can be harrowed and look as good as new.

Starting stalls are now commonly used around the world, and give a much fairer start. However, the position a horse is drawn can make a great deal of difference. On a tight track, for example, a low draw in a 5-furlong race can give several lengths advantage.

2 Equipment

Jockeys wear *silks,* the identifying colours of the owner of the horse. They also wear thin white breeches, paper thin black leather boots, a crash helmet and goggles to protect their eyes from the dirt thrown up by the horses in front. Each jockey also carries a whip.

Saddles vary in weight from a few ounces to 7lbs (3kg). If a jockey weighing 8 stone (50kg) rides a horse set to carry 10 stone (64kg) the extra weight in the form of lead is put into a *weightcloth* under the saddle.

Blinkers are fitted to a horse's head to ensure concentration and lessen distractions. Fitted for the first time, blinkers can make a marked difference to the horse's performance.

Jockeys' names are put on the number board before each race and young jockeys *(apprentices)* are entitled to claim an *allowance* to offset their inexperience. They can claim 7lb (3kg) until they have ridden 10 winners, then 5lb (2kg) until they have ridden 50 winners, and then 3lb (1.5kg) until they have ridden 75 winners. After this they lose their claim.

 Winning

The winner is the first horse past the *winning post.* The minimum distance required is a *short head* (always determined by a *photo finish*), then a *head,* a *neck,* ½ *a length,* ¾ *'s of a length,* and so on. A *length* is the distance between the horse's head and tail. In Britain, prize money ranges from £600 for the smallest race to £150,000 for winning the Derby. There are many levels of racing for all types of horses. *Maiden* horses (that have never won) run in *weight for age* races, where every horse of the same age carries the same weight. They then graduate to *handicaps,* where the best horse will carry *top weight* of 10 stone (64kg) and the poorest horse 7 stone (45kg). In theory this should mean they all finish together, though of course this never happens.

The lowest class of race is called a *selling race* where the winner will automatically be offered for sale. In many cases, the winner will be *brought in* or bought back by the owner who pays a specified amount of money to the racecourse for that privilege.

 Rules

The most common offences are *bumping and boring* in the final furlong. A horse may get tired and veer off a straight course, bumping into others and impeding their progress; or a jockey may go for an opening that suddenly closes. Although the horse may have won the race the *steward's enquiry* may show interference.

They may disqualify the horse, and if they see reckless riding, put the jockey under suspension. To make certain the horse runs with exactly the right weight, the jockey, with his saddle, must weigh out before the race and *weigh in* after it on the scales in the weighing room. If he has lost any lead weights, for example, he would be disqualified.

 Skills

The skill of the jockeys is vital. They ride with very short stirrups to lift their weight off the horses' back. American jockeys tend to crouch behind the neck, holding the reins very short; in Europe they tend to relax the horses more by holding the reins longer. Balancing the horse is most important; the horse and rider should look as if they are together in a smooth flowing action, so the horse moves faster.

Tactics

Top jockeys always know the past form of the horses they are riding. They know whether they like to lead or whether they like to be held up for a late run, and discuss all this with the trainer in the parade ring before the race. Horses are similar to humans — the nervous ones like to run on their own, while the tough ones like to get stuck in, in the middle of the bunch. The whip is used to make the horse run faster but the stewards are strict about a jockey hitting a beaten horse.

The horses hug the rails at the Curragh in Ireland, a typical European grass track.

HORSE RACING

Hurdles

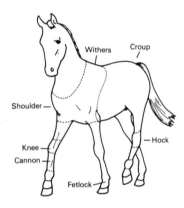

The 'points' of a horse

Horses often brush through the tops of the sloping hurdles rather than clear them — and they can actually flatten them without penalty.

7 Words

Allowance: the apprentice allowance for inexperience

Ante post betting: betting on a big race before the day of the race

Apprentice: a jockey who has not ridden 75 winners

At the distance: with a furlong to go

Colt: male horse, less that 4 years old

Draw: the place where each horse will start

Filly: female horse, less than 4 years old

Going: the state of the ground (firm, good, soft)

Handicap: a race where horses of different ability are weighted to finish together (in practice this never happens)

Jockey Club: racing's governing body. No jockeys would be members!

Members' Club: the most expensive viewing enclosure

Objection: when a jockey complains to the stewards, winning bets are suspended until the result of the *enquiry* is announced

Paddock: the parade ring where the horses are viewed

Photo-finish: used in close finishes to determine the winner

Plates: the horse's lightweight shoes

Put to stud: to retire a horse from racing and use it for breeding

Scratch: withdraw horse from race

Selling races: the lowest class of race; the winner is offered for sale

Silver Ring: the cheapest viewing enclosure

Spread a plate: lose a shoe

Starting price: the odds on the horses as they left the post, also SP

Stewards' Enquiry: to see if a horse has been interferred with

Sweating up: when a horse gets nervous before a race

Under starter's orders: when the white flag is raised, just before the off. ∎

The National Hunt season incorporates hurdles racing and steeplechasing and in Europe runs from August to May, with the top races between October and April. Horses carry from 10 stone (64kg) to 12 stone 7lb (80kg). Some horses are bred solely for National Hunt racing, with more stamina than their flat counterparts. Many flat horses, however, do graduate to hurdles.

Hurdle races range from 2 to 3¼ miles (3200m-5200m) and are for horses 3 years and older. The hurdles themselves are basically sheep hurdles with birch woven through the slats. They are 3ft 9in (1.15m) high but are sloped to give an average height of 3ft 6in (1.07m).

1 The Course

There are 8 hurdles in a 2 mile (3km) race and although they can be knocked down without penalty, it is better for both horse and rider if they jump them.

2 Equipment

Jump jockeys dress like flat jockeys but the silks are replaced by jerseys because of the cold winter weather. Inexperienced jockeys can claim 7lb (3kg) until they have ridden 15 winners and then 4lb (2kg) until they have ridden 30 winners. Some horses wear bandages or wrap-around *boots* to prevent their legs being injured if they hit the hurdle.

3 Winning

Although a horse can win a race by knocking down every *flight*, a horse will soon begin to feel the wear and tear if his jumping does not improve. Speed is obviously important but so is stamina, especially when the ground is heavy.

RIGHT: *Ice hockey is a fast-moving hard-fought game. Here, a Swedish forward battles for position in front of his US opponents' goal.* PAGE 126: *Flat out on the flat! The final furlong at Royal Ascot.*

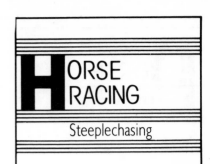
4 Rules

The rules of national hunt racing are very similar to those of the flat and are strictly adhered to by the same governing body, the *Jockey Club.*

5 & 6 Skills & Tactics

Over hurdles it is not surprising to find a horse well down the field early on *come through* late and win. Much depends on the *pace* of the race. If the pace is fast, winners tend to come from behind; if it is normal or slow, jockeys try to keep *handy,* in touch with the leaders. It is difficult to lead all the way especially when conditions are bad; then a jockey may go around the outside, which may mean the horse has to run further but on the firmer, faster ground.

7 Words

Come through late: come from behind
Flight: line of hurdles
Handy: in touch with the leaders
Pace: speed of the race. ■

A chaser is a horse bred for stamina and jumping for, unlike hurdles, steeplechase fences have to be jumped cleanly or the horse may fall or the jockey may be *unseated.* Horses have to be at least 4 years old before they start steeplechasing and some are still running at 15. Distances range from 2 miles (3km) to the 4½ miles (7km) of the world-famous Grand National Steeplechase at Aintree which demands great courage from both horse and rider.

1 The Course

Steeplechase fences are sloped to 4ft 6in (1.35m) high, and are made of birch pulled

LEFT: Britain's Mick Grant takes a corner at speed.

tightly together. There are 12 fences in a 2 mile (3km) race including 1 *water jump,* shallow but 15ft (5m) wide, and 2 *open ditches,* the toughest fences on the course. As well as the fence itself, there is a 4ft (1m) wide ditch on the take off side with a *guard rail* 18in (50cm) high in front. A horse must meet this fence just right: if he takes off too far away he will land on top of the fence: too close and he hits the guard rail. Either would mean a fall. Sometimes a horse jumps the fence well but crumples on landing.

2 Equipment

The horse normally wears a *breast plate* around his neck and shoulders to keep the saddle from slipping back. Bandages or boots help to ease the strain on his legs.

3 Winning

As usual the first horse past the post wins but he must have his jockey. A horse first past the post without a jockey does not win!

4 Rules

If a horse falls and brings down another runner it is bad luck and just part of the game. A jockey who falls off is allowed to remount and finish the race.

5 Tactics

Jumping is the name of the game and good jumpers are always worth following. Some may be faster but if their jumping is not 100 per cent they could fall or make a bad mistake which could unseat the rider. A good start is not as important as on the flat. There are no starting stalls for national hunt racing; instead, lengths of elastic *(tapes)* are suspended across the track. As there is no draw, a jockey can line up in any position. Although the inside is the shortest way round, many jockeys steer a wider course to keep clear of

HORSE RACING

Harness Racing

trouble. Top jump jockeys always give their horses a clear view of the fences — not always easy when there is a big field. Races tend to be won *out in the country* (far away from the grandstand) where 2 lengths gained at every fence through a good jump makes a good deal of difference. The jockey uses his whip to urge the horse on or to correct sloppy jumping.

 # 7 Words

Brought down: when one horse is tripped up by another
Chaser: a stoutly bred horse who runs over fences
Guard rail: the take-off rail in front of a fence
Under pressure: a horse being ridden hard by his jockey
Unseated rider: rider who has fallen off. ∎

The origins of harness racing are in the chariot races of 3000 years ago. In the modern version, horses are not allowed to gallop but have to trot or pace. Both are acquired gaits, not natural. In *trotting,* the left front leg and right rear leg go forward together, then the right front and left rear. In *pacing,* the left front and left rear move forward simultaneously then the right front and right rear, giving a sort of rolling motion to the gait.

1 The Track

The track can be anything from ½ a mile (800m) to 1 mile (1500m) in circumference, generally made of dirt although some of the country tracks are grass. The race starts with the horses in motion. A car with 2 wide, mechanical arms moves in front of the horses, while the jockeys manoeuvre so that the horses are nearly touching the mechanical arms; when all have reached the same position, the car pulls away and the race is on.

2 Equipment

Jockeys sit astride a *sulky* or cart which is attached to the horse. Very light, weighing from 30 to 40lb (15kg) sulkies usually have

hardwood shafts and bicycle-type wheels. For pacing, *hobbles* hold the horse on stride but trotters have no such aids. To keep the horse's head held high, a *check rein* is attached from the *bit* over the top of the head to the *saddle hook.* The higher the head, the more balanced and reaching the stride. Each horse wears a different number and jockeys wear distinguishing colours. They also carry a long, light whip.

 # 3 Winning

In the past there was a series of races with the best horse in 2 out of the 3 heats declared the winner. Now there is usually just the one race.

4 Rules

A trotter is trained to stay on the trot and to trot fast. If he breaks gait, going *offstride* and into a gallop, he must be pulled back into the trotting stride. This does not mean disqualification but usually eliminates any hope of winning. The same rules apply to the pacer.

5 & 6 Skills & Tactics

Harness horses are always warmed up before they race and they may cover up to 5 miles (8km) in the 2 hours before a race. A good start helps to get the inside position around the turns but a fast finish is also important.

 # 7 Words

Check rein: keeps the horse's head high
Gait: stride pattern of the horse
Green horse: one that has never trotted or paced in public
Hobbles: the leg harness that guides the horse's stride
Jog cart: heavier that the sulky, used for exercise and warm ups
Offstride: breaking out of the approved stride
Sulky: light racing vehicle. ∎

Trotters wear a special harness to pull the jockey, who balances carefully on his sulky.

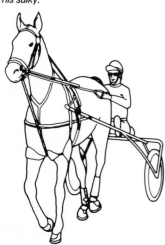

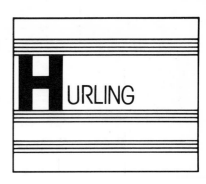

Hurling

Hurling is the oldest and one of the fastest ball and stick games in the world. It was first mentioned in 1272 B.C. in Ireland, where it is still the national game. It is played between two teams of fifteen players.

1 The Pitch

A hurling pitch is about 140m (150yd) long and 90m (100yd) wide, with a goal at each end. The goal looks like a cross between rugby and football goals, with its two tall posts joined by a crossbar and a net. A *parallelogram* or *square* (goal area) is marked out in front of the posts.

2 Equipment

The *hurley,* or wooden stick, is usually 90-105cm (3-3½ft) long and has a curved, broad, flattish blade 7.5-10cm (3-4in) at its widest point, rather like a field hockey stick. The ball is approximately 115g (4oz) in weight and 24cm (9½in) in circumference, with a cork core and a leather covering. The players wear shirts, shoes, socks and boots and some also wear protective helmets.

3 Winning

The idea is to hit the ball between the goalposts — over the bar scores a *point* (1 point), under the bar and into the net is a *goal* (3 points). The higher scoring team wins.

4 Rules

A hurling match has a referee, two linesmen and four goal umpires. The ball can only be kicked or struck with the hand when it is off the ground. The only way it can be thrown is with the hurley and it must not be carried for more than three steps — so an elaborate mid-air dribble goes on. To stop players from goal hanging, no attacker is allowed in the parallelogram before the ball. Although it looks a violent game, kicking, charging, pushing, tripping, holding, obstructing and charging from behind are all offenses, punishable by a *free puck,* or free hit. A player is only allowed to hit an opponent's hurley if both players are going for the ball. Violent conduct can result in sending off for an individual, disqualification or suspension for a whole team.

If the ball goes out of play over the side line, the team hitting it out loses possession and their opponents get a free stroke where the ball crossed the line. Other free strokes are given if a defender either hits the ball over the end line or commits a foul within the 21yd (19.2m) line. If an attacker sends the ball out over the end line, his side loses possession.

5 & 6 Skills & Tactics

Individual skills focus on controlling the ball with the oddly-shaped hurley. The ball can be struck on the volley or half-volley but cannot be carried on the blade of the stick, so an important skill is the *solo run,* a form of dribbling where a player bounces the ball on the blade while running. The ball cannot be picked up off the ground by hand so it has to be scooped up with the stick.

The team skills are similar to soccer or field hockey. Defenders (the *full-backs* and *backs*) mark attackers *(full-forwards)* who try to use the full width of the field to confuse their opponents by varying the length and direction of their passes. The two *wing forwards* are the quickest players and try to round the full-backs, then cross the ball for their teammates who are ready to try a shot at goal. The *half-backs* and *half-forwards* are the workers, trying to break up attacks in order to set up attacks of their own.

7 Words

Caman: (Gaelic) hurley or stick, traditionally made of ash
Pucking: hitting the ball with the hurley
Puck out: the defending side putting the ball back into play after it has been hit over the end line by an attacker
Side puck: bringing the ball back into play after it has crossed the side line
Free puck: a free hit, awarded for infringements of the laws
Carrying: travelling more than three steps with the ball on the blade of the stick. ■

Key: FF: full-forwards
HF: half-forwards
CF: centre-forward
MF: midfield
HB: half-backs
CB: centre-back
FB: full-back
B: backs
GK: goalkeeper

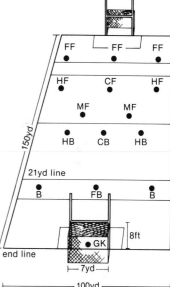

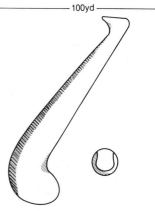

Stick and ball.

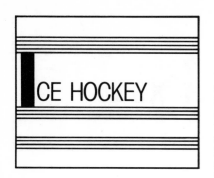

ICE HOCKEY

The 'world's fastest team game' aptly describes ice hockey and, because of this, it takes a little time to train the eye to follow the action. But the simple objective of scoring goals makes it as easy as soccer for the casual observer to understand. In both games, the intricacies of rules, such as offside and the use of substitutes, soon becomes apparent. Players skate about on the ice and, with the aid of sticks, try to shoot a small, hard *puck* or disc into the opponent's goal.

The game was adapted from field hockey, its separate identity dating from the first time a puck was used instead of a ball, reputedly in 1860 on the frozen Kingston Harbor in Ontario, Canada.

The ideal dimensions of a playing area are 61m (200ft approx) long by 26m (85ft approx) wide. The rink is surrounded by a continuous barrier board up to 1.22m (4ft) high, curved at the four corners. Play continues when the puck hits the board and bounces back onto the rink.

The goals at each end are 3.5m (10ft approx) inside the barrier, so play can continue on the strip of ice behind the goals. The goals are 1.22m (4ft) high and 1.83m (6ft) wide, with nets some 60cm (2ft) deep at the base. The goals are fitted into holes bored in the ice, so that they easily come loose when hit by a player going at top speed.

A red line divides the rink into two halves while two blue lines divide the rink into three equal zones. Other essential marks on the ice are the centre circle, four *face off* circles and *creases* in front of each goal which are marked by semi-circles or rectangles.

1 The Rink

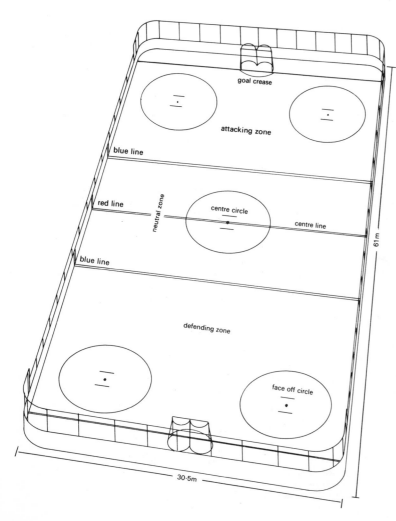

goal crease

attacking zone

blue line

red line

neutral zone

centre circle

centre line

blue line

defending zone

face off circle

61m

30·5m

2 Equipment

The most important piece of equipment is the stick. It is made entirely of laminated wood, with a blade limited to 37cm (14½in) in length. The goal-minder's is wider and heavier but the blades can be shaped to suit left- or right-handed players. Another point of variation is the *lie* or angle between blade and handle which can be adjusted to suit the player.

The disc-shaped puck, made of vulcanized rubber, is 7.6cm (3in) in diameter, 2.5cm (1in) thick and weighs approximately 156g (5½oz). The players wear a special ice hockey skate with a blade only 1.5mm (1/16in) thick, supported by lightweight hollow metal tubing.

The goalminder has special skates, wider and lower, which afford easier balance. They also have extra *stanchions* — the metal bars joining skate to boot — to prevent the puck passing underneath his feet. The ice hockey boot is more like a shoe in appearance, because it has a low ankle support which rises only 10-12cm (4-5in) above the sole. It has reinforced caps at heel and toe.

The players are heavily protected for this inevitably robust game — pads at knee and elbow, guards at shin and shoulder, thick gauntlet gloves and long stockings fitting over the knee-pads. Helmets are compulsory except in some

Players can skate round the back of the goal. Here two defencemen close in on the lone dark-shirted forward who is expecting a pass from the wing.

The well-dressed goaltender. He wears a helmet and facemask, padding under his shirt and pants, extra large pads and special boots to kick the puck away. His stick is broader than usual and he wears special gloves.

North American professional leagues. Special shorts and numbered sweaters in team colours complete the outfit.

The goalminder is allowed extra large leg-guards, added chest protection and special, well-padded gloves — not a matched pair because one kind is worn for holding the stick and another on the catching hand. Some goalies also favour a face-mask, lending a curiously grotesque appearance, as a protection from possible injuries.

A special machine clears and smooths the ice between periods.

3 Winning

Goal judges at each end indicate a score by turning on a red light behind the goal involved. A goal may be scored only by propulsion of the puck from the stick, not from kicking or throwing, and a goal does not count if an attacking player is within the *goal crease* at the time.

Goals are numerous enough in ice hockey for it to be a rarity when a side concedes none in a match. Such an achievement is termed a *shut-out* for the goalminder concerned and these are noted in the record books. Also in the books and scoring tables go not only the name of the scorer but also that of the player who passed the puck to him (unless it was a solo effort) who is credited with an *assist*.

If an attacking player is fouled when in a scoring position in front of goal, and

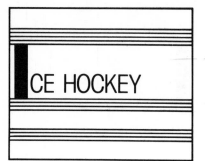

ICE HOCKEY

no other player apart from the goalminder is between him and the goal, the referee will award a penalty shot to be taken from the centre face off spot. Not a very common occurrence, it is exciting to watch a player carrying the puck up the ice with only the goalminder to beat. The goalminder cannot move out of his goal crease until the puck crosses the blue line. A miss ends the action and no goal can be scored from a rebound in this instance.

4 Rules

The very pace of the game is a major attraction and this dictates the need for substituting players frequently. Players

No. 20 is checked hard and high. This sort of physical contact often leads to fighting and brawling amongst the highly paid professionals in North America.

can tire after only a few minutes and tempers easily fray because of this, and the frenzied action. It is a six-a-side game insofar as only six members of each team are in opposition at any one time, but it is common practice for a senior side to carry up to a maximum of 20 players.

The line up comprises the *goalminder, two defencemen, right wing, centre man* (or centre *ice)* and *left wing*. The coach on the rinkside bench masterminds the timing of substitutions at any time during the game. Normally, he endeavours to keep defending pairs and forward trios intact. He may swap one forward line for another or the entire five outfielders at a time or merely replace individuals

as he thinks best. A substitute goalminder, though in attendance, is rarely used if the first choice stays in form because the position involves relatively little skating and is obviously less tiring.

A game is divided into three *periods* each of 20 minutes' actual playing time (the stopwatch is stopped whenever the puck is out of play). The teams change ends after each period. Play commences from the centre spot at the beginning of each period and after a goal is scored. This is done by a face off, when the referee drops the puck on the ice between the sticks of the opposing centre men. Play is also re-started at other times by a face off but on the nearest of the marked spots to the point where a foul occurred. The puck becomes *dead* (out of play) only when hit over the barrier or when the whistle blows for an infringement or at the end of a period.

A feature exclusive to the game is the use of a penalty box on the side of the rink, popularly termed the *sin bin*. Players are banished for four sorts of infringements. *Minor penalties* of two minutes in the sin bin are incurred for fouls like elbowing, charging, tripping, *high sticks*, deliberately hitting the puck out of the rink, *hooking* an opponent with the blade of a stick, *boarding* (pushing an opponent intentionally on to the barrier) and falling on top of the puck to stop play (which only a goalminder is allowed to do).

The team whose player is sent off in any of these cases is obliged to continue *short-handed* without a substitute for the player involved. A goalminder incurring a minor penalty is allowed to stay on the ice and his coach withdraws an outfield player. If a goal is then scored by the opposing team, the player can leave the sin bin and return to play before the two minutes are up.

Major penalties of five minutes are imposed for rough play, which is sometimes difficult to avoid in the heat of the moment when playing at such a furious pace. If any of the fouls that are usually penalized with a minor penalty are particularly violent, a major penalty is awarded. Substitutes are permitted for two opposing players when both are serving a major penalty simultaneously.

Misconduct penalties of ten minutes are for more serious cases of insubordination or abusive language but a substitute is permitted after two minutes so that the player rather than the team is punished. In this case, too, an offending goalminder would stay on the ice and a teammate would go off instead.

The most serious offences are disciplined by a *match penalty* which, as the term implies, means the player is sent to the dressing room for the remainder of the game. This is imposed in extreme cases of deliberate injury or intention to injure. A substitute is allowed five minutes after the offender has been sent off but the player banned cannot appear in any subsequent game until his case has been dealt with by a disciplinary committee.

To keep the game as attractive as possible, with an emphasis on attack rather than defence, ice hockey has an *offside* rule which is enforced by dividing the rink into three zones — *defensive, centre* and *offensive*. Essentially, a player can only pass to a team mate who is in the same zone so he has to skate with the puck into the next zone before passing. However, a

in a tight defensive situation he cannot ice the puck by firing it up to the far end of the rink. If he does all a defender has to do is touch it behind the goal line and the puck is brought back to where the player iced it.

 Skills

A top class ice hockey player must be able to skate forwards, sideways and backwards at high speed and with complete ease. He must be able to skate controlling the puck without looking at it. A good player has always got his head up, looking for his colleagues. Not only this, his control of the puck must be instantaneous. The slightest hesitation

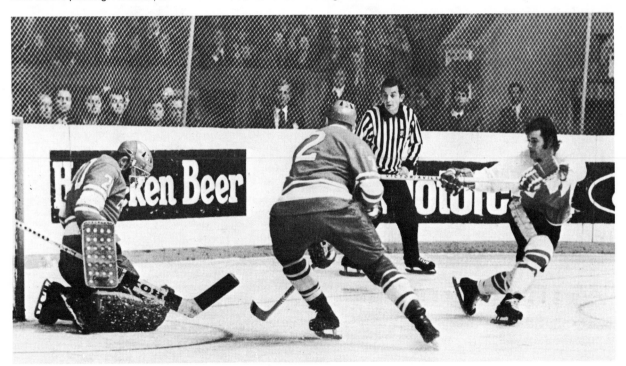

defender is allowed to pass to a team mate in his own half of the rink (marked by the red line). As some offside decisions can be quite marginal, the rules specify that the position of a player's skates on the ice dictate whether or nor he is offside (not the position of his stick or the puck).

When a side attacks, the man with the puck must skate into the attacking zone first. This is to prevent players hovering near their opponent's goal. Another rule to keep the game open is against *icing the puck*. When a player is

in stopping or dribbling it would leave him open to a defender's *stick checking* (tackling). Defenders might use the *poke check* to poke the puck away from an attacker. The *hook check* involves laying the stick flat on the ice to try to hook the puck from under the attacker's blade as he goes past, and then there is the *sweep check* where the defender uses his stick like a broom to sweep the puck away.

Although defenders tend to be bulkier and more robust than the attackers, they are still expected to be

The goalkeeper drops to his knees to save while the black-and-white-shirted referee looks on. The steel fencing is to protect spectators when the puck flies off the ice at over 160kmph (100mph).

ICE HOCKEY

The wrist shot. Note the curve of the player's stick, which helps lift the puck as it whizzes towards the goal.

able to score goals by making sudden breaks up the ice to take the opposition by surprise.

The most obvious tactic used in ice hockey is the *body check* where players are allowed to block opponents with their hip and shoulder. Players must try to force the opponents to skate round them so a body check from behind is illegal.

6 Tactics

Once a team has the puck inside the opponents' blue line, all five players would be up with the play. The wingmen go wide, or even skate round behind the goal, trying to create an opening before playing the puck back to a team mate for a shot on goal. This could be a defence man who would shoot from 15-20m/yd.

As soon as a team loses possession (possibly after an unsuccessful goal attempt), the defenders would skate back to defend their own goal but one forward would *fore check* and hustle the man with the puck while the other forwards try to cut out the chance of a pass. If the opponents move up the ice, the forwards continue to *back check*, trying to break up the play.

If a player is sent off to the sin bin the *powerplay* is used to take advantage of the fact that the opponents are one man short. The best five players go on the ice

and are expected not only to keep possession but to score. The short-handed team puts on its *penalty killers*, four men who play the *box system*, forming a square to keep the opponents away from the danger zone in front of goal.

Another tactic may be used if a referee spots a defender fouling a player who is not in possession of the puck. The referee puts his hand up but lets play continue as long as the attacking team has possession. Their goalminder would suddenly skate off the ice and a sixth attacker comes on, a terrific advantage. As soon as the attackers lose possession the whistle blows for the earlier offence so there is no fear of the opposition scoring while the goaltender is off the ice.

7 Words

Boarding: forcing an opponent onto the boards
Body check: blocking an opponent with hip or shoulder
Butt ending: hitting opponent with the end of stick; a major penalty
Flashing: chopping an opponent's wrists with the stick
Screening: blocking goalkeeper's view
Slapshot: full-blooded drive, not a flick-of-the-wrist shot
Spearing: driving stick into opponent's stomach. ∎

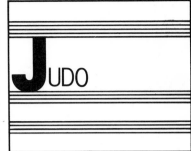

Both shoulders heading for the floor — Ippon! — and the contest is over.

Spectators have often referred to judo as 'two men in pyjamas fighting without pillows'; in fact, instead of throwing pillows, their intention is to throw each other to the floor.

As in boxing and karate, the two *players,* as combatants are called, fight for a fixed period of time unless a decisive throw ends the bout, like a knockout in boxing.

1 The Mat

The sport, which originated in Japan about 100 years ago, takes place on an area of matting 16m (17½ yd approx) square. A square *contest* area is in the centre of this, marked by a metre (yard) wide red band. This broad red line *(danger area)* warns contestants that they are at the edge of the contest area which is 10m (11yd approx) across.

The contest referee, as in boxing, is the only person allowed inside the contest area besides the players. His duty is to see that the rules are applied to award scores and penalties where deserved, and to ensure the safety of the competitors. However, any decision he makes may be overruled by the agreement of both line judges, who sit at opposite corners of the area. They judge if a player has moved outside the area and spot any infringements or scores that go unnoticed by the actual contest referee. Competitors never argue with officials . . . *ever!*

2 Equipment

The competitors wear white baggy trousers and a loose-fitting jacket made from strong cotton or nylon which is tied at the waist by a red or white belt, in order to distinguish one competitor from the other.

A buzzer, bell or hooter is used to indicate a contest is over.

3 Winning

The Japanese tradition of the sport is maintained in customs and language. Having stepped onto the mat, the players bow to the referee and each other. The referee then shouts *Hajime!* (begin). Judo means 'the gentle way' but the players attempt to get a good grip on the other's jacket (usually the lapel and the end of the sleeve), then try to upset the balance using a variety of throws and holds in order to throw the opponent onto the floor.

Although bouts are for a set time (for example, five minutes for preliminary rounds at the Olympics, seven minutes for the later rounds), contestants go out trying to win inside the distance, just as a boxer hopes to get a knockout to end a fight. In judo, a player would score an *ippon* (winning mark) by correctly

JUDO

executing a throw that hurls an opponent flat on his or her back; by holding an opponent down with his back to the ground for 30 seconds; or by gaining a *submission* when the opponent gives in or the referee decides the contestant is beaten, when held in an awkward or painful stranglehold or arm lock. The player shows that he has submitted by tapping either his opponent's body, his own body or the mat with a hand or a foot. A bout can also end when a player scores two *waza-aris,* or the equivalent.

A *waza-ari* is one grade lower than an ippon, and requires a high degree of skill. Perhaps an opponent is not thrown fully on his back or lands on his side; if an opponent is pinned to the ground for 25-29 seconds, this is waza-ari. A further grade down is a *yuko.* Again, a throw may not be executed quite as well as for a waza-ari or the perfection of an

ippon. An opponent held down from between 20 and 24 seconds would concede a yuko. The lowest score is a *koka,* which is quite common as it is awarded whenever a player is knocked to the ground or held down for 10-19 seconds.

As soon as a player scores two waza-aris, the fight is over, but any number of yukos and kokas can be amassed. In fact, one waza-ari is enough to beat any number of yukos and kokas, just as one yuko betters any number of kokas. If the scores are level at the end of a contest, the referee calls *Hantei!* and the two line judges pick as a winner the player who has been more aggressive and initiated more attacks. The referees raise their white or red flags, which correspond to the players' belt colour. Most contests finish decisively, with ippon or waza-ari. When the referee calls *sore-made!,* the bout is over.

If he lands on his side: Yuko!

4 Rules

The referee can award penalties during the contest against any player who breaks the rules or is not seen to initiate any attacks. The lowest penalty score is a *shido,* or caution that is the equivalent of a koka, followed by a *chui,* equivalent to a yuko. A *keikoku* warning is equivalent to a waza-ari and a *Hansoku-make* is a disqualification. So a combination of a waza-ari score with a keikoku penalty against the opponent would win the contest. Penalties are awarded for moving outside the contest area or any other breach of the rules (e.g. hitting, kicking, etc), or the use of techniques illegal to contest judo (e.g. bending the fingers, or attacking the face).

5 Skills

It is often difficult to spot which player is doing well, apart from looking at the score which is displayed on a board beside the mat. Look for the player who appears to be dominant and more aggressive, the one who takes a firm grip on his opponent's jacket first. Usually a superior judo player will stand more upright, while his opponent bends forward in order to prevent himself from being thrown; his attacks will look more decisive and stronger. As the contest proceeds, fitness begins to tell. The weaker player appears to be in pain, breathes heavily and does not attack his opponent. This is the one most likely to lose. As well as all the attacking moves there is a series of defensive ones designed to counter opponents.

Judo players talk about *throws* and *holds*. There are innumerable types and few, if any, people would be able to execute them all perfectly. They all have different names as players try attacks from the front or side or even use *sacrifice throws* where they drop to the floor before throwing an opponent. They use various parts of the body (legs, hips, hands, etc) as levers to throw their opponents. If the throw is perfect and merits ippon, the bout is over. Otherwise the contestants continue with *groundwork* where another wide range of *holding techniques, strangleholds* or *armlocks* are employed.

With holding techniques, the idea is to hold an opponent down on his or her back for 30 seconds. Strangles are only allowed on the neck (never the head) and even the loose *judogi* costume can be used to apply a strangle. Armlocks can only be applied to the elbow joint, so wrist locks and shoulder locks are illegal. There are straight and bent armlocks, both of which can be most painful and would enforce a submission.

 Tactics

If a player is better at groundwork than throws, he may concede a small score in order to get a chance of fixing a hold, strangle or armlock. All tactics are geared towards moving the opponent into a position where the strongest technique can be used. This is why there often appears to be little activity, apart from pushing and pulling, especially in cases where both opponents are familiar with the other's strengths and weaknesses. Then, much as in chess, a small mistake can bring disaster. Top-class players use *combination throws* where the first move is aimed at confusing an opponent before a quick change in technique puts him off balance and he is thrown.

Two players get to grips at the start of a contest. They compete in different weight categories, rather like boxers, and fight on the tatami or mats.

 Words

These are always in Japanese, the language of the sport.

During a bout the referee will shout the following commands:
Hajime!: Begin the contest!
Matte!: Wait! When a referee wants to halt a contest where the holds look inconclusive, when players go over the edge of the contest area, costumes become undone, etc; the players start again in the centre of the mat
Sono-mama!: Do not move! Freeze! If the contestants, locked together, are in danger of going out of the contest area, they are made to freeze and are physically pulled back to the centre of the contest area to resume fighting with the same holds still applied
Osaekomi!: a hold has been applied; the timekeeper starts the clock to time it
Sore-made!: That is all! The contest is over.

Other words:
Dan: a top degree of proficiency
Dojo: practice hall
Judogi: judo costume
Judoka: contestant, player
Kansetsuwaza: armlocks
Ne-waza: groundwork
Shimewaza: strangleholds
Shai: a contest
Tachiwaza: standing or throwing techniques. ∎

JUDO

KARATE

Karate means 'empty hand'. It was introduced to Japan from Okinawa in the 1920s and quickly gained popularity there. Competition karate developed late in the 1950s as a part of karate training. It has become increasingly popular — more so abroad than in its native land!

Competitions in karate involve strictly controlled punching and kicking techniques delivered with good form to within 5cm (2in) of the scoring areas of the body. These include the head and face, the trunk and the abdomen down to and including the belt.

Contests take place on an area measuring 8sqm (8 sqyd approx). The fight is controlled by a referee, with four corner judges and an arbitrator. In all cases of dispute the majority opinion is taken. The referee starts and stops the contest, awards points, or issues warnings and gives a decision at the end of the match. The corner judges use flags and whistles to signal scores, fouls, or other matters to the referee. All contestants wear an extremely light pyjama-type suit *(karate-gi)*, the jacket of which wraps over at the front and is

The taller man has used his reach to aim a successful kick to his opponent's midriff.

The player on the right has counter-attacked brilliantly. His opponent committed himself to a kick which left him off balance and open to a straight blow to the heart.

tied with a coloured belt, which picks out the grade of competitor. All *dan* or high grades wear black belts. One competitor will also wear a red sash around his waist, the other a white one, to help identify them. Correspondingly, each judge carries a red and white flag, and can indicate either a score or a foul by raising the appropriate colour.

Contest karate is scored in much the same way as judo, by issuing points or *ippons*. Ippons are awarded for technically excellent techniques to scoring

areas of the body. In all modern competition, the *Three Point System* is operated. This allows for the award of a maximum of three points during a competition and the first fighter to obtain a lead of two points is declared the winner. Where there is only a one point lead or no points scored in the competition, then the judges and referee will give their opinions and the majority decision will be taken.

The contest lasts for two or three minutes of actual fighting time. Up to three two or three minute extensions may be given in order to reach a clear win. The last extension is on *the first to score wins* or *sudden death* principle.

For safety's sake many techniques are excluded from competition karate. These include: headbutts, attacks to the eyes, throat or groin, direct attacks upon limbs or joints and dangerous throws. If a contestant commits a very serious foul, he can be disqualified for the rest of the tournament *(shikkaku)*. Less serious fouls can result in disqualification from the bout. So a referee might shout *Akahansoku* (red belted competitor disqualified), *shiro-no-kachi* (white wins).

The best karate players display coolness and motion and poise. Aggressive players who attack flat out with lots of yelling will never get to the top of the sport. Control is essential and top-class players will jockey for position, trying to get the optimum range — a man who favours kicks will stand further away than one who prefers to use hand techniques. The idea, as in boxing, is to be close enough to deliver attacks, yet far enough out of range from receiving them, perhaps by stepping to one side when attacked. The players keep their eyes fixed on their opponents, an eye movement will often signal an attack. If a player looks at one part of his opponent's anatomy, it could be a feint. A definite attack is always accompanied by a *kiai* or loud shout which has the dual purpose of adding thrust to the attack, tensing the body as well as drawing the attention of the judges. Good *karateka* (players) will never be caught off guard, responding automatically to any attack with well-balanced counters.

The referee will be heard shouting instructions during a bout:
Hajime!: Begin! To start the contest
Yamei!: Stop! The contestants rest as the referee asks the judges to confirm the award of a point by making a chopping motion of his right hand. If the point is awarded, he raises his arm indicating the successful player
Jogai!: Out of the area! ■

Modern pentathlon may perhaps be traced back to tests that 'King's Messengers' had to undergo before qualifying for duties in the King's service. To get their message through these men had to display the skills that now make up the Modern Pentathlon competition: show jumping; épée fencing; pistol shooting; swimming and cross-country running. Imagine a messenger setting off on his horse, jumping walls and hedges, defending himself with a sword and a pistol, and having lost his horse in a battle, swimming across a river and finally carrying his message to the King as swiftly as possible on foot.

The modern sport demands that the toughest and most versatile sportsmen have the ability to dominate a horse and at the same time form a partnership with it; the elegance, speed, balance and will to beat an opponent in fencing; the steady concentration and ability to divorce themselves from all else in the shooting; the strength and stamina required in the totally different activities of swimming and running.

Although traditionally a male sport, women enthusiasts now have their own competitions, though not at Olympic level.

Each of the five events uses the facilities of the individual sports of show-jumping, fencing, shooting, swimming and cross-country, which are covered elsewhere in this book.

The equipment required in pentathlon competitions is the same as that normally worn or used for each of the individual sports.

To find the best all-rounder, a standard performance is set in each event. Any competitor that can better that standard gets bonus points. Anyone who fails to equal the standard has points deducted. Team prizes are decided by adding together the totals of the three team members.

The five separate events are contested over five separate days. The order of the events is always riding, fencing, shooting, swimming and running.

Riding: each competitor draws lots for the horse which he will have to ride, a horse with which he is unfamiliar and whose temperament and ability is, for the rider, unpredictable. Having drawn

As well as pistol shooting and fencing, competitors have to swim, run and ride a horse in the five-day competition.

MODERN PENTATHLON

The most unpredictable event is the showjumping, because the quality of the horses can be so variable.

his horse, he is allowed twenty minutes, and six practice jumps, immediately before the competition proper. In the competition itself, he is faced with a ride covering 800 metres where he must negotiate 15 fences, one of which will be a *double fence* (two separate jumps set close together), and one a *treble* fence, a total of 18 obstacles in all. Quite simply, this is showjumping.

A time of two minutes is allowed to complete the course which earns the successful competitor a score of 1100 points. Points are deducted in the following way: two points for each second over the time limit of two minutes; thirty points for each fence that is knocked down, forty points each time the horse refuses the jump (the horse may refuse up to a maximum of three times at any one fence before the competitor must move on to the next). If a refusal occurs at any part of the double or treble fences, the whole obstacle must be jumped again.

Fencing: this is the most physically and mentally exhausting part of the whole competition. Using the classical duelling sword, an épée, each competitor takes on all the other competitors in turn, as many as 60 in world-class competition. The first *hit* wins the fight. Hits can be scored on any part of the body and are recorded by means of an electrical device that shows when the point of the épée touches the body. A green light comes on for one competitor, and a red light for the other. Each competitor can score a maximum of 1000 points, which can be achieved by winning 70 per cent of the fights. Depending on the number of competitors, each fight is worth a certain number of points; the fewer the competitors, the more points each win will be worth.

Shooting: an event that needs very little physical strength or stamina, but demands extreme qualities of mental concentration, coming the day after competitors have had to endure a gruelling session of fencing. Using a standard .22 hand pistol, they have to shoot at a revolving target which appears for only 3 seconds. The competition consists of 4 separate series, with five shots in each (20 shots in all), and prior to each shot the competitor must lower his arm below an angle of 45 degrees before raising it to shoot again. A score of 1000 pentathlon points is awarded if the competitor scores 194 (maximum would be 200). Pentathlon points are either awarded or deducted for scores above or below 194, each target point being worth 22 pentathlon points.

Swimming: unlike normal competitive swimming, pentathletes swim against the clock rather than against each other. The competition is arranged in heats in which each competitor must swim 300 metres freestyle. To gain 1000 points he must swim this distance in three minutes 53 seconds, and for every ½ second above or below this time 4 points will be subtracted or added. 'Winning' a heat does not secure any extra points as the fastest man over the distance gets the highest number of points, irrespective of which heat he swims in.

Running: each pentathlete runs 4000 metres across undulating country. Unlike normal cross-country races, every competitor runs alone, starting at one minute intervals. Therefore they are unlikely to see another competitor unless they make up the one-minute difference to catch the competitor in front or are themselves caught up from behind. Running against a clock often proves more difficult and exhausting than being paced by fellow competitors in a straight race. To score 1000 pentathlon points the competitor must cover the distance in 14 minutes 15 seconds, for each second above or below this time 3 points are deducted from, or added on to, the total score.

In the 1976 Montreal Olympic Games the winning total was 5520 points. Like most competitors, the winner was a little *below* the standard in riding (1066 points), and fencing (928 points), but was a couple of shots *above* average in the shooting (1044 points) and finished with a strong swim (1164 points) and a fast run (1318 points) to clinch victory.

Throughout the five days of the competition, it is often difficult to judge who is likely to win overall without being familiar with the strengths and weaknesses of each competitor. It is often the case that a pentathlete may achieve fantastic scores in the first three events, but then lose out, because of his lack of fitness or stamina, in the last two. Alternatively, a pentathlete may figure nowhere in the overall positions after the first three events, but may suddenly move up the rankings because of his prowess in the more physical events. Generally it is the athlete who achieves reasonable scores in each event who will figure in the medal positions; but it should be remembered that in the show jumping event even the best pentathlete can be unlucky enough to draw an unwilling and stubborn horse. It is this type of unpredictability that lends both excitement and frustration to this sport. ■

Motorcycles have come a long way since the first one was built in 1885. Modern racing machines have top speeds in excess of 275kmph (180mph) and the power turned out by the best 500cc or 750cc models is about 120bhp, twice that of a small family car! There are three main spectator sports — *road racing, speedway* and *moto-cross.*

ROAD RACING is motorcycling on hard surface tracks.

1 The Circuit

Although speed matters, most circuits test both bike and rider with a combination of sweeping bends and tight corners, linked by straights of varying lengths. The surface is tarmac. In North America, there are some high-speed, banked circuits, oval in shape.

2 Equipment

Tyres at international level are *slick,* with no tread pattern cut into them, so while the circuit stays dry (or at least only damp) the adhesion between the tyre and the track is still good. Heavy rain on the ground can lead to *aquaplaning,* when the tyre skates across the surface of the water. Therefore, picking the right sort of rubber compound is very important. A soft compound will give super grip while the rubber warms up and 'sticks' to the ground, giving tremendous traction round the corners. When the tyre starts to overheat or wear out as the rubber shreds away, it will start to slide on acceleration and cornering, forcing the rider to slow down, and lose ground on his rivals.

Using too hard a compound might ensure that the tyre does not wear out during the race. However, the adhesion is not so good and that, in turn, means slow laps.

Even more worrying for the rider are those days when showers leave the circuit alternately dry and wet. Grooves, hand cut into the softer *compound slicks* produces an *intermediate* or rain tyre. This is designed for wet weather, a dry track will rip the tyre to shreds.

The fuel used is normal petrol from the pumps, or a petrol/oil mixture.

3 Winning

Winning races is quite simply a matter of *lapping* a circuit in the fastest possible time, but that does not always mean the winner is the man with the fastest machine.

Before the start there is usually a one- or two-lap *warm-up*, depending on the length and type of circuit. This is not to warm up the engine, but rather the tyres. A couple of laps bring the temperature of the rubber on the tyres up to its working efficiency.

The bikes start from a *grid* marked out on the track, and the fastest man in practice is on the front row of the grid on the inside. The next fastest is next to him, and so on. In *Grands Prix* (major competitions) the engines are dead before a race. When the flag falls, the riders push their machines forward with the clutch lever pulled in against the handlebars. Then they drop the clutch to fire the engine as they leap on the machine, side saddle. This impetus helps overcome the high compression. In other international meetings, a *clutch start* is used, which means that the engines are running at the start.

When the flag falls (or at some tracks the traffic lights change from red to green) the riders increase the *revs* of the engine and drop the clutch.

Front wheels paw the air, and then drop as the rider changes into a higher gear. *Wheeling* is spectacular, but is unwanted and can be dangerous. Then the riders settle down to race, with the first bike home the winner.

The rider crouches low behind his windscreen, keeping his elbows and knees well in to achieve maximum streamlining as he hurtles down the straight.

MOTOR CYCLING
Road Racing

4 Rules

The major championships are for six categories of single-seat machines — 50cc, 125cc, 250cc, 350cc, 500cc and 750cc. The top speed of the 50cc machines is about 190kmph (120mph) and speed increases for each class up to about 290kmph (180mph) for the big bikes. There are also two sorts of motor bikes with sidecars, labelled B2A and B2B; both use 500cc engines, though there are some international events that have a 750cc limit.

5 Skills

A good start is very important, so that a rider can get away from the field and have a clear run in to the corners. Where the bike has to be pushed, the skill of *bouncing* on to the machine at the right moment, saves precious seconds. A rider with long, strong legs often has an advantage powering the bike off the grid. In events where the clutch start is used, if there is any delay at the start, some riders may become agitated. That isn't nerves, but a sign that the temperature gauges on the water-cooled two-stroke engines are climbing to boiling point. If left too long

on the line, modern high performance motors will overheat, or the clutch, trying to cope with all that power, will simply burn its plates away.

At the first corner, watch for the difference in riding styles. In the traditional style the rider sits on the bike, and blends into the machine, banking it over at incredible angles, while the present day experts throw their body over the side of the machine and keep the bike as upright as possible.

The current riders claim that their style leads to less risk of the bike *sliding away* from under them. However, the rider's knee usually touches the ground as he corners, so most competitors have plastic knee caps sewn into their one-piece racing leathers. Others even put metal studs on the knee patch to help reduce friction.

Some riders say the best method is to go into the corner as slowly as possible to safeguard against crashing, keeping the bike under control and upright, ready to accelerate earlier out of the bend.

Other riders prefer to go in very, very fast, brake late and hard, and then power the machine in a controlled slide round and out of the corner.

The *racing line* is important too. On most corners there is probably a fairly narrow strip of tarmac that could be considered the correct *line,* the fastest route round the corner.

Corners are always dangerous, because no mirrors are used. Sometimes, if a rider on the inside is slowing

Cornering is one of the most important skills. It is noticeable that the two bikes on the left have taken the same line, leaning hard into the bend, but behind, one rider is trying to gain time by going into the corner fast and braking hard to get through on the inside.

down because he has taken the wrong line, a rider on the outside could accidentally *knock away* his front wheel. Similarly, a rider on the inside who overshoots, could *torpedo* into the side of a rider on the outside. This can happen when a rider on a slower machine tries to pass on the inside by *outbraking* a faster opponent, relying on his tyres and brakes to follow a shorter and more difficult line.

On some tracks acceleration out of the corners is much more important than absolute top speed. With so much power at the rear wheel too much acceleration, too soon, can lead to disaster.

Down the straight, riders tuck the knees and elbows in, and put the body behind the clear perspex screen that acts as a windbreak. Coming in to a corner, riders sit up out of the air-stream to help with the braking effect.

The ability to stop quickly is import-ant too. If the bike cannot slow down quickly, and under control, a rider will lose valuable time.

6 Tactics

A rider may try an overtaking man-oeuvre for two or three laps just to see if it is possible, before actually passing in the closing stages. Look out, too, for the chance to take a wider line on the last bend, to give a faster run in to the flag.

7 Words

Earholing: cornering at top speed
On the limit: maximum speed
Paddock: assembly area for bikes and transporters
Privateer: rider not sponsored by manufacturer
Scratching: riding flat out
Shut the door: to prevent rider from overtaking
Slipstreaming: riding in draught created by another machine; being pulled by a faster machine
T.T.: Tourist Trophy — races on the 37 mile (60km approx) Mountain Circuit of the Isle of Man
Tear-offs: multi-layered visors that can be torn off when dirty
Wheelie: riding machine on back wheel: mainly done for show. ∎

Speedway racing is simple to follow, the races are short, the finishes often close, and the fans enthusiastic. There are variations on speedway around the world. Grasstrack, sandtrack and icetrack racing is popular on long 1000m tracks where two-speed gear-boxes are used. First gear is used only for starting and special spiked tyres are used on ice. The most organized type of speedway is on a cinder track. Team racing is the backbone of *dirt-track* racing, with seven man teams com-peting in a 13 heat programme on a league basis.

Each race is over four laps of an oval cinder-covered track, and lasts for not much more than a minute. Tracks vary in length from 300yd (275m approx) to 500yd (450m approx). Red lights around the track can be switched on to tell riders to stop at once to avoid accidents.

The machines are fuelled with methanol, but are tested at random to ensure that no additives are used.

Clocking speeds of close on 80mph (130kmph) down the back straight, speedway machines have 500cc four-stroke engines with no gearbox, but a clutch and a countershaft that can cope both with a blast of power as the starting tapes fly up, as well as flat-out motoring.

Points are awarded in each race, three to the winner, two to the second man home, one to the third, and nothing for the fourth.

In individual meetings, of course, it is every man for himself. In major events, where a rider competes five times to score a possible maximum of 15 points, starting positions at the tapes are decided by a pre-arranged formula to give everyone a fair chance from each of the four starting *gates*.

Riders must hold their line for the first 20yd (18m) of the race, before changing position. Most tracks favour the man on the inside line, the shortest distance around the track; but others can be ridden *round the boards* on the outside of the track giving a faster line.

Gating is important, as the rider who gets away from the starting gate first can dominate the race. He would be able to choose the best line for going round a bend and also be able to block other riders who try to overtake. However, watch for the good men coming from the back and passing on the inside when their rivals drift too wide at a corner and have to ease off the acceleration. Occasionally, a rider will go round the outside in a brave manoeuvre at top speed to try to take the lead. ∎

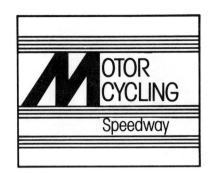

The leading rider keeps tight in to the bend so that his rivals cannot get by on the inside. Behind, another rider is trying to get past by going wide on the outside.

MOTOR CYCLING

Moto-cross

Moto-cross or Scrambling is motor cycle racing on a marked course across fields and up and down hills — like cross-country running.

The starting area is usually grassland, and hopefully smooth, but after that anything goes, and the men and machines must cope.

The moto-cross tyres are knobbly, with plenty of tread to find grip in sand or mud. The fuel is normal, straight from the pump.

The bike's suspension both front and back takes a tremendous pounding, and in recent years the amount of movement on front forks and rear suspension units has increased in a bid to improve the handling of machines.

Most moto-cross starts use a metal frame that falls away from the riders at the pull of a lever, or elastic tapes. Competitors have the engines running, but watch for itchy fingers dropping the clutch too soon, and jumping the start, because a good getaway is crucial.

Inevitably, because of the terrain, the bikes spend some of the time soaring through the air. Like road racing, if the back wheel isn't on the track, acceleration is lost, so the aim of the game is to keep the back wheel, at least, in contact with the ground.

The front wheel is a very different story. That needs to be *on the deck* to help cornering, but on a series of bumps the front wheel is kept in the air to help

The knobbly tyres are needed to get a grip on the sandy soil while a plastic mask protects the rider's face. The high front fork is characteristic of motocross bikes.

Springy suspension is needed to absorb the impact on landing.

Protective clothing is essential, and comprehensive. Tough leather jeans, plus a tough jersey padded on the elbows and chest is the minimum. Nowadays many riders have plastic protectors for the shoulders, elbows and chest, while the face is protected from painful pebbles by a mask.

Grand Prix events are based on time. Races last 40 minutes plus two laps and there are two races at each meeting. Points are awarded to the first ten finishers (15 points for 1st, 12 for 2nd, 10, 8, 6, 5, 3, 2, 1). There are four classes for Grand Prix, 125cc, 250cc, 500cc and sidecar machines.

control the bike, and on some tricky sections it is quicker to jump from one spot to another than ride through it!

Physical fitness is of tremendous importance because moto-cross is one of the most physically demanding sports in the world.

Delicate throttle control, and a fine sense of balance are crucial to a top moto cross rider. If he uses too much throttle, he crashes; too little and he loses the race.

Top moto-cross rider Jeff Smith used to say that if you did not fall off in moto cross — you weren't going fast enough! Painful advice indeed. ■

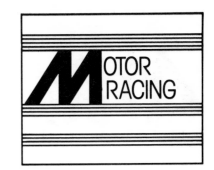

Motor racing is about the most spectacular, exciting and misunderstood of all sports. To the uninitiated, racing cars look like overpowered monsters being thrown round a circuit at stupidly dangerous speeds by lunatic men bent on killing themselves, wrecking the car, or both. In fact, racing cars is about sophisticated engineering development sparked by immensely skilful and sympathetic driving. Designers and builders of cars must be inventive, dedicated, tireless and inexhaustibly competitive. Their drivers must achieve extraordinary levels of fitness, perception, physical coordination and, of course, courage. Nothing less will bring success in a sport which is constantly growing throughout the world, with more different classes, more meetings, more spectators, and more television coverage every season. It's not difficult to see why: to watch a gaggle of Grand Prix cars ripping around the tight bends, fierce gradients and disruptive cambers of a circuit such as the classic round-the-houses track at Monaco is to witness one of the greatest thrills in all sport.

1 The Track

In the beginning motor racing took place on open roads, and some of the most famous races are still run on roads temporarily closed off — Le Mans, Long Beach and Monaco are obvious examples. But most races are now staged on special circuits, fully equipped with *barriers, run-off areas*, protected spectator facilities and instant access for fire and ambulance services if needed. The circuits are almost infinite in their variety, from the 23km (14 miles) of continuous bends, gradients, humps and dips of the Nurburgring in Germany to the simple rectangle with rounded corners of Indianapolis in the United States.

Some circuits test outright speed — at Indianapolis the cars average around 320kmph (200mph). Others provide a severe and exhaustive punishment for the gearbox, suspension, or tyres. To get around the twists and turns of the 3.5km (2 mile) Monaco serpentine and undulating circuit at anything over 135kmph (84mph) means howling through the gearbox (even down to the first of the five gears twice every lap), snaking through vicious and narrow bends, ripping the engine up and down

the *rev range* until it can stand no more. And in all that the driver must be looking for places to pass, judging whether he needs to pull into the *pits* to sort out a handling problem, change a deflating tyre or adjust a displaced wing. The spectators can share in those trials and traumas by being positioned where they can see the key action. That could be opposite the pits, so that tyre changes can be timed, or perhaps on the long straight where there is the best opportunity for cars to pass. Maybe it will pay to be on a particularly demanding corner — that will show not only who is going fastest by skilful driving, but also who is trying to sneak past by very late braking into the corner. It is in watching these finer points that the sports enthusiast can derive the real interest and fascination of motor racing.

2 Equipment

A racing driver's greatest fear is fire. Although racing fuel is kept in special safety tanks, and cars must have extinguisher systems, there are still crashes which create fires. The driver's clothing is mainly designed to protect against fire. It starts with cotton briefs, then fire-resistant underwear of long johns, knee-socks and a long-sleeved polo-necked vest. That is covered by an

In the pits, the mechanics are ready to change tyres, mend faults and re-fuel cars during races. Before a race, adjustments to the balance of a car are made here.

Formula 1

Formula 2

Formula 3

Formula Ford

Formula 5000

USAC

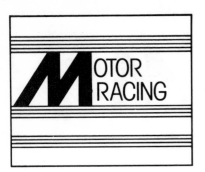

MOTOR RACING

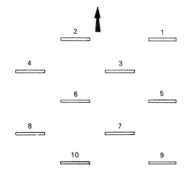

The starting grid: the car in number one spot is in the pole position.

Soon after the start, cars are still in their grid positions, as they come out of the first bend two abreast. The first two cars have open road ahead - a great advantage on a crowded track.

outer fire suit, usually triple-layered. All this is designed to resist heat; even the fastenings and thread used to sew on sponsor's badges are of special materials.

Fire-resistant boots — light like a boxer's — are matched by multi-layered gloves (gauntlet style) and a woven balaclava which covers all but the driver's eyes.

The crash helmet is very sophisticated, with a shatterproof visor and a life support system which incorporates a tube feeding compressed air into the helmet to sustain the driver if he is in fire or smoke. When he gets into the car, the driver is held snugly in by a six-point safety harness — two shoulder straps, two hip straps and two crotch straps — all linked to a central quick-release buckle. All that gear is very warm and it is not unknown for a man to be 4kg (10lb) lighter at the end of a Grand Prix in a hot country.

3 Winning

Of course the point is to get the car across the line before all the others — but there is much more to it than that. The vital importance of practice is the key to success. In almost all forms of motor sport there are official (timed) practice sessions in which drivers take their cars out on the circuit and try to establish as fast a practice lap as possible. This is crucial for two reasons. First it shows each team how they are doing compared with the opposition. Second, it establishes *grid positions*. As all the cars cannot line up at the start of a race a *grid* is marked on the track.

Two or three cars are in each row with the fastest car in practice starting in the *pole position* — the place on the front row of the starting grid which gives the best chance of reaching the first corner ahead of the pack. That is clearly an enormous advantage, especially on a narrow and twisting circuit, where overtaking is very hazardous.

4 Rules

The numbers and classes of motor racing are almost infinite. Everywhere in the world there is some sort of motor sport going on, whether it is an old car having a last fling before the scrap heap on a dirt oval, or the hugely expensive *Formula 1* racers of the Grand Prix

The design of Formula One cars changes from season to season, but this model shows the broad rubber tyres that have no tread on them, the aerodynamic aerofoils at the nose and above the tail. The driver's harness is buckled on to the cockpit.

circus which travel the world to bring the most refined form of racing to enthusiasts everywhere. These are some of the popular categories:

Formula 1: the cream of the cream, for cars with 3-litre unsupercharged engines or 1½ litres supercharged. The formula by which the Driver's World Championship is decided, the cars develop around 500bhp (brake horse power).

Formula 2: the stepping stone to

Formula 1, it is for cars with 2-litre engines and a maximum of six cylinders that develop 300bhp or a little more.

Formula 3: this is where the young talent emerges. They use 2-litre engines but with air box restrictors which reduce power to about 160bhp. Still remarkably fast.

Group 6: these are big sports cars that take part in classic races such as Le Mans. With an engine limit of 3 litres, typical examples are Porsche 936, Gulf-Mirage.

Group 5: sports cars which have been built in series. To be accepted, 200 cars of the same type need to have been built in 12 months. Typical example: Porsche 935 developed from 911 production car.

Group 1: this is for almost standard production saloons minimally modified for circuit racing. Balanced engines and modifications to suspension are allowed, but cars are really very close to showroom examples.

Formula Atlantic and Formula Pacific: small single-seaters with 1.6 litre engines provide intensive *open-wheel* racing on a modest budget. A good proving ground for young talent.

Can-Am: wide bodied sports cars with up to 5-litre engines based on stock production cylinder blocks. They contest a top series of races in North America.

Nascar: highly modified production saloon cars are used for dramatic racing on the high speed ovals of North America. Capable of 320kmph (200mph) or more.

USAC: all-out racing cars with few restrictions, these are built for the Indianapolis-type circuits of the United States. Many use the same Ford-Cosworth engine which powers so many Formula 1 machines.

5 Skills

Motor racing is a team sport. Yes, it's the *driver* who gets all the limelight, but the most brilliant driver would be totally unsuccessful without the dedicated and efficient backing of his team manager, car designer, mechanics and back-up administrators. The *manager* must be the inspiration: he must raise the finance to support the whole operation; he must help the designer to develop a car which is better than all the rest; he must organise cooperation from suppliers of tyres, engines, suspension and other vital components; he must super-

vise the building of cars; he must integrate the schedule of practice sessions, travel to foreign circuits, publicity appearances and so on; and he must enthuse the whole team to bear defeats, disappointments, long hours, boring travel, and inexplicable mechanical failures without complaint and still come up for the next race eager as ever.

The *designer* is vital. He must tread the tightrope between building a car heavy enough to last but still light to make it fast though possibly less reliable. He must be an expert in suspensions, braking systems, engine outputs, aerodynamics and exotic materials. And somehow he must blend them all together to make up a car which is as quick or quicker than anybody else's. It is especially difficult when — as in Formula 1 racing — most of your rivals are using the same engine as you are, so the differences are only subtle ones.

The *mechanics* are indispensable. They must be able to build a car, *tune* it to the limit, polish and prepare it lovingly and then bear up stoically when a split-second nudge at the start of a race can reduce it to a scrap-heap of battered metal and dusty debris. They must be able to work quickly but without overlooking a single detail — both for the safety of the driver and for the hope of victory. They must be able to work without rest, travel without complaint, improvise without proper facilities.

Finally, the *driver*. Of course, he must be skilful, fit, competitive and brave. But he must also be a technician and tactician. In very few races are the options straightforward. Think of all the complications which affect the planning of a race: the tyres may be wearing too quickly, a vital gear starting to jam, a broken suspension arm causing the car to bottom on some corners; a threatening rain cloud making the need to change tyres a possibility; a flock of *back markers* causing him to lose time against the man in his mirrors; a pit signal indicating that the man ahead is in trouble and should be attacked now. After all the preparation it is the driver's choices that lead to victory or defeat.

6 Tactics

In Formula 1, the top level of the sport, there are usually two cars to a team in single-seater forms of racing — and if two

MOTOR RACING

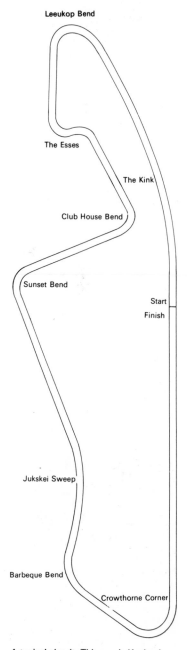

Leeukop Bend

The Esses

The Kink

Club House Bend

Sunset Bend

Start
Finish

Jukskei Sweep

Barbeque Bend

Crowthorne Corner

A typical circuit. This one is Kyalami circuit, South Africa.

MOTOR RACING

1

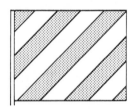
2

3

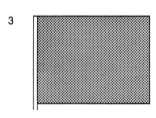
4

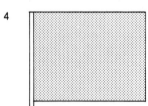
5

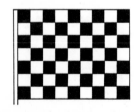

Flags are used to signal the drivers. A national flag starts the race; black requires a car to stop at the pits; white is ambulance on track; yellow, danger; blue (1) shows a car is close behind; yellow and red (2) means oil on the track; green (3) all clear; red (4) stop at once; black and white (5) signals the end of the race.

cars can drive line astern and very close, they are more than twice as difficult to pass than one car. Or one car can go all out at the start of a race to lure the opposition into an engine-smashing duel while the team's real potential winner is sitting back in the pack, waiting to ease through when the others have all been wheeled away to the *dead car park.* This happens more in endurance events such as the Le Mans 24-hour race, than in Grand Prix racing.

How do you tell if a particular car is doing well when watching a race? Of course, the main way is to see if it leads the race. The car which goes to the front and then pulls away from the opposition must be the fastest, but in a long race like a Grand Prix relative speeds change, and it is often fascinating to watch a low-placed car carving through the pack to get among the leaders. So it is often a question of watching gaps — is the man in fourth closing on that pair fighting out second place? Is the leader being caught down the straights or on braking for a corner?

The far-off watcher can also tell a lot by the way the cars go through the corners. A car that slices round the bend on a neat line lap after lap indicates a driver well in control and perhaps saving a little for a late push if necessary. But a racer that drifts a long way sideways on the bend and puts wheels up the kerb where the others do not indicates a man trying desperately hard and probably very near the ragged edge.

A car that lags after a slow corner indicates gearbox troubles — maybe selection difficulties or some gears defective — while one that can be passed on the entry to the corner shows brake troubles. Smoke usually means an engine which is not long for this world, and a driver's arm raised high out of the cockpit means 'avoid me at all costs, I'm about to stop'.

7 Words

Aerofoils: also called *wings;* the aerodynamic surfaces at both ends of a racing car which push the car on to the track and so give maximum traction on the straights and adhesion through the corners

Aquaplaning: happens when a car is racing on a wet track, especially on slick tyres; the tyre treads become separated from the road surface and ride on a film of water, meaning the car loses virtually all braking effect and directional stability

Armco: steel crash barriers

Electrical cut-off: an automatic switch to cut out the electrical supply in the event of a crash and so minimize the chance of fire

Fire extinguisher system: another automatic system, which distributes extinguisher throughout the car on a crash impact, or can be operated by the driver manually

Grand Prix: the top motor racing events, usually Formula 1

Ground effect: the aerodynamic effect obtained by the design of modern single seater cars, where the bodywork between the wheels is shaped to make the whole of the centre of the car one big wing, using the speed through the air to produce *negative lift* and so keep the car glued to the track surface through corners

Intermediates: treaded tyres used when there is a possibility of rain or when the track is wet

Monocoque: the construction system used for most racing cars, where the central cell of sheet metal is the backbone of the car and the other components — engine, suspension, transmission — are attached to it

Negative lift: the generation of a downforce to keep a car on the road by using wings or ground effect design

Open wheel: where the whole of the wheel can be seen, not covered in

Rip-offs: strips of plastic stuck across the driver's visor which he can rip off progressively as they become obscured by oil and dust thrown up by cars in front

Roll-over: a U-shaped tubular bar fitted to the back of the car's cockpit to protect the driver's head should the car roll over

Skirts: flexible sheets mounted along the side pods of a ground effect design car to enclose the central area beneath the car and enhance the ground effect of the air passing under it

Slicks: smooth racing tyres with no tread pattern — used for dry circuit racing

Stickies: specially soft compound tyres used by drivers in practice sessions to set up particularly fast times. They are too soft to stand up to a full race

Spaceframe: method of construction used for some sports cars, where a frame of welded lightweight tubes forms the main basis of the car and is then clad with light alloy or glass-fibre panels

Turbo-charge: method of boosting engine power by using exhaust gases. ∎

Drag racing developed in the USA from hot rod racing, where ordinary cars were fitted with more powerful engines for greater speed. After World War II would-be racers who could not get to official tracks began to race on the main streets (or "drags") of towns, using traffic lights as starting lines. Citizens' complaints and police disapproval led to the formalization of this sport.

MOTOR RACING
Drag Racing

1 The Track

The flat, smooth track or *strip* is ¼ mile (400m) long and at the start and finish there are electronic eyes to record *elapsed time* and *terminal speed.* Instead of a starting flag, there is a set of coloured lights, the *Christmas tree,* which moves from amber (ready) through to green (go). A red light flashes if a car jumps the start by leaving before the green light.

2 Equipment

There are several classes of vehicles ranging from everyday mass produced cars to *dragsters,* highly specialized racing machines. Some classes even require parachutes as part of the braking system. Most cars are rear-engined and these may be supercharged, turbocharged or run on nitromethane. The most obvious features of these cars are the rear tyres, *slicks,* which are enormous. Drivers must wear helmets, seat belts, fire-suits, gloves and fireboots. Breathers are required for certain classes.

3 Winning

In each race there are only two cars and the first across the line is the winner. A series of eliminating heats leads to a final and handicapping is used if cars of different classes are competing together.

4 Rules

The *strip* is divided into two lanes by a line down the middle. Crossing that line means disqualification, as does starting before the green light on the tree. It may be difficult to distinguish the different classes of cars because there are so many, but the categories are clearly defined. The formula is: car weight divided by advertised horsepower. For competition cars, the ratio is weight to cubic centimetre capacity.

5 & 6 Skills & Tactics

The start is all-important, so drivers aim for maximum acceleration. Engaging the clutch just as the green light appears gives an advantage but a second early and the driver is disqualified for jumping the start. The grip of the tyres is also important and cars are taken through the *bleach box,* where water or laundry bleach is spread in front of the slicks. When the car accelerates the wheels spin, the tyres smoke and a film of rubber is left on the track which gives better traction. Even with this technique, too much acceleration at the start leaves the rear wheels spinning.

7 Words

Burn-out: spinning the wheels in the burn-out pits or bleach box
Elapsed time (E.T.): the electronically measured time between start and finish
Fire-up road: side road where vehicles are started
Shut-down area: breaking distance, usually ¼-½ mile (400-800m approx) beyond finish line
Terminal speed (T.S.): electronically clocked speed as car crosses finish line
Wheelie: lifting front wheels off the ground, so car is balanced on rear wheels. ■

A dragster with its parachute out.

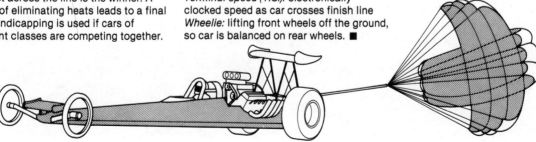

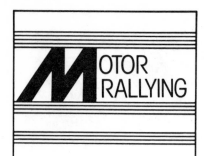

MOTOR RALLYING

Time was when the racing drivers who competed in track events also entered for rallies. Now the two sports are almost separate, with their own driving skills and star drivers.

In rallying, cars based on standard production saloons compete over every conceivable kind of surface and in every kind of weather condition. So a typical rally would have open road sections, which the cars cover at normal (legal) speeds, linking up *special stages* where the aim is to cover the length of the stage in the shortest possible time. There is no car-for-car racing; every driver is racing against the clock, on stages which can be over closed public roads (mainly in Europe) or even on private land, such as forest tracks.

At the other extreme, the Safari Rally in Kenya includes long high-speed sections on baked mud roads where the huge cloud of dust kicked up by a speeding competitor can hang in the air for an hour, or a sudden tropical squall can reduce the section to a quagmire in seconds. Many European rallies have cross-country sections or forestry stages, with hair-raising ascents and descents on treacherous surfaces. And often there is a solid boulder or immovable fir tree to block the car's path if the driver makes the slightest mistake. Or the danger could be a 60m (200ft) drop into a ravine.

Both driver and co-driver wear helmets inside the car, for protection and to hold the headphones for the radio communication. That's what the wire hanging between them is for.

1 The Route

Rallies can be staged anywhere in the world and the harder the going, the better. In the Finnish Rally of the Thousand Lakes the most skilful drivers produce incredibly fast times on farm tracks made up of small stones that roll like ball bearings. Equally, in the Arctic Rally in Finland even the solid ice of a frozen lake is used as a special stage.

2 Equipment

Rally drivers use much the same equipment as their track racing colleagues, though their defences against fire are less intense. The main difference is the helmet. A life support system is not essential, but an intercommunication radio is. Rally crews talk to each other by radio because the noise of engine and stones thrown up in the rough going drown the human voice. Radio is also used for communication with the team manager and service crews.

Winning

The winner of a rally is the car which has the fastest time over all the stages — and manages to avoid any penalties (time added on) for being late on the open road sections. Success or failure depends on both members of the crew — the driver has to be very quick on the special stages while the navigator must be immaculate in his route-finding and reading of *pace notes* based on earlier reconnaissance of the stage.

Rules

Rallying is a very complicated sport, with many classes and regulations. All a casual observer needs to be aware of is the fantastic skill and bravery of men who hurl 300 brake horse power machines down narrow forestry tracks between rocks and trees and slither skilfully over surfaces where even special chunky tyres provide only minimal grip. Some rallies are especially tough as no reconnaissance is allowed. An example of this is the RAC Rally of Great Britain which may be less spectacular than many events, but is more testing.

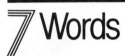 Skills & Tactics

Many of the top rallies are week-long events, where stamina and good back-up sevice are just as important as driving skills and faultless navigation. The crews must know how to conserve their strength, how to sleep on the move, how to arrange their meetings with service vehicles to keep their cars in peak order, when to drive all out and when to keep a little in reserve so as not to wreck the car. Many a rally is won or lost by seconds on the last special stage.

7 Words

Chunky studs: to give extra grip to tyres on loose surfaces
Co-driver: second driver
Drift: controlled four-wheel slide round corner, using throttle
Pace notes: used by navigator to guide driver along route at top speed
Spikes: tyres with very long studs to dig in to ice or snow
Yump: when car is airborne after bump; from Scandinavian pronunciation of 'jump'. ■

Although drivers are using rough, dirt roads, they go flat out and many rallies are covered at an average speed of 100kmph approx (60mph).

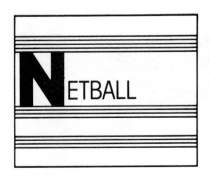

NETBALL

Netball is a woman's game combining individual skills of throwing, catching, running, jumping and turning with team tactics to produce a game that is fast-moving and tactically interesting, yet easy to follow.

A *bib* with letters indicating a player's position goes over the blouse. The ball should weigh 397-453g (14-16oz) and measure 68-71cm (27-28in) in circumference. It can be a netball or a size 5 Association Football.

1 The Court

Netball court showing the area of the court in which a player is allowed to move.

Netball is played on a hard surface 30.50m by 15.25m (100ft by 50ft) which is divided into three equal areas. The goal is a ring 38cm (15in) across on the top of a 3.05m (10ft) high goalpost. The game is controlled by two umpires who each make decisions in one half of the court, but control the game from the sidelines.

GS goal shooter   WD wing defence
GA goal attack   GD goal defence
WA wing attack   GK goal keeper
C centre   ▨ extent of playing territory

2 Equipment

Each player wears rubber-soled shoes and a skirt, tunic or pair of shorts and a plain blouse (usually in a team colour).

As no physical contact is allowed, defenders must time their jumps perfectly. Here GA has got her shot away before GD could intercept.

3 Winning

The winning team is the one that scores the most goals. A goal is scored when the ball is thrown through the ring. The Goal-Shooter (GS) and the Goal-Attacker (GA) are the only players allowed to shoot for goal and then only from INSIDE the shooting circle.

4 Rules

Each team consists of seven players who are easily identified by the bibs they wear which have initials rather than numbers on them. There are three attackers — Goal Shooter (GS), Goal-Attack (GA), and Wing-Attack (WA); three defenders — Goal-Keeper (GK), Goal-Defence (GD), and Wing-Defence (WD), and a Centre (C) who links the attack and the defence. Each player has a limited area of the court in which she may move and is not allowed in another area with or without the ball. This is called *offside*. The game lasts for one hour and is divided into four 15 minute quarters with the teams changing ends every quarter. Play begins with a *centre pass*. The first pass is decided by the toss of a coin and thereafter the Centres take alternate passes. Unlike basketball the players are not allowed to hold the ball for more than three seconds, or dribble the ball. When in possession a player may take only one step, so a team must combine to move the ball down the court by passing in a series of patterns of play.

Netball is a non-contact sport. Rough play, obstruction, intimidation and personal contact are penalized by the awarding of a *penalty pass*. If the defence commits a foul in the shooting circle, a *penalty shot* at goal is awarded. All other infringements on court (e.g. offside, stepping, etc.) are penalized by a free pass to the non-offending team. If the ball is sent out of court, play is restarted by a *throw-in* from the sideline by the opposing team.

NETBALL

WA is covering her opponent as the rest of her team stream back in defence. Note that she uses one arm to keep the regulation 90cm (3ft approx) away and the other to dissuade a high pass. As her opponent has only 3 seconds to pass, she must keep the pressure on.

5 & 6 Skills & Tactics

When a side is on the attack each player must try to outwit her defending opponent so that she is in a position to give or receive a pass. For the defence several alternatives are open: *zone defence,* in which each defender marks an area and tries to prevent a pass being effectively made or received in that area; and *one-on-one* marking, in which each defender marks one specific opponent.

7 Words

Bib: official part of uniform, showing initials of player's position on both front and back

Blocking: defending against a player who does not have the ball; no physical contact is allowed

Circle: actually the semicircle at each goal post where only the defending goalkeeper and goal defence as well as the attacking goal shooter and goal attack are allowed to set foot

Double bounce: illegal; as only one bounce is allowed

Dragging: illegal; as one foot must be kept still when player has the ball before passing or shooting

Free Pass: awarded to opponents in case of infringement

Obstruction: illegal; regarded as standing closer than the one yard (90cm) allowed

Partner: opponent marking a player

Stepping: illegal; lifting and putting down the landing or pivot foot when still holding the ball

Travelling: illegal; if player catches ball in midair outside circle, lands in circle and attempts shot at goal

Two lines: illegal; if ball crosses one-third of field (two cross lines) without touching a player. ∎

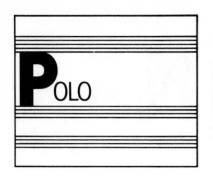

POLO

Teams of four horses and riders oppose each other in a game whose object is to score goals by knocking a small ball into a goal with a long, thin *stick* or *mallet.* The Persians played polo over one thousand years ago, but it only spread round the world when the British learnt the game in India and took it to North and South America.

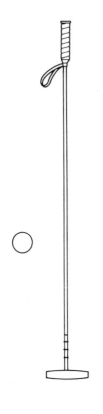

The polo stick (called mallet in the US) and its surprisingly small target — the 8.3cm (3¼in) diameter ball.

1 The Ground

Played on a huge, flat expanse of grass about 275m (300yd) by 183m (200yd), spectators are protected by low boards which keep the ball in play. The goal posts are wicker and bend or break easily if hit.

2 Equipment

The players ride horses which are always called *ponies,* though they may be any size or age. Wearing protective bandages or *boots* on all four legs, ponies must be tough and agile. Their riders wear helmets, a club jersey, white breeches and brown leather boots. Knee pads are often worn, too. The polo stick, or mallet as Americans call it, is 1.2-1.4m (4-4½ft) long with a slim, cigar-shaped head 23cm (9in) long. The ball is surprisingly small and made of solid wood 8.3cm (3¼in) in diameter, weighing 128g (4½oz).

3 Winning

A goal is scored when the ball is driven between the posts. Teams then change ends (except after a penalty goal) and again at half time. In order to ensure that matches are competitive, a handicap system is used. Each individual is rated from − 2 (ordinary) to + 10 goals (exceptional). To work out their handicap, teams add up the individual handicaps and subtract the total from the opposition to find out how many goals' start they are given. Teams rated 19 or more are very good indeed. A game lasts 56 minutes, broken up into eight 7-minute *chukkas* (periods). Played at speed, several ponies are used in the course of a game, which is controlled by two mounted umpires and a referee (off the field).

4 Rules

One of the most unusual laws in international sport insists that all players use only their right hands to hold the stick. Another important law concerns *right of way.* When two men are galloping after the ball, the one following the ball on its exact line or at a close angle to it has right of way as long as the ball is on his right or *off-side.* If any opponent forces him to check he receives a *free-hit.* There is no offside rule and players must not use their sticks dangerously. However, *hooking* an opponent's stick is allowed as long as he is about to hit the ball.

5 & 6 Skills & Tactics

The four players all have specific roles, even though the game is very fluid and fast-moving. The forwards are the No. 1 who spearheads the attack, and No. 2, the playmaker. Both Nos. 3 and 4 (the *backs)* are defenders, guarding the opposing Nos. 1 and 2.

The individual skills demand a high standard of horsemanship combined with the ability to hit the ball cleanly. Four main strokes are used. To hit the ball forwards, the *off-side forehander* and the *near-side forehander;* to hit it backwards, the *off-side backhander* and the *near-side backhander.* The variations of cut, pull and drive ensure that the rider can distribute the ball in any direction despite the angle and speed at which he approaches it. Spectators always enjoy shots under the neck or between the legs, watching the player *brace* himself in the saddle to give himself a firm base for hitting the ball.

A talented player can see the game two strokes ahead and move his pony accordingly.

7 Words

Brace: when a player stands up in his stirrups to play a shot
Crossing: cutting across right of way
Mallet: US term for stick
Near-side: left-hand side
Off-side: right-hand side. ∎

A test of sheer physical strength, powerlifting became separated from Olympic-style weightlifting in the 1960s and began to expand in popularity after the first World Championships were held in 1971.

Competitors must do three different lifts — the *Squat, Bench Press* and *Deadlift*. While records can be set in each, it is the heaviest total that wins a competition. The *lifter* has three attempts at each weight, and if two competitors lift the same weight, then the one with the lighter bodyweight always wins. An interesting extra dimension is added to the sport thanks to a formula worked out by Prof. Lyle Schwartz in 1978. The best lifter in any tournament can be worked out, irrespective of bodyweight, by the *SFT* (Schwartz Formula Total) which correlates bodyweight with weight lifted.

There are eleven categories for men— *up to 52kg* (114lb); *56kg* (123lb); *60kg* (132lb); *67½kg* (148lb); *75kg* (165lb); *82½kg* (182lb); *90kg* (198lb); *100kg* (220lb); *110kg* (242lb); *125kg* (275lb); *and over 125kg* (275lb).
There are nine weight divisions for women— *up to 44kg* (97lb); *48kg* (106lb); *52kg* (114lb); *56kg* (123lb); *60kg* (132lb); *67½kg* (148lb); *75kg* (165lb); *82½kg* (182lb); *and over 82½kg.*

The bar is the same as that used for weightlifting, 2.2m (7ft 2in) long, 28mm (1in) in diameter and weighing 25kg (55lb) with collars. The circular *plates,* or weights, are coloured blue (20kg), red (25kg), gold (45kg) and green (50kg).

THE SQUAT
Unlike Olympic weightlifting where the bar is always on the floor, in this discipline, the bar is rested on a stand at a height convenient to the lifter, who then takes the weight across his shoulders. With his feet set slightly wider than hip width, he keeps his head up, looking straight ahead. He then lowers himself into the squat position until the top of his thighs are "below

Although oils and greases are prohibited, powders are allowed on hands to help grip the bar. No clothing is allowed that would help the lifter, so elasticated vests and padded shorts are out. The main rules concern legal and illegal lifting.
parallel to the platform" as the rules require. Keeping his back straight and his knees pointing outwards, he must not squat completely, with his bottom brushing his heels but must start his *recovery* at once by standing up again. This is the toughest part of the lift, as the strong muscles on the inside of the thigh tend to pull the knees inwards, throwing the lifter off balance, straining the lower back. Keeping the knees apart ensures that the legs help to drive the lifter straight up. The head should be held back, looking up.

THE BENCH PRESS
For this lift, the competitor lies on a small, solid bench 45cm (18in) high. Buttocks, shoulders and head are braced against the bench but the feet are flat on the floor with the knees bent. As this lift tests the *pectoralis major* muscles between the chestbone and the collarbone, lifters have developed a way of arching the body, the *Collins Arch,* to get a more vertical push. Once in position, the barbell is handed to the lifter whose forearms will be as vertical as possible ready to take the weight down onto his chest. When the lifter is comfortable with it on him, the referee signals him to *press,* or lift, the bar. The lifter quite simply pushes upwards as hard as possible; as his triceps take over from the pectoralis major, the arms straighten and the bar must be held steady before the referee signals the attendants to remove it. The high arch of the back has to be maintained throughout the lift for maximum effect. Vast experience is needed for heavy weights.

THE DEADLIFT
With the full title of the Two Hands Deadlift, this is the ultimate test of strength, proving just how much weight a lifter can heave off the floor. The third and final discipline, it can decide the margins of victory or defeat. The lifter has to bend down, take the bar from the ground and then straighten up with his shoulders braced back. The bar is lifted only to thigh height in one continuous movement so the grip is vital. Using a method called *hooking,* the fingers are wrapped over the thumb, squeezing it tightly against the bar. The pull is so sudden and violent that the bar tends to roll in the hands and to counteract this lifters use an *alternate gripping method,* with one hand facing forward, the other backwards.

Placing his feet comfortably under the bar, with his hands well apart, the lifter cannot just pull vertically as this would pull his body forward and off-balance. Instead, a slight inward pull is used as the legs straighten. He has to keep his back straight and flat as he comes to the hardest part ... when the bar is knee high with pressure on the fulcrum of the hips and the muscles of the back. Lifters are not allowed to *lay back* as they take the bar up and should keep their heads up, the chest high, the shoulders braced and the knees locked. ∎

Bench press

Deadlift

Squat

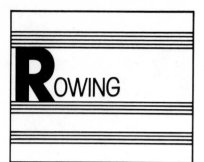

Rowing

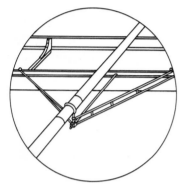

The rigger which supports the rowlock

Ask any top class rower why he enjoys rowing and he may have some difficulty answering. After a while, he may mumble something about striving 'to get everything right' and the satisfaction he gets when everything 'clicks' on the day of a big race. Eventually, he might get round to saying that at top-class level the difference between the winning boat and all the rest lies in the intricacies of technical prowess, and it is this ability to reach a level of competence and, more important, maintain it throughout a race, which makes rowing the fascinating sport it is. At least that's how the rower sees it.

For the spectator, however, the subtle differences between crews are usually missed. The boats flash past, there is a bit of splashing, some shouting and some colour and then it has all gone and the spectator knows very little about what was going on or why one boat was going faster than the other.

To understand and enjoy rowing, watching it on television can often be the best way to learn, because the camera can follow the crews right down the course, zooming in on particular crews or individuals, making it much easier to pick up mistakes.

1 The Course

At full international and Olympic level the standard course is dead straight and 2000m (1¼ miles) long. Women row 1000m, Juniors 1500m. The boats row six abreast in lanes which are clearly marked by buoys. At this level of rowing, boats usually steer straight and stay out of trouble, but to keep an eye on things, and adjudicate in the event of a protest, the race is followed by an umpire in a launch. If one crew is clearly infringing upon another, the umpire will hold up a white flag and tell the offending crew, through a loud hailer, that they are in the wrong. Should the crew fail to get back into position, the umpire may disqualify them. Usually there are standby launches at points along the course just in case the first launch breaks down. It happens surprisingly often!

Most courses at international and Olympic level are artificially made, rather like an immense but shallow swimming pool, so there is no current in the water. Therefore no one lane is better or worse than any other and this is why they are used at international level where the vagaries of a river current might distort the result. Plenty of top class rowing, throughout the world, is still held on rivers, which is where, after all, the sport started. There are two types of rowing competitions outside 2000m rowing. Firstly there are regattas, held in the summer part of the season, which follow much the same pattern as regattas on a 2000m course. Being on a river, there is usually only room for two or three crews to compete in each race. Perhaps the most famous of all these is the 'Henley Royal Regatta' in England.

The second type of competition on a river is known as a *head* race and these usually take place in the winter. Hundreds of crews, as many as 400 in the very big races, row down a fixed course starting at about 10 second intervals and their time is recorded. The fastest crew then becomes *head of the river*. Generally these races are several miles long, rather than a basic 2000m.

2 Equipment

As in all other sports using special equipment, the hardware used in rowing has become very sophisticated. *Oars:* many oars are still made from wood, but *composite* oars made from aluminium and plastic are now used. Some oars are reinforced with carbon fibre to make them less bendy when the pressure is put on them in the water. The *button* about which the oar pivots is adjustable to enable the *gearing* of the ratio of inboard to outboard length to be varied.

Boats: boats too are now very light — the oarsmen has to get himself and the boat down to the other end of the course, so the lighter the boat the better. Each oarsmen sits on a seat which runs up and down a *slide,* which has a slight angle or *rake*. Feet go into a pair of training shoes screwed into a rack across the boat known as a *stretcher*. The stretcher is adjustable both up and down and backwards and forwards, and sometimes for angle. Bolted to the outside of the boat, on one side for oars and both sides for sculls, is an adjustable stainless steel or aluminium frame known as a *rigger*, at the end of which is the *gate* that holds the oar. By a combination of all these adjustments each oarsman has his seat, oar and stretcher set up specifically for him.

3 Winning

The actual winning of a rowing race is simple: the first one to the finishing line beats the rest. International and Olympic rowing is, however, divided into various classes and categories, both of competitors and boats, who are allowed to race against each other.

There are three main categories of rowers:

Men's Heavyweight: men of any weight can take part, but, in effect it means the fastest and most prestigious crews, because in rowing bigger means stronger.

Men's Lightweight: which is for crews of an average weight of 70 kg (154lb or under) and where no individual in the crew weighs more than 72.5kg (159lb). There are annual International Championships for the Lightweight event.

Women: women have no segregation between lightweight and heavyweight. Until fairly recently they had no Olympic standing, but this has now been altered and standards have improved dramatically as a consequence.

There are also annual International Championships for Junior Men and Women. A rower may compete as a Junior until the end of the year in which his or her eighteenth birthday occurs.

Within these groups, oarsmen and women row in a selection of boats which are used at all levels from club rowing to International and Olympics. The categories of boats are as follows:

Eights: eights are the fastest and most prestigious of the various rowing boats, and, not surprisingly, the ones most people recognize. The crew consists of eight oarsmen, each with one oar, and a *cox* who steers. The oars are arranged so that four stick out on either side, though the patterns vary according to preference.

Fours: there are two types of fours. Both has four oarsmen, each with one oar, but one is *coxed* and the other is *coxless.* In the *coxless* four, the boat is steered by one of the oarsmen, usually the bowman, using steering lines attached to his shoes. As in an eight, the cox of a four usually sits at the back of the boat, but in many boats he lies in the front with just his head showing.

Pairs: once again there are two types of pairs, coxed and coxless. As in the fours, the cox of a pair is often lying in

the front of the boat, the theory being that he can get a better view of where he is going. It also results in a better distribution of weight in the boat and lowers the centre of gravity.

All the boats listed so far have been of the type where each oarsman has just one oar, held in both hands. In *sculling* boats the oarsmen (or *scullers* as they are known) have two oars (*sculls*), one in each hand.

Single Sculls: just one sculler in the boat, no cox — the loneliest of the rowing boats, and the very antithesis of an eight.

Double Sculls: as the name suggests, two rowers each with two sculls. Once again, no cox.

Quadruple Sculls: four rowers, four sculls on each side of the boat — probably the most sleek of all the boats to watch, but also one of the most difficult to row well. In women's rowing the quad-scull carries a cox, but not in men's rowing.

4 Rules

The rules affecting a boat when racing are basically very simple. It has to stick to its course and not interfere with any other boat. The rowers themselves are bound by the usual rules governing amateur status and are subject to the

At the start of a race, the rowers use sharp, powerful strokes to gain momentum.

The single scull is as sharp as a needle and narrower than the sculler himself. Here his sliding seat is well forward. When he straightens his legs he will slide backwards as the oars sweep through the water.

ROWING

serious rules forbidding the use of any stimulative drugs.

For a start of a 2000m course the six crews line up with the sterns of each held by a man lying on a pontoon sticking into the water. The *judge at the start* ensures that the bows of all the boats are correctly aligned before the start and when they have indicated that they are ready the starter starts them by saying 'Etes-vous prêt? Partez!' ('Are you ready? Go!' in French), and dropping a red flag to indicate the *off.* In top level racing, crews will usually try to jump the start, going off fractionally before the flag. The television viewer has a much better chance of seeing this and with all the boats in line it is something to watch out for. If the judge at the start sees a false start, he informs the starter, who calls the crews back by ringing a bell.

Starting instructions are given in French, the official language of the sport's international governing body — the Fédération Internationale des Sociétés d'Aviron (FISA), which is based in Switzerland.

Championship regattas commence with heats in which some crews qualify direct for the Semi-Finals or Finals. For those beaten in the heats there is another chance to qualify when they race in *repêchage.* This is to ensure that a possible medallist is not knocked out in the first round by coming third to the two best crews in the competition. The finals are always contested by six crews.

A sculler lying well back, having completed a stroke.

5 Skills

The power comes from the whole of the body, the legs doing as much as the arms and the torso. Each oarsman's seat is on small wheels and runs on a pair of tracks, called a *slide.* This contraption helps to lengthen the sweep of the oar in the water.

For the crew in general the most obvious thing to look for is whether the timing is good; whether all the oars are going into and out of water at precisely the same time. If the timing starts to get ragged in top class rowing it means competitors are tiring and starting to row badly. Usually this only happens towards the end of the race and it's always in this last 500m that mistakes start to appear. Most noticeably the *rating* will go up and then, if the crew is not really capable of doing the job properly, various parts of the rowing will deteriorate. The *cover* will go down. The beginning and end of each stroke begins to look ragged as the oarsmen try to pull the oar through the water too fast. Splashing is a tell-tale sign of tiredness. The rowers may also get *short on the slide.* When rowing well, the full length of the slide is used. The net result of all this is a slower boat. To the spectator, the controlled rhythm in the earlier part of the race is replaced by an uncontrolled rush, and the boat even appears to go backwards. A drooping head and jerky movements are also signs of tiredness. Good crews are those that have the mental powers and technical ability to overcome tiredness and maintain rhythm.

6 Tactics

The basic tactics are much the same for all crews. There is little manoeuvring because the strongest, most rhythmic crews will always come out on top. The first half minute of a race is spent in *getting the boat going.* The opening strokes should be rather short as the oars dig into the water to get the boat up to full speed. Some crews might take about half a minute to achieve this.

RIGHT: *Even rowing moves with the times. Here, the cox steers from the front.*
PAGE 162: *The lineout, unique to Rugby Union.*

When the boat is running well (after about 250m) the cox and stroke together try to *settle the crew down* to a steady rhythm by *lengthening the stroke out.*

At top level this would happen automatically. The pace would then be at about 95 percent of a crew's full capability. They would maintain this for the next 1250m, then with some 500m to go they sprint for the finishing line. They have no time to see what their opponents are doing. At a point picked out by the coach in the middle of a race, crews often put in a *burn,* either to test their opponents or to catch up if they are falling behind. The burst could be short and sharp or longer if the coach thinks his crew can draw clear away.

7 Words

Blade: the curved part of the oar that actually goes into the water
Bow: front of the boat — also the oarsman nearest the front of the boat
Burst: when a crew raises its rating to try

Clogs: old-fashioned name for the shoes in the boat
Cover: distance between two sets of puddles
Feathering: twisting the oar so that the blade is parallel to the water between strokes to cut out air resistance and the chance of hitting the tops of waves in rough conditions.
Gate: the device at the end of the rigger in which the oar is held
Pitch: the angle of the blade from the vertical — one of the tuning adjustments
Puddle: the whirlpool made by the oar as it leaves the water — a guide to the distance a boat travels before the next stroke
Rake: angle of inclination of the stretcher
Repêchage: the race for crews losing in the first round of a regatta so that they can still reach the final
Rigger: stainless steel or aluminium framework holding the oar to the boat. Highly adjustable
Shortening up: rowing too fast, at too high a rating, and not pulling the oar right through the water
Slide: the tracks on which the seat runs up and down

A coxed four rowing flat out but in full control. Note the size of the cox.

to burst clear of the field.
Button: the part of the oar that fits in the gate and holds it steady

LEFT: *The popularity of boardsailing has led to the introduction of a new Olympic class, the 'windglider'.*
PAGE 163: *A spectacular view of a skijumper, taken from the tower.*

Stretcher plate or bar: on which one's shoes and feet rest; adjustable
Stroke: the oarsman nearest the back (stern) of the boat who sets the pace which everyone follows
Stroke side: the side of the boat on which the stroke's oar is, as opposed to bowside; in the USA, port and starboard respectively. ∎

RUGBY UNION

Legend says that William Webb Ellis of Rugby School, England originated the game by picking up a football and running with it in 1823. Players run, pass and kick the ball in an attempt to score by grounding the ball behind their opponents' goal line, or kicking the ball between the posts at each end of the field. The side without the ball defends its territory by tackling the ball carrier and attempting to obtain possession.

Rugger, as it is often called, is an amateur game played with 15 players a side. The eight *forwards* are the men whose job it is to get possession of the ball. They are physically big and strong. The seven *backs* are the fast runners and slick handlers who expect to get the ball from their forwards and run with it.

The game starts and stops quite often, but on a good day the movement of the players and ball will range up and down and from side to side of the field.

The rugby field. A scrum has formed and the team at the far end is defending, with its backs lying 'flat', ready to tackle their opposite numbers if they run with the ball.

FB fullback
RW right wing
LW left wing
IC inside centre
OC outside centre
SH scrum-half
FH fly-half

1 The Pitch

The pitch can vary in size, but from goal line to goal line must not exceed 100m (or 110yd) and must be no wider than 69m (or 75yd). Like the pitch, the posts come in a variety of sizes. Most are made of wood, but some are of steel and others of whatever is available.

2 Equipment

Jerseys and shorts have to be strong. Some forwards protect their ears from becoming chafed in the scrum with bandaging, or a head band.

Forwards tend to wear boots with strong ankle supports, while backs prefer the low cut shoe-type of boot. The studs, made of leather, rubber, aluminium or an approved plastic, must be circular and conform to the dimensions laid down by the Rugby Football Union.

The ball is oval and conforms to rigid dimensions, weighing 380-430g (13-15oz).

3 Winning

There are two basic methods of scoring — the *try* and the *goal*. A try is scored when a player crosses the opponents' goal line carrying the ball and grounds it in the area between the goal line and the *dead ball line*. The try is worth four points. After a try has been scored the scoring team has the right to make a *conversion* with a *place kick* or *drop kick* at goal in line with the place where the *touch-down* was made. A place kick is made after the ball has been placed on the ground, a drop kick is made by letting the ball fall from the hands onto the ground and kicking it as it hits the ground i.e. on the half-volley. As with all kicks at goal, the ball must pass over the crossbar and between the posts. If successful, the conversion is worth two points, which are added to the four already gained for the try. Because of this it makes sense for the scorer to touch down as close to the posts as possible to *narrow the angle* and so to make it easier for the specialist kicker with his conversion attempt.

A *penalty try* can be awarded if the referee feels that a try WOULD have been scored but for some foul play by the defending side. A penalty try is awarded centrally, under the posts, so as to make the conversion easy.

There are two other methods of scoring a goal: the *penalty goal* and the *dropped goal*. Both are worth three points. For certain offences the referee can award a penalty which enables the non-offending side to kick at goal by means of a place kick or drop kick.

A dropped goal is often spectacular because it can be scored from anywhere on the field by any player while play is going on.

After a try has been scored and prior to the conversion attempt the kicker's team must all retire behind the ball. The opposing team must remain behind their goal line until the kicker begins his run; then they may charge in an attempt to prevent a goal. No charge is allowed at a penalty kick.

Laws

The laws are complex with many sub-sections and are constantly subject to scrutiny and change.

All senior matches are played over 80 minutes in two 40-minute halves. The *referee* is the sole arbiter but he can consult with the *touch judges* in international matches. Each half begins with a place kick from the centre of the half-way line. The game is also restarted this way after a goal or penalty goal, and by a drop kick from the centre after an unconverted try.

There are three ways of progressing towards the opponent's goal line: by passing (bearing in mind that a pass must move laterally, that is to say, it must be angled backwards), by carrying the ball, and by kicking the ball.

No blocking or obstruction is allowed and so the only way to stop an attack is to tackle the man with the ball. A player is considered to be tackled when he is held by one or more opponents so that the ball touches the ground. As soon as the ball touches the ground the player must release it; failure to do so produces a penalty.

If a team is to continue to go forward after such a tackle, it must get the ball again. If the ball is on the ground, then the forwards will form a *ruck* around it and try to *heel* it back. If the ball is still being held, then the forwards will join a *maul* around the player with the ball and try to wrest it free in order to gain clean possession for their side. The rucks and mauls sometimes develop into stalemate where neither side seems likely to win possession. In this case the referee awards a *set scrummage*. The team not responsible for the stoppage puts the ball into the scrummage.

It is not enough to get the ball over the opponents' line: the ball must be grounded. Here a fast-running winger has dived full length to make sure he evaded his opponent to score a try.

RUGBY UNION

The scrum

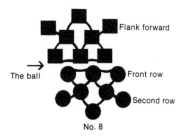

Flank forward

The ball →

Front row

Second row

No. 8

Three short powerful men make up the front row. The hooker is between two props. Note how the second row forwards get a good grip by grabbing the front of the props' shorts. A wing forward (6) binds into the edge of the scrum.

The most common scrummage formation is shown on the left: The front row consists of two *props* who have, in between them, the *hooker*. In the middle of the second row are the two *second row (lock)* forwards and they are flanked by the two *wing* or *flank forwards*. Isolated in the back row is the *number 8* forward. The backs align themselves ready to run with the ball. The *scrum-half* of the team awarded the scrum puts the ball into the *tunnel* formed between the two sets of forwards, who then try to hook the ball back as they push at each other. The ball must go in straight and no attempt to raise a foot must be made until the ball is in.

As a means of gaining ground or as a defensive tactic a player may kick the ball out of play and *into touch*. From within his own 22m (or 25yd) line he can kick directly into touch. A *lineout* will then follow at the point where the ball went into touch. However from outside his own 22m line he must make the ball bounce on the ground before going into touch. If he fails to do so then the lineout will take place opposite the point at which the ball was kicked. The lineout is formed by a minimum of two players from each side. The ball is thrown in normally by the hooker (or the winger). It must be thrown in straight and the players must maintain their relative positions until the ball is released by the thrower.

A player is *offside* in general play when he is in front of the ball and attempts to play it after it has been played by a member of his own team. There are specific laws defining *offside at a lineout* and a scrummage. At a lineout any player not participating in the lineout must stand at least 10m (or 11yd) from the line of touch. Players who ARE taking part can be offside if they cross the line in certain circumstances. At a scrummage a player is offside if he joins the scrum from his opponents' side, or if he is not part of the scrum and places either foot in front of the imaginary line while the ball is in the scrum.

The most minor passing and handling infringements are penalized by the awarding of a set scrummage with the non-offending side being given the advantage of the *put-in*. Technical offences at lineout and scrummage are punished by a *free kick* which can be taken straight into touch but not straight at goal. Whenever a free kick is awarded the offending side must retire 10m. If they fail to do so the free kick becomes a *penalty kick* from the same mark. The more serious offences produce penalty kicks which, if in range, can be aimed straight at goal for three points. Whenever a penalty kick is awarded, the infringing side must retire 10m immediately. If they fail to do so the place of infringement is advanced 10m. This rule discourages arguing with the referee!

5 Skills

The front row: the props are the pillars of rugby society. They support the hooker and form the foundation of the scrummage. Physical domination over their opponents is the name of their game and no pack of forwards can scrummage successfully without good props. Ideally they should stand under 1.80m (or 6ft) and weigh 95kg (or 210lb or over. The hooker tends to be lighter and his greatest asset is to be able to *strike* quickly with his foot when the ball comes into the scrummage. In many teams he is also employed to throw the ball into the lineout.

The locks: behind the front row are the two lock forwards — usually the biggest men in the side. They have to apply their weight in the scrummage, their height in the lineout. A good lineout jumper is of inestimable value simply because possession from this department of play gives the backs more room

to manoeuvre and therefore a great opportunity to attack. In a perfect situation the jumper would wish to catch the ball with both hands in order to control the possession he gives to his backs, but usually he *taps* or *palms* the ball back with one hand.

The back row: this consists of two flankers and the number 8, although nowadays the flankers often attach themselves to the second row.

The back-row forwards must work together. They have to be the fittest members of the side, their job requiring them to be as close to the ball as possible for as much of the game as possible. As the players nearest to the opposition backs they have a crucial role in defence while in attack they must attempt to be first to the loose ball in order to set up attacks for their own side.

Scrum-half: he is the link between forwards and backs, the man who puts the ball into the scrummage and the first to receive possession from the lineout. When the ball is heeled from the scrummage or the ruck, or comes back from the lineout or maul, it is the scrum half who has to make the initial decision on the play — whether to pass, kick, or take on the opposition himself.

Outside-half: also called a *fly-half* or an *out-half,* he is the pivot of the back division. He can control the play by kicking or passing or attempting a break by himself depending upon the prevailing conditions and the strengths and weaknesses of his team. He is the equivalent of American football's quarterback.

Centre-threequarter: in attack the two centres either serve the wingers outside them with passes, or attempt to run past their opposite numbers. Good passing is vital and a pass which is slightly off line can upset an attacking movement. Centres need the sort of acceleration which can take them past opponents in a confined space. Defensively, they must be secure enough to prevent their opposite numbers from breaking through.

Wingers: like the centres there are two — one on the left hand side of the field and one on the right. Ideally the winger should be the fastest member of the side with the ability to beat opponents by such subtle skills as sidestep, swerve and change of pace.

Fullback: the last line of defence with the positional sense to be in the right place at the right time. He must be able to clear his lines effectively by kicking to touch with either foot. He must be strong and courageous in defence with

good hand-eye coordination. But his duties are not confined to defence; occasionally he comes into the three-quarter line to provide an extra man.

6 Tactics

If a team has a strong set of forwards, play often revolves around them. When there is a scrummage, instead of passing the ball to the backs, the number 8 might pick up the ball then link up with his flankers or scrum-half. They interpass with the rest of the forwards who keep together as they power their way upfield. If the ball comes back quickly from a scrum, the scrum-half or outside-half can do a little kick ahead for his forwards to chase. He aims for the *box,* an empty area in front of the opposing fullback and behind the opposing forwards. From a lineout, the ball can be tapped down by a forward to a fellow forward who again tries to bull his way upfield supported by the other forwards. Another tactic from a lineout is to pass the ball to the outside half who does a *scissors* with his outside centre, who then links up again with the forwards. Alternatively, the scrum-half may kick consistently for touch, to gain ground.

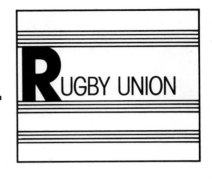

Instead of passing the ball, the fly-half will often kick the ball over the opposing backs for his own backs to chase. This can be especially effective when the ball is wet and it is difficult for players to turn quickly in defehce. In the play illustrated here, the attacking team's left winger has moved across the field to join the threequarter line.

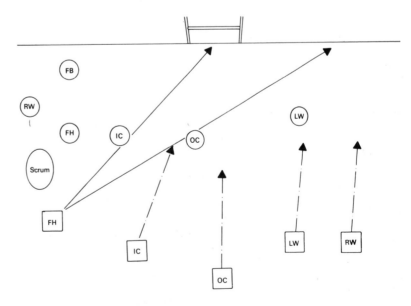

If the strength lies in the backs, then there are obviously many set ploys to try to fox the opposition — variations on the scissors move, using the fullback in the threequarter line, missing out one of the centres with a long pass.

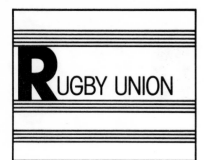

RUGBY UNION

But nothing can beat the element of surprise: the sudden acceleration, the sidestep or swerve at speed — these are the most potent of the backs' weapons and tend to be instinctive.

The weather plays an important role — the running handling game is best suited to sunny, windless days on dry, flat pitches, while rain and wind make passing a hazardous occupation and tend to discourage open play.

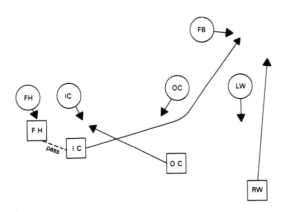

In the dummy scissors, the outside centre cuts inside, taking his opponent with him as he pretends to make a scissors move. However, the inside centre continues to run forward and goes through the gap that has opened between the opposition outside centre and wing.

7 Words

Advantage: if, from an infringement by one side, the other side gains some advantage, the referee may allow play to continue

Blind side: also called the *short, narrow* or *weak* side. When play is on the left hand side, the smaller area of the field between the ball and the left hand touch line comprises the blind side and vice versa when play is on the right hand side of the field

Dead: means that the ball is out of play

Drop out 22: if the attacking side kick the ball, or lose possession of it over their opponents' goal line, and the ball is touched down by a member of the defending side, the defending side are awarded a drop kick which can be taken at any point along the 22m (or 25yd) line; the opposing side can attempt to charge down the kick

Dummy: player feints to pass, but holds on to the ball = he *sells a dummy*

Engine room: commentator's description of the second row of the scrum

Five-eighths: Australian and New Zealand term for outside half and inside centre

Fly hack: a ball on the ground kicked along the ground

Front five: the three front row forwards and the two locks — also called the tight forwards

Grub kick: a drop kick which skids the ball along the ground; it is often employed by backs to make progress upfield, and is ideal in wet weather

Knock on: when a player drops or propels the ball forward in the direction of his opponents' line; a scrummage is awarded to the opposition for this offence

Lifting at the lineout: a highly illegal move — when one player in the lineout gives the colleague standing in front of him a helping hand to reach the ball

Loose forwards: the two flankers and the number 8; all very mobile players

Loose head prop: the prop standing on the hooker's left

Mark: also called a *fair catch* — when a player, standing with both feet on the ground, catches the ball cleanly from a kick by the opposition, and at the same time shouts 'Mark'; the player can only make a mark inside his 22m line and is awarded a free kick

No side: the end of the game

Pack: a collective name for the forwards

Punt: a kick made by letting the ball fall from the hand/s and kicking it before it touches the ground

Scrum five: the defending side can touch down behind their own goal line, but if they carry the ball over their own line before touching down, or if the ball crosses the defending side's goal line, having last touched a member of the defending side, and is then touched down, the referee will call for a scrummage 5m (5yd approx) from the defending side's goal line, giving the advantage of the put-in to the attackers.

Second phase: a deliberate ruck or maul after a set piece

The shove: the weight applied by the forwards when the ball comes into the scrummage

Strike: the act of hooking the ball in the front row

Strike against the head: when the opposition wins the ball from the other side's put-in at the scrummage

Threequarter line: made up of the two centre threequarters and the two wings

Tight head prop: the prop standing on the hooker's right

Up and under: a kick upfield high enough to allow the kicking side to follow it up and be underneath it when it comes down; also known as a *Garryowen.* ■

Rugby League is a version of Rugby which is played with 13-a-side and has professional leagues in several countries. It is arguably a faster and more open game than Rugby Union — partly because of the extra field space afforded by only 13 players a side and partly because of the rules.

A rough, tough game, it is a game of brain as well as brawn, which is why the skilful little player will always be appreciated just as much as the muscular he-man.

In Rugby League, as in Rugby Union, two teams controlled by a referee attempt to score points by running the ball over their opponents' *try line* or *goal line* and by kicking it between their goal posts.

The side without the ball defends its territory by tackling the ball carrier and attempting to obtain possession.

1 The Field

Rugby League is played on grass pitches. The posts are often padded at the base to prevent injury to players.

2 Equipment

Apart from the standard equipment of shirts, stockings, shorts and boots, all Rugby League players are encouraged to wear light protective shoulder padding because of the ferocious tackling.

3 Winning

As in most ball games, the team scoring the most points is the winner.

A *try,* the grounding of the ball over the opponents' try line, is worth three points and gives the scoring side the opportunity to add a further two points with a *conversion kick* at goal. The kick is taken from a point in line with the place where the try was scored and, as with all kicks, must pass over the cross-bar and between the posts to be successful. Sometimes a referee can award a side three points automatically if he feels that a certain try has been prevented because of an infringement by the defending side. This *penalty try* is awarded between the posts so that the conversion is taken from in front of the posts.

For some fouls during play a *penalty kick* can be awarded. If the offence took place near the opponents' goal, the kicker might try to score two points by using a *place kick* with the ball on the ground, and kicking it at goal. During play, a *dropped goal* worth one point can be scored at any time. Kicked on the bounce, a *drop kick* must also clear the bar, going between the posts.

4 Rules

The principal rule is that the ball must not be passed forward. It has to be

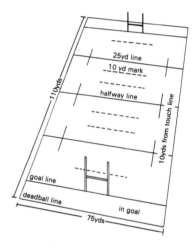

The field

Despite being tackled, the man with the ball has crossed the try line (or goal line). Now he must touch it down on the ground to score.

The ball must always be passed sideways or behind. This player has committed one opponent to tackle him and looks for a teammate who is free.

moved towards the opponents' line either with a sequence of sideways or lateral passes or else kicked.

A team consists of 13 players, plus two substitutes, who may be introduced or replaced at any stage of the game, which lasts 80 minutes. The players change ends after the first half of 40 minutes. A hooter sounds at the end of each half. In contrast to American football, obstruction of either attacking or defending players is not allowed and indeed incurs a penalty.

Each team is allowed to retain the ball for only the duration of six tackles. After that a *scrum* forms and the tackle count restarts with whichever team gains possession.

If a player with the ball runs over the touchline, play is resumed with a scrum in direct line with the point where he left the field of play.

If a player is effectively tackled on the field of play he invariably *plays the ball*

back with his foot to the acting *halfback*, though he is not restricted from playing the ball forward and resuming play himself.

If a player fumbles the ball forward and fails to regain it before it touches the ground, it is a *knock-on* and unless an opponent capitalizes by picking it up, a scrum is formed.

Ground can be gained by a forward kick but the ball must bounce inside the field of play before going out, otherwise a scrum is called from where the kick was taken. If the kick goes straight to the opposition, they would gain possession.

Although most forms of tackling are permitted around the ankles, legs, waist or body, a *head high* tackle is frowned upon and is often punished with the dismissal of the culprit from the field.

Other more common offences such as a player going *offside* (i.e. being in front of the play), *feeding* the scrum (putting the ball into the scrum incorrectly), *foot up* (trying to *hook* the ball back too soon) and *passing off the ground* (after a tackle) are all penalized.

5 Skills

Speed is important but a very different skill and equally effective is the *side step* to get past an opponent. All good halfbacks (the playmakers) must have acceleration from a standing start.

Positional play is also an art and the top class centres and halfbacks have an awareness of just where to be at the right time. The best can be seen inter-

After a tackle, the player gets up and plays the ball back to a teammate who gets play moving again. After six tackles a scrum forms.

cepting an opposition pass, then having a clear run to the line.

Positional sense is also a key requirement of the fullback — the last line of defence. In fielding a long clearance (catching a long kick) breaking up an attack, timing a tackle, or joining the threequarter line for an attack on the opposing line, a fullback must know exactly where to be at any given moment.

A powerful front or second row forward can often barge his way over the line from a *play-the-ball* or *scrum* situation 5 or 10yd (5 or 10m approx) out from the line.

The hooker is also a dominant figure in setting up attacks *in the loose* as well as by winning possession in the scrum.

And the *loose forward* in today's open game is at times almost as good as another threequarter if on top of his job.

6 Tactics

A club lucky enough to have pace in its back division and men with proven handling skills at halfback, will be able to play an open *running* type of game which is good to watch.

All the speed and craft in the world will count for nought if the opposition can keep on tackling hard and quickly. This has been achieved to great effect by less spectacular sides founded on a defensive basis.

Although the value of a dropped goal has been reduced from two points to one, it can still be a vital shot in the armoury, especially for the less talented sides.

Even if they lack the pace to break through opposing defences, they can often get close enough for the ball eventually to be transferred to a player who has the skill to drop a goal.

7 Words

Early bath: used whenever a player is sent off and heads for the dressing rooms

Making a scissors: a player on a decoy run going diagonally to the player with the ball to confuse the opposition

Play-the-ball: the act of an attacker who has just been tackled, but who then rolls the ball back with his foot to a colleague or plays the ball forward, picking it up himself

Stiff-arm tackle: an illegal tackle usually aimed at the head of an opponent and delivered, as the name suggests, with a stiff forearm

Up-and-under: a high kick put in by a player trying to gain ground and put an opponent under pressure; the kicker follows up his own kick with the aim of regaining possession immediately; the kick is also often referred to as a *Garry-owen.* ■

RUGBY LEAGUE

Tackling is always hard in Rugby League. Three men have made sure that the man with the ball has been stopped. He will then get up and play the ball to a colleague.

SAILING

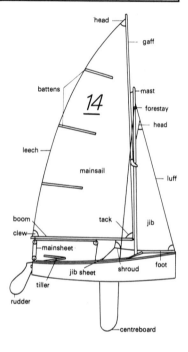

Sailing is an incredibly wide-ranging sport. It can mean tiny 'Optimist' dinghies on a small boating lake or the 236ft (72m approx) four-masted schooner 'Club Méditerranée', which competed in the 1976 Observer Singlehanded Transatlantic Race. In between there are hundreds of *classes*, types of dinghies and small keel boats, thousands of fully-crewed *off-shore* yachts which may race over courses of a few dozen or several hundred miles, and strong but sleek racing craft which battle over huge distances — even round the world in the 'Whitbread Round the World Race'. These capture the imagination of the general public and are frequently given big coverage by the media. But the sailing enthusiast will also be looking out for the less publicized but often more demanding competition in Olympic sailing classes or the main off-shore racing fixtures.

The idea of competitive sailing is to test a sailor's ability to get the most out of the boat as well as the wind. It is all a matter of angles, rather like snooker. A good sailor will be able to appreciate at which angle to sail in order to get the most wind to blow the boat along. When the wind is behind, the boat is *running, wind aft*. Since a boat can't sail straight into the wind, the sailor has to zig-zag or *tack* at a 45 degree angle to the wind, from left to right or *port to starboard* with the sails *close-hauled*. The *closer to the wind* a boat sails, the straighter the path and the faster it will reach the finish line.

tition because it provides a thorough test. The course is *laid* according to the direction of the wind so the fleet starts with a *beat to windward,* sailing into the wind, then turns the weather mark (the marker nearest the wind) before going off at an angle to a *wing mark* that is usually on the port side of the triangle. From the wing mark the boats return to the starting mark (the *leeward mark*). A second beat up to the weather mark is followed by a *dead run* (with the wind behind the boats) from the weather mark to the start point before a final beat to the finishing line, laid by the weather mark.

The 6m yachts have their spinnakers out to pick up every breath of wind.

Some fast classes — such as the Tornado catamaran — may have to do two rounds of the triangles. Sailors usually talk of these courses as consisting of *triangles and sausages,* so the standard Olympic course is a triangle, a sausage and a final beat.

The Olympic course: first leg is a beat to windward followed by two reaches, then a beat and a run; finally a beat to the finish.

1 The Course

Small boat sailors get afloat on lakes, rivers, reservoirs, disused gravel pits, estuaries and sheltered sea channels and bays. For the off-shore sailor, the seas of the world are there to be challenged. Of course, certain areas become favourite yachting places because of their sheltered waters or handy facilities. Many of them are associated with the classic contests of sailing. Newport, Rhode Island for the America's Cup; Sydney, Australia for the Southern Cross series; the Solent, England for the Admiral's Cup; Kiel, West Germany for the ever-attractive Kiel week.

The 'Olympic course' is the favourite triangular configuration for all boats racing in open water and is invariably used in the Olympic yachting compe-

2 Equipment

A yachtsman's main need is protection against wet and cold. For the off-shore sailor this will often mean tough, really waterproof *oilies* (they used to be made of oilskin, but these days are invariably of waterproof plastic) with welded seams and adjustable cuffs and hood, over a suit of woolly polar wear.

The dinghy sailor may be content with an old pair of jeans and a warm sweater, but the keener types usually have a lightweight all-in-one suit which keeps out the water and the wind. For winter sailing — and often used on warm days too when crews are on the water for a long time — a wet-suit underneath the outer layer of protection keeps the body warm even after a capsize.

Boots vary according to the type of boat being sailed — heavy ones with lace-up tops for the off-shore yachtsman, light and flexible ones for the dinghy sailor, with ribbing across the instep to prevent chafing from the toe-straps. Dinghy sailors also use buoyancy aids lighter than a life-jacket but able to support a waterlogged sailor after a capsize.

Off-shore sailors often use a safety harness in heavy weather. It consists of a harness around the body with a line that can be attached to a strong part of the yacht so that if a big wave comes over the top or the boat *heels* suddenly, the sailor cannot be swept overboard.

 Winning

In small boat classes, the first over the winning line takes the honours. At the Olympics, the winner is the boat with the best results over six races. Seven races take place but the worst result can be discarded and a points system decides the overall winner.

Dinghies are boats with lifting *centre-boards,* or flat plates of wood or metal that act as a keel. They are all built to class rules which are designed to make racing as close as possible by giving each boat the same potential. Then it is up to the *skipper* (captain) and crew to make the boat go faster or score tactical successes by skilful sailing to victory.

Some boats are *development* classes, where modifications to hull design, boat gear or sails are allowed to encourage ever-faster boats and ever-tougher competition. Other boats are *strict one design* classes where every boat is as nearly identical to the others as possible and only very limited modifications are allowed.

In off-shore boats, most are built to the International Off-Shore Rule (IOR). This is a *rating formula* from which a series of complicated calculations will produce a *rating* for the boat in feet. This is usually fairly close to the length of the boat measured along the water-line. When boats of different sizes are taking part in a race, this rating is used as a handicap figure and computed with the *elapsed time,* the time that a boat has taken to cover the course of a race. From that computation comes the *corrected time* — and the boat with the best corrected time is the winner. In

practice this means that the first yacht home (usually called the boat taking *line honours*) is seldom the actual winner of the race. Indeed, on a long race, such as the 600 mile (975 km approx) Fastnet classic which rounds off the Admiral's Cup series, it is quite possible for a smaller yacht which crosses the line many hours after the leader to emerge as the overall winner.

 Rules

Many rules cover the design of the boats themselves. There are hundreds of different classes of yachts sailing competitively. Some are only sailed in their country of origin; some are totally international and sweep through the sailing world with rocketing popularity. The Laser is the obvious example: though it was first sailed only in the early '70s, the number of these exciting singlehanded dinghies built is fast approaching the astonishing 100,000 mark. Here are the key classes sailing today.

IOR: yachts built to the *International Off-shore Rule.* This can mean any class of off-shore yacht from a *Mini Tonner* with a rating of 16½ ft (5.03 m), up to a *maxi-rater* with a rating of 70 ft (21.33 m) and usually over 80 ft (24.38 m) in length overall. Main performers, such as those in Admiral's Cup, Southern Cross and SORC series are between 35 and 55 ft (10.6-16.76 m) overall, with ratings between 30 and 40 ft (9.14-12.9 m).

Using the trapeze to keep the Tempest upright. A slight error of balance and the crewman will get a soaking and the boat would come to a halt.

SAILING

OOD: Offshore One Design: These are boats all built to one design so that they can race on level terms (no handicap correction).

Ton Cuppers: yachts built to the IOR formula but designed to rate at a specific figure in order to take part in *level rating* events on a boat-for-boat competition basis. Class divisions here are *Two Ton:* (IOR 32 ft); *One Ton* (27½ ft); *Three-Quarter Ton* (24½ ft); *Half Ton* (22 ft); *Quarter Ton* (18½ ft) and *Mini-Ton* (16½ ft).

Twelve Metres: offshore day racing yachts built to the complicated 12m formula which is used for the classic America's Cup competition. Elegant, expensive, very fast, and regarded by some as the cream of racing yachts.

Olympic Classes: 7 boats are used for the Olympic yachting regatta. Smallest is the *Finn* singlehander — a heavy, demanding boat which requires great strength and stamina. It measures 14ft 9in (4.5m) overall and has 108sqft (10sqm) of sail area.

Then comes the *470* two-man dinghy, a small but fast racing boat which uses a *spinnaker* and *trapeze* for the crew. It measures 15ft 5in (4m) and has a sail area of 140sqft (13sqm) plus a 140sqft (13sqm) spinnaker.

The Flying Dutchman is a fast two-man dinghy that measures 19ft 10½ in (6.05m) and has 200sqft (18.58sqm) of sail area, plus a 190 sqft (17.5sqm) spinnaker.

The Tornado is a catamaran and has two hulls. Here, one is in the water as the crew strive to keep the boat balanced.

These three centre-board boats are matched by two keel-boats and a racing catamaran. The two-man *Tornado* catamaran, fastest of all the Olympic classes, measures 20ft (6.1m) overall and has a sail area of 235sqft (21.83sqm). There is no spinnaker. The *Star* two-man keel-boat is the oldest design of all (1911) and measures 22ft 8in (6.92m) with sail area of 280sqft (26.13sqm) (no spinnaker).

Biggest boat of all is the three-man *Soling,* a very fast sloop which is 26ft 9in (8.15m) overall and carries 234sqft (21.7sqm) of sail.

In 1984, the seventh Olympic class, the *Windglider* will be introduced. A 14ft 9in (4.5m) mast stuck on a 12ft (3.6m) glassfibre surfboard, it is cheap and portable with its 59sqft (6.5sqm) sail. Competitors stand up on the 2ft (60cm) wide board and sail the Olympic triangular course. Harness and footstraps are only allowed in slalom and freestyle competitions.

Once the boats are racing, the main rules cover who has right of way going round buoys and markers. Basically, a boat with the wind on the port (left-hand) side must give way to one with the wind on the starboard (right-hand) side. Boats with the wind behind them that can manoeuvre more easily must keep out of the way of other craft.

 Skills

Sailing skills are much more numerous and varied than the untutored spectator might think. Clearly a good sailor must know how to make his boat go as quickly as possible on every point of sailing — that is, no matter from which direction the wind is coming. So when it is a question of sailing into the wind — *beating* — the skipper must be able to sense how close he can sail to the wind, how to adjust for wind shifts, how to sail the close-hauled course without *pinching* and so losing power, and how to use his own and the crew's weight to keep the boat sailing as near upright as possible and thus keep the sails full.

Sailing with the wind on the beam, from behind, he must know how to balance the boat properly, how to use the crew's weight to induce the hull of a dinghy to *rise on the plane* (to skim along the surface), how to set and control a spinnaker for maximum speed and how to balance his other sails to keep the spinnaker drawing at its best.

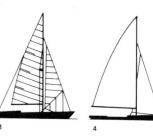

1   2

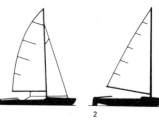

6 Tactics

A good start is essential for success but unlike athletics or motor racing, boats cannot line up at a starting line. They have to be moving so by manoeuvring they try to cross the starting line as soon

The Flying Dutchman is generally accepted as being the fastest two-man dinghy in the world. She has a long, light hull, a trapeze and the largest sail area among conventional dinghies. Teamwork between the helmsman and his crew has to be perfect to win the Olympics.

The start of a race. All these Stars have timed their runs to perfection and are crossing the line together. The start line runs across the picture, from left to right.

as possible after the gun goes off. A good start gives the advantage of sailing into *clean air* — not disturbed by boats ahead. Skippers will practice starts for many hours, timing their sail away from, and up to, the line to the split second, with all sheets hard in and the boat really moving quickly.

In match racing events such as the America's Cup, where there are just two boats and each tries to *cover* the other, the yachts may manoeuvre warily in circles behind the start line for some minutes after the gun. But in fleet racing you will see 20 or 30 boats coming up to the line, all on starboard tack, all battling for that extra ounce of speed.

Then the sailors must choose the correct side of the course to get the best wind or avoid the adverse tidal flow. They must calculate the approach to the next mark to have the tactical advantage of being on starboard tack (with right of way). They cover close rivals to blanket the wind and prevent other boats getting away on a sudden *lift* or gust of wind. Boat handling skills are legion, and sometimes very subtle. It can make all the difference between winning and losing if a split second can be taken off the time it takes to break out a spinnaker or if a trapezing crewman can adjust rapidly to slight changes in wind.

But most of the skill of sailing is having a refined sense of strength and direction of the wind: the man or woman who adjusts most efficiently to the infinite variations of the wind and water is the one who wins yacht races.

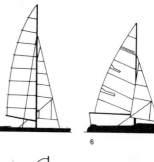

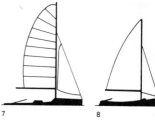

1   *Flying Dutchman*
2   *Finn*
3   *Soling*
4   *Scorpion*
5   *Tornado*
6   *470*
7   *International Canoe*
8   *Cadet*

Sailing

7 Words

Aback: when the wind presses on the wrong side of a sail
About: a boat goes about when her bows pass through the wind
Anemometer: a device to measure wind strength
Athwart: across the boat's width
Backstay: a rope from masthead to stern
Beam reach: sailing with the wind at right angles to the fore-and-aft line of the boat
Bear away: alter course away from the wind or another yacht
Beat: a course which requires the yacht to sail close-hauled and tack

The fastest and most expensive sailing boats to take part in ocean racing. They have specially designed equipment to withstand the wind and waves as they negotiate races of 600 miles or more.

Block: a pulley through which a rope passes over a grooved wheel
Boom: the horizontal spar at the foot of a sail
Burgee: flag flown at the masthead showing club or organisation colours
Centreboard: hinged or sliding moveable keel in small boats which balance boat
Class: type of boat

Cleat: wood or metal T-shaped fitting used for securing rope
Close-hauled: a boat is close-hauled when her sails are sheeted in tight and she is sailing as close to the wind as possible
Ease: slacken a rope
Fetch: a sailing course which does not require a yacht to tack
Genoa: a large triangular foresail
Goosewinged: said of a boat sailing before the wind with sail set on both sides
Gybe: to bring the wind through the stern so that the boom swings to the other side
Halyard: rope or wire for hoisting sails
Harden in: to haul in sails
Headsail: sail set forward of the mast
Helmsman: the man at the tiller or wheel
Knot: one nautical mile per hour (equals 1.852 kmph)
Leeward: side of a boat furthest away from the wind
Mainsail: the sail aft of the mast
Mizzen (mast): the after mast of a yawl or ketch
Painter: rope attached to the bow of a dinghy by which she may be secured
Port tack: a boat is on port tack when the wind is blowing on her left side
Quarter: the after-part of the side of a vessel
Reef: to reduce sail area
Run: to sail before the wind — also called sailing downwind
Shake out: to free a reef from a sail
Sheet: a rope used to trim a sail
Shroud: a wire rope used to support the mast
Skipper: captain, sailor that controls boat
Spinnaker: a full-bellied triangular sail set when reaching or running to take advantage of good wind
Spreaders: or crosstrees — spars extending from the mast to spread the rigging for greater support
Starboard tack: a boat is on starboard tack when the wind is blowing on her right side
Stay: a wire rope giving fore and aft support to the mast
Tack: to beat to windward on a zig-zag course
Tiller: a bar from the rudder which the helmsman uses to turn the rudder
Trapeze: where a crewman wears a harness attached to a wire and hangs over the side of the boat to try to balance it
Waterline: where the surface of the water and the boat's hull meet
Windward: the side of the boat against which the wind blows. ■

Of all sports, shooting undoubtedly makes the most stringent technical demands, without neglecting the importance of good physical form and strength. Every competitor displays the qualities of endurance, precision, plus *skill at arms* as well as the *killer instinct* required by all sportsmen engaging in top level competition. Modern shooting, alongside many other sports, may be regarded as *art without malice*.

The gun, of course, has developed in many different forms, ranging from the hand pistol (traditional duelling device) to the large shot gun (traditional *game hunting* device). Each was designed with particular qualities and for a particular purpose; and there is a competition that tests the use of each weapon.

Few can visualize the finesse, steady nerves and extraordinary muscle control required to hold a gun at arm's length and score a *bull's-eye* from a distance half the length of a football field, especially when the centre of the target *(bull)* is the size of a small coin. The slightest distraction, the smallest amount of fatigue, or nervousness, could cause the competitor to miss the target completely.

1 The Target

In all but the shotgun competition, a target of varying sizes is used that has a bull's-eye at the centre and a number of circles around it. Each circle or ring is allocated a different number of points: hitting the bull's-eye scores the maximum number of points; hitting the outer ring scores the minimum number of points. However in some events the target is only exposed for a few seconds at a time and sometimes the target itself moves.

2 Equipment

Apart from the gun itself, the equipment used by each competitor may vary greatly. Quite often, competitors wear peaked hats, to shade them from the light, and some employ goggles or an eye-patch to blank out the eye that is not being used to sight on the target. In rifle shooting padding is often used on the elbows of the jacket, the

thickness and position of which is strictly governed by the rules; a telescope may be used by a competitor to see where he hit the target, so that any corrections can be made.

3 Winning

Quite simply, the only sure way of winning is to hit the bull's-eye every time a shot is fired, no matter what type of gun is used, and no matter what the target. But each event has its own individual competition requirements and its own system of scoring.

4 Rules

The majority of rules in shooting are concerned with the safety of both competitor and spectator (e.g. the gun may only be pointed and fired in a certain direction). Other rules determine the number of shots that are allocated, the time allowed for each individual shot or each series of shots and the way in which a score is awarded. Generally, if a hole on the target cuts through one of the lines surrounding the bull's-eye, then the higher score will count. Special gauges are used to judge this.

Rapid Fire Pistol
Only a standard .22in calibre pistol, using special low velocity ammunition can be used. The international target is divided into 10 scoring zones and has a

diameter of 500mm (20in approx). Five targets are set up .75m (30in approx) apart, 25m (27yd approx) from the shooting position. The targets are sideways on, but mounted on pivots and are turned simultaneously to *face* the

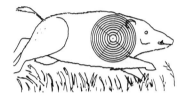

Top: running boar target
Above: rapid fire pistol target

The shooter about to fire in the standing position. He is not allowed to use a sling, but a thick glove is permitted to help support the rifle.

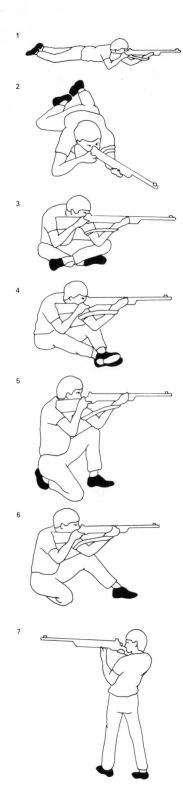

competitors for a few seconds at a time.

The competition consists of 60 shots. Firing is divided into two parts of 30 shots each. Each part is sub-divided into six series of five shots each; two series in which the targets are exposed for eight seconds for each shot, two series at six seconds and two in four seconds. Competition lasts about 2½ hours.

To sum up, in each series of five shots the competitor is faced with five targets that will turn to be exposed for only a certain number of seconds. During this short time a shot must be fired at each target, before they turn away again. The total number of points is calculated from the 60 shots of the competition and the highest number overall wins.

Free Pistol
This is similar to rapid fire, but the targets do not turn away from the competitor so there is no time limit, other than 2½ hours for the full course. This, again, is of 60 shots which are fired, but at a distance of 50m (164ft approx) from the target. The competition consists of six series of 10 shots each. A .22in free pistol is used with no restrictions on weight, barrel length or trigger. The grip may be specially moulded to the competitor's hand but cannot support the wrist. No optical sights are permitted and the standard 10 ring target is used.

Running Game Target
This is the modern version of boar hunting. The weapon used is a standard .22in rifle weighing less than 5kg (11lb approx) and with a trigger that requires at least 0.5kg (1.1lb approx) to operate. Any type of sight, including telescopic, is permitted.

The running game competition is conducted at a distance of 50m (55yd approx) with the target moving at a constant speed across an opening 10m (11yd approx) wide. The target is in the shape of a boar with a round bull's eye and scoring rings, counting from 1 to 10 points, superimposed on it. The 10-point ring (bull's-eye) has a diameter of 60mm (24in approx).

The target will move across the opening when the competitor is ready to fire. Two speeds are used. For the first, or *slow* run, the target takes five seconds to cross the gap; for the second, or *fast* run, the target takes only 2½ seconds. The competition consists of three 10--shot series at the slow run target and a further three 10-shot series at the fast run target, a total of 60 shots. Points are

awarded for each shot, depending on what part of the target is hit. The highest number of points wins the competition.

Small Bore Rifle, 3-Position
The small bore rifle is a standard .22in rifle and is classified as *free*. The competitor must shoot from three different positions: standing, kneeling and prone. A *palm rest* for the hand can be attached underneath the barrel of the rifle to help support it when in the standing position. Another device can be attached to the butt of the rifle so that it hooks underneath the armpit and a sling can be hooked onto the competitor's jacket for extra stability.

A standard international target is set 50m (154ft approx) from the shooting position and the competition is made up of four series of 10 shots in each position for a total of 120 shots.

Small Bore Rifle — English Match
Using a standard .22in small bore rifle, 60 shots are fired at a standard 10-ring target over a distance of 50m with the competitor in the *prone position* (lying chest downwards) throughout. The competition consists of 60 shots fired in six series of 10 shots each. Only one shot is fired at each target and points are awarded for each shot with the highest score overall winning.

Clay Pigeon Shooting
Live pigeons were used to practise the new sport of shooting in the 18th century. The birds were released from boxes or *traps* but by the turn of the century clay targets, looking like large ash trays, were replacing birds. These were hurled into the air by mechanical springs. However words like *bird* (for the target), a *kill* for a successful hit, and *lost* for a miss have been retained.

The idea of a modern competition is to test the marksman by hurling the clay pigeon up in the air at different heights and angles. In *down-the-line* shooting, the clays are projected from a *traphouse* about 15m (16yd) in front of the marksman. The clay flies away from the shooter, who fires from each of five positions.

At international and Olympic level, down-the-line is superseded by the more complex *Olympic Trap*, previously known as *Olympic Trench* because the traps are set below ground level, in a trench, in five groups of three.

Six competitors take part at any one time, but one rests while the other five shoot. A shooter stands at each position (station). Each in turn calls 'Pull!' or

Firing positions: 1 and 2 prone; 3 cross-legged sitting; 4 open-leg sitting; 5 and 6 high and low kneeling; 7 international standing

even just grunts which is enough to release a target with the microphone-activated system! The target could be thrown by any one of the three traps in front of each station. After each shot the competitors move one position to the right.

Twelve-bore shotguns fire shells containing a charge of lead shot. The saucer-shaped clay target measures 11cm (4in approx) in diameter and is 2.5cm (1in approx) thick. Two shots may be fired at each target and a *hit* is scored if the target is broken while in flight. Competitors often discharge both barrels to make sure the clay is shattered. A *round* (series) consists of 25 targets per competitor, five from each of the shooting positions. International competition consists of eight rounds of 25 for a total of 200. Competitions normally take place over three days, shooting 75, 75 and 50.

Skeet Shooting

Skeet shooting developed in the USA although *skeet* comes from a Scandinavian word meaning 'to shoot'. Originally the idea was to have a more complicated form of clay pigeon shooting based on a huge circle like a clockface with competitors shooting from the twelve points of the clock. Eventually they settled down to using just the lower half of the clockface. The clay pigeons are released from the *high house* (on the left, at 'nine-o'clock') and from the *low house* (on the right at 'three o'clock'). The shooters move counter-clockwise, their skills being tested as the directions, angles and heights vary from station to station.

The competitors shoot in *squads* of six starting on the left side of the field at Station 1. Each shooter in turn fires at a single target from the left traphouse (high house), and then at two targets thrown simultaneously (a *double*) from each traphouse. When the squad has completed Station 1, the shooters move on in sequence. At Stations 2 and 3 they have one *high* and one *low* target, then a double; at Station 4, just a *single* from the high and the low; at Stations 5 and 6, one high, one low and a double; at Station 7 a double and the shooters finish at Station 8 with a single from the high and low houses to make a total of 25.

International rules insist that the gun is lowered, with the stock touching the shooter's waistline, until the target appears.

The competition is made up of eight rounds of 25 shots, a total of 200, spaced over three days, shooting 75, 75 and 50.

5 & 6 Skills & Tactics

Because shooting is a highly technical and controlled activity there are no tactics which can be used during a competition. Electronic scoreboards are kept up to date throughout the competition, but it is easy to gauge someone's performance by looking at the target. In the shotgun events it is easy to see a good shot because the clay target will shatter when hit. In all the others, the target will clearly show where the bullet had entered and, at the end of a series of shots, a *wand* or pointer is used by the judges to indicate the position and number of points each shot has scored. In the case of the running boar target, a clock face will be displayed, and where the hand is on the clock will indicate the position at which the bullet hit the target (e.g. score of three equals a hit on the 3-point ring; hand on six means a bullet hit at six o'clock position in that ring). Generally a good competitor will have very little *wobble* (movement) while the gun is being aimed, and he will endeavour to *group* all of his shots together — hopefully in the bull's-eye!

7 Words

Birds: the targets in clay pigeon shooting
Bull: bull's-eye, the centre of a target
Clays: targets, birds — short for *clay pigeons*
Double rise: two targets thrown in the air at once
Offs: 'how many offs did you have?' How many points did you drop by not hitting the bull?
Possible: the highest possible score, hitting all the bull's-eyes
Puller, pusher: the man who activates the traps; he used to *pull* a lever, now he *pushes* a button!
Round: a series of 25 targets — a *round of skeet;* also a round (one) of ammunition in .22 shooting
Straight: 'He's gone straight', he's hit 25 consecutive targets
Traps: the machines that hurl out the targets
Zero: a miss, 'How many zeros did you get?' ■

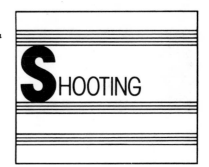
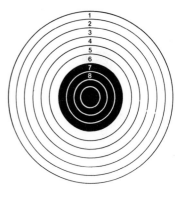

An air pistol target

Skeet shooting

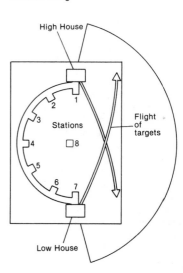

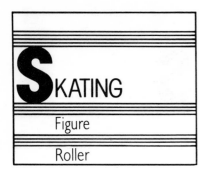

SKATING

Figure

Roller

Figure skate with serrated toe-pick

Roller Skate

ROLLER SKATING is experiencing a boom around the world thanks to better skates and disco-dancing. It has the same disciplines as ice skating but there are subtle differences. For one thing, the skates themselves have different characteristics. While the ice skater has to have strong ankle support, the roller skater stands, in effect, on a platform that moves easily, so less effort is needed to build up speed. The jumps, however, require more work to lift the 3 kg (7 lb) skate into the air. The ball and heel of the foot are used to steer the skate in a wriggling motion and it is harder to spin on the edges of the wheels than on an ice skate.

The grace, beauty and precision provided by ice skaters as they jump, spin and glide in time to a wide variety of music makes compulsive televiewing for countless armchair fans, many of whom thoroughly enjoy what they see with little knowledge of the rules or technicalities.

But the majority of spectators, whether at home or at the rink, watch only half or two-thirds of the contest. It must be a unique feature of figure skating as a sport that only a handful bothers to observe the first third of the competition. Yet the preceding *compulsory figures,* tedious and monotonous to all but the avid connoisseur, command 30 per cent of the competitor's total points.

1 The Rink

The usual area for international competitions is 60 by 30m (200 by 100ft approx) of flat ice. Competitors are expected to use the whole of the rink during their performances.

2 Equipment

Unlike the skate used for speed skating or ice hockey, the figure skate has *teeth* at the front end of the blade, which are known as a *toe-rake* or *toe-pick*. This is important in spins and jumps. The blade itself is about 3mm (⅛in) wide and fractionally longer than the boot to which it is screwed, with a hollow groove along its underside which forms two edges. This is important because most movements have to be performed on an *inside* or *outside* edge.

3 & 4 Winning & Rules

A world or Olympic championship meeting in FIGURE SKATING is made up of four events. These are: men's and women's singles; pair skating; and ice dancing. Unlike a racing sport, where the outcome is determined by the clock, the result of a figure skating competition depends on the opinions of a panel of nine judges, each from a different country.

The championship for solo performers is divided into three sections — the *figures,* followed by two sessions of *free* skating. In the first, *compulsory figures,* each skater has to trace on the ice three specific shapes or figures, the three having been chosen by a draw the night before from an international schedule of figures.

Each is composed of a prescribed pattern in the form of either a two-lobe or three-lobe figure of eight. The skater starts from a stationary position and leaves a clearly visible tracing on the ice which is repeated twice. The judges award marks based not only on the accuracy of the *tracings,* but on the way in which they are performed. They take into account the skater's degree of control, style and posture, also the neatness of turns and changes from one foot to the other. Using decimal tenths, each judge marks out of six for each figure and their aggregates are adjusted so that this section makes up 30 per cent of the total marks to be given.

The second section of the contest is the *free skating short programme.* For this, each competitor is allowed two minutes to perform seven obligatory movements (specified jumps, spins, spirals and so on) to music of his or her choice.

A fault in any of these elements is penalized in two sets of marks, each out of six; one for technical merit and the other for presentation. These marks for the short programme are worth 20 per cent of the overall total.

The third section is the one which generates the widest interest, the *final* (or *long*) free skating programme. In this, the skaters are free to devise performances to show off their best moves, in whatever order they choose and to whatever music they like. This performance lasts five minutes for men and four for women. Again, there are two sets of marks, separately assessing technical merit and artistic presentation, and these amount to half those awarded for the whole event. The judges consider the variety of moves, their degree of difficulty and their execution.

The pair skating championships are much simpler to follow because there are only two sections, the short and long free skating programmes. As in the singles, for the short programme each pair has to link specific moves (six in all) within a two-minute time limit. Their skill in performing them is worth a quarter of their total marks.

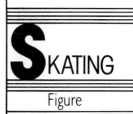

In recent years the freeskating part of the figure skating programme has become more artistic as competitors not only move with the music but also try to interpret it.

The long free skating for pairs allows five minutes for each performance, but the basic difference is that the programme comprises specialities like lifts, spins and spirals which obviously require two people. These pair special-ities are interlinked with synchronized solo movements while skating apart, known as *shadow skating,* the whole being assessed for harmonious unison of movement as well as style and degree of technical difficulty. There are separate sets of marks for technical merit and artistic impression.

Pair skating demands good teamwork and understanding as well as antici-pation and split-second timing.

ICE DANCING is an off-shoot of figure skating, but the layman may be confused about the real difference between them. Pair skating depends more on strength and athleticism, with spectacular lifts. Ice dancing must *look* like dancing on ice and any moves that look more like pair skating are marked down by the judges.

Ice dance championships comprise three sections. In part one, there are three *compulsory dances* such as the Viennese Waltz, Yankee Polka and the Blues. The middle section of a championship is called the *set pattern dance.* While the sort of dance is chosen months in advance, so that couples can practise, they can pick their own music.

The judges award one set of marks for each of the three compulsory dances, worth 30 per cent of the total, and two sets for the set pattern dance (compos-ition and presentation), worth another 20 per cent. The remaining 50 per cent is given for the final section, *free dancing.* For this, each couple devises its own four-minute programme to music of their choice. They may include

several different dances and changes of tempo. As usual, two sets of marks are awarded, for technical merit and artistic impression.

5 & 6 Skills & Tactics

Top skaters are as at home on skates as most people are on land. They can skate backwards and forwards, sideways and in curves. Some moves are more im-pressive executed at speed, others quite slowly and gracefully. What are more difficult are the *spins,* which must be done on the spot, without *travelling.* The spin should look effortless. The *sit-*

In pairs, the death spiral is one of the many spectacular moves executed by couples. The woman often ends up with frost on her hair as she sweeps low over the ice.

SKATING

Figure

Halfway through an upright spin, the competitor must still have complete control over hand, arm and head movements and must spin on the spot, without travelling.

Apart from obvious moves such as spins and jumps, skaters are expected to use different edges of their skateblades. These 8 edges are abbreviated as follows: LFO, LFI; LBO, LBI; RFO, RFI; RBO and RBI. The L and R refer to the left or right foot; the F and B mean forwards or backwards and the I and O, inner and outer. Each skater glides over the ice in a curve with the weight on the inside or outside of the foot, travelling forwards or backwards. To accentuate this, the skate blade is hollow ground to give an inside and outside edge.

spin where the skater starts upright then sinks slowly spinning on one leg is a tremendous test of strength and control. The jumps are another feature of skating. Height is important, using a proper take-off and a *clean* faultless landing with no wobbling. Top skaters can rotate either clockwise or counter-clockwise in midair and then land going forwards or backwards. At no time should there be any obvious signs of effort or strain.

Once a skater has mastered every technique, the fine improvements come from the position of the head, the carriage and movement of the body and the way the hands are held. It is the only sport where men as well as women are judged on artistic interpretation. Working with music, the skater's grace and balance must always conceal the all-round physical attributes of strength and suppleness.

7 Words

Arabesque: long sustained gliding edge with body stretched forward and free leg raised high
Axel: jump from outside forward edge, with one-and-a-half midair rotations, landing on back outside edge of opposite blade
Bracket: half-turn from one edge to the opposite edge of the same blade

Salchow Jump

Lutz Jump

Toe Loop

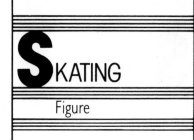
Broken leg spin: sit spin with free leg extended to side or behind

Camel: spin in arabesque position

Chasse: three-step dance sequence without disengaged skate passing the other

Cherry flip: another name for toe loop jump

Choctaw: dance turn wherein blades and direction are changed simultaneously to opposite edges

Counter: half-turn, entering like a bracket, exiting like a three, maintaining the same edge

Cross-foot: spin executed on flat of both blades, with legs crossed, toes together

Crossover: a stroke where the free foot crosses in front of the skating foot

Death spiral: pair skating move, with man acting as a pivot while girl rotates around him

Double jump: any jump with an extra midair rotation

Flip jump: same as toe salchow jump

Flying camel: jump variation of a camel spin

Flying sit spin: a long loop jump landing into a sit spin

Lasso lift: pair move involving side-by-side, hand-to-hand position from which girl is lifted overhead to rotate one-and-a-half times while man's arm is outstretched in lassoing pose

Layback: one foot spin with torso bent backwards

Layover: one foot spin with torso bent sideways

Loop: figure in which a circle is inscribed within another on a continuous edge, with no break

Loop jump: take-off from outside back edge, rotating once before landing on outside back edge of same blade

Lutz jump: counterwise jump from a fast back outside edge of one blade, using the other toe as lever to achieve a reverse midair rotation, landing on back outside edge of opposite blade

Mohawk: dance half-turn when skates and direction change simultaneously to opposite edges

Overhead axel: pair lift begun from girl's forward outside edge, from which girl is rotated one-and-a-half times above partner's head, his arm supporting her armpit, landing on back outside edge of girl's opposite blade to the one from which she began

Parallel spin: executed on flat of the blade, with upper body and non-skating leg parallel to the ice (also called camel spin).

Rocker: one-foot turn, reversing direction with no change of edge

Salchow: jump executed from inside back edge of one blade, rotating once before landing on outside back edge of opposite blade

Sit spin: executed with the free leg extended forward and the skating leg well bent, with body crouched over the skating knee

Spiral: any gliding movement with body in sustained pose

Split jump: in which the skater achieves a splits position

Split lutz lift: pair move achieved from backward side-by-side position, beginning and ending on a girl's back outside edge

Spreadeagle: heel to heel and in line

Three: one-foot turn involving change of edge

Throw axel: spectacular pair move achieved by the man throwing the girl through the air from the force of his axel jump, his partner landing on a true edge

Toe jump: any jump attained by assistance from the saw-teethed point of the blade

Triple-lobed figure: compulsory figure where skater turns and rotates in order to come out of turn on the same edge but in a different direction

Triple jump: any jump with two extra midair rotations

Twist lift: pair move involving one or more midair rotations by the girl while descending to land on a true edge

Twizzle: one-foot dance turn involving a full 180 degrees rotation of the blade,

almost on one spot

Walley jump: the only major counter clockwise jump apart from the lutz, begun from a backward inside edge and landed on the backward outside edge of the same blade. ∎

Couples must always achieve perfect balance and line, moving as one.

SKATING

Speed

Rounding a curve, the skater keeps just one arm behind his back and swings the other to help balance himself.

Watching a long distance speed skater at full stretch can give an impression that he is travelling much slower than in reality. This is because his graceful movement, even when racing all out, is based on an energy-conserving style with maximum wind assistance. Surely no racer in any other sport can look so elegant in action, yet speed skaters are the fastest self-propelled humans over level terrain.

Speeds faster than 48 kmph (30mph) have been achieved by sprinters, who can cover a kilometre or mile about a minute quicker than a track athlete.

A men's world or European championship, now usually a two-day meeting held at the weekend, comprises events over four distances, two each day. In order, the distances covered are 500, 5000, 1500 and 10,000m. The women's championships are normally held at separate venues, the only basic difference being their distances — 500, 1500, 1000 and 3000m. In each case, the best overall performer in the four events, calculated on a points basis, becomes champion. The times are divided in such a way as to bring every race down to 500m, i.e., the 5000m time is divided by 10, and so on. Then, by a simple addition of the points arrived at over each distance, the overall winner is the competitor with the lowest total points. Individual distance winners do not win separate titles, which is peculiar to this sport, which does not differentiate between sprint and long distance specialists. However, world sprint championship meetings are held, with men's and women's titles won by the best overall performances over 500 and 1000m events.

Olympic events are contested over the four distances for women, and five for men, with the addition of an event over 1000m. Unlike the world championships, no overall title is recognized in the Winter Olympics, medals being awarded for each distance. So, there are five men's and four women's Olympic gold medallists.

1 The Ice

At its best this has to be an outdoor sport because the internationally accepted oval circuits of 400m, even when artificially frozen, cover too vast an area to house under a roof.

Major events today are held on mechanically frozen open-air circuits which, although increasing steadily in number, are still not numerous, and this means that training opportunities for some competitors are very restricted. The majority of speed ovals are in Scandinavia, Holland and other parts of northern Europe. There are only three in North America. Not surprisingly, the best racers tend in the main to be Dutch, Norwegian, Russian and American.

In Norway and Holland, the numbers of supporters thronging the rinksides are comparable to the size of football crowds elsewhere. The scene is made more colourful and exciting at international events by the presence of usually very good-humoured and well-informed Dutch and Scandinavian fans, who travel abroad in large groups wearing rosettes and coloured hats and scarves, and armed with cow bells, motor horns and sometimes even kites. They certainly contribute to the atmosphere and spur on their compatriots in no uncertain manner.

2 Equipment

The steel speed-skate blades are appreciably longer than those used for figure skating, usually between 30 and 45cm (12 and 18in) and also much thinner, something like 0.8mm (1/32in). The blades are straight, whereas those used by figure skaters are slightly curved. The thin leather shoes have lower heel supports and are lighter in weight than figure boots. Close-fitting tights, sweater and protective woollen headgear add to the racer's streamlined appearance. A red or blue armband is worn to distinguish competitors, who tend to look alike in their tight-fitting clothing.

3 Winning

Time was when everyone raced in a bunch, with first past the post the winner, which might have been reasonable on huge expanses of natural ice on which most, if not all, of the distances could be straight. Pack-style racing stayed in vogue longer in the United States than elsewhere, but nowadays the time of each competitor decides the winner and entrants are drawn to race in pairs and in separate lanes.

4 Rules

Each of the pair of racers is obliged to stay in his own marked lane, except when changing from inside to outside lane (or vice versa) within a stipulated length once each time round the circuit. It is the responsibility of the skater moving out from the inner lane to avoid a collision or baulking his opponent. A racer deemed to have been baulked through no fault of his own may afterwards be allowed a re-run, in which case the better of his two times would count. Skating in the wrong lane would mean disqualification and, as in athletics, after a third false start, the offender is eliminated.

5 Skills

The speed skater's technique is based very much on energy-conserving styles over the longer distances, the skater often racing along much of the straight with both hands clasped behind his back. But his long, measured strides are eating up a remarkable distance while he appears to be making little effort. His stride may exceed 10m (32ft) and the lazier he looks, the better he is probably performing.

The long, smoothly gliding stroke is begun on the outside edge of the blade, which rolls to the inside edge as the stride is completed. An impressive

body-roll action results. The body *relaxes* over the thigh of the skating leg. The more direct the line a racer skates along the straight, without undue straying from side to side, the better is his style and the faster his likely time.

As the bend approaches, the racer eases into a different style, leaning in to the left (they race anti-clockwise) and bringing the right arm into play with a rhythmic pendulum swing, bending more forward from the waist in a downhill skier's *vorlage* posture.

6 Tactics

A trend to specialize has prompted a keen controversy about the wisdom of a policy encouraging racers to enter all events, but some outstanding all-rounders capable of winning over the shortest and longest distances (the latter twenty times as far as the former) have maintained fascination and admiration for the elite few capable of achieving this distinction.

Nearly all world records are now attained on rinks at mountain resorts at altitudes above 500m. This is because the air is thinner and the ice purer and faster.

Another form of speed skating, known as *short track racing,* is that which is performed on indoor rinks. Essentially different styles and techniques have developed in this because of the much shorter lap of 110m. International short track championships are held over distances of 500, 1000, 1500 and 3000m. Only recently has the International Skating Union approved standardized rules for these events, enabling indoor title holders and records to be recognized.

7 Words

Armband: worn to identify skaters who tend to look alike in their skin-tight suits. The skater starting in the outside lane wears a red armband, the skater on the inside, white
Crossing line: where the skaters have to change lanes on the back straight
Pre-start line: a mark 75cm behind the starting line where skaters must stand still before the start
Stroke: the long, rhythmic skaters' stride. ■

S KATING
Speed

To cut down the wind resistance the skater keeps his arms behind his back, and leans forward.

Skiing

Alpine

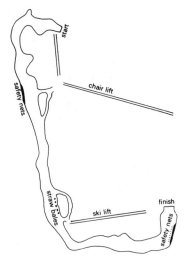

A typical downhill course. Because of the high speeds achieved, the course has to be wide, and has safety nets and straw bales to protect skiers and spectators alike. The course drops some 800m as competitors cover about 4000m.

Hurtling down prepared courses on skis in the snow, one competitor at a time against the clock — that is the essence of alpine ski racing. Now practised in more than 40 countries, the sport derives its name from its origins in alpine countries, where the steep slopes offer ideal terrain.

Championships comprise three events — *downhill, slalom* and *giant slalom* — with titles awarded for each and a fourth for the best overall performer in the three, known as the *combined* or *alpine combination title* and calculated on a points basis.

1 The Course

International downhill courses are the most demanding and challenging, requiring more courage than the slalom. With no particularly sharp bends, the track is selected to test skiing at speed over varying gradients, bumps and gullies. Its length can vary between 3500 and 4500m (2 and 3 miles approx) for men and between 1500 and 2500m (1 and 1½ miles approx) for women, according to local conditions. It is calculated to produce a best time of around two minutes for men and a little less than that over the shorter women's course.

The vertical drop may fluctuate between 750 and 900m (2500 and 3000ft approx). Wide gates, pairs of poles with flags not less than 8m (26ft approx) apart, are positioned to keep the skier within bounds and away from dangerous obstacles. Average speeds have exceeded 100kmph (60mph approx). Competitors must practise on the course the day before the event, to familiarize themselves with its characteristics in the interests of safety.

Whereas the downhill is primarily a display of speed and daring, the slalom is devised to test control in turns. Slalom courses are appreciably shorter than those for downhill and the gates in this event play a more vital role. They can be as narrow as 3m (10ft approx) and are shrewdly placed at contrasting angles to test quick judgement, fluency of movement and skill in pace-checking and turning.

Gatekeepers are positioned beside each gate to check whether a racer passes correctly between the poles. Any who do not must climb back to do so or face disqualification. International courses for men have between 50 and 75 gates and a vertical drop between 200 and 300m (650 and 975ft approx). Women's courses are shorter and usually less steep.

The giant slalom is something of a compromise between slalom and downhill, blending the characteristics of both. The course is longer than the slalom, with wider gates set farther apart. The course conditions are, more often than not, better for the early starters in a race. The run deteriorates as the event progresses, at a rate depending on snow conditions. With this fact very much in mind, the best racers are given the best opportunities by being allowed to race first, an established tradition which is sometimes challenged by the argument that all competitors should be given equal chances.

Parallel slalom or *dual slalom* is a newer, separate event of alpine ski racing which does not form part of the conventional championships but which is included in at least one meeting of the World Cup series.

On two adjacent courses of as similar length and character as the terrain will allow, racers start simultaneously — one on each course — and the first past his finish line wins the first round. The skiers then change runs and come down again. Knock-out competitions leading to a final can be easily arranged.

By dividing the TV screen into two pictures, the viewer is able to watch both racers at the same time and gets a different sense of racing thrill to that derived from watching racers clocked one at a time.

2 Equipment

The trend to specialize has escalated in recent seasons, so equipment has been specialized too. Whereas the early racers used to wear a similar pair of skis for all three events, they now have different ones for each. They also have a staggering choice of boots and safety toe-release and heel-release gadgets. Intense rivalry between different manufacturers, each bidding to persuade the stars to use and thus popularize their products, has sparked off revolutionary progress in high-precision equipment.

Wooden and metal skis have given way to fibre-reinforced plastic, the result of much scientific research.

Shorter lengths of ski are gaining preference. Sophisticated plastic boots have superseded leather and clip fastenings have replaced laces. The shafts of ski sticks (poles) are of lightweight tubular metals rather than the once-fashionable bamboo. Stretch trousers and anoraks have been discarded in favour of close-fitting cat suits which reduce wind resistance.

A wide variety of ski waxes, applied to the ski soles to aid speed and control according to the snow conditions, is a crucial accessory for the star performer. Equipment is completed by gloves, a protective helmet, and goggles with adjustable ventilation.

A downhill ski is usually wider and longer than the slalom ski. Fractionally longer than its wearer's height, it needs to be extra stable and durable, stiffer near the tail and more flexible at the tip, in order to negotiate bumps more easily at fast speeds. With theses qualities, however, it is less manoeuvrable in turns.

The slalom ski is designed mainly with easier turning in mind. It is shorter, with a stiffer tail, but is less controllable for fast, straight running.

The giant slalom ski needs to be suited equally for turning and speed and therefore incorporates some of the extreme characteristics of the other two It is more of an all-purpose ski and more like the one the recreational skier uses.

3 Winning

The downhill event is won by the competitor who legally completes the course in the fastest time.

Slalom events comprise two runs on different tracks, the fastest aggregate time deciding the winner. Competitors are not allowed to practise on the course, so must memorize the gate positions while ascending to the start point. The slalom demands less courage than the downhill and tends to suit a calmer temperament.

4 Rules

Apart from those governing the proper course that should be followed, the rules are straightforward. A competitor in any alpine event is naturally elimi-

nated if both skis come off, but a racer losing only one is not disqualified if able to finish the course on the remaining ski, though the time would be so much slower than the rest of the field that there would be little point in taking the risk.

It is usually an advantage to ski early on in a competition, but racers have to earn their right to ski early in an event and this is done by grading the competitors in groups of 15 or so, the first group comprising those with the best records in previous races. In events with two runs, the same order of groups is retained for the second run, but chance is evened out within each group by reversing the order in the group.

For the purpose of establishing an order of merit for starting in major events, the International Ski Federation, popularly called FIS (the initials of the French translation, Fédération Internationale de Ski), has devised a system of FIS points which top-placed racers earn at stipulated international meetings according to the position in which they finish. The number of FIS points a racer collects determines his qualification to enter an international event as well as the group in which he starts. The *lower* the number of points the better, like a golf handicap.

One advantage of this scheme is that the quest to improve their points rating provides a constant incentive for racers to do their level best every time they perform, even when they know they cannot make the first three.

Downhill skiers rely on flat out speed, balancing perilously on the edges of their skis at times.

SKIING

Alpine

There are three types of freestyle or creative skiing involving ballet, skiing over moguls and doing tricks in mid-air off a jump. Ballet incorporates the skills of skating and gymnastics, while off the jump it's like diving — with skis on! Music usually accompanies performances.

5 & 6 Skills & Tactics

The downhiller is the fastest-travelling ski racer and, the quicker he goes, the more pronounced is the crouch in the *egg position,* with the weight thrown back so that the skis are almost planing. An icy surface will encourage pace, but softer, powdery snow will make the going slower and cause the skier to straighten his posture to transfer extra body weight to the rear of the skis. The emphasis is always on transfer of weight to the side for turning, but with prudent economy of upper body action to minimize wind resistance.

The slalom technique, perfected notably by the Austrians, Swiss and French, accentuates a hip-swinging, *tail-wagging* style which, when accompanied by a pronounced forward lean during the faster sections of the run, is a spectacle to enjoy as gate after gate is negotiated with an artistry which looks more graceful the better the slalomer performs.

Also promising to make increasing impact on television is *freestyle* or *creative skiing,* an offshoot from, rather than an official part of, alpine racing. Now a competitive sport in its own right, freestyle skiing is a highly specialized, fast-rising form of spectacular acrobatic and balletic skiing which, while still in its infancy, has made more rapid headway in North America than in Europe.

Some of the somersaulting involved is incredible. Achievements which few would have believed to be humanly possible a few years ago are performed with much style and grace in this mainly professional branch of the sport.

Giant slalom course

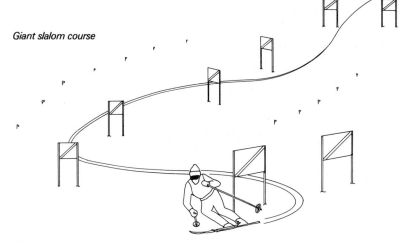

7 Words

Basket (Ring of Wheel): circular attachment near the point of a ski pole to prevent its excessive penetration into the snow
Camber: the arch of the ski from tip to tail
Christie (or Christiania): a medium-to-fast swing turn with skis parallel
Edging: tilting the skis so that the edges dig into the snow to gain a firm grip
Egg position: a crouching, compact stance for downhill, with elbows and hands tucked well in to lower wind resistance
Fall-line: direction of steepest descent
Gate: two poles with flags in matching colours between which racers must pass
Hairpin: a sharp turn in a slalom course forced by two gates in close proximity
Herringboning: method of climbing with tips of skis turned outwards, leaving a fishbone pattern in the snow
Mogul: a pronounced bump in the course created by constant use
Piste: a prepared downhill trail made firm by pressure of many feet or by machines
Pre-jumping: a technique used to clear bumps of sudden changes in gradient
Safety bindings: accident-prevention devices which automatically release the foot from the ski when falling
Schuss: a straight downhill run at speed without turning
Schussboomer: a racer who skis out of control
Seelos: a special series of three slalom gates, with the middle gate at right angles to the other two
Shovel: the upturn of the forward tip of the ski
Sideslipping: method of controlled sideways or diagonal sliding by raising the ski edges
Sidestepping: climbing sideways with skis parallel
Sitzmark: depression in the snow made by a skier when falling
Stemming: pushing out the heel of one or both skis to achieve an angle to the direction of movement
Stem-christie: turn initiated by stemming and ended by a christie
Swing: a high-speed turn with skis parallel
Vorlage: a pronounced forward lean with weight of the body well over the balls of the feet
Wedeln (or *Godille*): technique involving rhythmic succession of linked, hip-swinging turns. ■

This form of skiing developed in Scandinavia. Thus the sport is known as *Nordic skiing* as opposed to the downhill racing version which is called Alpine skiing. The name has grown to incorporate *cross-country skiing, biathlon* and *ski jumping*.

Cross-country skiing, also known as *Nordic racing* or *langlauf,* is really just walking on skis across undulating terrain or relatively low gradients.

As the cross-country competitor picks up one ski he is sliding along on the other. Note how the heel is free on the very light, long ski.

Dedicated training and peak fitness are vital for this rigorous sport, which relatively few women outside northern Europe even attempt, though female participants from North American and southern European nations are now more numerous than a decade ago.

Of course, there is a great difference in physical demands between Nordic skiing for pleasure, which Scandi-navians proclaim to be as simple as walking, and racing against the clock.

1 The Course

Men's championship races are contested over distances of 15, 30 and 50km (9, 18 and 31 miles approx). Women's races are over 5 and 10km (3 and 6 miles approx). There are also relay races — comprising four 10km legs for men and four 5km legs for women.

2 Equipment

The equipment is essentially different to that used for the Alpine style. The skis are longer, narrower and much lighter, with a bigger upturn at the tip. An average pair weighs about 1.4kg (3lb 2oz). The bindings fasten only at the toe of a light, flexible shoe, so that the heel moves freely up and down.

The sticks or poles are also longer and are constantly used to help push the skier along, whereas the alpinist's poles are used for balance. The bottom of the skis are waxed and a knowledge of the right kind to apply is vital. According to the prevailing snow conditions and gradient of climb or descent, waxes can give more grip or more slide.

3 Winning

A good racer averages over 16kmph (10mph) when the going is favourable, so the shortest race over 15km approx can be covered in about 50 minutes while the long distance 50km takes something like 2¾ hours. Food and non-alcoholic drink is permitted during the 30 and 50km events.

Competitors begin one at a time at half-minute intervals. The course is roughly circular and in a world championship or Olympic event arranged so that competitors do not use any part of it more than twice. It is marked clearly at regular intervals by flags and each race finishes at the same point as the start.

4 Rules

The rules stipulate that the course should consist of ever-varying sections of uphill, downhill and level terrain. The course-setter must avoid including climbs which are too long or steep, or downhill sections too difficult or hazardous. Monotonous open stretches are avoided so that the trail is kept as interesting as possible, with no artificial obstacles.

The first section is made intentionally easy, to minimize early strain, and the

SKIING
Nordic
Cross-country

SKIING

Nordic

Cross-country

most strenuous part starts about half-way. The course is also devised to avoid sharp changes in direction likely to affect unduly the racer's rhythmic stride.

5 & 6 Skills & Tactics

The secret is the rhythmic regularity of long strides. A kick-off from one ski alternates with a glide through on the other and this is assisted by alternately planting each stick firmly in the snow as the leg on the opposite side begins the kick action.

Turns are achieved by using a diagonal stride rather like skating, putting weight on the inside edge of the ski. A similar technique applies when climbing a gradient, the *edging* off-setting any tendency to slip back. The movement is rather like the *herringbone* of an alpine climber, with ski tips turned outwards and heels kept close, leaving the tell-tale fishbone pattern in the snow behind.

The accent on rhythmic movement is energy-conserving and the thrusts with the ski poles need to be coordinated. When climbing and turning, extra propulsion is achieved by planting both poles in the snow at the same time and leaning further forward to a near-crouching position. As in most sports, the best performers make it look deceptively easy and in this case they do so because of the rhythm which, in turn, fosters the much-admired grace of a seasoned racer.

Although generally safer than the alpine style, Nordic racing is more gruelling and stamina-demanding. As in track athletics, the longest distance favours the slightly older competitor who often acquires a more reliable staying power when approaching 30.

Harmonious coordination of movement is required, allied to deep, steady breathing, plus that will to keep going when on the verge of exhaustion.

Many races will be decided not during the race but before it, when the skier or his team manager decides on what wax should be used on the bottom of the skis. There are several waxes which react both to the temperature of the air and the condition of the snow. If the correct wax is chosen, the skier will glide more easily while getting a firm grip climbing uphill. The wrong choice will result in the skier working harder and tiring faster.

When the biathlon competitor arrives on the range he has to put his ski poles down, unsling his gun, put his ammunition in the tray provided, load, fire, then strap his rifle on again, pick up his poles and set off again. Top class competitors can do all this in less than 1½ minutes.

7 Words

Bumbag: used by cross-country skiers for carrying refreshments
Critical point: a line marked on the landing area of a ski-jump, beyond which it is dangerous to land
Diagonal stride: where both arms and legs are used to push the skier along — right arm and left leg would go forward together; left arm and right leg would be back
Double poling: where skis and legs are kept together as the skier drives himself along, planting both poles in the snow at once
Scaffold, tower: where skijumper begins run down skijump
Vorlage: skijumper's forward lean in mid-air, with knees straight and arms by the side
Waxing: the secret of success in many skiing events — wax is applied to the ski bottoms to aid both glide downhill and grip uphill. ■

Biathlon world championships did not begin until 1958 and the sport was first included in the Winter Olympics of 1960.

The biathlon combines cross-country ski racing and rifle shooting. It is a unique test of skiing and marksmanship and, not surprisingly, members of the armed forces make up a large proportion of participants. Nations without snow are at less of a disadvantage in the biathlon, because they can practise shooting before going abroad to ski.

In the Olympic Games there are three biathlon races:

20km Individual Race: each country may enter up to four racers who are required to ski 20km (12½ miles approx) during which they have to stop four times at a 50m (55yd approx) range. There they fire five shots. The score works on penalties, 0 penalties for a bull, 1 minute penalty for an inner, 2 minutes penalty for any other misses. The order of shooting on the various ranges is lying, standing, lying, standing. The winner is the man whose running time is the least after shooting penalties have been added.

10km (Sprint): the second individual race. Covering 10km (6¼ miles approx), there are only two bouts of shooting, one lying, one standing. However, this time the targets are breakable or of the metal falling type. After five rounds have been fired the competitor is required to run a *penalty loop* of 150m (165yd approx) for every target remaining. The winner is the man whose running time is the least.

Relay 4 × 7.5km: this is for teams of four men, each of whom runs an identical course, similar to any normal track relay. Each country lines up its first racer and there is a mass start, the winning team being the one whose final skier crosses the finishing line first. During the race, each skier fires twice, at targets similar to the sprint's, only this time having eight rounds with which to knock down the target. Once again penalty loops are run for any targets remaining.

The competitor's overall time, both while skiing and shooting, is recorded. Then penalties are added on — two minutes for each shot which misses the target (one minute for an outer).

The ability to unsling the rifle, fall flat and take steady aim immediately after skiing all out and still keeping the skis on, all with the minimum possible delay, is clearly a challenging task, but on a 20km course it is still possible to complete both skiing and shooting within an hour and a quarter. ■

The other branch of Nordic skiing is skijumping, surely the most spectacular and awe-inspiring. Courage and grace are interwoven in this very specialized sport, which is as different from holiday skiing as is high diving from ordinary swimming.

The world's most famous skijumping site is the Holmenkollen Hill on the outskirts of Oslo, where Holmenkollen Week every March provides the highlight of the Scandinavian winter sports season. What Wimbledon means to tennis is what Holmenkollen means to Nordic skiing fans. The jumping finale each season is attended by crowds of more than 100,000 including members of the Norwegian Royal Family.

Most of the world's other main jump hills were originally erected for the Winter Olympics — notably at Innsbruck, Austria; Cortina d'Ampezzo, Italy; Sapporo, Japan; St. Moritz, Switzerland; Garmisch-Partenkirchen, West Germany; and Lake Placid, USA. But the biggest is at Oberstdorf, West Germany.

SKIING

Nordic

Biathlon, Skijumping

For 1 to 4 see page 194; 7 see page 192

The shooting range. Competitors have to change pace from the effort of skiing to the calm concentration of shooting.

NORDIC SKIING
Skijumping

1 The Jump Tower

There are two categories of world championship and Olympic jumping — *90m* and *70m* (100 and 80yd approx). This does not denote the height of the jump towers but the calculated length that can be jumped from them. Higher towers are only used for *ski-flying,* the name given to a non-Olympic ski jumping event.

The ski jumper swoops down the ramp, crouching low to cut down wind resistance in order to get maximum speed into the air.

2 Equipment

The skis are long and heavy with three grooves in the sole — all of which aid stability. The boot is attached firmly in front but the heel is left loose to permit *forward lean* in the air. (The official distance of a leap is measured from the lip of the ramp to the point between the feet of the jumper where he lands).

3 Winning

Jumpers are viewed from below in an atmosphere of suspense akin to watch a trapeze act in a circus. A hum of expectancy is silenced as the skier is seen to leave the top of the jump tower, crouched low as he gathers momentum down a narrow ramp until suddenly he becomes airborne.

Thousands of pairs of eyes are focused on that brave jumper, but none more keenly than those of five judges whose job it is to award marks for technique. The winner is not necessarily the one who clears the longest distance because the competition is based on both distance and style. The highest and lowest marks of the judges are subsequently discarded, leaving only those of the middle three to count.

4 Rules

The judges are watching to see whether the jumper slackens pace while he descends the ramp and how he times his spring into the air. As he soars, they like to see pronounced foward lean from the ankles, with hips and knees very nearly straight, and arms held parallel, either close beside the body or straight out in front, but not uneven or to the sides.

Minimum mid-air motion is expected. The skis should be held parallel, close together and inclined upwards, so that the air resistance presses under the skis. Just before landing, the jumper flexes the body to take the impact.

He should land without falling or stumbling, moving into what is called a *telemark stance,* one foot in front of the other, with arms at the sides and knees partly bent. Any unsteadiness or undue stiffness after landing can still lose points. Finally, spreading arms to aid balance, he skis along the level outrun area and skids to a halt. This is one time he may wish he had ski poles, which jumpers do not use because poles would play havoc with wind problems while in the air. ∎

Snooker is played by four million people in the British Isles, extensively throughout the Commonwealth, and to a lesser extent in the United States. It has a long grass-roots tradition ranging from its invention in 1875 through the inauguration of the English Amateur Championship in 1919 and the World Professional Championship in 1926 to a peak of interest and activity in the age of television.

The idea is to use a long wooden stick (called a *cue*) to knock balls into holes or *pockets* around the edge of the special cloth-covered table. The balls have different values, indicated by colour.

1 The Table

The table is very solid, and must be absolutely level. The *bed* is of slate, covered with finely woven green baize cloth which also covers the hard, rubber *cushions* which edge the playing area. The quality and weave of the cloth can affect the delicate spin of the ball.

2 Equipment

The cue is made of wood — the shaft of ash, the butt often of ebony which gives it weight and rigidity. Each player will have a cue that 'feels comfortable', is about shoulder high and weighs about 450g (1lb). A small round *tip* of leather is stuck on the cue and is always rubbed with special fine chalk during play to give a slight grip in the ball. If a ball is out of reach of a player a *rest* is used to support the cue.

The balls were originally made of ivory, but are now made of crystallate and are quite heavy for their size. They are 5.23cm (2¹⁄₁₆in) diameter, but in North America 5.39cm (2¹⁄₈in) in diameter.

3 Winning

Success at snooker demands a high degree of concentration, for the sport combines both physical and cerebral elements and takes place in a confined arena, producing a dramatic atmosphere.

A game of snooker (referred to as a *frame*) is won by the player who scores the most points. A match consists of a specified number of frames with victory going to the player who wins the most.

Points are scored by *potting* (knocking the balls into the pockets around the table) and acquiring penalty points conceded by the opponent. At the start of each frame 22 balls are on the table with the 15 reds arranged in a triangle and six *colours* — yellow, green, brown, blue, pink and black placed on allotted spots. The white or *cue ball,* is the only one which may be struck directly by the cue and is used to knock other balls either into pockets or into another position on the table. A red ball (worth one point) must be potted or *sunk* first, and then the player must hit a colour. If it is potted, he tries for another red and so on in red/colour sequences. The reds remain pocketed (off the table) but colours are replaced on their spots until all the reds are sunk. The player then goes for the colours in ascending order from yellow (two points) through green (three), brown (four), blue (five) and pink (six) to black (seven). The frame ends when the black is finally potted and only the white cue-ball remains on the table. Sometimes a player goes through the entire sequence without the opponent ever having a chance to strike a ball. The maximum possible score is 147 points, achieved by pocketing all 15 reds (15 points) alternating each time with the black (15 × 7 or 105 points) and ending with each colour in sequence (27 points).

4 Rules

At the beginning of each frame, the cue-ball may be placed anywhere in the 'D' for the first stroke but after that it is played from wherever it comes to rest, unless off the table, when it is again placed in the 'D' for the next shot.

Although the sequence for scoring shots known as a *break* is easy to follow, the way penalty points are awarded after a foul is more complex. Basically, the minimum penalty is four points but if a ball with a higher value (blue, pink, black) is involved, then the penalty is the value of the colour concerned. These points are *added* to the *opponent's* score.

If a player misses the red altogther or hits the wrong ball, the penalty is four points, rising to five, six or seven

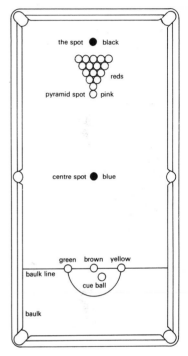

The player lines up the white cue ball with a red which he is trying to pot. He makes a firm bridge with his fingers and upturned thumb.

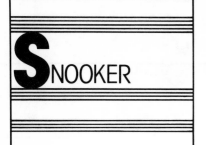

SNOOKER

points if the ball struck by mistake is blue, pink or black. When the cue-ball is sunk, either directly or bouncing in-off another ball, the opponent receives at least four points.

At expert level, penalties tend to be the result of deliberate *snookers,* rather than mistakes. A player is snookered when the direct path from the cue-ball to either side of the target is blocked by a ball which cannot be hit legally. This can happen if one or more balls are in the way or even if the cue-ball comes to rest on the *lip* of the pocket and the cushion effectively prevents a direct shot, when a player is said to be *angled.* If after a foul a player is snookered, he can ask his opponent to play again or can elect to play a *free ball.* That means that he can take any colour as a red (or colour when no red remains on the table) and this ball has the value of the ball which would normally be hit. If a colour is potted it is replaced on the table.

There are other fouls, such as striking the cue-ball twice and playing before all the balls have come to rest, but these are rarely seen in competition.

If the scores are level at the end of a frame, the black ball is replaced on its spot and the toss of a coin decides which player has first shot. The cue-ball is played from the 'D' and the winner is the one who pots the black or is awarded penalty points as a result of his opponent's foul.

Once all the reds have been potted, the players try to sink the colours in ascending order starting with the yellow (left), the green (on the right of the D), then the brown (centre), blue, pink, and black.

 Skills

Snooker is a game of *angles.* The balls are rarely in exactly the same spot from one game to another, so a player has to have a 'feel' for the table and the balls. By hitting the cue-ball a litte off centre, he can make it spin. He can make it swerve to the right or left, he can *stun* or *screw* it so that it stops dead after hitting the object ball, or he can even make the cue-ball spin backwards after hitting the object ball. This is done by hitting it low down, which produces *reverse spin.*

The idea of these special shots is to not only pot the object ball, but to manoeuvre the cue-ball into position for a pot on the next shot. So a player is never thinking just of the immediate objective, but is planning a series of moves.

With rubber cushions, there is plenty of scope for bouncing the cue-ball round the table — or *doubling* it off two or even three cushions to pot it, or manoeuvre it into a snooker or into a good position for a pot. Again, it is a matter of understanding the angles as well as knowing how hard the ball has to be struck to end up in the right position on the table. At top level, this includes an appreciation of the effort produced by the *nap* on the cloth which can slow down a ball or assist it to swerve.

 Tactics

In tournaments, the opening or *break off* shot is invariably a *safety shot,* the primary object of which is to leave a difficult position for one's opponent, by leaving the cue-ball either lying against a cushion (thus making it more difficult for a player to strike the cue-ball accurately) or behind a colour, usually the green, brown or yellow.

In reply to the break off shot, the second player sometimes attempts a pot but more often there will be an exchange of safety shots as each player in turn tries to gain the advantage. At this early stage, the importance of snookering is predominantly tactical: its object is to force the snookered player to concede an opening. Pure potting ability is very important but even with players of the highest standard there is invariably a calculation between the benefit of a successful pot and the consequences if the pot is missed.

Some frames are decided with a single large break but most combine a series of smaller breaks with safety shots and snookering.

The closing stages of a frame produce many absorbing tactical battles, either when the scores are close or when one player trails by a greater margin than the combined values of the balls remaining on the table. If, for instance, a player is 30 behind with only the six colours remaining (value: 27 points) he is said to *need a snooker.* In this situation, he must attempt to lay a snooker in such a way as to force a foul (four points or more) from his opponent, thus reducing the points margin to 26, sufficient to allow him to win by potting the remaining colours.

RIGHT: Off to a racing start! A good dive saves crucial fractions of a second.
PAGE 198: Diego Maradona of Argentina — the world's most expensive soccer player.
PAGE 199: 1981 world ice dancing champions — Jane Torvill and Christopher Dean of Britain.

7 Words

Break: a sequence of scoring shots
Break-off: the first shot of a frame in which the striker plays at the unbroken triangle of reds
Clear the table: sequence of shots in which a player pots all the balls left on the table (also known as a *clearance*)
Cue-ball: the white ball
Double: a shot by which a ball enters a pocket after striking the opposite cushion
Free ball: if a player is snookered after a foul shot by his opponent he may nominate any colour in place of the snookered ball
Full ball shot: a contact in which the cue-ball strikes the object-ball full on
Half ball shot: a contact in which the cue-ball strikes one half of the object-ball
In hand: the situation after an in-off when a player may place the cue-ball anywhere in the 'D' for his next shot
In-off: when the cue-ball enters a pocket (usually after striking another ball)
Maximum break: a sequence of shots in which a player pots all 15 reds, 15 blacks and all the colours, to score 147
Natural angle: the angle which the cue-ball takes after striking an object-ball at medium pace without spin of any kind
Plant: a position in which one object-ball is played onto another in such a way as to make the second ball enter the pocket
Pot: propelling the cue-ball onto an object-ball to send it into a pocket
Safety shot: a shot in which a player makes no attempt to score but intends to leave his opponent unable to score
Screw: backspin; applied by striking the cue-ball below centre
Set: a position in which two object-balls are touching in such a way that the second ball will be potted when the first is struck
Shot to nothing: position in which a player attempts a pot in such a way as to leave himself in position to continue his break if successful but in which he will leave the cue-ball in a safe position for his opponent if he fails
Side/side spin: applied by striking the cue-ball either to the right or left of centre, to make it swerve
Stun: a shot in which the cue-ball is stopped dead by striking the cue-ball just below centre when hit full ball. ■

LEFT: Tracy Austin, tiny US tennis star, hammers a two-handed backhand over the net.

SNOOKER
Billiards

Billiards was the forerunner of snooker, pool, and indeed all billiard table and pool table games. The variety which is played on English billiard tables (that is, those tables which have pockets) boasts a substantial following in Britain and the Commonwealth. The billiards which is played on pocketless tables is confined to Europe, the United States, South America and parts of Asia and Africa.

At the top level, billiards is a cultured, rhythmic, artistic game, though the best players have perfected scoring systems which, to those who are not committed followers of the game, appear repetitious. It is for this reason that billiards does not lend itself to television coverage as readily as snooker.

For 1 and 2 see page 195.

3 Winning

Billiards is played with three balls, two whites and a red. One white, distinguished by two black spots, is called *spot* and the other *plain*.

The game starts with the red on the spot (see diagram). Players spin a coin for the choice of playing first from the 'D' and for the choice of the spot or plain white ball.

The first player must play away from the 'D' and hit the red with his opening shot. If he pots the red or if his white goes into the pocket *in-off* the red, he scores three points. If he misses the red, his opponent is awarded one point but if he misses the red and the white and goes into a pocket his opponent gets three points. The break ends when the first player fouls or fails to score. The second player then places his ball anywhere within the 'D' and can aim at either the red or his opponent's white, provided it is not *in baulk* (the area between the baulk line and the baulk cushion).

A player can drive his opponent's white into a pocket (pot white), cause his own white to enter a pocket after striking his opponent's white (in-off white), or cause his own white to strike both the red and his opponent's white *(cannon)*. If successful, any of these shots is valued at two points.

The game proceeds with players taking turns until one reaches a pre-arranged points target (e.g. 100 or 1000 points) although, in championships, competitors play a stated length of time, usually an agreed number of two hour sessions.

SNOOKER
Pool

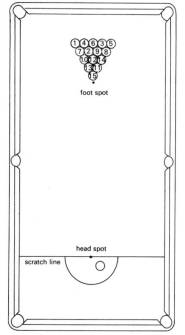

foot spot

head spot

scratch line

4 Rules

Each time a player scores an in-off, he replaces his ball anywhere within the 'D' for his next shot. This is known as playing *from hand.* When doing so, the player's own ball (cue-ball) must initially leave baulk before striking another.

Each time the red is potted, it is returned to its own spot, but if a player pots the red from its spot three times in succession (in professional championships twice) it is placed on the middle spot until potted again. If a player pots his opponent's white, it remains in the pocket until his opponent's turn.

Players of high standard have to watch for the *15 hazards* rule (a hazard is an archaic term for a pot or in-off). This rule limits a player to 15 consecutive pots or four in-offs, so to continue his break he must play a cannon at least once every 16 shots. The referee warns a player after 10 consecutive hazards.

5 & 6 Skills & Tactics

The larger the breaks the better the players are playing. Top competitors will show their class by making one easy shot lead to another. Tactics tend to play a less prominent role than in snooker, as championship games resolve themselves largely into a test of scoring breaks.

7 Words

Coup: striking the cue-ball into a pocket without contacting another ball
Drop cannon: a cannon played from hand taking the first object-ball from the middle of the table and contacting the second object-ball at the top of the table to gather all three balls in that area
Hazard: a pot or in-off
Long jenny: an in-off where the cue-ball is struck with extreme side before striking an object-ball near a side cushion and entering a top pocket
Nursery cannon: a cannon or more

usually a sequence of cannons in which the cue-ball runs the two object-balls gradually along a cushion
Short jenny: an in-off in which the cue-ball is struck with extreme side before striking an object-ball near a side cushion and entering a middle pocket
Top of the table: a scoring sequence in which a break is compiled by a combination of pot reds and cannons at the top of the table. ■

Pool is a generic term which covers all games played on pool tables. There are many such games and standardization of rules, particularly internationally, is incomplete. Table sizes also vary. In America, though, the championships organized in the '14.1' continuous version of the game carry the most prestige.

The object of the game is to reach an agreed points target, usually 150. Fifteen balls are initially racked in a tri-angle. A player scores one point for each ball he pockets. He must *call* or nominate each ball and pocket in advance.

When 14 balls have been pocketed they are replaced in the triangular shape with the apex ball missing.

As he takes the fifteenth ball the player attempts to send the cue-ball into the triangle so that it scatters the balls and leaves an opportunity to continue the scoring sequence.

There is a penalty of two points for failing to break properly and of one point if the cue-ball enters a pocket. Safety shots are permissible if the player calls *safe* prior to striking and causes an object-ball to hit a cushion. Breach of this rule involves a one-point penalty.

Another popular version, Eight Ball, dominates the British pool scene, largely because it lends itself to a coin-operated commercial operation. One player attempts to pot balls numbered one to seven while the other attempts balls nine to fifteen. When a player has completed his sequence, he is entitled to pocket the eight ball. Whoever does so wins the game. ■

Pool Term	Snooker Equivalent
Bank	Cushion
Draw	Screw
English	Side
Run	Break *(i.e. scoring sequence)*
Scratch	In-off

Anyone can play soccer. Anyone can understand it. There are no huge barriers to prevent anyone from appreciating the highest skills. Soccer is the world game, played everywhere and enjoyed everywhere. It quite simply involves kicking a ball.

Every four years, when the best countries come together in the World Cup finals, television carries the games to all quarters of the earth.

In 1978, when the finals were staged in Argentina, the River Plate stadium in Buenos Aires could hold only 77,000 spectators. But, with China joining the international audience for the first time, the opening ceremony was watched by an estimated 600 million viewers. It was the biggest television audience there had ever been.

There are good reasons why soccer has become the world's most popular sport. Anyone who has ever kicked a ball, or even a stone in the street, knows the 'feel' of the game. Also, the laws are simple, the playing field can be almost any piece of more or less level ground and the basic equipment is inexpensive and readily obtainable.

Everyone can play but some play better than others. At the highest level, soccer calls for many qualities: skill in controlling the ball, balance, speed, anticipation, physical courage. Yet these are all accessible qualities. There

is no mystique to stand between players and watchers.

Nor is this a sport which makes any special requirements of physique. Given a certain level of fitness, there is scope for the short as well as the tall, the wiry as well as the muscular. Ball sense and ball skill — the instinct for the telling movement and the ability to make it — are paramount.

The spectators at a big professional game themselves contribute to the entertainment. Their cheers and chants, their colourful banners and dress all combine to produce excitement and tension as the balance of the game swings. The explosion when that tension is released by the scoring of a goal is what attracts the fans.

Skilled television presentation can show soccer to its very best advantage. A high camera with a wide-angle lens discloses the pattern of play and team combination. Lower cameras capture individual artistry in close-up. Slow-motion replays reveal in detail the technical mastery of the best players.

1 The Field or Pitch

The markings on a soccer field are quite simple. The goal area is used to position the ball for goal-kicks. The goalkeeper can only handle the ball inside the penalty area. If a defender commits a serious foul in the penalty area, he is punished by a penalty kick. The centre circle on the halfway line keeps opponents 10yd from the ball at kick-offs. The length and breadth of the pitch may vary, but it is always a rectangle.

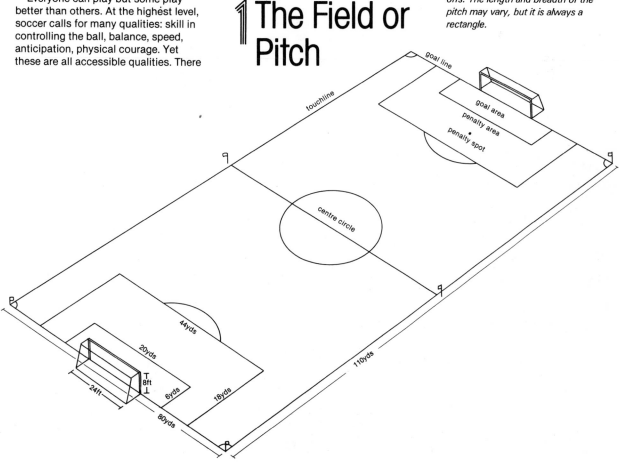

SOCCER

2 Equipment

Soccer kit is not complicated. Outfield players need matching shirts, shorts which may be a different colour from the shirts, socks and boots. The goal-keeper must wear a shirt or jersey of a colour that distinguishes him from team mates, opponents and the referee.

Modern boots are low cut and light in weight. To give a good foothold, the boots will have either moulded rubber bars or studs (cleats) or provision for screw-in alumiumum studs. The latter allows the choice of studs appropriate to the conditions; the softer the pitch, the longer the stud. Where matches are played on dirt pitches or synthetic surfaces, flat-soled boots with a patterned grip are preferred.

Shirt designs can be plain and simple or colourful and fancy. Europe tends to be orthodox. The United States has set fashions in bright and intricate styles. Everywhere there is increasing probability that shirts will also bear the name of the commercial sponsor. Professional soccer is a business as well as a sport and the players, who take most of the money in wages, must expect to earn some of it by becoming mobile advertisements.

The ball is round and made of tough leather with a circumference of between 27 and 28in (68 and 71cm). At the beginning of a game it must weigh 14-16oz (400-450g). In wet or muddy conditions it can get much heavier but the same ball is used throughout the match unless it is punctured or is somehow lost (kicked out of the ground perhaps!). Nowadays balls are coated with a plastic film to stop them soaking up moisture.

3 Winning

A soccer team consists of 11 players, only one of whom, the *goalkeeper,* is allowed to handle the ball. In most competitions a limited number of substitutes is permitted. The normal duration of a game is 90 minutes. The team which scores the greater number of goals in that time is the winner.

Scores are achieved by propelling the ball into the opponents' goal, usually by kicking or heading it. Sometimes in a melee of bodies and legs it is difficult to tell which part of the anatomy applies the final touch. Only the deliberate use of hands or arms is prohibited. Under pressure, a defender may concede an *own goal,* turning the ball into his own net. Sometimes the ball may be *kicked off the line, headed away* or bounce down from the crossbar on to the line, before being kicked upfield. For a goal to be awarded, the whole of the ball must cross the whole of the line.

The most common form of competiton for a number of teams wishing to compete with each other is by means of a *league.* Usually, each team plays all the others twice, once on home ground and once *away* with two points for a win, one for a draw, none for a defeat; but in England three points are now given for a win.

When all matches have been played, the team with the most points wins. If two teams finish with equal points superiority is decided either by sub-tracting the goals conceded by a team from the goals it has scored (*goal difference*) or by dividing the goals scored by the goals conceded (*goal average*). The winner would be the team with the better (i.e. higher) goal difference or average.

Another very popular form of compet-ition is the *knock-out tournament.* Teams are paired by means of a draw. The winners, either after a single match or after the scores in home and away matches have been added together, pass into the next round and a fresh draw is made.

Goalkeepers are crazy, it is said. When goals have to be scored attackers are ruthless. Goalkeepers have to be equally tough to meet the challenge.

If the scores are still level after two games, an extra period of play may be allowed. If that fails to produce a result, competition rules may allow for the teams to take alternate penalty kicks until one is eliminated. It is customary for the ultimate winners of a knock-out tournament to receive a silver cup, and so this type of competition has come to be called *Cup* football.

From time to time, the sudden death element allows a lesser unfancied team to beat more distinguished opposition. Knock-out competitions provide the drama of the unexpected. League contests, in which all play all, reduce the element of chance and generally reward the best team over a long period.

4 Laws

Soccer is governed by only 17 *laws.* The first six merely define the field of play, the ball, the equipment, the players and the officials who will arbitrate during a game. These last comprise a *referee* and two subsidiary officials known as *linesmen.* Other laws relate to such technicalities as the duration of the game and the start of play. Before a match, the two team captains spin a coin to decide who has the choice of either *kicking off* or picking which end to defend. A strong wind or sun in one direction could influence this decision. Teams play 45 minutes each way, with a 10-15 minute break at half-time.

In general, only two laws give rise to argument but they are enough to make refereeing no job for sensitive natures. One concerns fouls and misconduct. In theory, this forbids all forms of violence — kicking, punching, tripping, etc — as well as handling the ball and less physical offences such as swearing and time-wasting.

If the transgression is serious or persistent, the offender may be officially cautioned or even dismissed from the game. The referee may display a *yellow card* to indicate a caution. If he shows a *red card,* the offending player must leave the field for the remainder of the game, *sent off.*

However, soccer is a game frequently played at speed and invariably with determination. Some body contact is inevitable and not all of it is illegal. Often the referee has to decide whether an act committed in a split second was accidental or intentional. In addition to

acting as judge and policeman, he must also be a mindreader.

The second source of contention is Law XI, which takes 225 carefully chosen words to explain when a player is *off-side.* In essence, this law prevents attacking players from waiting close to the goal for chances to score from short range. Basically, if a player is in front of the ball in his opponents' half of the field and does not have two players between himself and the goal line, he is off-side, as soon as the ball is played forward by one of his team mates, except from a throw-in, a goal-kick or a corner-kick.

Certain offences within a penalty area are punished by a penalty kick — in effect, a free shot from a spot marked 12yd (11m approx) from the goal, which can be defended only by the goalkeeper. Otherwise, play restarts after a foul with a free-kick: the team offended

Heading is a great football skill. Not only is it a way of getting past a defence by going above it, but it's also invaluable for passing and deflecting the ball to a colleague.

SOCCER

against resumes play with a stationary ball at the place where the infringement occurred. The opponents must be 10yd (9m approx) away from the ball at one of these free-kicks.

If the ball goes over the side-line (*touch-line*) a *throw-in* is awarded there against the side that last touched the ball. Any player can take it, and throws the ball two-handed over his head and back into play. If a defender is the last person to touch the ball as it goes over the goal line, then a *corner-kick* is awarded to the attacking side, taken on the side of the field that the ball went out of play. If, however, an attacker is the last one to touch the ball before it goes over the goal line, then a *goal-kick* is awarded to the defending team. The goalkeeper usually takes this (though anyone is allowed to), placing the ball in his goal area and either booting it upfield, or often just tapping it to a colleague (who must stand outside the penalty area) who plays it back to the goalkeeper. He then has the easier job of kicking the ball downfield.

5 Skills

Goalkeeper: must be agile and brave. Needs good judgement in jumping, diving, catching or punching the ball, and especially in taking up the best position in relation to an attack. Once he has the ball in his hand an accurate kick or an overarm throw to one of his team mates can often turn a defensive situation into an attacking one in a matter of seconds.

Defenders: must have the strength to tackle firmly and, ideally, the pace to match the speed of opposing attackers. Ability to head the ball well is also important.

Midfield players: must be complete all-rounders, reinforcing defence or attack as required. Stamina, imagination and accuracy with long and short passes are essential. The best midfield players are also goal scorers.

Attackers: must be fast, skilled in controlling the ball with head and feet, capable of turning in restricted space and confident of their ability to take the ball past opponents.

6 Tactics

Professional footballers often say that their game is 'all about winning'. When your income depends on it, victory will inevitably play a prominent part in your thinking. Modern soccer is, therefore, intensely competitive. But, because it is easier to defend with organisation than to attack with imagination, much football strategy is negative.

Cynics argue that league competitions virtually invite caution. While a goal-less *draw* (tie) remains worth one point, a hard-headed coach may, in certain circumstances, feel justified in adopting tactics primarily designed to keep the score sheet blank.

Nevertheless, teams that have captured the imagination of the soccer public have been notable not only for winning but for winning with flair and style. At various times the national teams of Hungary, Brazil and Holland and such club sides as Real Madrid, Manchester United, Honved of Budapest, Ajax of Amsterdam and Bayern Munich have shown a spirit of adventure in which skill and resolution have been thrillingly blended.

Changes in playing formation have reflected over the years the trend towards reinforcing the defence. One of

Formations

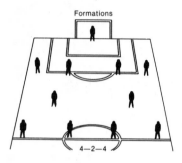

4—2—4

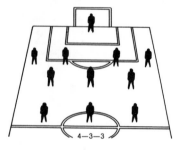

4—3—3

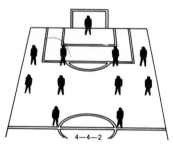

4—4—2

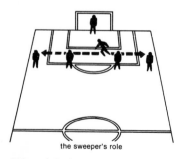

the sweeper's role

Although he has six colleagues forming a defensive wall to stop a freekick, the goalkeeper has still had to dive to his left to punch the ball away.

the earliest formations for outfield players was based on two fullbacks, three half-backs and five attackers: 2-3-5. The Brazilians modified that to 4-2-4.

When others tried to copy, they could not match Brazil in finding two outstandingly gifted players to bear the heavy burden of forming the midfield link between the four attackers and the four defenders. So there has been further evolution: to 4-3-3 or even 4-4-2.

None of these formations can be rigidly maintained during play. They provide a basis, allotting players areas of responsibility on the field. The more flexibility there is within the framework, the more versatile players can be at interchanging roles, the better the team is likely to be.

 Words

Banana shot: an attempt at goal in which the kicker makes the ball swerve through the air

Bench (also *dug-out*): Place at the side of the pitch for the team coach, physiotherapist and substitute players

Bicycle kick: a technique by which a player throws himself backwards in order to kick the ball at head height in the opposite direction to which he is facing

Centre (also *Cross*): a ball kicked into the penalty-area from near the touch-line

Corner-kick (also *Corner*): a means of restarting play after the defending team has played the ball over its own goal line; the attacking team kicks the ball from a quarter-circle at a corner of the pitch

Direct free kick: a free kick from which a goal may be scored without another player also touching the ball

Full-back (also *Back*): a player with defensive responsiblities on one flank (thus, left- or right-back)

Goal-kick: a means of restarting after the attacking team has played the ball over its opponents' goal line; the ball is kicked from the goal-area and must be kicked hard enough to leave the penalty area; although the goalkeeper usually takes the kick, anyone on his side is allowed to

Indirect free kick: a free-kick from which a goal may not be scored until a second player, from either side, has touched the ball

Kick-off: the beginning of a game

Marking: shadowing an opponent, particularly when the opposition has possession of the ball

Obstruction: when a player blocks an opponent when the ball is not within playing distance; if however, a player has the ball at his feet he can 'screen' the ball with his body; this is NOT obstruction

One-two (also *Wall pass*): an exchange of passes between two players in which the second player instantly returns the ball to the first

Passing: transferring the ball from one player to a team mate

Penalty: means a 'penalty kick' awarded for a serious offence by a defender in the penalty area; the attackers select one man to have direct shot at goal from the penalty spot with only the goalkeeper to beat

Square ball: a lateral pass

Striker: an attacking player

Sweeper: a spare defender without specific marking responsibilities. Usually the last man in defence in front of the goalkeeper

Tackle: a challenge to an opponent in order to win the ball from him

Target man: a central attacking player, usually tall, towards whom team mates can aim passes in the penalty area

Through-ball: a forward pass between opposing defenders

Throw-in: a means of restarting after the ball has crossed the touch-line. The ball must be thrown from behind the head with both hands

Winger: an attacking player who operates mainly near the touch-line (thus left- or right-winger). ∎

If the man on the ground plays the man rather than the ball it is a foul. But if the white shirted team keeps possession, then the referee should play the advantage law and let the game flow on.

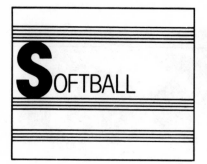

SOFTBALL

Softball is the little brother of baseball. Although there are still nine players a side, only seven innings are played. Once largely confined to company outings and summer picnics the game has made a place for itself in the American sporting scene and grows in stature across the world.

Softball is really two games; the *fast-pitch* variety which is closer to baseball in its intent and strategy, and *slow-pitch,* the more popular version among most players because it favours attack

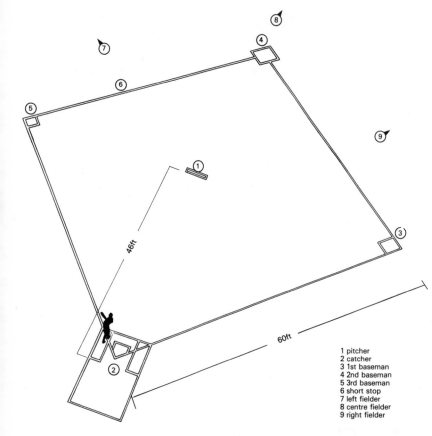

1 pitcher
2 catcher
3 1st baseman
4 2nd baseman
5 3rd baseman
6 short stop
7 left fielder
8 centre fielder
9 right fielder

at the expense of defence and produces more opportunities to succeed at bat. Fast-pitch is the game which is played at World Tournaments, but slow-pitch is developing its own tourney structure.

1 The Field

The softball diamond needs about 250ft (75m) of *fair territory* down each of the two foul lines and about 330ft (100m) to straight centre field. This is smaller than a baseball diamond, but all other features are similar.

2 Equipment

Players need a minimum of equipment — a bat, a batting helmet and a fielder's glove, not to mention some type of uniform, which depends on the formality of the league and the occasion. The softball itself is larger and softer than a baseball and is about 12in (30.5cm) in circumference, weighing about 6½oz (185g).

3 & 4 Winning & Rules

The difference between the games centres on the pitcher. As in baseball, pitching is a major portion of the skill of the sport and softball's shorter distance between the pitching rubber set in the ground and home plate means that good pitchers can be totally dominant in the fast-pitch game. Throwing underhand in a quick, whip-like motion, pitchers have approached, or even surpassed, the speed of fast-throwing baseball pitchers. They can also deliver a pitch unknown to baseball — the rise ball, which can leap abruptly at the batter just before crossing home plate. The easier throwing motion (underarm from a flat surface as opposed to overarm off an elevated mound) is easier on the pitcher's arm, so great teams can be built around two pitchers, since they

The characteristic underarm delivery of a softball pitcher who has only a small pitching rubber set in the ground, as opposed to a baseball pitcher's mound.

will be able to pitch every other day, often twice in the same day before taking a rest. No baseball pitchers perform so frequently.

The fast-pitch game, then, is controlled by these pitchers. A good softball hitter may bat 250 — as opposed to an average 50 points higher for a baseball batter — to be considered unusually proficient. The number of batters retired on *strikes* is significantly higher in fast pitch softball and the number of runs scored is, not surprisingly, much lower. Games that finish 1-0 are common, even though extra-inning games between two excellent pitchers may extend for unusually long periods; a normal game consists of seven innings, but top-level tournament play almost always includes games in the 15-18 inning range that finish with the scoring of a single run.

The paucity of scoring and the dominance of the pitchers in fast-pitch has led directly to the creation of slow-pitch, which emphasizes lots of hitting, base running and very high scores. The difference is achieved by a single rule change which alters the entire manner of pitching: instead of being able to deliver the ball in a straight line to the batter, the slow-pitch delivery must come to the plate in an arc, so it is delivered upward when leaving the hand and reaches the batter on its downward arc. This rule eliminates any real pitching speed; so the number of strike-outs declines, the base hits fly all over the park.

Scores in the slow-pitch version of the game are higher than those averaged in baseball and the spectators enjoy the fact that although a team may be quite far behind, the opportunity for a come-

back is always a possibility.

The main differences between baseball and softball are that the field of play is smaller, the ball is larger, pitching is underarm, players are not allowed to *steal* runs and games last seven innings instead of nine.

In fast-pitch, the pitcher dominates play, but in slow-pitch the fielders hold the key. With the batters hitting consistently, field positioning is important. Once the ball has been scooped up, fast accurate throwing is vital to try to put out base runners. Although players can be tall or short, speedy or slow, a *good arm* is essential. ■

Softball is rapidly growing in popularity as a spectator sport. Here, the catcher takes a high pitch.

For 5, 6 & 7 see pages 47-49

The baserunner must be out, as the second baseman already has the ball snugly in his glove.

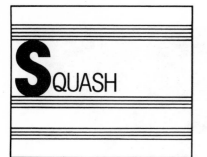

SQUASH

Squash is essentially a participant sport. It has never been easy for a large number of spectators to see what is going on, although with the advent of glass-walled courts it was immediately possible to offer more seats to spectators. It is a tense and exciting game, usually for two players, and has been successful from the playing point of view because it combines the need for intelligence, determination and courage on the mental side, and great physical fitness on the practical side.

In the USA, Canada and Mexico, however, there is a different version of the game, known as *hard ball,* as opposed to the *soft ball* version played in the rest of the world. The court is 2½ft (75cm) narrower and the ball, as the name suggests, is hard and travels around at a tremendous speed. The difference between the two games has been summed up in the remark that the 'international game' consists of two gentlemen chasing a small black ball round a court, and the American game consists of a small black ball chasing two gentlemen around the court. Over the years there have been various experiments at bringing the two games together, but all have failed, as they merely resulted in creating a third, and inferior, game.

1 The Court

Imagine a tennis court; now build a wall 15ft (5m approx) high where the net is, another wall 7ft (2m approx) where the baseline is, and two more walls down the inner tramlines, and you have a squash court. Now bring the opponent from the other side of the net to the same side of the wall, exchange your tennis rackets and balls for the lighter squash rackets and smaller squash balls, and the game can start. The equivalent of the net is the *tin,* a strip across the bottom of the front wall, with a red painted board above it, the top of which is 19in (48.3cm) from the floor. The floor is wooden, the walls smooth and hard.

2 Equipment

The squash racket is usually of wood and the handle has a leather or toweling grip, and overall the racket is 24in

A squash racket is much lighter than a tennis racket, with a smaller head. Wood is still popular, though steel shafts are also common.

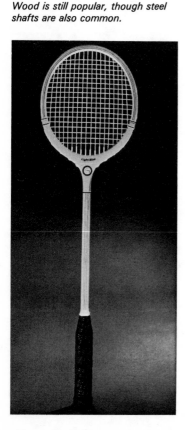

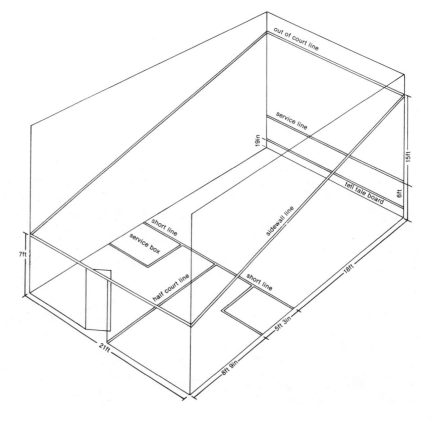

(61cm) long. The head is strung with man-made gut, so it is really a smaller, lighter version of a tennis racket. The ball used in the international game is made of rubber and is hollow, weighing just under an ounce (23.3-24.6g) with a diameter of 1½ in (40mm approx).

③ Winning

Like tennis, one person serves, and the rally continues until one of the players hits the ball a) into the tin, b) fails to hit the ball before it has bounced twice, or c) hits it out of court. Any shot that touches the tin or board is *down* and loses the rally. To be *out* a ball must hit or go over one of the top lines on any of the walls, hit any part of the ceiling, or go over any beam or rafter.
A squash match is normally the best of five games, and a game is the equivalent of a set in tennis. A game is won by the first player to reach nine points. However, if the score reaches eight all, the person not serving must choose either *no set* or *set two.* If the player chooses no set the game continues to nine, and someone wins it, nine-eight; if the player choses set two, the game continues to ten, and someone wins it ten-nine or ten-eight.

Points can only be scored by the server (referred to as *hand-in*) when he wins a rally. If his opponent (referred to as *hand-out*) wins a rally, he does not score a point, but takes over the service and becomes hand-in. While the server continues to win points, he has to serve each new rally from alternate sides of the court. The score is always called with the server's score first (say 'three-two'). If he wins that rally the score is 'four-two' and if he loses it, the score is called, 'Hand out, two-three', the words 'hand out' being put in to indicate that the service has changed over, and therefore the score will be reversed.

④ Rules

The service rules in squash are rather complicated. Remember the number three; the server has to get three things right before his service is correct, there are three types of fault, and three types of crime so dreadful that he loses the service at once! The three things he needs to get right are 1) to have at least one foot touching the floor inside the service box at the moment of serving, 2) to strike the ball directly on to the part of the front wall between the out of court line and the *cut line* (the one across the front wall at a height of 6ft (2m approx), and 3) for the ball to land within the opposite back quarter of the court, after touching the front wall.

The footfault rule says that you have to have at least one foot — both if you like — in contact with the floor, entirely within the small service box area, at the moment when the racket makes contact with the ball. It need only be the toe or heel, and it need not be stationary, but no part of the qualifying foot may be touching any of the lines.

Then the ball has to go directly from the non-racket hand into the air and be struck by the racket before it touches either wall or floor, direct to the correct part of the front wall, and rebound so as to land in the opposite back quarter. On the way back it can hit the other side wall or the back wall, but it must land on the floor within that quarter. However, hand-out is allowed to *take* (hit) the ball on the *volley* (before it bounces) if he thinks it is to his advantage. If he does, he has *taken* the service.

A *fault* is when hand-in has 1) served a footfault, 2) hit the ball on or below the cut line on the front wall, as long as it is above the board and tin, or 3) the ball has bounced on the short or half court lines, or outside the opposite back quarter. Any combination of two or all three types of fault counts as just one fault.

If hand-out does not choose to play the ball, hand-in will serve again,

A shot played parallel to the side wall forcing the opponent to vacate his position in the middle of the court.

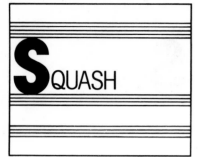

SQUASH

but two consecutive faults will lose him the service. However, hand-out may take a fault on the first service, and frequently does so, if it presents him with an easy return, and if he accepts the fault, he makes it good, and the game is under way, just as if the service had been correct.

The errors that lose hand-in the service at once, 'instant double faults' so to speak, are 1) services which do not even reach the front wall above the board before touching the floor, 2) are out of court, or 3) hit another wall before striking the front wall.

Because squash is played with both players in the same fairly small arena, moving at high speed and wielding potentially lethal weapons, the rules do their utmost to ensure that accidents will not happen. Basically, a player who has just played his shot must, in the words of the rule, 'make every effort' to get out of his opponent's way, in order to give him a fair view of the ball, a clear run to it and complete freedom to play the stroke of his choice at it. If the player fails to do this, the referee awards that rally to the opponent. Furthermore, even if a player has done all in his power to get clear, but has not succeeded in doing so, and has prevented his opponent from playing a probable winner, he will still be penalized by the referee.

5 & 6 Skills & Tactics

Squash has been likened to chess played fast. At a good standard of play it is seldom possible just to hit winners. They have to be earned. So, the aim of the players during a rally is to combine safe strokes, which run no risk of becoming losers, and at the same time, to hit the ball where the opponent least wants it played, which is normally to the corner of the court furthest from his last position.

Unlike tennis, the ideal service is a *lob,* aimed to rebound from the front wall so that it hits the opposite side wall just below the out of court line behind the rear line of the service box. It should then land on the floor between the side and rear walls, and if allowed to reach the rear wall, will not rebound far enough to be returned. The more frequent defensive service is a *drive,* which hits the front wall just above the cut line, and is aimed to strike the side wall

roughly opposite where hand-out is waiting to receive it, and is again aimed to a good length in the rear of the court.

After every stroke, including service, players aim to get to the centre of the court, known as the *T* because the lines there join as a 'T'. From that central position, a player can dominate the court and give his opponent no obvious space open to aim at. In order to get to the 'T' a player has to hit the ball to a position close to a side wall or into one of the corners, so that his opponent moves away from the central position. He can do this by *drop shots,* which are softly played shots into the front corners; *angles,* which are shots that strike one of the side walls on the way to the front wall, and so hopefully *wrongfoot* (unbalance) the opponent again with shots near the front of the court; *drives,* which are hard hit strokes usually down the nearest side wall, but sometimes across court; or *lobs* which are high strokes looping over the 'T' position and dropping awkwardly in the back corners.

The object of drives and lobs is to play the ball *to a good length,* which means causing it to bounce on the floor for the second time so close to the back wall that the opponent does not know whether to rush his shot and try to take it before it reaches the back wall, as it may not rebound far enough to be retrieved, or to leave it to hit the back wall and hope that it will come out far enough.

7 Words

Angle: stroke making ball hit side wall before the front wall
Boast: an angle shot that is played defensively from the rear corners of the court
Drop shot: a softly hit stroke that usually touches the front wall just above the tin and drops straight to the floor
Game ball: possibly the last serve of the game, when the server needs to win the rally to win the game
Nick: the angle between the foot of the wall and the floor; also the junction of two walls; if the ball strikes the nick it will rebound unpredictably
Reverse angle: a stroke where the ball hits the far side wall before rebounding on to the front wall
Tin: the strip on the front wall below the board which makes a noise when the ball hits it. ■

Gliding over the face of a huge wave at speed while standing on a long board takes balance, courage and lightning reflexes. The sport originated in the Pacific, was popularized in California and now features professional competition with enough good prize money to attract top Australians and South Africans to compete in the USA.

The shape of the land over which the waves travel affects the size and shape of the waves that surfers look for. There is a *beach break* on an open beach, a *point break* where the waves hit a point of land, or a *reef break* where the waves crash down before reforming. The most famous surf in the world is in Hawaii where 'The Pipeline' produces consistently good surfing conditions with the *tubes* that surfers get excited about. These are waves that curl over to form a long pipe or tube through which surfers ride.

Although long boards 7ft-7ft 6in (2.25m) are still used in Hawaii for the big waves, most top surfers use 6ft-6ft 6in (2m approx) boards made with a polyurethane foam core, sealed with glassfibre and resin. The core, or *block,* is handshaped to suit the individual; for example, a heavier competitor would need a thicker board. As in snow skiing, participants seize on the newest ideas and designs in the hope of improving their performances. Many use twin fins underneath the rear of the board which give manoeuvrability in small waves. The standard shape is like a fish, while in bigger waves the board might be more spearshaped with a narrow tail. Channels may be grooved into the underside ... new always seems to mean better!

The most effective development came in the mid-70's when a *leg-rope,* or *leash,* was introduced, joining the ankle to the surfboard. Now when a surfer falls off, he doesn't waste time recovering the board but can paddle out again ready for the next wave.

Amongst professionals, the prize money is growing so the need for consistent performances means there are fewer spectacular tricks. Fields of up to 150 are whittled down to a two-man final on a knock-out basis. Starting in groups of six at the most, the winner of each group goes through to the next round, and so on to the final. With each heat lasting 20 to 30 minutes, surfers are judged on the basis of their best 3 or 5 rides. Spotters look for competitors who wear different coloured vests for easy identification. "Red's up!" might be the cry and then the judges on shore watch that surfer come in. So that he doesn't have to take his eyes off the water, the judge tells a marker at his side what score he has given out of 20. Ten is average; fifteen or more is very good. The final would be much longer, perhaps an hour, so that the best two surfers get a good chance to display their abilities.

The main rule concerns interference. Basically, once a surfer is on a wave, standing up on his or her board, no other surfer can get in the way at the risk of being penalised. A surfer must stand up to score; kneeling down does not count.

The surfer stands sideways on the board so that a slight transference of bodyweight alters the direction — again, rather like a snow skier. Called a *natural* if his left foot is forward, he's a *goofy-footer* if he stands right foot forward. Extra weight on the nose accelerates the board, weight at the back slows it down but there is little room to move about on the short boards. A typical run would involve the surfer paddling out lying chest down on the board beyond the point where the waves break, then turning round and waiting for the swell to come. When a *peak* comes along, the surfer paddles into it, drops down onto the *wall,* or face, of the wave, does a *bottom turn* . . . and then begins the zigzag moves. He could go back to the lip, or if there is a tube, go for that . . . if, of course, he falls off, he is *wiped out!*

Top-class surfers can do a *360,* spinning the board round in a circle, or a *180,* where they reverse direction; but the tube ride is the ultimate experience even though it may last no more than five seconds. Swooping up and down the face of a wave, riding it as long as possible, the surfer also gets points for style, grace and timing.

Tactically, it makes no sense to dazzle the judges with clever moves which end in disaster. A surfer's score depends on his best 3 or 5 runs (whatever the rules require), so it is essential to complete that number successfully. Once this minimum is achieved, a surfer can then pull out all the stops in order to improve his points total in the time left in the heat.

SURFING

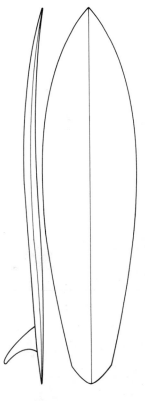

The competitive surfboard is fish-shaped. Underneath there is a fin, sometimes two fins, for stability.

Belly-board: a short board used by beginners
Cut back: turning at an angle at the back of a wave
Deck: top of the board
Goofy footer: Surfer whose stance has the right foot forward
Hang five/ten: standing with toes over the edge of the board; not often seen now
Kick out: at the end of a ride, letting wave go under board at the top of the wave
Pop-out board: cheap, moulded board for beginners
Rails: edges of board
Soup: whitewater where waves have broken
Stoked: a good ride
Wipe out: fallen off. ∎

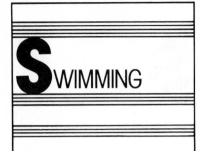

SWIMMING

Competitive swimming is based on four strokes — *front crawl, butterfly, back crawl* and *breast-stroke*. There are also *medley* events, in which individual competitors swim an equal distance in all four strokes.

Individual races for men and women include:

Freestyle — 100m, 200m, 400m, 800m (women only) — 1500m (men only)
Backstroke — 100m and 200m
Breast-stroke — 100m and 200m
Butterfly — 100m and 200m
Individual Medley — 200m and 400m

Team races: these are 4 × 100m freestyle and 4 × 100m medley for both men and women, plus a 4 × 200m freestyle for men. In medley team races the order of strokes is backstroke, breast-stroke, butterfly and freestyle. The 4 × 200m freestyle and the 200m individual medley for both men and women are not in the current Olympic programmes.

1 The Pool

An Olympic-size 50m swimming pool. There is a spare ninth lane as well as extra room at both sides to let the waves subside.

All long course international competitions must be held in a pool exactly 50m (164ft approx) long and at least 21m (70ft approx) wide. The other requirements are as follows:

1. The water must be 1.8m (6ft approx) deep overall for Olympic Games and World Championships.
2. The pool must be fitted with electronic timing before world records can be ratified.
3. There must be at least eight lanes each 2.5m (8ft 2½in approx) wide.
4. There must be floating lane dividers stretching the full length of the course. These are designed to absorb the waves made by swimmers.
5. The starting blocks must be between 0.5m and 0.75m (1ft 8in and 2ft 6in approx) above the surface of the water.
6. There must be backstroke turn indicators (a line of flags across the pool) 5m (5yd approx) from each end of and 1.8m (6ft approx) above the surface of the water. They must be removed during races of other strokes.
7. There must be a quick release *false start* rope across the pool 15m (15yd approx) from the start, which is released if a swimmer starts before the gun.
8. The water temperature must be a constant 24°C (75°F) and the water level must be constant with no appreciable movement.
9. There must be a distinctive line on the floor of the pool in the centre of each lane, running the length of the lane to a point 2m (2yd approx) from each end. There must be similar target lines on the end walls (or on the electronic timing pads) in the centre of each lane.

2 Equipment

Goggles: these are undoubtedly the most significant addition to a swimmer's kit in recent years. Not only do they cut out the annoying effects of chlorinated water on the eyes, but they also improve a swimmer's performance by allowing him to see where he is lying in a race and also to prepare properly for turns. They are made of plastic, cushioned around the edges to avoid chaffing the eye socket.

Swimsuits: even a woman's costume weighs only 1oz (30g approx) and is highly streamlined in design to prevent *drag.* Suits must be one-piece, though recent experiments with two-piece suits have increased competitors' speeds.

3 Winning

The winner of the race is the swimmer who starts properly, completes the required number of lengths making contact with the wall at each end, touches the final wall first and throughout the race observes the rules governing the stroke.

Seeding: all major championships operate a system of seeding. The official best time for each competitor is submitted in advance and if there are five heats, the five fastest swimmers will be placed in separate races and so will the next five fastest swimmers and this system continues until all swimmers have been assigned to a heat.

Within each race, including the final, a *spearhead* system of seeding is operated. The fasted swimmer is always placed in the lane immediately to the right of the centre of the course, which is lane 4 in an eight-lane pool. The next fastest swimmer is placed in the lane on the left, which is lane 5, and the next fastest swimmer is placed in the lane on the right, which is lane 3. This alternative system continues until the slowest swimmer is placed in lane 8.

The faster qualifiers get a slight advantage because they are able to see competitors on either side and also the centre lanes have marginally less turbulance than the outside lanes.

Timing and judging: at all Olympic Games and other major regional championships the judging of race placings is done electronically. Although the electronic equipment can often measure to .001 of a second, the smallest division is 0.1 of a second. This means that, although swimmer A may touch first in 48.981 seconds and swimmer B in 48.987 seconds, they will both be deemed to have dead-heated in 48.98 seconds. If this time were a new world record, they would be credited jointly with that record.

4 Rules

Freestyle: note that these events are not called 'front crawl' because that is a specific swimming stroke. In a freestyle event there are no rules laid down about which stroke has to be used. In practice, however, competitors use some version of the front crawl which is the fastest stroke so far developed.

Backstroke: the principal technical requirement here is that swimmers must remain on their backs throughout the race, except during the turn when they may leave their *normal position* on the back after the hand has touched the end of the pool. This concession allows backstrokers to do a *screw somersault* turn during which they are on their side, but they must be properly on their backs again before their feet leave the wall as they push off.

Breast-stroke: this stroke is rigidly controlled by technical regulations. The body must at all times be *on the breast* and both shoulders must be horizontal except at the turn after the touch has been made. The hands move forward from the breast and are brought back at or under the surface of the water. The leg kick must be performed under the surface of the water with the feet turned outwards in the backward movement. Hands and feet must work in pairs simultaneously and in the same horizontal plane without any alternating movements. Part of the head must at all times be above the general level of the water, except after the start and turn when the swimmer may take one arm stroke and one leg kick while wholly submerged.

This last rule was introduced about 20 years ago to eliminate a competition technique whereby many races were being swum largely below the surface, which produced faster times! Nowadays, there is still controversy over this rule because many swimmers lie so flat

SWIMMING

A sprinter swimming the crawl. The elbow is high with the body rolling round a longitudinal axis. Competitors breathe to the side and look across at rivals in other lanes.

even when swimming on the surface, that the water breaks over their heads.

When turning in breast-stroke and at the finish of the race, the wall must be touched by both hands simultaneously and at the same level.

Butterfly stroke: this is the newest swimming stroke, having been added to the Olympic programme only in 1956. The rules are similar to those for breast-stroke, except that the arms must be brought forward and together over the water and pulled backward simultaneously. A breast-stroke kick was used originally, but nowadays all leading butterfliers use a *dolphin* or fishtail-like up-and- down action with the legs together. The legs must not kick independently as in front crawl and the touch rule in butterfly is identical to that in breast-stroke.

Individual Medley and Team Events: all the above stroke regulations are strictly applied during individual medley and team events.

NB: one controversial swimming rule insists that two *false starts* (when a swimmer starts before the gun goes off) are allowed, but that whichever swimmer or swimmers is guilty of the third false start is disqualified, whether he or she was a previous offender or not.

5 Skills

In general, the best swimmers always appear to have a regular rhythm and to be in control of their stroke. Movement through the water is steady.

Front crawl: as the arms give most of the propulsion in this stroke, the efficiency of their action is essential. Imagine standing with your arms stretched out in front. The hands should be 15cm (6in) apart for the ideal entry position for each hand. The elbow should always be higher than the hand as it comes out of the water, so that the good swimmer *catches* and holds the water all the way back under his body to the exit point at each thigh.

The function of the legs is to give balance and rhythm rather than propulsion. There are three common leg kicks — the 6-beat, the 4-beat and the 2-beat, according to the number of individual leg kicks to each stroke cycle of two arm pulls.

In general, the fastest swimmers in the world use a 6-beat kick, but usually only over the shorter sprint distances, because the speed is won at the cost of considerable oxygen consumption by the very vigorous leg kick. Over the longer distances, from 400m (440yd approx) upwards, the two or four beat kicks are much more common, as swimmers aim to conserve their fuel (oxygen) principally for use by the more efficient 'propellers' (the arms).

Back crawl: the good performer carries the head absolutely steady with very little shoulder or hip sway, and usually looks the most elegant of swimmers.

As in the front crawl, the arms are the more powerful propellers. They should be brought out of the water straight but in a relaxed manner, and the hand enters well beyond (but not behind) the head. After the initial catch and short pull, the best swimmers will bend the elbow and push down to below the hip.

The legs give more power than in the front crawl kick and almost everyone uses a consistent 6-beat rhythm with toes pointed, flexible ankles and a 'whippy' action.

Breast-stroke: the arms and legs give roughly the same amount of propulsion but unlike the other strokes they are not all moving at once. Basically, the arms pull while the legs are stretched, then the arms stretch forward as the propulsion comes from the legs, as they kick backwards. This unique char-

The relaxed action of a world-class backstroker. The hips are just below the surface, the ears are barely submerged, the legs whip more than in the front crawl.

acteristic of breast-stroke means that timing is of paramount importance in achieving a fluent action, otherwise a very obvious *dead spot* develops when the body is not being pushed or pulled along the pool.

A good breast-stroker keeps the action compact, timing exactly the changeover from pull to kick so that impetus is maintained, and really stretching when the arms go forward to allow maximum benefit from the kick.
Butterfly: this is the most vigorous of all the strokes. The power ratio between arms and legs is very similar to front crawl and there are normally two kicks to each armpull. The main skill is to keep the body flat with the hips high, even when the head lifts to breathe. As in backcrawl, the kick should be *whippy* with very flexible ankles and feet pointing slightly inwards. Only strong, very competent swimmers can perform this stroke successfully.
Starts: at the command 'Take your marks' the swimmer takes up his or her preferred stance at the edge of the starting block. Nowadays most swimmers favour the *grab start* where they hold the front or edge of the block with both hands and coil the whole body in a tense, spring-like posture. At the pistol shot or klaxon, they release all the tension and drive upwards and outwards with all their force. Some swimmers *pike* or *tuck* in the flight before entry, which increases their momentum on entry, and at an angle which guarantees a shallow glide, although breast-strokers will go slightly deeper to gain maximum benefit from the full stroke permitted under water.

In backstroke events the start is made in the water with the swimmer's back facing the direction of the race. The gutter, or special handgrips, are held firmly and the feet placed together on the wall, but below the surface. On the 'Take your marks', the good backstroker will bunch up like a coiled spring and then on the pistol shot drive most of his body upwards and outwards clear of the water as the arms are flung back beyond the head into a stretched and streamlined position. In front and backcrawl and butterfly, the legs should always begin the stroke before the arms, while the reverse is true in breast-stroke.

It may seem contradictory to kick before pulling on frontcrawl, backcrawl and butterfly, the three strokes in which the arms are always dominant. The advantage lies in maintaining the very streamlined spear-like position of the body until the swimmer commences his

pull and breaks surface simultaneously.
Turns: all top-class front crawlers nowadays use a kind of *tumble* turn. The aim is to maintain forward momentum by somersaulting straight into the wall at top speed and twisting on to the side or front position during the final quarter of the somersault, as the swimmer pushes off. A good turn will actually gain time and *short-course* (25m pool) times are invariably faster than *long-course* (50m pools) because of the additional turns. The advantage is two-fold. The swimmer need not touch with the hand when swimming freestyle, so the turn is actually executed nearly a metre from the pool wall, just close enough for the feet to make contact with sufficient knee bend for a good push-off. Then the power of the drive off the wall increases the normal swimming speed for the next couple of strokes.

The back crawl turn is similar to the front crawl, except that the swimmer must push off on his back and the hand must touch the wall. In breast-stroke and butterfly the swimmer turns at the surface after the obligatory double-handed touch and then leads out with one shoulder. The swimmer has to resume the horizontal position on the breast when the arms start pulling.

The butterfly or dolphin stroke is the newest of the swimming styles. Here the swimmer takes a breath as she brings her arms forward, while her legs kick powerfully.

It is important to judge correctly when to start swimming again after the turn, when the propulsion of the push-off begins to wane. Only constant practice and the swimmer's own feel produces the ideal timing at all stages of the turn.
Relay Race Takeover: the first swimmer in a relay race will do a perfectly normal

start, but subsequent swimmers will have the advantage of a *flying start*. This means that they can actually judge when to launch themselves forward by watching the incoming swimmer. This is a distinct advantage worth as much as 0.8 seconds in a really outstanding take-over, because waiting swimmers can commence their start before their colleague has touched the end of the pool, provided that both feet remain on the block. In the ideal takeover the hand touch and feet leaving the block are simultaneous. It is a sign of a poor take-over technique if a relay squad does not swim about two seconds faster than the aggregate time of their best individual performances with a normal start.

The breaststroke swimmer tries to keep as low in the water as the rules permit, pushing the arms forward as the legs kick back.

6 Tactics

Competition swimming is not as rich in tactics as many other sports as it is basically a speed sport. The competitors are restricted to their own lanes, so that shoulder-to-shoulder jockeying for position with the physical and psychological intimidation of track and field athletics is not possible. Nor can there be sudden changes of speed and posi-

tion within the space of a few yards as in cycling. Nevertheless, the established system of seeding does mean that the best competitors are always close to each other.

The most valuable tactic is an accurate knowledge of a swimmer's own ability to pace a race. It is surprisingly easy for swimmers to go through the early stages of a race far too fast for their own good without realizing it. The cost is inevitably paid for later in the race with considerable interest! A swimmer noted for stamina rather than finishing speed might set a fast early pace to entice his rivals into his trap. But an ability to take pressure is necessary, because, as with most racing sports, it is easier to *sit on someone's tail* as they set the pace than to take the initiative.

7 Words

Negative splits: the practice, quite common in distance events, whereby the second half of a race is swum faster than the first

Shave-down: excessive body hair can have a very slight drag effect on a swimmer's speed. In recent years it has become common for swimmers to remove all body hair (even from the head in some cases) before a big event. The actual physiological effect may be slight, but the psychological one can be considerable. The shaved-down feeling in the water gives a swimmer a real boost

Split times: the times taken for each individual 50m or 100m in a race of any length, or the times of each individual swimmer in a relay

Stroke-shortening: when swimmers begin to tire, each individual stroke loses its optimum efficiency. To compensate for this, the swimmer will often speed up the stroke rate, but without increasing overall speed

Taper: an important part of race preparation, it is the period of from one to three weeks immediately before a big competition during which workload is decreased, so that the swimmer may be sharpened up and rested for the selected day and event

Tying up: this expression will often be used alongside *stroke shortening* as another clear indication of fatigue. It describes the condition when the muscles *tie-up* and lose efficiency, because they are not getting enough oxygen. ∎

able tennis is the slickest, quickest, deftest and most sleight-of-hand sport of them all. Labelled as *ping-pong,* this bat-and-ball game demands a vast range of qualities from a player, and at international level involves spectacular hitting over large distances. The Chinese have amazed television audiences with the accuracy with which they can project gigantic lobs onto the table from positions occasionally even outside the barriers.

For sheer speed, skill and reflexes table tennis is without parallel. The great variety of spins imparted by the wrist on a ball of less than half an ounce (15g) can be missed without the television action replay to illustrate the artistry in slow motion. To employ these and to counter them requires animal cunning, and to go on doing so while the score mounts needs a robot's control of nervous strain.

From its origins in Britain late last century it has spread from twin centres of development in Europe and the Far East to the Third World.

1 The Table

The table is only 2½ft (0.76m) off the ground; 5ft (1.52m) wide and 9ft (2.74m) long with a net only 6in (0.16m) high. Small though it may be, it is frequently the centre of great activity and hence the minimum arena space for

major tournaments is nearly 40ft (12m) long and nearly 20ft (6m) wide.

Despite regulations to standardize tables, they may vary importantly. The top must be of dark matt (preferably green) with a ¾in (2cm) white line around the edges. The small centre line is for the service in doubles which must land in the diagonal half.

The table may be made of anything, but is usually wood. Hard ground or a sprung floor may make the ball bounce that little bit more and enable attackers to get in and hit. Even the varying hardness of the ball, depending on the make, and the temperature of the air in the hall can affect the speed of the ball and top class players are sensitive to such differences.

2 Equipment

Players wear coloured clothing. White is banned because it would be difficult to see the white celluloid ball, only about 1½in (3.8cm) in diameter. The equipment that has changed the game has been the variety of materials attached to the surface of the bat giving great assistance to spin. The blade may be of any weight, size or shape but must be of wood of even thickness, flat, rigid and unperforated. Sponge rubber outer surfaces are banned, but plain pimpled rubber can be stuck on the bat with the *pimples* outward. Players often have a

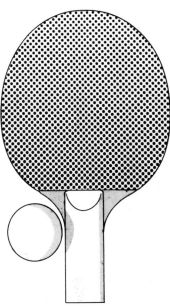

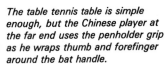

The table tennis table is simple enough, but the Chinese player at the far end uses the penholder grip as he wraps thumb and forefinger around the bat handle.

TABLE TENNIS

layer of sponge rubber plus pimpled rubber facing inwards — a *sandwich* — as well as sponge and a layer of rubber with pimples out. The first of these is rare today. Both sandwiches give spin, but the trend is towards pimples reversed, which gives more spin but less speed. Different sized pimples and different materials on each side of the blade enable the server to twiddle the bat below the table to deceive as to the amount of spin on the ball. One player has been known to stick his head under the table at the other end to see what's going on!

3 Winning

Scoring is pleasantly simple compared with other racquet sports. The winner is the first to get 21 points. If the score reaches 20-20, play goes on further until one player has a two point lead. Matches are usually the best of three games but often of five in international tournaments. Players change ends after each game, and in the deciding game as soon as the first player has scored ten points.

Both these doubles players use the western or shakehands grip. The lady is a left-hander, so complements her right-handed partner. Unlike tennis, doubles partners must play the ball alternately.

4 Rules

No volleying is permitted, a rule unique to table tennis. The ball must bounce once before being returned except on the service where it must bounce on both sides of the table. Each player has five services in turn unless the score reaches 20 all, when one service is taken alternately. If the service touches the net but hits the far side of the table it is a *let* and is taken again. If the same happens in a *rally* the shot is legal. It is also legal if the ball passes round the net, as it may with a big *sidespin loop*.

Viewers are sometimes concerned when they see a player stop or catch a ball that is missing the table. Unlike tennis, this is legal provided the ball has clearly passed the end of the table.

One rule has created special controversy in recent years. The service must start with the ball on the open palm of the hand and be projected upwards without spin. It is the player's responsibility to make sure the umpire sees this. If the player's body shields the ball he runs the risk that a fault may be called. Another rule is the *expedite system* to counteract defensive play. If a game is not over in 15 minutes, service alternates after every point and the server is allowed a maximum of 13 strokes to win the point — or else it goes to the opponent!

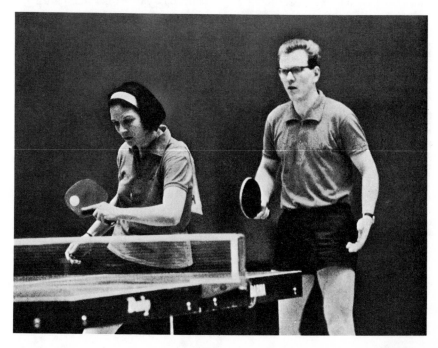

5&6 Skills & Tactics

Asia's great rivalry with Europe mirrors the two main styles that divide the game. The *western grip* and the *eastern penholder* could hardly look more different or represent more distinct ideas about playing. The western is sometimes called the *shakehands grip.* The penholder describes itself, and one of its main advantages is that the same side of the bat is used all the time, so taking a vital fraction less time to move around in fast attacking rallies. In the western grip the bat has to be turned around from the backhand to the forehand. It is hard to defend with the penholder but increasingly in the men's game the player who attacks first wins anyway. Nevertheless, many more Asians use the western than Europeans the penholder, and the Hungarians who took away China's world title in 1979 highlighted another flaw in the penholder. They attacked the penholder backhand with the *loop.* This is a shot hit with such exaggerated topspin that the ball lurches violently off the table. Cross court backhand looping tends to find out weaknesses in the penholder capacity to block, defend or lob on that side.

The loop may be prevented by a short *push,* denying room to prepare for the shot. Or it may be countered by *blocking,* a difficult skill to master. Many players feel that this loop, a spectacular form of attack, often produced with a highly athletic action of arm, wrist and body, can only be stopped by attacking first. Hence the increasing importance of service to win the initiative and the great variety used to keep the receiver guessing.

The classic style associated with the western grip is defence played with *chop* to impart backspin, sometimes at big distances from the table. This tends to drag the attacking shot down in to the net. Chop is less effective and less common than it used to be as it needs hard work to succeed against the loop compared with the flicked and rolled topspins predominating before the '60s. Whatever stroke is used the ball should never land in the middle of the table, where it would be easy to *kill:* players always aim for near the end or just over the net.

Doubles play makes extra demands on the players who have to understand each other perfectly.

Because service is so important, the player is concentrating on the ball - almost willing it over the net!

7 Words

Backhand: played across the body, when back of the hand faces opponent
Chop: defensive move chopping down on the ball, imparting backspin and returning the ball low
Counter attack: attacking an attacking shot, forgetting all ideas of defence
Drive: attacking shot with topspin
Forehand: played wide of the body, when palm of the hand faces opponent
Loop: greatest stroke in modern game — a drive with lots of extra top-spin. Often hit as ball is dropping low and therefore losing spin
Paddle: slang term for a table tennis bat
Penholder grip: the Oriental style of gripping bat handle as if it were a pen or chopstick
Push stroke: just that, forehand or backhand, a simple return without spin
Shake-hand grip: conventional Western grip, like holding a door-handle
Sidespin: ball will bounce sideways on landing if bat is stroked across it
Smash: hard attacking shot, hit flat
Topspin: ball spins towards opponent, dips suddenly and shoots through on landing
Western grip: see *Shakehand grip.* ■

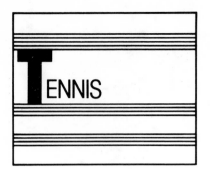

TENNIS

Top professional tennis players are rich celebrities who travel the world throughout the year. They enjoy the fruits of the game's rapid growth as one of the most glamorous and rewarding segments of the sporting entertainment business. Modern tennis can be a recreation, a career, or each in turn. In 1978, 10 years after the introduction of open competition, 32 men and nine women won more than $100,000 each in tournament play.

This racket-and-ball game can be played indoors or out, and features either *singles* (one against one) for men or women, *doubles* (two against two) and *mixed doubles,* where a pairing of one man and one woman take on another man and woman.

1 The Court

The net hangs from a metal cable (*net cord*) which is suspended from two posts 3ft 6in (106cm) high. It sags slightly in the middle, where it has to be 3ft (91cm) high.

The *tramlines* on each side of the court, making it 9ft (2.74m) wider, are used only for doubles play. The only aspect of courts which varies is the surface. The differences are due mainly to climatic variations, and fluctuations in the supply and cost of materials. The diversity of surfaces encourages a diversity of playing methods — extreme examples being the *ground-stroke* specialist, educated on *slow* courts, and the *serve-and-volley* specialist educated on *fast courts.*

The three major championships provide showcases for all the main outdoor surfaces: roughly distinguished by the generic terms *hard* (used for the United States championships), *clay* (the French), and *grass* (Wimbledon). The first two are composite courts consisting of several layers of material. The difference between them is that clay courts have a loose, sandy top dressing made by crushing shale, brick or stone. Clay courts vary according to the texture and depth of the top dressing, but basically they are slow enough to give players time to run down most of their opponents' shots. So openings must be created by tactical manoeuvring. Players accustomed to firm surfaces may have difficulty in timing their clay-court slide, so that they arrive in the right place at the right time, properly balanced.

The *topless* hard court — often known as a cement — is usually medium to fast and produces a more consistent bounce and a safer foothold than clay or grass. This pace is a compromise, because men's tennis tends to be at its most attractive on slower surfaces, women's tennis on quicker surfaces. Grass, from which *lawn* tennis took its name, was soon reduced to minority status. Because of its speed, it demands a high level of basic skill, fast reactions and a capacity for improvization, but it makes tennis too much of a gamble unless the courts are in perfect condition — and

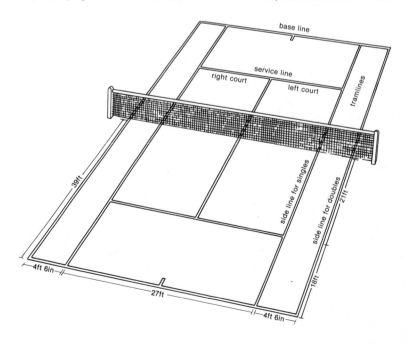

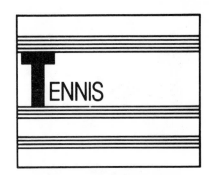

The server has twisted his racket on impact to produce the kicker, or American twist, which will make the ball rear up on landing.

ment and nowadays there is a third choice — composite frames (for example, graphite) which tend to last a long time. Less muscular players are more likely to look for flexibility rather than stiffness in a racket.

The tension of the stringing is also a personal matter. Those who hit hard prefer tightly strung rackets providing a rebound at maximum speed, whereas those specializing in deft ball control have their rackets more loosely strung so that the ball will *stay longer* on the strings. Natural gut is generally considered to have the best playing qualities, but is expensive, vulnerable to dampness, and does not last as long as nylon or *hybrid stringing,* a combination of gut and nylon.

Balls must measure 2½-2⅝ in (6.35-6.66cm) in diameter and weigh 2-2⅛ oz (56.7-58.5g).

The air pressure within the balls is varied to suit differing conditions. The greater the air pressure, the harder and faster the ball and the more suitable it is for slow courts. The balls are often kept in a refrigerator so that they are cool and have a consistent bounce when they are used.

Clothing must be comfortable and capable of absorbing sweat. It should neither be so tight as to inhibit free movement, nor so loose as to flap about. Modern socks and shoes are made with cushioning material.

Although metal framed rackets are used by many players, the traditional wooden frame is still the most popular.

maintenance is difficult and costly.

A wide range of synthetic courts have been developed for indoor play and some have been adapted for use outdoors. Rather like a thick carpet, their playing qualities differ according to the texture and thickness of the materials used and the surface on which they are laid. In general, though they reflect the general modern tendency to reduce, by means of elasticity or friction, the speed at which the ball rebounds from the court. Excessive speed takes most of the finesse out of tennis and makes it less interesting.

2 Equipment

The frame of the racket may be of any material, size, shape or weight. However, in tournament play, a heavy racket would weigh 14-14½ oz (400-410g) but most players use something about 13-14oz (370-400g). Wood used to be prevalent and to a great extent still is. Metal frames were successfully developed after half-a-century of experi-

3 Winning

It is generally accepted that the original scoring system for tennis, going back hundreds of years, was based on the quarters of a clock: thus 15, 30, 45 (corrupted to 40), and the hour (game) is used instead of the more logical one, two, three and four. The use of the word *love* may have arisen from the French 'l'oeuf', the egg representing the figure 0. *Deuce,* possibly from the French 'á deux', indicated that one player must win two consecutive points. A margin of two runs through the entire scoring system.

To win a game, one player must win four points unless the score reaches three each (deuce), in which case a two-point lead must be established. A deuce position can thus recur repeatedly. Similarly, the first player to win six games wins a set, unless the score reaches five games each (*five-all*), in which case the set continues until a two-

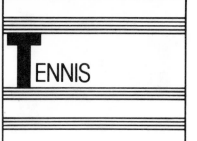

Tennis

game lead is established. The first player to win two sets (often three is demanded in men's events) wins the match.

The *tie-break* game is now widely used when a set reaches six games all. The player due to serve next serves the first point and the players then serve two consecutive points in turn. The game — and set — is won by the first player to score seven points: but if the score reaches six points each, one player must gain a two-point lead to win. Numerical scoring (rather than any extended use of the 15, 30, 40, system) is used throughout the tie-break.

A dramatic feature of the scoring is that point and games vary in impor-

This player shows the tremendous power he can get into his service as his racket arm twists back before hitting the ball. By pulling the face of the racket across the ball as he hits it, he will impart spin on it.

tance. For example, it is more important to win a 30-40 point, which could end the game, than it is to win a 15-all point. Equally, winning a game matters more at 4-5 down than it does at, say, 2-3 down.

Players serve alternately and when men are playing, especially on a fast court, it is easier to win games when serving. Indeed, one lost service game (a *service break*) should logically lead to the loss of that set.

4 Rules

Every game begins with a *service,* which puts the ball in play. The *server* stands just behind the baseline, to the right of the centre mark, and tries to hit the ball over the net into the service court that is diagonally opposite. The server throws the ball up into the air and hits it at full stretch. Players must not run or walk up to hit the shot, though they are allowed to jump into the air as they hit the ball. They must not step on or over the baseline or centre mark, or a *foot fault* is called and the serve counts as a *fault.*

A server is allowed two attempts to get the ball into the correct court. If the first goes in, play continues. If the first serve is judged a fault, the player serves again. If both serves are faults (a *double fault*) the opponent wins the point and the server begins again from the left-hand court. The position of the server continues to alternate throughout the game, as does the position of the opponent who always receives the serve in the court diagonally opposite. Similarly, after one player has served a game, the opponent then serves and so on until the set is won. Players change ends after each odd game — after the first, third, fifth, and so on. In doubles play, not only does the service alternate after each game, but also between each player every fourth game. However, unlike contestants in table tennis, doubles players need not take it in turn to play the ball. Either player can hit it.

The serve is the only shot which must bounce before the opponent hits it. The point is then lost by the player who hits the ball into the net or outside the court, allows the ball to bounce twice before returning it, or fails to hit it altogether.

Other rules, which would rarely be broken at top level, dictate that the ball must cross the net before a player can hit it, that players must never touch the net, and that a player must not hit the ball twice in succession.

A ball falling on any part of a line is regarded as falling within the court. The difficulty of making consistently accurate line calls causes controversy at every level of tennis: not least because the difference between hitting a line and hitting the ground fractionally beyond it can represent the difference between a perfect shot and a lost point. There have been many experiments with electronic devices, but reseach and development are both complicated and expensive, and no entirely satisfactory system has yet been devised. If there are no line judges, the responsibility for making line decisions rests with the umpire.

Much has been done in recent years to clarify the rules so that they cover every contingency that may arise during a match. But the need for self-discipline and good manners remains. Anyone can behave properly when things are going well. The test of character and conduct comes when a match is going badly.

tent toss is essential to service control, whether a player is using the basic flat serve, or one of the spin variations. With the former, the aim is usually to hit it deep into the opponent's service court. By using spin, the ball can be made to swerve in the air before and after bouncing.

Ground strokes (so called because they are played after the ball has hit the ground) must be accurate whether they are hit *down the line* (parallel to the side line) or across the court. *Lobs* and *drop shots* are extensions of the basic ground strokes: the lob should soar over the reach of the net player, and the drop shot should drop just after crossing the net. The *half-volley,* played just after the bounce demands particular care. The

The two-handed backhand can be tremendously powerful when used by base-line specialists. It can be restricting when trying to reach shots wide to the backhand.

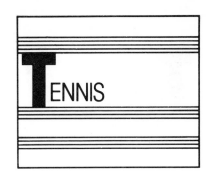

5 Skills

Much can be learned by analysing the professionals: their positioning, footwork, stroke-preparation, posture, wrist-work, adjustments to the angle of the racket head and so on. The greater the variety of strokes, speeds, and spins at a player's command, the greater the chance of winning — as long as the variety is shrewdly used and soundly executed. The basic shots are the service and ground strokes. A consis-

volley, played just before the bounce, is more of a punch than a swing. The *smash* is similar to the service, and must be carefully timed and placed.

There is a diversity of spins — hitting flat (with the racket head vertical), slicing under or across the ball, or rolling the racket over it (*top spin*). All these swings demand a good swing and wrist-work, and controlled adjustments of the racket head. This last point is especially important when taking the ball *early* — with a volley, a half-volley or on the rise — or when playing on grass, which demands shorter and quicker swings and faster reactions. A player must always be able to change

Tennis

gear, to hit hard or gently in turn, with equal accuracy.

The growing popularity of slower surfaces, giving players more time for their shots, has coincided with a wider acceptance of two-handed hitting (usually on the backhand). From a short swing, the shot is given more power, control and disguise. However, the two-handed shot restricts a player's reach; and two-handed players are seldom outstanding volleyers.

A high backhand volley played at full stretch. The ball is punched back over the net with a stiff wrist.

rallies with consistently accurate shots hit long and hard. It is difficult to hit outright winners on a slow court so their main asset is patience, as they wait for their opponent to make an error. But also, they must continually be prepared to run from side to side, always ready to spring to the net if tested with a drop shot.

The all-court player obviously combines both qualities and can adapt a variety of strokes to any surface, or force an opponent to hit a loose shot which can be put away for a winner.

Tactical manoeuvring is designed to create court space for a winning shot. The basic tactical decision is whether to stay back or go to the net; a player should never be trapped between the baseline and the service line. If the player stays back, he or she will usually return to the middle of the baseline between shots, as this is the tactical centre.

When rallying, a player usually tries to hit the ball just over the net, and as hard and deep as possible. This puts the opponent under pressure. Change of pace is used to create openings. This may be done by hitting the ball harder or more gently, or by taking the ball earlier or later than usual. There are also general points to remember, for instance the lob is usually most effective when played to the opponent's backhand.

The tactics of tennis are clearest in doubles. With two opponents to fox instead of one, the skill of opening up the court for a winning shot demands deft manoeuvring. Good doubles play thoroughly explores the court's length, width and air space. There are continual adjustments from attacking to defensive positions. Everything is geared to the need to get to the net, which is where doubles matches are won. The idea is to make the opponents return the ball upwards, so that it can be put away with a volley or a smash. Doubles offers great scope for subtlety and finesse.

 **Tactics**

Players can be categorized as *serve-and-volley, baseline* or *all court* players.

The serve-and-volley is most effective on fast surfaces. It involves serving hard, and then coming straight to the net looking for the opportunity to *put away* a volley, for a *winner*.

The baseline players are usually happier on a slower surface where they can wear down an opponent in long

 **Words**

Ace: a service the opponent cannot even touch

Approach shot: a deep drive (usually hit with underspin to keep the ball low), designed to justify an approach to the net

Break point: a rally in which the player receiving service is within a point of winning the game

Chalk, raise: when a ball hits the white

line, a puff of chalk dust usually shows that the ball is in

Chip: a shot with underspin — usually gently and often to a sharp angle

Choke: a player is said to choke when his stroke is inhibited by nervous tension

Dink: a short, gently-hit shot usually played to a sharp angle

Drop shot: a gentle shot, hit with underspin, designed to drop steeply, and die quickly after landing just beyond the net

Elbow: players are said to 'get the elbow' when they choke

Forecourt: the area between the service line and the net

Grand Slam: a grand slam is achieved by winning the championships of Wimbledon, France, the United States and Australia in the same year

Let: a service that touches the net before landing in the correct court, or any other point that has to be replayed

Lob: a shot designed to soar high over an opponent at the net and drop near the baseline

Match point: a rally in which one player is within one point of winning the match

Passing shot: a shot that passes an opponent who is in the forecourt hoping to volley

Percentage tennis: a deliberate discipline of hitting only shots on which the percentages suggest success; no risks are taken

Placement: a shot so placed that the opponent cannot reach it. Usually associated with ground strokes

Poach: in doubles, 'trespassing' in order to play a shot that would normally be the partner's prerogative

Rally: the exchange of shots between the beginning and end of a point

Receiver: a player receiving service

Retriever: a player who specializes in returning the ball rather than hitting winners

Seeding: the practice of placing leading players in separate sections of the draw so that they cannot meet until the later rounds

Service winner: a service which is touched by the receiver but is good enough to prevent a return being played

Set point: a rally in which one player is within a point of winning the set

Scrambling: the practice of running down and returning shots that looked like being winners

Tennis elbow: a common term for all ailments that cause an ache, and possibly pain, in the elbow of the racket arm

Weight of shot: usually refers to a shot that — because of the player's strength or timing, rather than obvious muscular effort — feels unexpectedly heavy on the opponent's racket. ∎

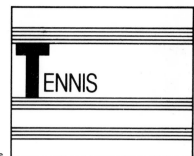

TENNIS

Weight on the front foot, this player is set to play a backhand and could opt for a shot down the line or back across court, depending on the position of her opponent.

TOBOGGANING
Luge

Although both tobogganing and bob-sledding are concerned with sliding on sleds down icy courses, the fundamental difference is that the tobogganist has no mechanical means of steering or breaking.

There are two distinctive forms of tobogganing. One is *luge tobogganing,* in which the rider is lying on his back going down the course feet first. The other is *skeleton tobogganing,* where the rider lies face down and travels head first.

Developed from a recreation traceable to the 16th century, the racing sport took root in Switzerland around 1879. It flourished mostly in central Europe until Olympic status in 1964 escalated worldwide participation.

1 The Course

The course is similar to that used for bobsleigh, but is usually steeper, with narrower corners. It averages 1000m (1100yd approx) in length, with at least a dozen bends. At Igls and Konigsee the bobsleigh courses are used for tobogganing.

2 Equipment

Luge riders wear special aerodynamic suits, crash helmets, goggles and visors, gloves with small wire brushes on the knuckles and lightweight shoes which should be reasonably aerodynamically

The modern artificial course racing sled is reinforced with fibreglass and the woods are made of glued layers of ash. The rein is used for steering.

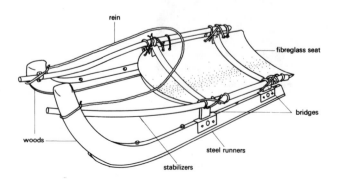

shaped. When starting off the rider sits on his luge with his legs along the runners. He then *pulls away* from the start using two metal hoops set in the ground and uses the wire brushes on his knuckles to give himself an extra push on the ice for the first few yards. It is very important to get a fast start. The luge is made of wood with twin metal runners, and has one or two seats made of fibreglass or canvas. Competitors spend a lot of time polishing the runners.

The single seater luge is restricted to 22kg (46lb) approx) and the double to 24kg (53lb approx). The width between the running (inner) edges of the steel runners is restricted to 45cm (17.7in) — therefore the overall width is a little more. The overall height is approximately 30cm (11.8in) but the height of the stabilizer bars over the bottom of the seat is restricted to 15cm (5.9in) between the bridges.

If the rider (stripped) weighs less than the maximum weight allowed he/she may add half of the difference by wearing a weightbelt of some sort — usually around the waist. It is not usual for riders to wear padding in competition as this can reduce aerodynamic efficiency and restrict movement. However, various forms of padding are usually worn in practice and when nursing an injury of some sort.

In top level competition, events are won and lost by hundredths of a second, even after four descents, so all these seemingly small points of preparation and aerodynamics are very important.

3 Winning

There are standard single-seater championships for men and women and also two-seater events for men. As in bobsleigh, results are decided by lowest aggregate times achieved during four descents.

4 Rules

Treating the runners with ski waxes is permissible, but heating them to gain extra speed is forbidden. The maximum weight for a male competitor is 95kg (209lb approx), for a female 85kg (187lb approx).

5&6 Skills & Tactics

The luge is flexible, so the riders steers by pulling up the runner on the side to which he intends turning, at the same time pushing the front end of the opposite runner inwards. If the driver puts his weight over the outer runner, it will slide faster than the inner runner. As the luge is travelling so fast (about 75mph/120kmph) only the slightest correction is needed to alter its course — just tilting the head one way is often enough!

Course familiarity is a key factor in championships and accidents are caused, more often than not, by lack of experience on the track or attempting to go faster than the competitor really knows how. This is always a danger in Olympic events, which tend to attract some relatively inexperienced riders from those countries without courses of their own. ∎

Skeleton tobogganing is so called because there is no superstructure on the sled. It is a sport which is usually associated with one place — the famous Cresta Run in St Moritz, Switzerland. Twice included in the Olympics in the years when St Moritz played host, the Cresta run style of tobogganing was probably more widely known than lugeing until the 1960s.

First built in 1882, the Cresta run is 1250m (¾ mile approx) long. Its major classic event is the Grand National and its most successful rider has been an Italian, Nino Bibbia. Skeleton riding does take place at other tracks.

It is a dangerous sport and certainly *flying off* at corners at St Moritz is an accepted part of the sport, but skeleton riders are seldom more than superficially hurt in this way. Tracks used by bobsleighs and luges must not allow any possibility of the toboggans or riders coming out of the track, as this is very dangerous to riders and spectators. Keeping riders in the track even in severe crashes is brought about principally by banking the corners much higher and in some cases they curve right over to form a roof — so that an out-of-control rider goes up the wall, touches the roof, and falls back in the track — painful but far preferable to going head first at high speed into the trees!

Nicknamed 'The Championship of Thrills' it looks the most daring of all the sled sports but luge riders might disagree! On tracks such as Igls, used by both sorts of toboggans, the luges are faster, and lying on their backs looking between their toes gives competitors a greater impression of speed.

As well as the protective equipment used by the luge rider, the skeleton tobogganist wears, significantly, a chin guard, and has boots with metal *rakes* or spikes to aid steering. A skeleton rider also has strong hand/wrist guards as there is considerable risk of badly damaging a hand if it is caught between the ice wall and the skeleton.

The sled comprises two steel runners attached to a simple, flat platform fitted with a sliding seat.

Lying chest down, the rider grips the upper bow of each runner and control is entirely dependent on body weight transference. A change of direction can be made merely by hitting the head as the skeleton touches 85mph (140kmph).

The seat slides back when cornering, throwing weight to the rear of the runners. Finding the best angle of approach and exit at each corner is the fine art which helps to clip off those all important split seconds. At the start the rider stands beside his toboggan some 10ft (3m) behind the timing line, then he gets his sled in motion and jumps on. ∎

TOBOGGANING

Skeleton

A course has a series of bends to both the left and the right to test competitors' ability to control their tiny toboggans as they hurtle downhill on the ice.

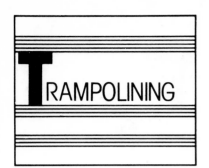

TRAMPOLINING

When the American George Nissen invented the first trampoline in the 1940s, a new sport was born that was, and is, graceful, fun and demanding. Competing indoors, performers use the trampoline as a springboard to jump, roll, leap, somersault and twist in the air in intricate routines that demand perfect execution and artistic interpretation.

Rather like a bed, a trampoline consists of a solid steel padded frame about 1m (3 ft) off the ground, 3.6m-4.3m (12-14 ft) long and 1.8m-2.15m (6-7 ft) wide. So that air can pass through it, a criss-cross series of interwoven nylon straps are used to form the *bed,* and these are affixed by strong springs to the frame. The minimum head room of 6.7m (22 ft) gives an idea of how high competitors can jump! Four *spotters* stand ready to catch any of the competitors who makes the slightest error.

Trampoliners wear what gymnasts wear — long white trousers over a leotard for men, leotards for women.

Individual competition is based on two disciplines — compulsory exercises and a voluntary routine. There are usually two rounds of competition with the top ten in the first going through to the next where another voluntary routine takes place. Team competitions are based on the performances of four members. In *synchronized* competitions, the idea (as in pairs skating) is for two trampoliners to execute their routines in time with one another on separate beds, placed side by side.

Ten movements form each section. Known as the *ten-bounce routine,* competitors are told what moves to carry out in a compulsory section and, of course, a competitor shows off his or her best skills in the voluntary section, just as an ice skater, diver or gymnast might. Each move has a *degree of difficulty,* or *tariff rating,* which is added to the points awarded for the execution of the move to get the score. Because of this, a perfectly executed simple move may be as effective as a poorly executed complex move.

Performers must give judges a list of their voluntary routines beforehand; if they then vary the moves, they do not lose points, as this is only an administrative aid.

Once performers get going, they adopt the three positions used by divers (straight, tucked and piked), seeking the same perfection of position in mid-air, with toes and fingers properly pointed, the correct number of rotations, twists and somersaults.

For a relatively young sport, trampolining has more jargon for its moves than any other. The skill lies not in remembering all the names, but in working out a routine that links them all together smoothly and rhythmically, called *swing-time.* Top-class jumpers work 6m (20 ft) in the air throughout routines.

 Words

Adolph: forward somersault with 3½ twists
Barani: forward somersault with half-twist
Barani-in: double forward somersault with ½ twist in first somersault
Barani-out: double forward somersault with ½ twist in second somersault
Checking: flexing the knees, ankles and hips to absorb recoil from the bed
Double: double somersault
Double-full: backward somersault with double twist
Fliffus: double somersault with full twist
Free bounce: straight bounce, with no movement in the air
Front: forward somersault
Full: denotes the number of twists in a somersault — e.g. front-full, back-full
Kill: see checking
Knee drop: basic landing position on knees and shins; from knees upwards, the body is vertical
Miller: named for its originator, this is a triple-twisting double back
Out bounce: free bounce at the end of a routine. This shows that the performer is still in control
Randolph/Randy: forward somersault with 2½ twists
Rudolph/Rudy: forward somersault with 1½ twists. ∎

Elementary trampolining moves show a piked back drop (left) and a piked front drop (right). In both moves, the competitor executes a pike — hands touching toes in mid-air — before dropping to the trampoline.

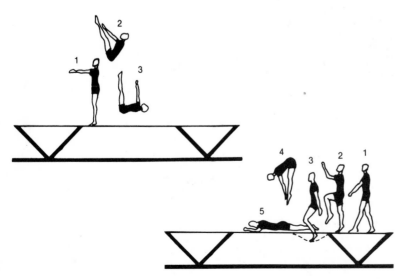

Volleyball is a team game that can be played indoors as well as outdoors, though top matches are nearly always played indoors. An exciting game combining fitness, stamina and agility, coupled with a high degree of skill, it requires concentration, quick thinking and continuous movement. An all-action game, players on court are involved all the time, unlike some team games where they are often involuntary spectators. In spite of the exciting spectacle the advanced game can create, volleyball is essentially simple, involving two teams of six players hitting a ball over a net.

1 The Court

The court is a rectangle measuring 18m by 9m (59ft by 29ft) marked with a centre line under the net; each half of the court is further divided into a *back court* and *attack zone.* The posts are outside the court, pulling the net taut between them so that the height at the centre is 2.43m (8ft) for men and 2.24m (7ft 4in) for women. The extremes of the court are marked with thin *antennae* which are fixed to the net above the sidelines.

2 Equipment

Players may wear protective pads on their knees. These help when diving to retrieve the ball. The amount of skill required in this particular action is sometimes under-estimated, particularly when players can be seen to dive, roll and still return to their feet within a matter of seconds.

The ball must weigh between 260-280g (9.2-9.9oz) and is about the same size as a football with very light strips of leather stuck on to a rubber bladder.

Light shoes with a good grip are essential and most players favour long-sleeved shirts for greater protection.

3 Winning

Before the match starts the two captains toss a coin. Whoever calls correctly has the choice of serving first or choosing the side of the net in which to play. The two teams line up on the base line facing the net and are called onto court by the *first referee* who is on a tall chair or ladder, level with the top of the net. The serving team starts the game from the service area behind the base line. The hand is used as a racket to hit the ball and the service should go over the net and into the opposite court.

The easiest way for a team to win a rally is to ground the ball in the opponent's court. Points can also be won by forcing the opponents to hit the ball out of court or by making it impossible for them to be able to return the ball with the three permitted passes. Points are only added to the score if a *team wins a rally while serving* and a player continues to serve as long as the team wins rallies and therefore points. If the receiving team win the rally, they win the right to serve. The rotation system means that all players in a team have the chance to serve. In international matches and most important games teams play the best of five sets. A set is won as soon as one team reaches 15 points but if the score is 14-14 then a margin of two clear points is required.

Teams change ends after each set, and when one team reaches eight points in the fifth and final set if the match goes this distance. Service, however, stays with the team that was serving before the change of ends.

This smash looks successful, as the ball is on this side of the net. There are many sophisticated moves now at the net, when players fake smashes to confuse opponents.

4 Rules

A team is allowed to touch the ball a maximum of three times on its own side before returning it over the net. The only exception is if the ball is not *blocked* cleanly at the net and goes on into the defender's area. They can then have their three touches, so altogether four would be allowed. As the ball is being served, all the players must be in position, with three players in the front part of the court and three directly behind them lined up in the rotational order announced at the beginning of the game.

As soon as the ball is in play, players may move into any formation they choose. However, those in the back court are not allowed to take part in a *block* or attack the ball above the level of the net. These rules, along with the one dictating that everyone moves round one position each time the serve

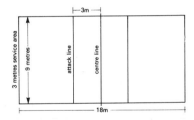

Court markings

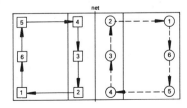

Rotation of players on court

VOLLEYBALL

changes sides, ensure that all players develop all-round skills.

Players must not obscure their opponents' view of the server (*screening*), they must never touch the net (*net fault*) and they must keep their feet behind the service line when serving (*foot fault*). During play, they must also stay in their half of the court. If two players foul simultaneously the point is played again. Players must not touch

suddenly, unlike a conventional serve where the ball travels in an arc. The *hook* service is powerful and puts spin on the ball, but is difficult to execute properly.

The most usual way to receive a serve is with the *dig,* where the forearms are used to control the ball. Then it will be directed towards the net to position two or three. The dig takes the speed out of the ball and controls it so that a counter attack can be built.

The second pass is the *volley* or *set* which may be directed forward or overhead. The fingers of both hands make contact with the ball just above the forehead and due to the speed of the ball, players often tape their fingers around the joints to prevent dislocating them. This pass is played cross-court to set up a *smash* or *spike* which is hit downwards with the open hand. The smasher jumps as high as possible in order to get above the defence and to make it more difficult to retrieve. Top smashers hit the ball in excess of 90kmph (60mph). The smash must be hit cleanly, not pulled with the arm and an effective smash requires a good volley. If a set is not good enough, the smasher may have to go for an accurate *placement* shot between defenders instead.

The opposing team will try to *block* a smash by forming a wall of hands where the ball is likely to cross the net. The only players that can form the block are front court players (numbers two, three and four). Formed correctly, the block will force the ball to rebound straight back into the other team's court, so they have to reform their attack at once. Receiving players will go to any lengths to keep the ball in play, diving and rolling to keep the ball off the floor so that is can be set for an attack.

Using the W formation, these players are waiting for the service. On the left, three women crouch at the attack line while the two on the right act as sweepers for any balls hit deep. Out of the picture, to the left, is the setter who hovers below the net waiting for the dig.

the ball twice in succession though they can make the first and third touches as long as a team mate makes the second. The rules also insist that the ball is *volleyed* (played cleanly) and never caught, or held for an instant. It must not touch a player below the belt though it can bounce off any part of the body above the belt. So punching or even heading the ball is allowed, although not recommended!

Teams are allowed up to six substitutes in any one set. A coach may want to rest a hard-working player or simply take-off one who is not playing well. A coach may also call two 30-second *time-outs* in any one set, to correct or alter his team's pattern of play.

The pattern of play

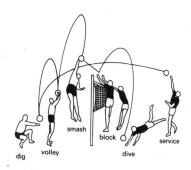

dig · volley · smash · block · dive · service

5 Skills

At top level, good serving is vital. A player may serve underarm but is more likely to serve overarm like a tennis player, using a *float* service. This wobbles in the air, coming down very

6 Tactics

The three touch volleyball of dig, set and smash is always the basic tactic but teams vary the way in which these passes are linked. A ball may be smashed on the second pass or perhaps from different positions on court. Only a frontline player is allowed to smash the ball within the attack zone so the setter may set a ball behind the attack line for a back court player to smash. The setter is the playmaker of any team and will try to steer the ball in front of the smashers wherever they are. Positioned in the centre of the court the setter goes for the middle of the net with *short sets* and combinations. This may involve one smasher dummying and another player looping round and hitting the ball. The setter will try to present the ball away from the block and may use *shoot sets*, much faster and flatter in trajectory than normal, to take the opposition by surprise. He may even play the second ball over the net himself.

A player should always try to play the dig with both forearms but it is necessary at times to use one arm when diving for the ball. A quick recovery is essential after diving so that the opposing team cannot exploit the extra space. The formation of a team on court is also important, and most top teams use a penetrating setter who will always make his way into positions two or three from wherever the rotation system places him, in order to create an extra attacking player on the front line. No player may move into a new position until after the ball has been served. Whilst it is a great advantage to have tall players at the net in positions two, three and four, it is equally important to have fast players both for making an attack and in forming the block to counter the smash. In using a penetrating setter a team's defensive formation has to be sound and it is vitally important to know which player will cover what area on court. For example, when the block is formed a defensive player will need to be covering the space behind it in case of a *dump* or *tip*, a deceptively soft shot.

Words

Attack line: this line is 3m (10ft approx) from the centre line and runs across the width of the court. Players in the back court may not attack from in front of this line.
Back line player: a player who is in position one, six or five at the time of service
Block: a wall of hands is created to prevent the opposing team's smasher from hitting the ball over the net
Dead ball: the rally has finished
Dig: a pass made by using the forearm
Dive: a means of retrieving the ball
Double touch: a fault incurred when a player is adjudged not to have played the ball cleanly
Dump: a fake smash sometimes called a *tactical ball* which involves a player usually placing the ball over the block with his fingertips
First pass: usually the dig played back to

the net which commences a rally
Float service: a type of service that makes the ball move in the air and drop suddenly
Front court player: a player in position two, three or four at the time of service who is allowed to attack
Penetrate: a back court player moving into the front court to set; this creates three attacking players to smash
Rotation: the movement of players in a

clockwise order when service has been regained
Side out: when a serving team loses a rally they lose the right to serve. No points are recorded
Set: a set is won when one team reaches 15 points and is ahead by two points
Setter: the player who volleys the pass (usually with both hands) near to the net for his attackers to smash into the opponents' court
Shoot set: a fast volley pass with a low trajectory
Short set: a volley pass made close to the setter which tends not to go very high above the net
Smash (spike): the act of hitting the ball downwards into the opponents' court with force
Switching: players in either front or back moving to alternative specialist positions after the ball has been served
Volley: the act of playing the ball with the fingertips of both hands overhead
Time out: a 30-second break in play called by a coach to talk to his players. Each team may have two time outs in any one set. ∎

The vicious smash or spike by the woman on the right appears to have been blocked effectively by one of the two blockers at the net, who timed their jump perfectly. Note the taped fingers, which take a battering in this deceptively simple game.

WATER POLO

About 100 years old, water polo is one of the toughest sports ever invented. On the surface it is a bit like soccer played in a swimming pool, but under water it is more like wrestling, and anything goes! A fast-moving team game, the seven players on each side must have strong swimming and ball-handling ability, as well as the stamina to put up with constant *dunking* under water as players tackle each other in search of the ball. It is not surprising that the four substitutes allowed are needed and used, because the *35 second rule* demands that players try a shot at goal within 35 seconds of getting possession.

1 The Pool

At international level, the pool must be at least 1.80m (6ft approx) deep because players are not allowed to touch the bottom during play, 30m (100ft approx) long and 20m (65ft approx) wide. There is a small goal at each end of 3m (10ft approx) wide and 0.9m (3ft approx) high. Lines on the side of the pool show the goal lines (1ft approx) from the end of the pool as well as the 2 and 4m (6½ and 13ft approx) lines.

Any free throws awarded for fouls that take place between the goal line and the 2m line must be taken from the 2m line. The 4m line marks off the area in which the goalkeeper is allowed to do things forbidden to other players.

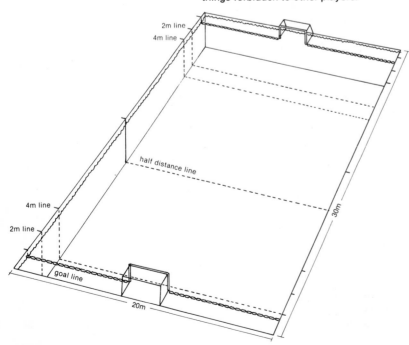

2m line
4m line
half distance line
30m
4m line
2m line
goal line
20m

2 Equipment

The teams are identified by the caps they wear — dark blue or white, numbered 2 to 11. The goalkeepers wear red caps with number 1 on them. The referee walks up and down the edge of the pool and indicates decisions quickly with a blast on his whistle. He shows which side has a free thow by holding up either end of a stick which has a blue flag on one end and a white flag on the other.

The ball is round and waterproof, weighing 400-450g (14-15oz) with a circumference of 68cm (27in).

3 Winning

Players move the ball about by *dribbling* it, swimming in a front crawl style, and using their arms and chest to control it. They also pass and throw the ball about, but only *one* hand can be used. Goals are scored when the whole of the ball enters the goal. The team that scores the most goals wins the match, which is divided into four seven-minute periods. After a goal is scored, the team that conceded it is awarded possession.

4 Rules

No player, except the goalkeeper in his 4m area, can touch the bottom of the pool, punch the ball or use two hands. Splashing water at an opponent or striking him, holding the ball underwater to keep it away from an opponent and *pushing off* from the side of the pool or goal posts are also illegal. The penalty for those offences is normally a free throw, taken from where the infringement took place. However, for more major breaches of the rules a player will be sent out of the pool for 45 seconds. Another punishment is a *penalty throw,* awarded for major fouls on attackers in the 4m area. A direct shot at goal, with only the goalkeeper to beat, it is taken in front of goal from the 4m line. Just as in soccer, no other players can be in the area, and if the ball rebounds off any part of the goal, play continues. No player may advance into the opponents' 2m area unless the ball goes into this area before he does; this stops players goal-hanging.

Water polo's 35-second rule keeps the game open and exciting. If a shot is not taken within 35 seconds, the opponents gain possession of the ball.

5 Skills

Good players paddle hard enough under water to keep the top part of their torsos well above water. They shoot and pass the ball with a *cocked* wrist and elbow, whipping the ball away. The speed of the ball can be increased by spinning the body through 180 degrees before unleashing a shot. However, a *lob* is useful as well as the *backhand* shot, used when a player has his back to the goal. The *pull-on* shot quickly flicks a pass on its way, while the *bounce* shot is really a trick shot where the ball skips along the surface of the water. Once a player gets near to goal, he can often deceive the goalkeeper with his eyes, by looking one way but shooting another!

Defenders must know which is the stronger throwing arm of each opponent and keep him under pressure by hovering close by that shoulder. When his opponent has possession, a defender usually puts one hand on his chest to push him down into the water, then his other hand reaches high in the air to try to block a pass. But, as in all sports, the ability to move quickly over a short distance is vital for players to get away from an opponent and have room to pass or shoot.

6 Tactics

Like soccer, water polo uses various set formations but again, like soccer, the most advanced tactics have players constantly changing position. Although players are nominally called left, right and centre back, left, right and centre forward, the top class teams keep the opposition guessing by swimming almost continually until one man can get away from his marker. This sets up other chances and a team mate then swims in front of the goal in the *man-in-the-hole* position of centre forward, which puts pressure on the defence and

opens up other gaps. The counter to this non-stop swimming is the *zone defence,* where defenders guard an area of the pool rather than a particular opponent. This system can be broken by five attackers swimming in a *figure of eight* pattern which tests defenders to the limits, but the 35 second rule puts pressure on both teams. Extra pressure is brought to bear on the team playing with a man out of the water. The attacking side must take every advantage of this situation.

7 Words

Corner: taken by attacker from 2m line at poolside when defender deflects ball over his own goal line
Field goal: scored from open play, not from a penalty throw
Personal fault: any player committing three major fouls (including conceding penalties) is banned from the rest of the match
Swim-up: to start play the ball is either thrown in by the referee or released from an underwater cage and teams swim at top speed from their own lines to try to get possession. ∎

The classic position for a goalkeeper, high out of the water, narrowing the angle by coming out of the goal and spreading his arms wide to cover as much as possible. His eyes are fixed on the ball. The attacker's elbow leads the ball in the shot, helping to get maximum power when the wrist flicks the ball away.

WATERSKIING

The sport splits into three distinct disciplines — slalom, jump and tricks. At top competition level, some of the men skiers are jumping two bus lengths further than Evel Knievel, rounding buoys on a slalom course, throwing up spectacular plumes of water and performing seemingly impossible feats on the trick run. That is why waterskiing is such an exhilarating spectator sport.

1 The Courses

The first is the *slalom* event. The course consists of six *turning buoys* laid diagonally on the water. The idea is for a skier to begin the course through the entrance gate, complete successfully the rounding of the six buoys and exit through the gates at the far end. The boat maintains a straight course and constant speed.

A skier who completes a run is dropped into the water, the rope is then shortened a specified amount and the skier then re-enters the slalom course. This procedure continues until the skier either *misses* (fails to round) a buoy or falls.

Trick or *figure* skiing is the most artistic form of waterskiing, combining strength and flexibility. In this discipline the skier performs a rehearsed programme of consecutive tricks over

two 20-second runs. These usually include turns, such as the 180 degree front-to-back turn, where the skier pivots to face backwards before turning back the way he came, and the 360 degree turn, where the skier completes a full circle at the end of the rope.

The tricks are performed either on the surface of the water, jumping over the wake of the boat, stepping over the tow rope, with one foot in the *toehold,* or a combination of these moves. Each movement has a predetermined points value and is marked on its degree of difficulty. No trick can be repeated, and

For the tricks part of the competition, this skier shows good balance as he stands on one leg and is towed along. The other foot is in the toehold.

a movement not executed to the satisfaction of the judges does not receive any points. Tricks may vary in value from 20 to 450 points.

At top-class competition level, skiers will be trying to execute 30 tricks within the 40-second time limit. Some will be backwards, on one or two skis, and spinning round on the end of the rope.

The *jump event* has possibly the most spectator appeal. Here, the skier cuts across the wake of the boat at about 100kmph (65mph approx) then travels over the ski ramp and leaps into the air. The skier is allowed three attempts at the jump. The farthest distance counts.

2 Equipment

Different waterskis are used in each event, but the length and construction depend on the skier's weight and preference.

The slalom ski has two bindings for the leading and trailing foot. The trick ski is much shorter and wider to allow maximum manoeuvrability.

The pair of jump skis tends to be slightly longer and wider than

Slalom course

68m
82m
82m
27m
23m

This skier throws up the characteristic plume of water as he cuts back diagonally after rounding a slalom buoy. His body is almost parallel to the surface of the water.

the slalom ski. The helmet in this discipline, although the personal choice of the skier, is made of a light but tough plastic.

The ski rope used is a 6mm (⅛in) braided polypropelene with a 29cm (11⅜in) rubber-coated metal handle. For flotation, a thick nylon or ensolite ski vest is used and wet-suit pants should be worn in the jump event.

For competitions, specialist tournament waterski boats are used. These leave a smooth wake, which is a help to the skier.

3 Winning

In international competitions the scores are calculated on the number of buoys rounded in the slalom, the total points from the tricks, and the longest distances covered in the jump.

From these placings an aggregate score is calculated. To win at this level, the skier must have a mastery of each discipline, and score consistently high points.

4 Rules

In the slalom event the boats must keep a constant speed of 58kmph (36mph) in the men's event and 55kmph (34mph) for the women. The initial length of the rope is then shortened as follows: 16m (52⅜ft approx), 14.25m (46ft approx), 13m (42⅜ft approx), 12m (39ft approx), and 11.25m (36ft approx) for the 5th *cut*.

In the jump event the boat runs at 56kmph (35mph approx) for the men and 48kmph (30mph approx) for the women. The jumping height is raised to 1.8m (6ft approx) for the men and 1.5m (5ft approx) for the women.

5 Skills

Waterskiing requires great strength in both jump and slalom, but coordination and agility are the key to the trick event. The sport at this level requires all-year round practice.

Waterskiers are all-round athletes who exercise and do weightlifting.

Although they have strength in their thighs, they need strong but flexible muscles in their upper body and stomach area too.

6 Tactics

Tactics do not really apply in this sport. It is the luck of the draw on running order and competitors just have to go out and do their best.

7 Words

Armsling: an attachment used by some skiers, to keep their arms tightly into their body while jumping

Backwash: when the wake of the boat hits the river bank or wall, and rolls back onto the course, sometimes affecting the skier

Balk: when a skier has cut too late for the jump and has to release the handle without attempting the ramp

Binding: a rubber shoe attached to the waterski for the skier's foot

Buoys: buoys can be red and orange in colour, made of plastic and are used to mark out the various courses

Cutting: a skier *cuts* when he pulls away from the boat with his skis on an edge

Gates: the buoys placed at the beginning and end of the course

Half a buoy: if a skier has just rounded a buoy but fallen, the judges will award half a buoy

Observer: sits in the tow boat, to acknowledge the skier's communications and assist in the recovery of the ski line

Pass: a successful run in any of the disciplines

Quick release: an attachment giving a quick release to the tow rope should the skier fall

Shortening or line-off: when the rope is shortened in the slalom event

Spring: when the skier reaches the top of the ramp, the instant straightening of the skier's legs gives extra height

Toehold strap: a strap attached to the trick handle for the skier's foot during toe tricks

Wake: the formation of the water caused by the boat and engine while the boat is moving

Wake tricks: crisscrossing the wake, there must be daylight between ski and wake to meet judges' approval. ■

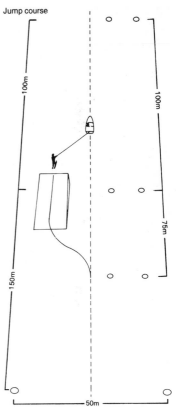

Jump course

100m

100m

75m

150m

50m

Landings can be hard. Losing control in mid-air, a skier hitting the water at 65mph (100kmph) feels as though he has bumped into a brick wall.

Two hands clean and jerk, split style. The lifter wears a belt and knee bandages for support.

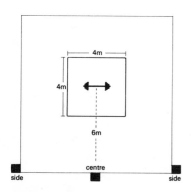

Referees' positions marked around the platform

People have been interested in feats of strength since time immemorial and strong men were often regarded as national heroes. Modern weightlifting competitions are still popular and one of the reasons for their appeal is their simplicity. The winner is simply the man who can lift the most weight overhead, but to make the sport fair for small men and large men, there are ten weight categories for the competitors, as in boxing:

Flyweight, up to 52kg (114½ lb)
Bantamweight, up to 56kg (123¼ lb)
Featherweight, up to 60kg (132¼ lb)
Lightweight, up to 67½ kg (143¾ lb)
Middleweight, up to 75kg (165¼ lb)
Light-heavyweight, up to 82½ kg (181¾ lb)
Middle-heavyweight, up to 90kg (198¼ lb)
Heavyweight, up to 100kg (220¼ lb)
100kg class, up to 110kg (242½ lb)
Super-heavyweight, over 110kg (242½ lb)

1 The Platform

The competition area consists of a wooden platform 4m (13ft) square. The barbell is placed in the centre of the platform and the lifter must perform his lifts in that area. If he steps off the platform during the performance of a lift, it will not be passed by the referees.

2 Equipment

At the beginning of this century methods were devised for adding to the weight of a *barbell* by means of disc loading and this kind of barbell is now standard equipment all over the world. Very stringent rules control the design and dimensions. The overall length must be 2.2m (7ft 2¼ in). The bar is *knurled* along most of its length which helps the weightlifter to get a better grip. The maximum diameter of the discs is 45cm (18in). The discs are coloured to help the officials who load the bar (*loaders*) and the referees to recognize quickly the weight of the larger discs which are similar in shape. The largest disc weighs 50kg (110lb) and is coloured green. The next largest disc, the red one, weighs 25kg (55lb) and the 20kg disc (44lb) is col-

oured blue. The range of discs continues in smaller sizes in heavy rubber or metal — 15kg (33lb), 10kg (22lb), 5kg (11lb), 2½ kg (5½ lb), 1¼ kg (2¾ lb). After the discs have been loaded on to the ends of the barbell which are made to revolve independently of the bar in the middle, the discs are locked in position on the *sleeves* by means of *collars.* The barbell together with the two collars weighs precisely 25kg (55lb) unloaded.

3 Winning

The competition lifts are the *Two Hands Snatch* and the *Two Hands Clean and Jerk.* The Snatch is a 'one movement' lift, that is, the lifter must take the barbell from the floor to arm's length above his head in one single movement. The lifter is allowed to move his body and feet to help lift the barbell and fix it in the finishing position above his head. The Two Hands Clean and Jerk is a two part lift. In the first part the lifter raises the barbell on to his upper chest or collarbones and this must be done in a single clean movement. This is why the first part is called the *Clean.* As in the Snatch, you will see the lifter first driving with his legs as the bar starts to rise, then he extends his whole body and swiftly drops into a squat to catch the barbell on his shoulders and upper chest. He returns to the erect position with the barbell firmly fixed across his upper chest. Then he bends his knees in a short dip and with a fierce leg drive, hoists the barbell above his head.

Each lifter in the competition has only three attempts in each of the two lifts. At the beginning of the competition he decides with which weight to start and informs the official announcer who controls the order of lifting. The competition begins with the lowest weight requested by the lifter concerned, then the weight is increased as the better lifters come on to make their attempts. All increases of weight must be in multiples of 2½ kg.

If a lifter succeeds with his first attempt, he must take at least 5kg more for his second attempt. If that is also successful, he must take at least 2½ kg more for his third and last attempt. If he fails in his first or second attempt he can either take the same weight again or risk increasing it. If his opponent is getting ahead, a lifter might take more than the minimum 5kg or

2½kg in an effort to catch or over-take the opponent. The best of the three attempts is counted for the final score.

When all lifters have finished their three attempts in the Snatch and Jerk, the best results of these two lifts are added together and the lifter with the highest total is the winner. If there is a tie in the totals, the lifter with the lighter bodyweight is the winner. In world championships and some other important events, medals are given for 1st, 2nd and 3rd in Snatch and Clean and Jerk, and points given for team competition.

4 Rules

The referees must first check all the competiton equipment to see that it accords with the official measurements etc. After weighing in the competitors, all three of the referees must inspect the lifter's competition clothing. This must consist of a leotard or vest and trunks under which an athletic support or second pair of trunks are worn. A strong pair of sports boots or shoes and socks completes the official costume. Additional items which can be worn are T-shirts to help keep the shoulders warm and bandages or elastic supports on the wrists and knees. You will also see the lifters applying powdered chalk to their hands before each lift. This is to dry their palms so that their grip on the bar will not slip.

The referees are seated around the competition platform where they have a perfect view of the lifts. They judge each attempt in accordance with the technical definition of the lift. They must be at least 6m (19½ft) from the lifter standing in the centre of the plat-form. The chief referee sits directly in front of the lifter and the other two dia-gonally at the side.

When the lift is completed and the lifter is standing motionless with the barbell fixed at arm's length overhead, the chief referee gives the signal to re-place the barbell on the platform, by shouting 'Down!' and at the same time waving his arm in a downward motion. However, a newer system of lights is slowly replacing the need for the referee to shout out. After the barbell has been replaced on the platform, the three ref-erees indicate if the lift has been done properly by means of a system of lights controlled by the two switches on the table in front of the referee. If a referee

considers the lift is good, he will switch on a white light. There are 11 faults listed for the Snatch and 15 for the Clean and Jerk, and if the lifter commits any one of these faults, his lift must not be passed. So if a referee observes one of these faults during an attempt, he will switch on a red light. The lights are arranged in two rows where they are visible to the lifters, to all officials and to the spectators. A majority decision is sufficient either to pass or fail a lift. Three or two white lights means the lift is passed. Two or three red lights means the lift has not been passed. A time-keeper is also appointed to help control the competition and he must hold a referee's qualification. When a lifter is called to the platform for his turn by the announcer, the time-keeper starts his clock. The lifter has two minutes in which to prepare himself mentally, chalk his hands and make the lift. If the two minutes are up before the lifter has lifted the barbell from the plat-form, that attempt will be disqualified. If a lifter is taking two lifts in succession on his own, he is given three minutes by the time-keeper for the second of the successive attempts.

5 Skills

The Snatch: a good lifter will pull the barbell close to his body because the closer the pull is to the vertical, the more accurately it can be fixed in the finishing position. Half-way through the pull you see the lifter drop under the

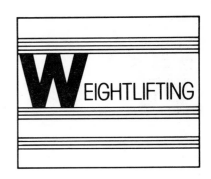

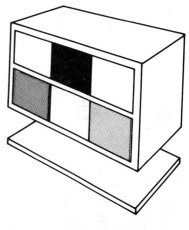

The referees' light signals indicate whether a lift was good or not. Here the majority decision is in favour with two white lights (bottom row) and one red on (top row).

Two hands snatch, split style.

WEIGHTLIFTING

barbell into a squat position. This helps him get his trunk, shoulders and arms under the barbell and to support it with straight, locked arms. When the lifter has fixed the barbell above his head and is in a balanced position, he must rise to an erect finishing position. As soon as he is standing up straight with the barbell firmly above his head, his feet on one line and all parts of his body motionless, the *chief referee* will give him the signal to replace the barbell on the platform.

Many lifters manage to pull the barbell fully to arm's length overhead as they squat under it, but then drop the barbell either in front or behind. The referees will not accept such an attempt as a good lift. Failures of this kind are usually due to a misdirected pull, either too far forward or swinging out of line too far back over the head. It is also a common fault for a lifter to mistime his squat by going down too soon instead of driving with his legs and trunk into a fully extended position first before making the swift descent under the barbell.

Two hands clean and jerk, squat style.

If a lifter is slow in locking his arms and has to finish the lift by *pressing* the barbell to arm's length (straightening his arms) the referees will not pass the lift. The pause in the ascent of the barbell, followed by the pressing movement means that instead of the single movement required by the rules, the lifter has used two movements to fix the barbell. Similarly if, during his recovery to the erect position, the lifter relaxes and lets one or both arms bend and then straighten again, the referee will not pass the lift. An alternative method of *snatching* is using the split, described below. *The Clean and Jerk:* to help fix the barbell in the ideal position directly above the shoulders in line with a vertical trunk, the lifter uses a *split* jump to get immediately below the barbell with one foot going forward and the other foot simultaneously backward. As in the Snatch, this jerk movement to fix the barbell overhead must be a single uninterrupted movement without any pause or straightening of the arms at the last moment. Again the direction of the barbell must be very precise. If the drive is only a fraction forward, which is a common fault, the barbell will be in an unsupported position and will crash to the floor. The splitting movement of the legs, a critical part of the technique, must place the lifter in a balanced position directly under the barbell. A badly directed split can cause him to lose his balance and fail to maintain the barbell in its overhead position. Finally the lifter carefully brings his feet back into one line and stands erect and motionless, awaiting the referee's signal to replace the barbell on the platform.

6 Tactics

Because of the strenuous nature of a weightlifting competition, it is essential that the lifter warms up thoroughly before taking his lifts on the competition platform. A warm-up area is provided close by. It is furnished with several platforms and barbells of the same design as those used in the competition and all the lifters in that competition warm-up together. In his warm-up a lifter gradually works-up until he reaches a weight 15 or 10kg below the one that he will take on his first attempt on the competition platform. When there are several lifters competing with him, he may have to wait some time before his competition attempts.

Two hands snatch, squat style. Perhaps more difficult technically than the split style

Therefore he continues warming-up with lighter weights to ensure that his technique is still *in the groove.*

The lifter is accompanied by team officials. His coach will primarily check his technique and correct any faults that appear and will also help him to choose his warming-up and competition weights. The team manager will follow the progress of the competition and join the coach in discussing tactics and choice of weights that may be needed in order to beat the opponents. Thus the warming-up room becomes a hive of activity as the lifters and their attendant officials work together, lifting, exercising, consulting, exchanging notes, 'psyching up' etc. The atmosphere in this room and around the competition platform rises to a high pitch of tension and excitement as the weight of the barbell goes up and down and only two or three lifters are left battling for first place. The competition rises to a climax of excitement in parallel with the rise of the weight. Quite often, in order to win, a lifter has to attempt a weight he has never lifted before and in many cases it will be more than double the weight of the lifter. This introduces the element of courage to add to those of skill, speed and strength, which are the requisites of a champion lifter.

7 Words

Bench press: in powerlifting, the lifter lies on his back and raises the barbell off his chest to arm's length

Clean and press: no longer recognized as a competition lift; after the clean the barbell is raised above the head by straightening the arms

Dead lift: in power lifting the lifter heaves the barbell off the floor to thigh level

Dumb bell: not used competitively, this is a weight lifted in one hand

IWF: International Weightlifting Federation, the sport's governing body

Lifter: a competitor

No lift: lift that does not satisfy the rules and therefore does not count

Powerlifting: variation of weightlifting that demands strength rather than skill and speed. The three lifts are the bench press, dead lift and squat. The sport has its own world championship

Press: to straighten the arms

Squat: or deep knees bend, is used in powerlifting; in a squatting position, the barbell is across the back of the lifter's neck and he has to stand up. ■

WRESTLING

Amateur

Amateur wrestling is one of the oldest, most basic and natural of sports. There are numerous regional styles of wrestling, such as Cumberland and Westmoreland in Britain, Kushti in Iran and Sumo in Japan, but only three have been recognized by the International Wrestling Federation (FILA) the world governing body. These are Freestyle, Graeco-Roman and Sambo, all of which have annual world championships. American inter-collegiate wrestling is similar to Freestyle and its popularity is a major factor in the country's continuing success in Freestyle at the Olympic Games, where the communist countries, in particular the Soviet Union, are the most formidable power. The main difference between Freestyle and Collegiate wrestling is in the rules rather than the technique. For example, in Collegiate wrestling, only two officials, a referee and a timekeeper, control the bout, rather than four as in Freestyle and Graeco-Roman.

Sambo is a Russian form of jacket wrestling. The word is composed from 'samozashchita' (self defence) and the initial letters of the words 'bez oruzhiya' (without weapons). Its similarity to judo has meant that a number of Sambo's outstanding fighters have won international honours in judo, and increasingly Sambo fighters have concentrated on judo because it forms part of the Olympic programme and Sambo doesn't.

Freestyle and Graeco-Roman are therefore the pre-eminent wrestling styles, having been a regular part of the modern Olympics. The difference between styles is that in Graeco-Roman a wrestler is not allowed to seize his opponent below the hips nor to grip with the legs. Otherwise the rules are the same. Both styles have 10 weight categories:

Light flyweight — up to 48kg (106lb)
Flyweight — 52kg (115lb)
Bantamweight — 57kg (126lb)
Featherweight — 62kg (137lb)
Lightweight — 68kg (150lb)
Welterweight — 74kg (161lb)
Middleweight — 82kg (180lb)
Light-heavyweight — 90kg (198lb)
Mid-heavyweight — up to 100kg (220lb)
Heavyweight — over 100kg (220lb)

A spectacular throw with one wrestler about to hit the mat, shoulders first. To obtain the pin, the wrestler on the mat will put his weight on to his opponent to hold him down while the referee counts the mandatory 4 seconds.

1 The Platform

At international meetings, both styles take place on a raised platform with sloping sides. No ropes are used. The mat has a circle 9m (10yd) across, which has a red strip 1m (1yd) wide inside to show wrestlers that they are near the limit of the circle. This is called the *passivity zone*. The contests are controlled by four officials — a mat chairman, who supervises the bout from a desk outside the area, a mobile referee, a judge on the edge of the mat, who can give a second opinion on the referee's actions, and a timekeeper.

2 Equipment

Amateur wrestlers wear leotards leaving the upper chest and shoulders bare. One competitor wears a red

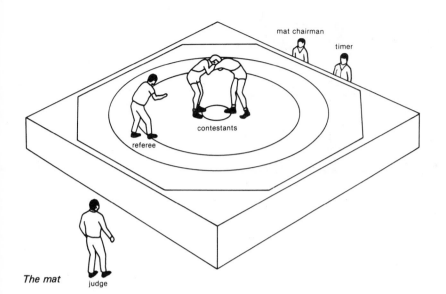

mat chairman

timer

contestants

referee

The mat

judge

WRESTLING
Amateur

The wrestler on the mat is 'bridging' on his head and toes to try to get out of the hold. If his shoulders are held down on the mat for 4 seconds, he would be pinned and lose the bout.

costume, the other blue to aid in identification for officials and spectators. Light boots and socks are usually worn. Competitors in Freestyle and Graeco-Roman, unlike the other styles, may not have oil or grease on their bodies.

3 Winning

Ideally, a bout is won when a wrestler *pins* both his opponent's shoulders on the mat for one second. This is termed a *fall* and immediately ends the bout, being wrestling's equivalent of a knock-out in boxing. Invariably, however, a wrestler wins on a decision given for his domination of the bout. Points are subtracted for passivity, foul holds and other infringements of the rules. The competitor with more points, allocated by the referee as the bout is in progress and confirmed by the judge and mat chairman, is the winner at the end of three rounds.

4 Rules

Fouls include unfair tactics such as pulling hair, ears or even the opponent's costume and applying holds that are likely to injure opponents; so is twisting an opponent's arm behind his back more than 45 degrees or using a

IN bild

competent performances in the other style. The skills are closely allied although there is greater flexibility in Freestyle, where diving at the legs is a common technique, as are trips and sweeps involving the feet. Many Freestyle wrestlers, particularly the Japanese, have acquired their throwing technique from judo.

There is frequently valuable cross-fertilization between these two sports. *Strangles* and *armlocks* are not allowed in amateur wrestling as they are in judo but in groundwork (on the mat), wrestlers excel in levering an opponent onto his back. Amateur wrestlers are rarely thrown cleanly as is common in jacket wrestling, because it is difficult to maintain a firm grip on an opponent's unclothed body. Many are talented at evasion techniques. In Graeco-Roman, competitors grasp each other round the top part of the body and use sudden body movements to unbalance their opponents.

The wrestler on top is applying a toelock. Note how he is in fact holding the top of the foot. If he put pressure on the toes, this would not only be dangerous, but illegal. He is also bracing his right leg against the body to prevent the opponent from rolling over to escape from the hold.

The man facing the camera is escaping from a hold by using a reverse leg-lock. He was underneath his opponent, but by intertwining his leg and using it as a lever, he has reversed the position and will end up on top!

scissor grip on the head or body. Further rules insist that wrestlers lessen the likelihood of injuring an opponent who is being thrown to the floor. For example, a competitor must drop to one knee when throwing an opponent to lessen the impact.

 # Skills & Tactics

Most competitors concentrate on either the fluid Freestyle or the more static Graeco-Roman, but they can still put up

 # Words

Ankle-and-leg dive: common technique whereby wrestler takes his opponent off balance by grabbing one leg
Cradle hold: hold in groundwork where the wrestler pins his opponent with one hand over his head and another through his crotch
Double-thigh pickup: take-down when a Freestyle wrestler scoops up the legs of his opponent from the front by catching him behind his thighs
Fall: another name for a pin, when a competitor has both his shoulders pressed to the floor
Full Nelson or Double Nelson: hold in amateur wrestling, in which a wrestler places both arms beneath his opponent's neck. Nelson holds using only one arm as a lever (*half Nelson*) are allowed and are widely practised
Pin: holding an opponent's shoulders on the mat. This automatically ends the contest both in Freestyle and Graeco-Roman
Standing arm-roll: a throw widely employed in Freestyle where a competitor clasps his opponent's arm, and wraps it round his own body and rolls him to the ground
Take-down: technique whereby a competitor brings his opponent from a standing position onto the mat
Wing: method of grasping an opponent tight to one's body and then levering him over his back. ∎

Television has made millions of professional wrestling fans around the world. Compared with the strict rules of amateur wrestling, professional wrestling has all the elements of show-business — paid performers, glamorous stage names, flamboyant attire, and spectacular acrobatics.

1 The Ring

Rings vary in size between a minimum of 14 ft (4.25m) square and 21 ft (6.4m) square. Four posts, well-padded with about 2 in (5 cm) of foam rubber, support the three ropes which, unlike boxing, have no vertical tape in the centre. The floor of the ring is covered with canvas which has to have a minimum of ½ in (1.2 cm) of foam rubber or felt underneath it. This prevents cuts and lacerations when a wrestler is hurled to the canvas.

2 Equipment

Although some individual wrestlers wear distinctive outfits, most have two sets of trunks, an elasticated support, a pair of soft leather wrestling boots which measure some 12 in (30 cm) from the heel to the back of the calf. Wool socks absorb the sweat. They take two towels into their corner and wear a dressing gown or robe. Some prefer one-strap to the usual two-strap leotards for comfort. Knee bandages, arm supports and so on are all allowed subject to the referee's discretion.

3 Winning

An afternoon or evening programme consists of four or five bouts. The *preliminary bout* is usually 6 rounds of five minutes each. The *supporting bout* is 8 × 5 minute rounds, the *main bout* is 10 × 5 minutes and the *bottom of the bill* match is 8 × 5 minutes.

Because there is limited time on television, championships are usually tailored to fit in specific slots. British and European titles are decided over 12 three minute rounds, world titles over 15 three minute rounds. The winning wrestler is the first to achieve *two falls, two submissions*

or a *knock out*. In the unusual event of a draw, the referee can ask the wrestlers to continue for one or two rounds. This may happen when there is a return bout and a decision is important.

A *fall* is given when both shoulder blades are held down on the canvas for a three second count. A *submission* occurs when one wrestler secures his opponent in a hold that is not only unbreakable but also painful. To stop suffering the wrestler taps the canvas to acknowledge defeat. However, a referee may have to intervene to prevent a stubborn wrestler being injured. A *knock out* is awarded if a wrestler, like a boxer, does not recover in ten seconds. If he is thrown out of the ring, he has to climb back before the ten-second count is over.

4 Rules

Wrestlers are divided into weight categories to ensure equal matches:

Lightweight — up to 11 stone (154 lb/70 kg)
Welterweight — up to 11 stone 11
(165 lb/75 kg)
Middleweight — up to 12 stone 8
(176 lb/80 kg)
Heavy middleweight — up to 13 stone 5
(187 lb/85 kg)
Light heavyweight — up to 14 stone 2
(198 lb/90 kg)
Mid-heavyweight — up to 14 stone 13
(209 lb/95 kg)
Heavyweight — has no weight limit

The referee must not allow any *choke holds,* which cut off the air supply in any

WRESTLING
Professional

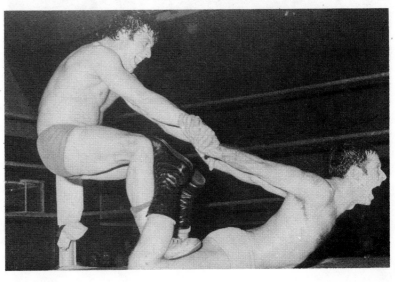

Aiming for a submission with the 'surfboard'. The hold can be even more effective when the aggressor rolls backwards and uses his own body as a cradle to lift his opponent into the air. The submission does not form a part of amateur wrestling.

way. European wrestling is not too keen on *sleeper holds,* although they are allowed in North America. These are executed by putting pressure on the side of the temple which cuts off the blood supply to the head and renders a wrestler unconscious quite quickly. Eyes must not be gouged but ears tend to take a pounding. *Forearm smashes* to the head cause cauliflower (swollen) ears with the bone at the point of the elbow causing the damage. As long as breathing is not hampered, no-one worries too much about noses!

While forearm smashes to the chest or head are allowed, punches with the fist are not. Chops or blows with the side or the flat of the hand are common.

The body slam. The westler on the right drives his opponent head-first into the canvas.

All forms of wrestling are based on physical strength. Both men are in the same weight category, so each tries to overpower the other by seeking out his weaknesses. The first move is to engage the *wrestler's hold* when the two link up by putting one arm round the opponent's neck and grabbing the other arm. They then try to pull each other down to the canvas or try to throw each other by using a variety of throws such as a *standing cross buttock.* This is the throw that many children use naturally in the playground, using a hold round the neck and the hip as a pivot. A *standing flying mare* is executed by throwing an opponent over the shoulder after grabbing an arm as a lever. A *neck mare* involves a hold around the neck and a throw over the shoulder.

All wrestlers have favourite holds and some prefer to grapple on the floor. The *single leg Boston crab* can be a very painful hold putting pressure on the knee as well as the base of the spine. To carry out the *standing full Nelson* a wrestler has to slip round to the back of his opponent where he puts his hands under the opponent's arms and then grips them together at the back of the man's neck, clasped in an unbreakable *butcher's grip,* with the fingers interlocked.

More spectacular is the *drop kick.* As an opponent moves into attack, the wrestler throws his feet up into the air, trying to plant them flat on the attacker's face or body. Also effective is the *monkey climb.* Clasping his hands behind his opponent's neck (facing him), the wrestler jumps up and puts his feet on the outside of the groin. By pulling backwards, the opponent shoots into the air!

6 Tactics

Physical condition plays an important part in all forms of combat, as the body tires quickly under the battering it receives. A wrestler tries to tire his opponent so that he *blows up,* or *runs out of steam.* If he feels he is fitter, he will use the ropes more, throwing his opponent and making him run, good tactics for the *counter wrestler.*

Much is down to *psyching,* gaining a psychological advantage over an opponent, weighing him up and out-staring him. The most lethal move is the *piledriver* which requires tremendous strength as a wrestler picks up his opponent, turning him upside down, with one hand holding the crotch, the other the shoulder in the *bodyslam* position — with the feet

5 Skills

Basically, in a good wrestling match, as in a boxing match, aggression is important. Look for the man who goes for a hold, the man on the attack. Unfortunately, there are some wrestlers who tend to be on the defensive.

pointing at the lights and the head down at the canvas. Trapping the unfortunate opponent's head between his knees, the wrestler drops to his knees, thus hitting the head on the canvas, like a *piledriver*. Not surprisingly, this usually produces a knockout.

 Words

Arm lever: bending elbow joint the wrong way
Arm lock: basic wrestling hold on arm
Body hold: basic wrestling hold on body

Forearm smash: wrestling's answer to boxing's right hook
Head lock: when opponent's head is held under armpit
Knock-out: as in boxing, the wrestler has 10 seconds to recover his senses
Leg lock: basic wrestling hold on leg
Monkey climb: hanging on to opponent's head, wrestler climbs up him!
Nelson: twisting arm up behind back ■

Arm and wrist locks are basic to the professional game. Here the wrestler on the right decides to move from a straight arm level to a double wrist lock on his opponent, who throughout will be looking for a counter move.

Just about anything goes in wrestling, including forearm smashes and chops — though not the straight use of the fist — in an effort to please or goad the spectators … and often a television audience.

Body slam: opponent is held vertically and driven head first into the canvas
Choke hold: illegal as it cuts off air
Drop kick: flying two-footed attack on head or chest with feet flat
Fall: when both shoulder blades are held down on the canvas for 3 seconds
Figure four: combines an arm lever, back stretch and leg lever to achieve submission.
Flying mare: opponent thrown over shoulder through the air

Sleeper hold: cuts off blood supply to head; wrestler passes out
Submission: when wrestler in unbreakable hold, gives in
Surf board submission: wrestler rides opponent, pulling his arms backwards and standing on the back of his thighs
Tag: contest between two teams of two, who take it in turn to wrestle
Toe hold: where toes are bent back painfully
Wrist lock: bending wrist wrong way. ■

Acknowledgements

The Publishers gratefully acknowledge the assistance of the following in the preparation of this book:

Tony McCarthy, Editor of *World of Sport*
Goodwin Dorman Design
Photo-typesetting by Bi-print Studio Ltd.
Colour origination by Culver Graphics Ltd.

Illustrations supplied by Studio Briggs Ltd.

All colour photographs in this book and on the cover were supplied by All-Sport Photographs Ltd.

Black and white photographs supplied by:
All-Sport: 2C, 7R, 9, 11L, 13, 23, 24L, 24R, 25B, 26, 27, 28, 29B, 30L, B, 31(2), 32, 36, 41B, 45, 46R, 47, 48, 51T, 64, 75, 79, 84, 85, 87R, 98, 105L, 106, 107, 109(2), 110(2), 111, 112(2), 113, 114R, 154, 155, 159T, 160, 184, 185, 190, 195, 196, 211, 219, 232, 236R
AMF International Ltd: 61, 62
The Australian Information Service, London: 21B, 46L, 65, 142, 178, 224, 225, 226, 227, 236L
Colorsport: 73(2), 74, 77(2), 118, 119, 120, 121, 147, 152, 153, 167, 168, 171, 172(2), 173, 218
Dale Martin Promotions: 245, 246, 247(2)
Dunlop: 105R, 223R
Embassy of the Federal Republic of Germany: 2L, 3L, 6(3), 7L, 21T, 25T, 29T, 33, 34, 35(3), 37, 38, 39R, 50, 59, 66, 69
David Finch: 2R, 137, 138
Gray's of Cambridge: 40, 210
Esso Gunnarsson: 3R, 143, 144
High Commission for New Zealand: 39T, 108, 209(2)
Irish Tourist Board: 103, 123, 124
Japan National Tourist Organization: 140(2), 192, 193, 214, 229
London Weekend Television Ltd: 5
McLaren Racing: 148R
Mallinson: 146(2)
Trevor Meeks: 145
National Film Board of Canada: 15, 22, 30R, 49, 67, 71(2), 78, 114L, 133(2), 134, 135, 136, 139, 141(2), 174, 183T, 216
New York Jets: 11R, 12
Frank Page: 177T
T.I. Raleigh: 82
Mervyn Rees: 41T
Louis Ross: 42, 43
Royal Netherlands Embassy: 177B, 186, 223L
Oscar State: 238, 239, 240, 241
Swiss National Tourist Board: 58
Team Talbot, Guildford: 51B, 52(2), 57
UK Frisbee Disc Association: 102
US Softball Association: 208
US Travel Service: 10